French Country Wines

FRENCH
COUNTRY
WINES

ROSEMARY GEORGE

faber and faber
LONDON · BOSTON

First published in 1990
by Faber and Faber Limited
3 Queen Square London WC1N 3AU

Printed in Great Britain by Richard Clay Ltd, Bungay, Suffolk

A CIP record for this book is available from the British Library

ISBN 0 571 13894 2
0 571 15311 9 (pbk)

Contents

Acknowledgements		ix
List of Maps		xi
Introduction		xv
1	A Brief Outline of Viticulture and Vinification	1
2	Wines of the South West	8
	Haut-Poitou	12
	Bergerac and the wines of the Dordogne	15
	Pécharmant	19
	Monbazillac	20
	Bergerac	24
	Rosette	28
	Saussignac	28
	Montravel	29
	Côtes de Duras	30
	Côtes du Marmandais	34
	Buzet	38
	Cahors	42
	Côtes du Brulhois	62
	Lavilledieu	63
	Côtes du Frontonnais	65
	Gaillac	69
	Vins de pays of the South West	79
	Vin de Pays Charentais	79
	Vin de Pays des Côtes de Gascogne	81
3	The Lost Vineyards of the Lot, Aveyron and the Landes	84
	Glanes	84
	Queyssac-les-Vignes	86
	Entraygues et du Fel	87

	Estaing	89
	Marcillac	90
	Tursan	92
4	The Foothills of the Pyrenees	95
	Jurançon	95
	Madiran and Pacherenc de Vic-Bihl	104
	Côtes de St-Mont	111
	Irouléguy	113
	Béarn	115
5	Wines of the Midi	117
	Introduction to *vins de pays*	130
	Roussillon	132
	Côtes du Roussillon and other table wines	134
	Rivesaltes	143
	Maury	148
	Banyuls and Collioure	149
	Fitou	154
	Corbières	158
	Minervois	166
	St-Jean-de-Minervois	174
	Blanquette de Limoux	176
	Côtes de la Malepère	181
	Cabardès	184
	Coteaux du Languedoc and Clairette du Languedoc	187
	Quatourze	192
	La Clape	194
	St-Chinian	198
	Faugères	203
	Picpoul de Pinet	206
	Cabrières	208
	St-Saturnin	208
	Montpeyroux	210
	St-Georges-d'Orques	211
	Pic St-Loup	213
	Méjanelle	214
	St-Drézery	215
	St-Christol	216

CONTENTS

Coteaux de Vérargues and Muscat de Lunel 216
Muscat de Frontignan 219
Muscat de Mireval 222
Vins de pays of the Midi 223
Costières de Nîmes and Clairette de Bellegarde 233

6 Wines of Provence 240
Cassis 241
Bandol 246
Palette 255
Bellet 258
Côtes de Provence 262
Coteaux d'Aix-en-Provence 272
Coteaux Varois 280
Coteaux de Pierrevert 282
Côtes du Lubéron 284

7 Wines of Corsica 288
Ajaccio 293
Sartène 294
Figari 296
Porto-Vecchio 296
Vin de Pays de l'Ile de Beauté 298
Coteaux de Cap Corse 300
Patrimonio 301
Calvi 304

8 The Upper Reaches of the Loire, and the Lyonnais 307
Côtes du Forez 307
Côte Roannaise 310
Côtes d'Auvergne 313
St-Pourçain-sur-Sioule 318
Coteaux du Lyonnais 323

9 Wines of Savoy 326
The Combe de Savoie 329
Chautagne and Jongieux 333
Roussette de Savoie 335
Seyssel 336

CONTENTS

Ayze   338
Crépy and the vineyards of Lake Geneva   339
Bugey   342

10   Wines of the Jura   349
     L'Étoile   352
     Château-Chalon and *vin jaune*   352
     Arbois   356
     Côtes du Jura   359

11   Wines of the North   363
     Côtes de Toul   363
     Vin de Moselle   367
     Paris   369

     Appendix 1   What is Grown Where   371
     Appendix 2   Outline List of Vins de Pays   375
     Glossary   383
     Abbreviations   385
     Bibliography   386
     Index   388

Acknowledgements

Many people contributed to this book. My thanks go first to Julian Jeffs whose idea it was. Little did I realize just what I was embarking on, but I am very grateful to Julian for giving me the opportunity to spend so much time exploring my favourite country.

Catherine Manac'h of *Food and Wine from France* deserves a very special thank-you for putting me in touch with various regional organizations in France, all of whom contributed vital help and information about their respective wines, namely the Comité Inter-professionnel des Vins de la Région de Bergerac, the Comité Inter-professionnel des Vins de Savoie, the Societé de Viticulture du Jura, the Groupement Interprofessionnel des Vins de Corse, the Syndicat des Costières du Gard, the Conseil Interprofessionnel des Vins de Fitou, Corbières et Minervois, the Syndicat des Coteaux du Languedoc, the Comité de la Promotion Économique Varoise and the Comité Interprofessionnel des Côtes de Provence. Catherine's efficient organization also arranged several vineyard visits, notably a wonderful week in Corsica, and, not content with that, I have constantly pestered her on the telephone for additional information. I am quite certain that without her help this book would never have been written at all.

Friends in the wine trade in both England and France provided introductions and information: Anthony and Novella Lacey, Hetty Sookias, David Withers, David Zeitlin, Lance Edynbry, Angela Muir, Andrée Ferrandiz, Simon Farr and Nick Belfrage.

My travelling companions on my various research trips also deserve thanks for all their help and constructive comments, not to mention map-reading abilities and entertaining observations: Colette Bayaud, Monique Dorel, Marie Lum, Yan-Kit So, Aileen Hall, Maggie MacNie, Helena Harwood, Gabrielle Shaw, my mother, May

ACKNOWLEDGEMENTS

George, and last, but certainly not least, my husband, Christopher Galleymore, for all his support and encouragement both in France and back home at my desk.

Finally, a very big thank-you to all the wine-growers who made this book possible by their willingness to discuss their work and share their wines with me. Without them there would be no book.

List of Maps

_____

The Country Wines of France   xii and xiii
The South West   10 and 11
Bergerac and Monbazillac   16
Cahors   44
Gaillac   70
The Pyrenees   96
The Midi   118 and 119
Provence   242 and 243
Corsica   290
The Upper Reaches of the Loire Valley 308
Savoie and Bugey   327
The Jura   350

The Country Wines of France

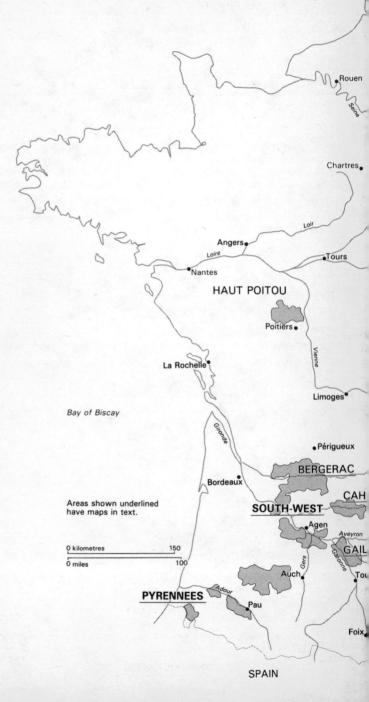

Rouen

Seine

Chartres

Loir

Angers

Loire

Tours

Nantes

HAUT POITOU

Poitiers

Vienne

La Rochelle

Limoges

Bay of Biscay

Gironde

Périgueux

BERGERAC

Bordeaux

CAH

SOUTH-WEST

Agen

Aveyron

Areas shown underlined
have maps in text.

GAIL

Garonne

Gers

Auch

Tou

0 kilometres   150

0 miles   100

Adour

PYRENNEES

Pau

Foix

SPAIN

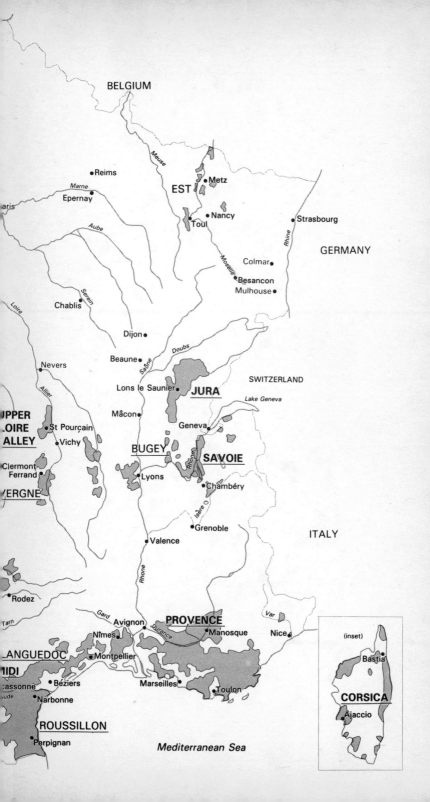

Introduction

The first thing to do is lay down the parameters. What exactly is meant by the country wines of France? The term French country wines seems to appear on merchant and restaurant wine lists with increasing frequency these days as it is used to cover all those wine regions that do not slot conveniently into the classic areas of Bordeaux, Burgundy, the valleys of the Loire and the Rhône, Alsace and Champagne. That leaves a rather large part of France, nearly two-thirds of the country's vineyards.

So my journey through the country wines of France has taken me first to the vineyards of the south west and the Pyrenees, where the wines bear a certain resemblance to Bordeaux, but none the less retain their own individual character, and then on through the vast vineyards of the Midi, beginning close to the Spanish border and travelling gradually round the Mediterranean coast. This is a lotus land for vines. They have grown prolifically here on the fertile plains, but now the winds of change are blowing through the area with growing speed in a drive towards quality and character. Then I crossed the Rhône into the sun-soaked hills of Provence, where pink wines are common, but where in contrast the reds, from the same grape varieties, are so much more exciting.

From there, Ajaccio in the island of Corsica is a short flight from Nice. Corsica has few similarities with 'the continent' as the island prefers to maintain its solid independence, and its best wines are quite individual and made from grape varieties that are not found on the mainland of France. From the rugged hills of Corsica I went to the uppermost reaches of the Loire, to the very first vineyards of the river, the Côtes du Forez and the Côte Roannaise, and those lost vineyards of the Massif Central, and then through the Coteaux du Lyonnais on to the lush pastures of the Savoie, where the vines grow on steep hillsides and the cows graze in green valleys. The wines here have more affinity with those of Switzerland.

Mountains seem to enhance individuality. They cut the region off from other influences, which may explain why the Jura, which is not on the way to anywhere, has one of the most distinctive of all French wines, *vin jaune*, as well as grape varieties that are rarely grown elsewhere.

From the Jura I headed north, to some of the most northern vineyards of France, to the forgotten wines of the Côtes de Toul and the Vin de Moselle. The Moselle is so much a part of German, and even Luxembourgeois, viticulture that we tend to overlook the fact that it rises in France. Finally Paris represents the epilogue, the symbol of all those vineyards that once lined the banks of the Seine but have long since disappeared.

This book is the result of ten journeys to France, amounting to over six months of visiting vineyards and talking to wine-makers and tasting their wines, between June 1985 and October 1987. Vineyards are not always on the main tourist routes. My researches have taken me to unexpected parts of '*la France profonde*', to lost corners of the Aveyron and the Massif Central and to sleepy villages around Toul or in the rugged hills of Roussillon. It has been the most exciting voyage of discovery for there was always the unexpected to be uncovered, the unknown wine to be found, like the thrill of tasting Chardonnay in the Massif Central, or discovering the flavour of Mançois in Marcillac.

Wine-growers tend to be friendly people. They are happy to talk and taste, to discuss their wines, and tell you their problems and joys and share their experiences. This book is about the people who make the country wines of France. I have tried to convey their hopes and doubts, their problems and rewards. Inevitably I will have omitted many favourite growers, for one reason or another. It is impossible to see everyone in a large appellation, while in a small appellation the choice was sometimes determined by who answered the telephone. However I have done my best to track down those about whom there was a general consensus of quality, those who are doing things and going places with their wine. As it was, at the final count, constraints of space did not allow for the inclusion of all the growers I visited.

The country wines of France encompass all categories of wine, from long-established appellations such as Arbois and Cassis which, along with Châteauneuf-du-Pape, were the first to be created, to those recently promoted from VDQS (Vins Délimités de Qualité Supérieure), and others hoping for promotion; to *vins de pays* of all kinds, from the conventional ones that offer little more than a regional *vin de table*, to wines that would merit an appellation if they did not defy the authority of the Institut d'Appellations d'Origine and plant unconventional grape varieties.

I have visited all the appellations and Vins Délimités de Qualité Supérieure that do not belong to any other wine region. However, *vins de pays* are more problematic. France is covered with *vins de pays*. At the last count there are 133 in existence, but many of them travel no further than the statute book. They may have been created where one grower had influence, or maybe they are produced by one co-operative in the south. Many of them are singularly anonymous and will remain so, while others, especially where there is no parallel appellation, will be the object of experimentation and searches for quality. And then there are wines that fit into no classification, such as the *clairet* of Paris and the *vin de paille* of the Aveyron.

The viticultural map of France is complex and complicated and yet it is possible to see three broad areas, determined by grape variety. Western France is dominated by Cabernet Sauvignon for red wine and Sauvignon for white wine, with a variety of grapes of similar character that are suited to the mild maritime climate of the Atlantic seaboard. All the wines of the south west have an inevitable affinity with Bordeaux and Cabernet Sauvignon, with certain regional variations. There are Tannat in Madiran and Auxerrois in Cahors, but the taste has the rigid structure of Cabernet Sauvignon.

The Midi, from Perpignan to Nice, is the land of prolific Carignan and Cinsaut and improving Syrah and Mourvèdre. The former give quantity while the latter provide flavour and structure. Syrah is found at its westerly limit in Gaillac and Mourvèdre needs the heat and humidity of the Mediterranean. Both demand warm ripening sunshine. However the more adaptable grape varieties of the east and west have encroached into the vineyards of the Midi. Cabernet Sauvignon is now an intrinsic part of many of the Midi *vins de pays* and permitted in the appellations of the Côtes de Provence and Coteaux d'Aix-en-Provence while Chardonnay too is being planted with some success in the south.

Eastern France, with its continental climate of severe winters and sharper seasonal contrasts, is the home of Pinot Noir, Gamay and Chardonnay. These are the grape varieties that form the link between areas as ostensibly diverse as, say, the Côtes de Toul and the Jura. Each region, however, also adds its own spice of individuality, with, for instance, the Savagnin of the Jura and the Jacquère of Savoie.

The east meets the south quite abruptly in the Rhône valley. There is, however, a country wine on the edge of Provence, Coteaux de Pierrevert, that includes grapes from the south as well as Pinot Noir. The Atlantic meets the Mediterranean in the Côtes de la Malepère and Cabardès. Here there is a successful blend of Cabernet Sauvignon and Grenache, for both can grow side by side in the variety of microclimates to make the transition from the structured wine of Aquitaine to the warmth of Roussillon.

In French, country wines can translate literally and confusingly as *vins de pays*. *Pays* means country but as I have said the term encompasses so much more than *vin de pays*. Another translation could be *vins régionaux*. That however lacks colour. Other suggestions were made to me and the one I liked best was '*les grands inconnus*', the great unknown wines of France. For these are the wines that are going to become known in the course of time. If you look at a wine merchant's list of twenty years ago, the wines that were put in the category of what we would now call country wines included such well-known names as Sancerre and Pouilly-Fumé, and it was not so long ago that Muscadet was considered a country wine. Look how things have changed. What wine merchant today would be without Sancerre or Muscadet on his wine list? It is with the country wines of France that the future lies. As Bordeaux, Burgundy and the Rhône grow in price and demand, we must look elsewhere for more accessible drinking, to the unknown areas of France that are waiting to be discovered. There are unexpected treasures to be found and new flavours to discover. The wealth of vinous delights among the country wines of France is legion.

I

A Brief Outline of Viticulture and Vinification

====

This chapter is intended as a brief guide to the standard procedures of viticulture and vinification, that are common to many of the vineyards of France. Anyone who is already familiar with these is invited to skip the next few pages hastily, for they will learn nothing new.

Phylloxera affected virtually all the country's vineyards at some time towards the end of the last century. This disease first appeared in the Gard in the 1860s, inadvertently brought to France from the United States. It is caused by a tiny aphid, the *phylloxera vastatrix*, which attacks the roots of the vines so that they eventually die. American vines are generally resistant to the aphid and so the only remedy is to graft French vines on to American rootstock. Although this solution was discovered by the turn of the century, untold damage had been done to the vineyards of France. Enormous areas of vines were abandoned and never replanted, or were planted with varieties like Aramon that produced large quantities of indifferent wine. Phylloxera was responsible for a considerable decline in the quality of many French wines and for their virtual disappearance. For instance, only a few dedicated growers continued to produce Auxerrois in Cahors and Mourvèdre in Bandol. Fortunately, as will be seen, there has been a revival in the fortunes of many areas in this century.

The first appellations were created in 1936 and all the better wines of France are recognized as *appellation contrôlée*, which entails a conformity to regulations regarding grape varieties, yields, the precise vineyard area and methods of pruning, viticulture and vinification. Each appellation is delimited vineyard by vineyard, a procedure known as the *délimitation parcellaire*. This delimitation considers the *terroir* of an area, a definition that includes not only the soil, but

1

also the aspect and microclimate. The second rung of the hierarchy is the small group of Vins Délimités de Qualité Supérieure, most of which are aspiring to an appellation. Their regulations are equally strict and both categories have to submit to tasting and analysis before they can be sold. These are called *labelle* tastings, which give the wine its *agrément*, indicating that it conforms to the appellation. Several appellations and VDQS consist not only of the basic wine, but also of several *crus*, which are often based on specific villages where it is considered that better than average wine is produced. Normally an appellation consists of a number of *communes*, a word which best translates as village, or parish in the case of a small or not so small country town.

The most recent arrivals in the hierarchy of French wines are the *vins de pays*, which in official terms are seen as superior *vins de table*. The very simplest wine, without any regional characteristics whatsoever, is a *vin de table*, and a *vin de pays*, because it has some regional character, is considered to be a superior *vin de table*. In fact, as will be seen, it may be a more exciting wine than the parallel appellation.

There is a distinction to be drawn between different types of grape varieties. When the French refer to 'noble' grape varieties, they mean ones like Chardonnay, Cabernet Sauvignon and so on. 'Hybrid' varieties are crossings between two vine species, usually *vitis vinifera* and *vitis labrusca*, and are not allowed in appellation wines. *Teinturier* varieties, like Alicante Bouschet, have red juice as well as red skins, and are used to boost the colour in wines that would otherwise be pale and insipid. The most common combination in the Midi is Alicante Bouschet and Aramon. In some vineyards in the Midi where they are making efforts to improve quality, *cépages améliorateurs* have been planted – 'improving' grape varieties, notably Syrah and Mourvèdre as well as Chardonnay, Cabernet Sauvignon, Merlot and so on.

The *viticulteur* is responsible for cultivating vines and growing grapes, which he usually delivers to a village co-operative, while the *vigneron* or wine-grower has a cellar and vinifies his own wine. He may bottle it himself, or sell it in bulk to a *négociant* who deals in wine, treating, bottling and selling it. The various activities of the *négociant* are referred to collectively as *la négoce*. Sometimes two or more members of a family or a small group of growers may form what is called a GAEC, a Groupement Agricole d'Exploitation en Commun.

Viticultural techniques vary little throughout France. Everyone is aiming to produce healthy ripe fruit. The vines are trained and pruned in various ways, the two most common methods being *gobelet* and *guyot*. The *gobelet* system is common throughout the Midi. The vine needs no support and consists of a single trunk with several small branches. The *guyot* system necessitates training on wires, the single *guyot* having one arm, and the double *guyot* two. A vineyard technique on which there is some experimental work in France, but which is more common in the New World, is T-budding. This is a means of changing the composition of a vineyard more quickly than by completely replanting. The fruit-bearing part of the vine is sawn away and a bud of the new grape variety is grafted into the trunk. In this way, if the graft is successful, only one year's fruit is lost.

Vines suffer from disease. Chlorosis is caused by an excess of calcium in the soil, which prevents the vine from assimilating iron. It can be combated by using chalk-resistant rootstock or by adding iron to the soil. *Coulure* is a disease to which some grape varieties, notably Grenache, are particularly susceptible. If the flowering takes place in unsatisfactory weather the berries fail to develop.

In bad weather, particularly in humid conditions, vines are susceptible to rot and are always treated for this. Oidium can be a problem too. This is a powdery mildew that attacks the leaves and berries, and a sulphur spray is the usual remedy. Another treatment favoured particularly by those who practise organic viticulture, abstaining from all chemical fertilizers and treatments, is the *bouille bordelaise*, or Bordeaux mixture of copper sulphate. Another occasional climatic problem is spring frost, against which the grower has little redress. Sometimes *chaufferettes*, small heaters fuelled by gas or oil, are lit in the vineyard to warm the air and keep it above freezing-point.

At vintage time the *état sanitaire*, or general health, of the grapes is all-important and a criterion by which a co-operative judges the quality of its members' work. Mechanical harvesters are becoming increasingly common in French vineyards, except where the appellation regulations dictate the need for whole bunches of grapes – for instance, where sparkling wine is made or the vinification technique of carbonic maceration is used. Mechanical harvesters shake the ripe grapes off the vine and suck them up on a conveyor belt. If you are making sweet wine from grapes affected by the noble rot (which dehydrates the grapes to give you rich, sweet, concentrated juice), you will have to practise *triage* at the harvest: this means that your pickers will have to go through the vineyards several times, making several *tris* or selections of grapes.

In the cellar the wine-maker is faced with several choices. For white wine the grapes will be pressed as quickly as possible and the juice cleaned. This process is called *débourbage* and is done by chilling the juice or must and allowing it to fall clear over a few hours; or a centrifuge may be used, which spins the juice, throwing off any solids. Alternatively, a fining agent such as bentonite, which is a kind of clay, may be added to clean the must. Occasionally the juice may be allowed to remain in contact with the skins for a few hours in order to give the wine more flavour, in a process called 'skin contact' or *macération pelliculaire*.

Fermentation is the process whereby yeasts convert the sugar that is present in the grapes into alcohol and carbon dioxide. Many growers are equipped to control their fermentation temperatures very accurately. Sometimes a technique called *ruissellement* is practised, whereby cold water is run over the outside of the vats in order to reduce the temperature inside. In the case of white wine about 20°C is considered the optimum, while for red wine the fermentation may reach as much as 30°C or more. Very modern wine-making plants may have stainless tanks equipped with a glycol blanket as an extra layer covering part of a vat containing glycol, which enables the wine-maker to control the temperature of the fermentation more efficiently. In the case of white wines the malolactic fermentation, the conversion of malic acid (as in apples), into lactic acid (as in milk), may or may not take place. It has the prime effect of reducing the acidity level of the wine, which may or may not be desirable, and can also change the basic taste of the wine.

Red wine-making presents the wine-grower with different choices. If he has picked with a mechanical harvester, his grapes will already be destalked. If, not, he has to decide whether or not *égrappage* or *éraflage*, both terms meaning the removal of the stalks, is necessary. The stalks can add extra tannin to the wine, which may not be required. If the fermentation is slow to start, a *pied de cuve* may be used to encourage it. This is prepared by taking the grapes from a few vines and warming the must until the fermentation starts and a large quantity of yeast develops. Yeast will only operate at a certain temperature. Some growers rely on natural yeast, while others use specially prepared cultured yeasts, which can be obtained from oenological laboratories.

If the grapes are not fully ripe and are deficient in sugar, chaptalization (the addition of cane sugar to the fermenting must) is permitted. This is carefully controlled and there are specific regulations for each appellation laying down the maximum level of chaptalization. In the Midi chaptalization is forbidden for appellation wines, but not for *vin de pays*. Tartaric acid is an essential component of wine, but if a wine is left for any period of time in a cold place, the tartaric acid is likely to precipitate and form unsightly crystals in the bottle. Well-equipped cellars will have machinery to carry out what they call a *passage au froid*, or cold stabilization treatment, whereby the wine is kept below freezing-point until the tartaric acid precipitates, and then the crystals are filtered out of the wine.

An essential requirement of red wine-making is to obtain enough colour from the grape skins. Often this necessitates a process called *remontage*, whereby the juice is run over the *chapeau* or cap of grape skins at least once, if not twice a day. Some well-equipped cellars have rotating vats, which can be programmed to turn so that the juice does not need to be pumped over the grape skins. A more traditional way of extracting colour is by *pigeage*, the time-honoured process of treading the grapes with your feet. You do still find this in the heart of deepest France. The length of time that the grape skins remain in contact with the fermenting juice is called the *cuvaison*. This, of course, is fundamental to the depth of colour in the finished wine. The fermentation may last longer than the *cuvaison*. If you wish to make a *vin de garde*, a wine that will last for a few years, your *cuvaison* will be longer than if your objective is a *vin de primeur*, a wine for early drinking.

A relatively new vinification technique has developed in France for red wine, called carbonic maceration. This is explained more fully in subsequent chapters, but necessitates the picking of whole bunches of grapes which are then put into a tank full of carbon dioxide. Contrary to normal rules of vinification the pressed juice, or *vin de presse*, is considered better than the free-run juice or *vin de goutte*.

Once the fermentation is finished, various choices have to be made. Some wines are made from a blend of different grape varieties, with an *encépagement* determined by the appellation regulations but also allowing the grower some flexibility. Each grape variety may be fermented separately and then the final blend or *assemblage* is either made in the spring following the vintage or, if the wine is to be aged in wood, before it is put into barrels. Barrel sizes vary in France. Most common in the south west are the Bordelais *barriques* of 225 litres; in order to avoid an excess of italics, I have tended to refer to these simply as barrels. In eastern France you find Burgundian *pièces* of a similar size, while in the Midi very much larger barrels are common. These may be *demi-muids* of 600 litres and even larger *foudres*. There is no specific size for a *foudre*, and for simplicity's sake I have called them casks. Often they are used for storage, rather than to give the wine any specific effect of oak ageing. The keeping of wine in oak barrels leads to loss by evaporation, which necessitates constant checking of the level of liquid and frequent topping up or *ouillage*.

Before bottling wine needs to be clarified. If it is aged in oak, it may be racked from one barrel to another as any sediment falls to the bottom of the barrel. The wine may also be fined, most commonly with bentonite. Filtering is also necessary although occasionally a wine may be bottled off the fine lees of the fermentation, as these may be considered to give the wine a desirable extra dimension of flavour.

The depth of colour of a pink wine depends on how long the juice is left in contact with the grape skins. Otherwise the vinification method is the same as for white wine. Pink wine in the Midi is often called a *vin d'une nuit*, for, as the name implies, the juice has remained with the grape skins for only one night.

The production of sparkling wine entails another set of procedures. The earliest and most traditional way of making sparkling wine in France was the *méthode rurale*, whereby the first fermentation was stopped for a sufficient length of time to allow the wine to be bottled. Then the fermentation started again, often the following spring, and the bubbles of carbon dioxide remained in the bottle, as did the sediment remaining from this second fermentation. Nothing more was added to the wine.

The champagne method was born of the need to remove the sediment from the second fermentation from the bottle, and so the processes of *remuage* and *dégorgement* were developed. The bottles are placed in *pupitres*, wooden racks with holes which allow the bottles to be rotated so that the sediment eventually settles on the cork and can be removed or disgorged with a minimum loss of wine. Normally the neck of the bottle is frozen so that the sediment is contained in a small ice pellet, but unsophisticated producers still practise what is called *dégorgement à la volée*, whereby a little wine containing the sediment flies out of the bottle when the pressure is released. At this point the dosage, which determines the level of sweetness of the wine, is added. More modern producers have *giropalettes*, large wooden or metal cages which can be programmed to rotate automatically with the bottles. A cheaper way of producing ordinary sparkling wine (*vin mousseux*) is by the *cuve close* or *charmat* method, by which the fermentation takes place in a tank and the wine is filtered under pressure before bottling. An intermediate process is called the transfer method. Here the second fermentation takes place in bottle, but the wine is transferred into a vat for filtration before final bottling.

The method of making *vin doux naturel* is elaborated upon in the relevant chapters. However, it must be pointed out that the name is a misnomer in that the wine is not natural for it is fortified with grape spirit. The fermentation is stopped at the required moment, when there is the right balance of natural alcohol and sugar, by the addition of grape brandy. It is the sweetness in the wine that is natural, not its alcoholic strength.

Subsequent chapters will explain the regional variations in these basic procedures.

2

Wines of the South West

Bordeaux is the inevitable starting-point for the wines of the south west. Claret provides the model for the red wines of the region, for Cabernet Sauvignon is the principal grape variety of so many of them. Not so long ago many of these wines were blended with those of the Gironde to be sold as claret, and in the Middle Ages they shared a history of commercial strife and rivalry that gave rise to an endless series of taxes and privileges.

The appellations closest to Bordeaux are now only separated from it by the departmental boundary. For centuries wines like Bergerac, Côtes de Duras and Buzet have been overshadowed by their big brother and only now are beginning to establish some individual identity. The further you travel from Bordeaux the more are differences apparent, with the inclusion of grape varieties not found in the Gironde. While Bergerac, Duras and Buzet are firmly Girondin, the Côtes du Marmandais allows for a local, otherwise unknown grape, Abouriou, which gives a distinctive regional flavour.

Travel east along the Lot to Cahors and the emphasis changes again. Auxerrois, otherwise known as Malbec or Cot, is the principal grape variety here. There is Merlot too, but no Cabernet Sauvignon. Further east still in Gaillac there is a wealth of different grapes, some Bordelais in origin, like Cabernet Sauvignon, but there is also the influence of the south with some Syrah, and individual local grapes like Duras, and for white wine Loin de l'Œil and Mauzac. Nearby Fronton boasts a unique grape variety and flavour in Négrette, while Lavilledieu and the Côtes du Brulhois borrow flavours from both Bordeaux and the Pyrenees.

Further south towards the foothills of the Pyrenees is the red wine of Madiran, where Tannat is the principal grape variety. However, there is Cabernet Sauvignon too. The tough, sturdy Tannat also dominates the red wines of Béarn, Tursan and Irouléguy and Côtes de St-Mont.

There is a parallel trend amongst white wines. The sweet wines of Monbazillac are like those of Sauternes, with Sauvignon, Sémillon and Muscadelle, while the dry whites of Duras, Bergerac and Buzet are also based on Sauvignon and Sémillon. Travel further east and they are mixed with local grapes like Mauzac and Loin de l'Œil, while the white wines of the Pyrenees have distinctive grape varieties of their own. Sweet Jurançon comes from Petit Manseng, while Pacherenc de Vic Bihl is also made from Gros and Petit Manseng, as well as the distinctive Arufiat, whereas the main grape of Tursan is Baroque.

Even further east in the upper reaches of the Lot valley are the three tiny VDQS of Marcillac, Estaing and Entraygues et du Fel where an extraordinary mixture of grape varieties has been retained, some local, some from the west of France and some from the east.

The most important *vins de pays* of the south west are those born of the decline in the consumption of Cognac and Armagnac, so the grape varieties here are those that were destined for the still.

Climate is an important factor in determining the choice of grape varieties. Bordeaux and south western France essentially enjoy a maritime climate, neither too hot in summer nor too cold in winter, with a moderate amount of rainfall. The further east and further south you go, the hotter and drier the weather becomes as you approach the Mediterranean. Cabernet Sauvignon does not like extremes of temperature, nor do Sauvignon and Sémillon, and these grapes flourish in the south west.

The historical development also reveals the influence of Bordeaux. Throughout the Middle Ages the power of the Bordelais dominated the commercial fortunes of the wines from the valleys of the Dordogne, Garonne and Lot, notably from around Gaillac and Cahors in the area that was known as the Haut-Pays. The history of these wines is a sequence of trading conflicts and grants of privilege, and their situation was not finally resolved until 1776 under Louis XVI. After that, many of these wines were used as '*vin de médecin*' to boost the more feeble wines of the Gironde. This was undoubtedly the role of the famed but quite undrinkable black wine of Cahors.

My journey through the vineyards of the south west began close to Bordeaux, in the vineyards of Bergerac, but first I deviated from the southbound motorway to explore the wines of Haut-Poitou,

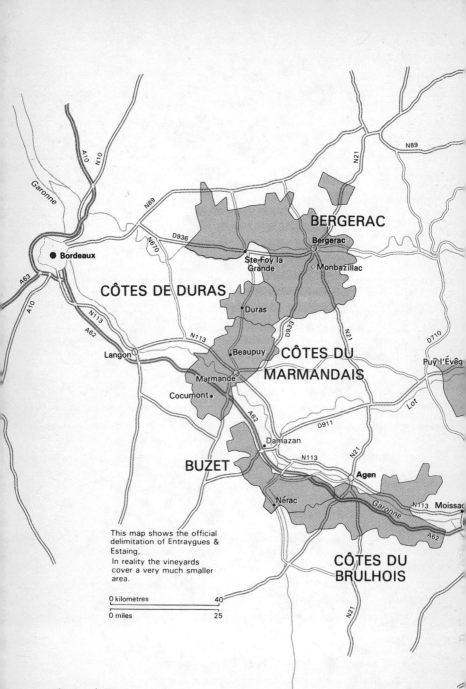

BERGERAC

Bergerac

Ste-Foy la
Grande

Monbazillac

CÔTES DE DURAS

Duras

Beaupuy

CÔTES DU
MARMANDAIS

Langon

Puy l'Évêq

Marmande

Cocumont

Damazan

BUZET

Agen

Nérac

N113 Moissac

This map shows the official
delimitation of Entraygues &
Estaing,
In reality the vineyards
cover a very much smaller
area.

CÔTES DU
BRULHOIS

| 0 kilometres | 40 |
| 0 miles | 25 |

The South West

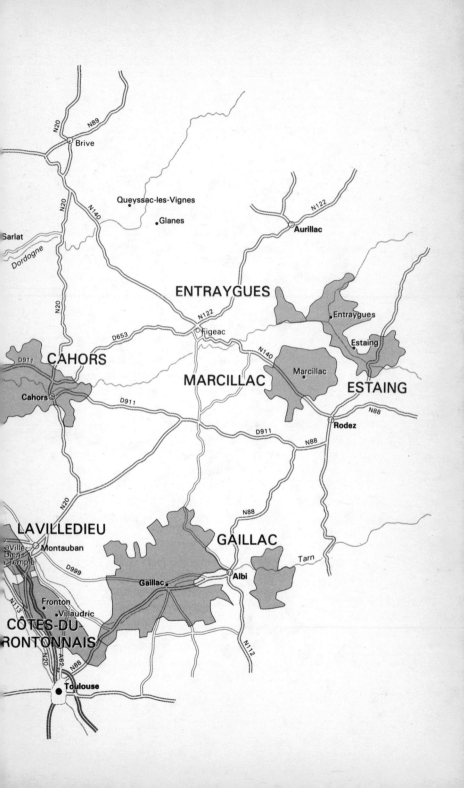

which have some affinity with Aquitaine in the use of Sauvignon and Cabernet, but also include Chardonnay and Gamay, the grape varieties of eastern France.

HAUT-POITOU

When you leave the Loire valley behind you and head for Bordeaux and the south, you would not expect to find vineyards before Cognac, and certainly no serious wine before Bordeaux. But if you take the motorway exit at Poitiers Nord, for the village of Neuville-de-Poitou, you will encounter one of France's most successful wine co-operatives, which is responsible for virtually the entire production of the Haut-Poitou.

Unlike so many of the vineyards of France, those of Poitou were not Roman in origin. Unusually, they were not heard of until the Middle Ages. Roger Dion, in his admirable history of French viticulture, attributes the growth of the vineyards of Poitou to a climatic advantage. The area was less subject to the climatic adversities of Burgundy and the Ile de France and could thus supplement a small harvest in the valley of the Seine; and the proximity of the port of La Rochelle enabled the wines to make the sea voyage to Flanders and England. It is recorded that in 1199 the wine of Poitou was one of the most widely consumed wines in England, where it was sold at lower prices than the wine of Anjou and of France, meaning the Ile de France. In the year that King John fixed the maximum price of wines drunk in England, he mentioned first the wines of Poitou, coming from La Rochelle, then those of Anjou and finally those of France. There was no mention of Bordeaux at all.

From then on little is known of the region's viticultural history. Vines remained there, but in obscurity. Like every other wine region of France, they suffered from the ravages of the dreaded phylloxera louse that attacked the roots of vines and destroyed so many vineyards in the late nineteenth century. The first hint of cohesion came with the creation of the Cave Co-opérative du Haut-Poitou in 1948. Some organization was necessary, for after the phylloxera crisis the vineyards had been replanted with indifferent grape varieties like Folle Blanche and hybrid reds for worse than ordinary table wine. There were seventy-two founding members of the co-operative. At the outset membership rose dramatically to over 1200, but it has now fallen back to 900. The trend is for this figure to decrease as many small farmers give up their land, so that a membership of around 250 is expected in ten years' time. This is a region of polyculture, with cereals, rape and tobacco all grown on the plains. Only a quarter of the co-operative members have more than five hectares of vines and for most the average holding is just one hectare.

Vin du Haut-Poitou was first recognized as a VDQS in 1970 and then promoted to an appellation with the 1989 vintage, and called simply Haut-Poitou. The final delimitation of the vineyard area was completed in 1983 and includes fifty villages, forty-eight in the department of Vienne and two in Deux-Sèvres, mostly to the west of a line drawn between Poitiers and Châtellerault. Neuville is at their centre but the most important villages are Doux, Blaslay and Vonzailles. The countryside is green and undulating, with fields of wheat on the plains and vines at about 100 to 120 metres on gentle slopes that rarely suffer from frost. There are now about 1,000 hectares of vines in the appellation, of which the co-operative is responsible for 95 per cent. About a dozen growers produce their own wine, but they mainly sell it in bulk to local *négociants* and are of no commercial significance. It is indisputably the co-operative at Neuville that has created the wines of Haut-Poitou as we know them, encouraging the replanting of the vineyards with noble grape varieties and fostering commercial demand.

The soil is mainly a mixture of clay and chalk, in two geological layers. There is chalk tufa as in Saumur, which suits white grapes, and a larger amount of pebbly clay mixed with a type of stone known locally as '*cosse*', which contains iron, a mineral beneficial for red wines. The climate is mild, with some maritime influence. The mixture of soil has allowed for a considerable diversity of grape varieties to be planted, but in its reconstruction of the vineyards the co-operative has followed an energetic policy of concentrating on specific grape varieties, with the result that most of its wines are made from single varieties.

Situated between Bordeaux and the Loire valley, its vineyards reveal the influence of both regions. Its most characteristic wine, which first established its reputation, is Sauvignon du Haut-Poitou. Sauvignon is a traditional grape variety of the area, as of the Loire valley, and it grows here with notable success, accounting for 60 per cent of the white grapes. Some Chardonnay has been reintroduced and now makes up 30 per cent of the white vineyards, although there were traces of Chardonnay here before phylloxera. Perhaps surprisingly as it is so common in the Loire valley, Chenin Blanc does not thrive in Haut-Poitou. There is a little but it is being abandoned in favour of Chardonnay. As for red wine, Gamay has always grown here, accounting for 60 per cent of the red grapes and producing a successful fruity red for early drinking. Cabernet, a blend of 60 per cent Cabernet Franc, as in the Loire reds of Bourgueil and Chinon, and 40 per cent Cabernet Sauvignon, as in Bordeaux, is a little more substantial. There are also a few hectares of Pinot Noir, but for the moment purely as an experiment and as yet of doubtful success.

The vinification equipment at the co-operative in Neuville is impressive. They have a cellar built between 1981 and 1983 for red vinification, with twenty-two horizontal rotating vats. These vats take away the need for daily *remontage*, the running of the fermenting juice over the skins, and give a better extraction of colour and flavour. In addition they are self-emptying and equipped for automatic temperature control. They can be programmed to rotate as desired, every day for Cabernet and less frequently for Gamay. Gamay usually takes five days to ferment and Cabernet a little longer. A semi-carbonic maceration method of fermentation is used for the Gamay, whereby the grapes are not crushed, although because of mechanical harvesting not many are still intact and there are no stalks present. Gas builds up inside the whole grapes so that they burst.

White grapes are usually fermented in stainless steel vats, with careful temperature control, at around 16–20°C for about twelve days. The juice is first cleaned with a centrifuge. Red wines always undergo a malolactic fermentation, but the whites do not, so that their natural acidity is retained. They are also treated for tartrates.

Apart from the Cabernet all the wines are designed for early drinking, with the bottling of the new vintage beginning in December. As well as red and white wines some pink is made, a *vin d'une nuit*, which (as the name implies) means the juice was left on the skins to absorb colour for just one night. There are also two sparkling wines, a white from pure Chardonnay and a pink from Cabernet. Both are sold under the brand name of Diane de Poitiers, Henri II's colourful mistress, whose home for many years was the beautiful château of Chenonceaux. Sparkling wine made by the champagne method is a recent addition to the Haut-Poitou range. For the moment it is a co-operative at St-Cyr-en-Bourg in the Loire valley that turns the base wine into bubbles. Wine usually spends fifteen months on the lees of the second fermentation, depending upon demand.

The achievements of the co-operative at Neuville-de-Poitou are impressive, and have resulted in a range of well-made wines with fruit and flavour. The Sauvignon is pungent with good varietal character, the Chardonnay lightly buttery, the pink pretty and fresh and the Gamay an attractive fruity glass of red wine. There is an aura of optimism and success about the place. The wines of Haut-Poitou deserved their recent promotion to appellation status, though in practice that will make little difference to their situation. More vineyards could be planted, but it is unlikely as there is a good market balance and so little incentive. Tobacco and cereals are easier to cultivate, and as Roger Barthon, the technical director of the co-operative observed, 'The people of the land are prudent; they see; they observe; they decide.' Maybe they will decide to plant more vines; maybe not. Whatever their decision it is certain that the wines of Haut-Poitou have established their place on the French wine scene.

BERGERAC AND THE WINES OF THE DORDOGNE

Bergerac is an attractive country town and prefecture of the Dordogne; the River Dordogne itself, crossed by bridges old and modern, flows through the town. Busy main roads run through the newer districts, but there is an attractive old quarter, with timber-framed houses and a square graced, not surprisingly, by a statue of Cyrano de Bergerac. Rostand's famous play was based on a real person, who may or may not have come from Bergerac. The Maison du Vin occupies one of the loveliest of Bergerac's old buildings, in the Place du Dr Cayla. It was built during the thirteenth and fifteenth centuries as a convent, the Couvent des Recollets. There is an arcaded courtyard with a polonia tree; at the back a terrace overlooks the Dordogne, which at this point is wide and majestic.

The department of the Dordogne is rich in agriculture. Not only are there vines, but strawberries and tobacco – Bergerac even has a museum of tobacco. There are other gastronomic delights, too: walnuts, *cèpes* and the famous black truffles. It is thought that the popularity of the truffle was established in the late 1870s, after the outbreak of phylloxera, when the wine-growers turned to truffles instead of vines for their livelihood. The countryside around Bergerac

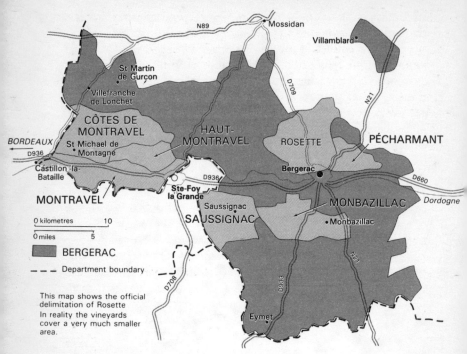

Bergerac and Monbazillac

is gentle, with undulating hills that are a natural continuation of those of St-Émilion.

The wines of Bergerac are, like all those vineyards dependent upon Bordeaux, Roman in origin. The Roman poet Ausonius, who gave his name to Château Ausone, praised the wines from the banks of the Dordogne. However, it was during the Middle Ages that the wines of Bergerac really established themselves in importance; they were reaching London as early as 1250. They were amongst the many wines of the Haut-Pays that competed with Bordeaux and fought against the privileges claimed by the city of Bordeaux to protect its own wines from the competition of vineyards further upstream. Edward III supported the Bordelais in the trading struggle, putting an embargo on all goods coming from Bergerac, but the Bergeraçois were not deterred. The Plantagenet overlordship of Aquitaine meant that the wines of Bergerac were certainly known to the English until the Hundred Years War was ended by our defeat at the battle of Castillon in 1453. The modest little town of Castillon, to which the epithet 'la Bataille' was added in 1953 at the 500th anniversary of the battle, to distinguish it from the many other Castillons of France, lies between St-Émilion and Bergerac. There is an insignificant monument on the bank of the Dordogne, just outside the town, to commemorate the defeat of John Talbot, Earl of Shrewsbury. It is a grey stone column, with a madonna perched on top, and bears the words:

> *Bataille de Castillon*
> *17 juillet 1453*
> *En ces lieux*
> *Mourut le général*
> *J. Talbot*

It is a surprisingly discreet memorial of a battle that was to have a dramatic effect on the development of south west France, ending three centuries of English influence. For Bergerac it meant that the Dutch replaced the English as their most important customers. This was to continue for several centuries. In 1520 François I removed trading restrictions and allowed the wines of Bergerac free passage down the Dordogne. Trade was at its height in the seventeenth and eighteenth centuries. It is recorded that in 1682 Bergerac exported a total of 106,000 *tonneaux*, of which 63,500 went to the Low Countries. The Revocation of the Edict of Nantes by Louis XIV in 1685 also had an effect, for many of the local Huguenots left to settle in Holland and naturally encouraged the export of the wines of Périgord to their new home. At that time most of the wine was white and sweet. Roger Dion writes that the wines of Bergerac and Ste-Foy were suitable only for the Dutch market in the eighteenth century. They were mixed with sugar or syrup to make them sweeter before being sent to Holland, where the Dutch even added *eau de vie* to give body and strength to the weaker wines. In contrast, Bergerac today means red or dry white, while Monbazillac is the sweet wine of the region.

The origins of Monbazillac are monastic. In 1080 the abbey of St Martin was founded in Bergerac and the monks planted vines on land belonging to the abbey at a place called Mont Bazailhac. In the Middle Ages the wines of Monbazillac were famous. A story is told of a band of pilgrims who were presented to the pope. 'We come from Bergerac,' they said, which awakened no response in the pontiff (the story does not relate which pope); 'from Bergerac, near Monbazillac,' they added. The reply was immediate, 'Ah, Monbazillac, an excellent wine,' and the papal hand was raised in blessing.

In their enjoyable book *Food and Wine of South West France*, Michael and Sybil Brown suggest that the sweet wines of Monbazillac and the method of their production, relying on the effects of noble rot, were appreciated during the Renaissance, well before those of Sauternes, which only became popular under the Second Empire; so maybe the growers of Sauternes learnt from those of Monbazillac.

In the early nineteenth century Jullien recorded viticulture as one of the most important activities of the department of the Dordogne, especially around Bergerac and Sarlat. 62,000 hectares of vines produced 525,000 hectolitres of wine, half of which was consumed locally. Some was exported. He described the reds as dry, elegant and full-bodied, with an agreeable bouquet. In the best category he ranked Terrasse, Pécharmont, Les Farcies, Campréal and Sainte-Foy-des-Vignes; some of these names are still reputed today, notably Pécharmont, or Pécharmant as it is now spelt. As for white wines, he said that Monbazillac, St-Lessans and Sance were renowned for the quality of their white wine, known as Bergerac, and that they were the same price as those of Langon, i.e. Sauternes.

Cavoleau, writing a little later, described the Dordogne as one of the big vineyards of France, dividing it into Périgueux, Nontim, Riberac, Sarlat and Bergerac. He said that the Dutch used to take the sweet wines but now preferred the wines of the Languedoc, so that there had been a change from white to red. The best reds resembled those of St-Émilion, which of course is the adjoining area, and he compared the whites to those of Frontignan, saying that they were rich and perfumed, with a strong bouquet of Muscat.

Rendu, writing a few years later still, also described Bergerac as the best of the Dordogne, with elegance and finesse, while Monbazillac was without a rival in its region. He explained that the Muscadelle grape, called Muscat Fou, gave a fine, alcoholic and very perfumed wine on the upper slopes, while Sémillon grown on the lower slopes had less finesse. Monbazillac could be aged in wood for six years or more and the old wines could be mistaken for excellent *vins d'Espagne*. Rosette was also mentioned as good, but less *liquoreux*, while distinguished reds included Tiregand and Pécharmant, as well as some now unknown names.

Mouillefert, at the beginning of this century, described Bergerac as being in a class of its own. He gave Cot Rouge as the main grape variety and said that the wine was often sold as St-Émilion. That indeed is one of the problems of Bergerac today, that it has been overshadowed by its more prestigious neighbour and is only now striving to establish a separate identity as a wine with its own characteristics, distinct from Bordeaux.

The vineyards of the Dordogne shrank considerably after the phylloxera. Those of Sarlat, Brantôme and Périgueux have disappeared completely, while Bergerac has consolidated its situation. Red and dry white wines have gained in importance, while Monbazillac has improved its quality by stricter production regulations. As well as Bergerac, there are Côtes de Bergerac, Saussignac, Montravel, Rosette and Pécharmant, and of course Monbazillac.

Pécharmant

It is generally considered that the best red wines of the Bergerac region come from Pécharmant. 'Pech' is a dialect word for a hill, so Pécharmant means quite literally 'the charming hill'. It is a small area to the east of the town of Bergerac, covering about 210 hectares. The total delimited area is 500 hectares, and there is a gentle increase of about ten hectares per year. Pécharmant distinguished itself from red Bergerac by a difference in soil, which is mainly clay and limestone with some gravel on the slopes, and also by the blend of grape varieties, which includes some Malbec. The vineyards of Pécharmant are on south-facing slopes, in four parishes: Bergerac, Creysse, Lomblas and St-Sauveur. The grape varieties are Cabernet Franc, Cabernet Sauvignon, Merlot and Malbec, the last being called Cot Rouge locally. Malbec rounds out the Cabernet, but not everyone grows it, as it is also rather fragile and sensitive to *coulure*. Pécharmant is a more solid, substantial wine than red Bergerac, and unlike most Bergerac, which can be drunk young, it needs some ageing.

Château Tiregand is one of the leading properties of Pécharmant. It is owned by the St-Exupéry family, who are cousins of the author of *Le Petit Prince* and also of the owners of Domaine de Pech Céléyran at La Clape. They have been here since 1830 and have thirty hectares of Pécharmant, and two hectares of Sauvignon. The proportions of grape varieties in the vineyard are 45 per cent Merlot, 15 per cent Cabernet Franc, 30 per cent Cabernet Sauvignon and 10 per cent Malbec. Each grape variety is vinified separately, and the *cuvaison* lasts about fifteen days (which is longer than for Bergerac) at a temperature of about 27–30°C. A little chaptalization is sometimes necessary. The malolactic fermentation takes place in November and the final blending, usually including some pressed juice, is done immediately afterwards. Xavier de St-Exupéry is the only producer in Pécharmant to have a *chai de vieillissement*, enabling him to age his wine in wood. It is a lovely old cellar with the date 1668 over the door. He has 225-litre barrels which are bought from Château Mouton-Rothschild and kept for about twelve years, as well as some 600-litre barrels which are older. Most of them are made of oak, but some are of acacia and chestnut. The wood no longer gives the wine any flavour, but there is still the process of gentle oxidation, which does not occur if the wine is kept in a cement or stainless-steel vat. The barrels are topped up every week in summer and every fortnight in winter, and the wine is racked every three months during the first year and every four months during the second year. Usually it is kept in wood for twelve to eighteen months, and then benefits from a further seven years' ageing in bottle. M. de St-Exupéry firmly believes that the longer a wine spends in wood, the better it will be in bottle.

Château Tiregand was originally one of the feudal castles of the region, and was destroyed as an act of submission, like most of these fortresses, when Aquitaine became part of France. The present château is more like a manor-house, but one wall of the old château is still standing and you can see the holes from which arrows were fired. From the terrace there are views of the vineyards, looking over the valley towards Monbazillac.

Monbazillac

The vineyards of Monbazillac cover an area to the south of the River Dordogne. Perhaps surprisingly, many of the vineyards face north, but in that way they are most susceptible to the river mists that cause the much-sought-after noble rot. Some people in the area make Monbazillac alone, while others also have red wine. The total area of the appellation is about 2,500 hectares, with the Cave Co-opérative de Monbazillac, the largest producer, accounting for a third of the appellation. It was founded in 1941 and has members in all five villages of the appellation: Colombier, Pomport, Rouffignac, St-Laurent-des-Vignes and Monbazillac itself. This is not a region of polyculture, so that most of its members have vines alone on their land, with an average holding of about nine hectares. However, as well as Monbazillac they also make Bergerac, red and dry white, and sweeter Côtes de Bergerac, Bergerac Rosé and even some Pécharmant (the owner of the twenty-two-hectare Pécharmant estate of Château Renaudie is one of their members). They also have five individual Monbazillac châteaux, of which Septy is their flagship. The others are Château La Brie, Château Pion, Château Marsalet and the imposing fourteenth-century Château de Monbazillac, which over-looks the valley towards the Dordogne. It is now used for official receptions and dinners given by the regional wine brotherhood and merits a star in the green Michelin guide for its historical interest.

Monbazillac, like Sauternes, is made from Sémillon, Sauvignon and Muscadelle. The co-operative has 80 per cent Sémillon, an increasing 15 per cent of Sauvignon and 5 per cent Muscadelle. They practise a careful selection of their grapes at the vintage, designating them for one of three qualities of Monbazillac: the Tête de Cuvée, the Cuvée Sélection and the Cuvée Supérieure which, at the bottom of the range, did not appear to be superior to anything. Wines with insufficient alcohol and sugar for Monbazillac can be declassified into Côtes de Bergerac. It is a well-equipped co-operative, with stainless-steel fermentation vats. The fermentation, for which the temperatures for Monbazillac reach 25°C, lasts about six or eight days. It is stopped when the right balance of sugar and alcohol is reached, usually 13° alcohol plus 3° sugar for the best wines, and for the basic Cuvée Supérieure 12° alcohol to 2° sugar. To stop the fermentation they either add sulphur dioxide, or preferably pasteurize the wine to avoid an excessive use of sulphur. The château wines spend three or four years in vat and bottle before sale, and they are considering an experiment of ageing in wood for the Château de Monbazillac.

In contrast, at Clos Fontindoule just outside the village of Mon-bazillac lives Gilles Cros, one of the most traditional producers. He is an old man with nearly sixty years' experience of making wine. The very first time he helped with the vintage was in 1929, and he remembers the great years of 1934, 1942, 1943, 1947, 1949, 1955, 1959, 1964, 1967, 1970, 1976 and, more recently, 1982 and 1983. He has never seen one vintage the same as another. He reminisced about the harvest, recalling the colour of vintage time. Young people from the north of the department, where there are no vines, came to help. There were also itinerant Spaniards, and a grower would have twenty or twenty-five people to feed and lodge. They danced in the evenings, and in the morning the alarm clock sounded long and hard. He is rather sad to see the folklore disappear. Mechanical harvesters could never be used in Monbazillac for they would turn the grapes into jam, but nonetheless the harvest does not have the same atmosphere and festivity as in the old days. Conscientious growers still go through their vineyards many times while others have reduced the number of *tris* or pickings to two or three.

The Cros family have been at Fontindoule since the time of Napoleon. The name of the estate has an interesting origin: *fontin* was the Celtic word for fountain – there still is a spring on the property – and a *doule* was the large open vat used for fermenting the grapes at the vintage. Altogether they have seventeen hectares of vines, Monbazillac only, no red or dry white. The vineyards are all round the property and are planted with 60 per cent Sémillon, which gives the wine its alcohol, weight and body, and 20 per cent each of Muscadelle and Sauvignon, which provide the perfume. They are all vinified together.

You can chaptalize in Monbazillac, but for the appellation the wine must have a minimum potential of 13°, composed of 12° alcohol with 1° of sugar. Conscientious growers would even declassify that into Côtes de Bergerac and M. Cros only bottles his wine at 13° plus 3° and ideally likes a total of 18° – 14° plus 4°. He stops the fermentation with sulphur dioxide, which he says fades as the wine ages. His father was one of the first to put his wine in bottle, back in 1934, and also bought one of the first tractors back in 1928, but they still kept their animals until the mid-1950s. It was the rural exodus that really established the use of tractors in the vineyards. M. Cros's cellar contained a mixture of barrels and vats, although his father installed cement vats in 1934 to replace the large old casks. He has added steel tanks and also has some old oak barrels. His wine is aged for three or four years before bottling, including a brief period in some old wood.

The perfectionist amongst the producers of Monbazillac must be M. Vidal at Château Treuil de Nailhac. He is insistent upon the importance of quality, that 'it is the only thing that can save us'. In years like 1984 he makes no Monbazillac at all, for years in which you need to chaptalize are not good years for Monbazillac. It is not with 13° that you make good Monbazillac; you need at least 14° or 15°, and 17° or 18° is even better – giving 13.5° alcohol plus 3.5° sugar, or 14° plus 4°. In 1955 he remembered potential degrees of 20° and 21°. With higher alcohol there is less risk of refermentation, so that you need less sulphur. 'The more you force the wine, the worse it will be. You cannot make wine with sugar-beet, but chaptalizing to increase the potential alcohol from 17° to 18° will improve your wine.' His yields average about 25 to 30 hectolitres per hectare, although the appellation regulations allow 40 hl/ha.

M. Vidal's Monbazillac is made from 60 per cent Sémillon, 20 per cent Sauvignon and 20 per cent Muscadelle. The fermentation is slow and gentle so that when 14° alcohol is reached, he adds 200 grams per litre of sulphur dioxide, racks the wine and leaves it until the spring. Then it is put into wood for one or two years and bottled after three years. He has an attractive cellar of oak barrels where his Monbazillac quietly matures. M. Vidal's wines certainly demonstrate the quality of Monbazillac. We began our tasting with a 1980, which had no botrytis and which had therefore not been aged in oak. It was lightly honeyed and elegant. The 1979, with 30 per cent botrytis, was golden in colour, with a taste of concentrated honey and quite a dry finish. The 1981 had 70 per cent botrytis and was richer, with 14.5° of alcohol plus 4.5° of sugar; botrytis was present on the nose and there was even more flavour of concentrated honey, but a balancing dry finish saved it from being cloying. In 1975 the noble rot was total and gave a potential 22° of alcohol (15.5° plus 6.5°); the wine was deep golden in colour, with botrytis on the nose, and almost unctuous and oily – a superb glass of wine. Best of all, however, was the 1964 which had a rich, honeyed flavour and the mature taste of botrytis that M. Vidal called *le goût de rôti*.

In all, 430 people give a declaration of yield in the appellation of Monbazillac, and of those 160 belong to the co-operative. Of the remaining 270, about half sell their wine to *négociants* in bulk, while the other half put their wine in bottle. The latter group is increasing as young people take over from their parents. The quality of the wine is improving generally and the co-operative has made considerable progress in the last few years, although it suffers from the usual problems of a co-operative. There is still a lot of bad wine around in the appellation, but the bulk producers are more often to blame than those who put their name and reputation on a label. To give the last word to M. Vidal: 'Monbazillac does not suffer mediocrity.' A good Monbazillac is undeniably a delicious wine with which to begin or finish a meal.

Bergerac

The basic appellation of Bergerac covers a total of ninety-three villages, a large area stretching from the easternmost vineyards of St-Émilion to beyond the town of Bergerac. Bergerac can be red, white or pink, though in fact very little pink wine is made. For white there is an increasing trend to make crisp dry Sauvignon, usually labelled Bergerac Sec, although white Bergerac is made traditionally from 70 per cent Sémillon blended with 30 per cent Sauvignon. Sémillon, Muscadelle and even Ugni Blanc are allowed in the appellation. If the white wine is *demi-sec* or *moelleux*, it is called Côtes de Bergerac. Sometimes the word *moelleux* appears on a label, but there is no fixed rule about this.

For red wine the difference between Bergerac and Côtes de Bergerac is one of alcoholic degree – a minimum of 11° as opposed to 10°. The grape varieties can include not only Cabernet Sauvignon, Cabernet Franc, Merlot and Malbec, but also Fer Servadou and a little-known and ordinary grape called Mérille. In practice most people have Cabernet and Merlot, and there is a little Malbec, particularly in the vineyards of Pécharmant.

One of the most exciting producers of Bergerac is Nick Ryman at Château la Jaubertie. He tired of life with stationery and bought the elegant sixteenth-century château, with its eighteenth-century façade, just in time for the vintage of 1973. As a newcomer he has been prepared to question many of the accepted practices of the area; his son Hugh has spent time with one of Australia's leading wine-makers, Brian Croser at Petaluma in South Australia, so that the Australian influence is now apparent in the wine-making. At the château I tasted his 1984 white Bergerac, a blend of 80 per cent Sauvignon and 20 per cent Sémillon. It was quite unlike any other – a rich, fat, full-flavoured wine with a taste reminiscent of the New World, but without the heavy alcohol. Nick Ryman attributes the distinctive flavour to the slow fermentation, which takes about a month in stainless steel vats at 8°C or 9°C, whereas before it used to take ten days at 18°C.

As for red wines, he planted Cabernet Sauvignon when he arrived at Jaubertie, so that the vines are now well established. His wine is made from 65 per cent Merlot, 25 per cent Cabernet Sauvignon, 5 per cent Malbec and 5 per cent Cabernet Franc. Each is vinified separately and since 1981 he has experimented with ageing in new oak. He reckons to use each barrel for four years, with the wine spending about three months in wood, depending on the age of the vines and the age of the barrels. The taste was rich and fruity, almost redolent of blackcurrants.

Nick Ryman's experimental approach extends to planting Chenin Blanc as well as some Chardonnay crossings. The INAO (Institut National des Appellations d'Origine) will not permit pure Chardonnay and the crossing of Chardonnay and Raffiat de Moncade is only allowed on land outside the appellation, just to see what happens. His vines around the château are trained for a mechanical harvester which he reckons is the best thing that has ever happened. With a mechanical harvester you can plan the vintage more efficiently and you can pick seven or eight hectares a day, as opposed to just one hectare with pickers. The interval between the grapes leaving the vine and arriving in the cellar is not more than ten or twelve minutes, whereas with pickers it may be as much as an hour and a half, which greatly increases the risk of oxidation. The grapes would be destalked anyway, so nothing changes there. He follows the Médoc practice of planting roses at the end of each row of vines, which looks pretty, but also has a practical purpose. Roses are even more susceptible to oidium than vines and will act as a warning of the need to spray the vines.

Another leading property is Château Belingard, owned by the Comte de Boisredon who also has three other estates, all adjacent (Château Boudigand, Château Chayne and Château St-Mayne), making a total of 60 hectares of vines. They make three types of white wine: a dry, a *fruité*, which is slightly sweet, with a high proportion of Sémillon, and a Monbazillac. Their white vineyards are planted with 60 per cent Sémillon, 20 per cent Sauvignon and 20 per cent Muscadelle, while for red they have a third each of Merlot, Cabernet Sauvignon and Cabernet Franc, as well as a few plants of Malbec. The vines are planted in widely spaced rows, 2.5 metres apart, with one metre between the plants, giving a total of 2,800 plants per hectare. The plants are trained on wires, 1.8 to 2 metres high, with the *guyot double* type of pruning.

The history of Belingard is fascinating: the name means garden of the gods, and the site was apparently associated with Celtic religious rites. There is a stone seat that faces the sunrise at the spring solstice. It is probable that the Celts knew about wine before the Romans. They did not actually know how to cultivate vines, but made wine from the grapes of wild vines that grew as creepers in the oak forests of the area. Near by are the remains of an eleventh-century chapel, where monks first planted vines, and also a Celtic tumulus.

Vinification methods are exacting. For Bergerac Sec they macerate the juice on the skins for twelve or fifteen hours in the absence of oxygen. They consider that this skin contact allows the development of enzymes which will give the wine better aromas than if the grapes are simply pressed. The fermentation takes six to ten days at 15°C, sometimes using natural yeast, and sometimes cultured yeast from Alsace. They usually need a *pied de cuve* to start the fermentation, and when it is finished, they leave the juice on the lees for three weeks for the wine to absorb the aromas. No malolactic fermentation occurs as they consider it unnecessary, their white wines not having a high natural acidity. The wine is then bottled in the spring or early summer and they expect it to age for two or three years in bottle. The blend of their Bergerac Sec is 60 per cent Sauvignon, 30 per cent Sémillon and 10 per cent Muscadelle; it has a rich, perfumed flavour, fairly grapy with an almost honeyed character and quite fresh acidity, but not at all aggressive.

For the *fruité* wine, they aim to keep 7 to 10 grams of residual sugar in the wine; to stop the fermentation at the desired moment they use a centrifuge, which removes most of the yeast. Then they chill the wine and add a little sulphur dioxide. Like Nick Ryman, they are constantly questioning their methods. They have compared wine made with and without skin contact and the relative merits of centrifuges or chilling for cleaning the juice before fermentation, to encourage it to fall clear naturally.

They have a separate cellar for their Monbazillac, which is made from 70 per cent Sémillon, 15 to 20 per cent Muscadelle and 15 to 10 per cent Sauvignon, using grapes that are either overripe or affected by noble rot. In fact they consider there is much less noble rot than there used to be, as its development has been deterred by the extensive treatment of the vines. They usually do two pickings in their Monbazillac vineyards: a first picking in which the grapes are carefully selected, and a second picking for all the remaining grapes a few days later. Again they stop the fermentation at the desired point by centrifuge and then add sulphur to the wine – as little as possible, about 250 grams per litre, whereas a few years ago 400 g/l was the norm. After a year in vat, the wine is aged in wood for a further year. Usually the colour is a pale gold. It seems that less reputable producers have been known to increase the colour of their Monbazillac by adding caramel.

For their red wine, Belingard ferment each grape variety separately at a temperature of 28–30°C for about eight days. The reds are not wines to age. They would like to reintroduce wood ageing and give the wines the hint of vanilla that comes from wood; M. de Boisredon would like to buy new barrels each year, but use each barrel for as many as three or four different wines during the year. The price of Bergerac Rouge, however, is not such as to justify the expense of new oak barrels. Instead the wine is kept in cement vats lined with epoxy resin, and bottled thirteen or fourteen months after the vintage.

Charles Mournaud at Château La Plante is one of the appellation's enthusiasts. He cares passionately about his wines and his mood is infectious. On the western edge of the appellation, he is almost surrounded by the vineyards of Bordeaux. On the opposite side of the valley are the Côtes de Castillon, and he is only 4 kilometres from Puissguin St-Émilion. As he put it, we are 'in a little lost corner'. He has 9.5 hectares of vines, from which he makes Bergerac Sec, Bergerac Rosé, Côtes de Bergerac Rouge, Côtes de Bergerac Moelleux and some champagne-method sparkling wine. For him the three tools of the wine-grower are the heart, the brain and the hands: wine is a work of art. Most of his red wine spends three or four months in old oak barrels. 'It is brought up like a child and we taste it religiously.' He buys his oak barrels second-hand from a grand cru in St-Émilion. His vineyard has monastic origins, having once belonged to monks from the abbey of Lascaux in the Gironde, which had a chapter at Villefranche-de-Lanchat. His methods are fairly traditional: he does not have a mechanical harvester, nor does he use any weedkiller or chemical herbicides in his vineyard, and his vinification is standard, with fermentation in cement vats and ageing of the reds up to three years, but more in vat than wood. As he says, 'We have stayed traditional,' but he is not against modern technology. His dry white Bergerac was crisp and fresh, while his red wines perhaps had more in common with some St-Émilion than with other Bergerac, having a good balance of fruit and tannin.

Rosette

It is surprising that the other individual appellations of Bergerac should be based on this style of *demi-sec* white wine. Obviously the reasons are historical, but the wines of Saussignac and Montravel have little popular appeal today. Rosette, indeed, has all but disappeared. The Comité Interprofessionel des Vins de la Région de Bergerac ignores it altogether, telling me that to all intents and purposes there is no more production of Rosette. The Guide Hachette gives one property, Château Puypezat, which I was unable to visit. Officially the appellation covers a few villages to the north west of Bergerac, but in practice the growers here call all their wine Bergerac or Côtes de Bergerac.

Saussignac

Saussignac, which was formerly called Côtes de Saussignac, is a *moelleux* wine made in five villages to the south west of Bergerac: Saussignac itself, and also Gageac, Rouillac, Monestier and Razac-de-Saussignac. The name has little popular appeal and the wine is often sold as Côtes de Bergerac Moelleux, even though it is considered to be a better wine than Côtes de Bergerac from other parts of the appellation. The production is small, about 1,000 hectolitres. A little is made by the co-operative at Sigoulês, but the most important producer is Pierre Sadoux at Château Court-les-Mûts. His father bought the property in 1960 on his return from Algeria and they now have 23 hectares of vines, of which Saussignac forms a small proportion. It is made from Sémillon alone, whereas their dry Bergerac includes 30 per cent Sauvignon. Vinification methods are meticulous and precise, for Pierre Sadoux also runs an oenology laboratory for several other growers and applies the same precision in laboratory and cellar. They are well equipped to control their fermentation temperatures. The grapes for Saussignac are picked later than the others for the ideal balance of alcohol and sugar is 12° plus 2.5°, and to achieve this the fermentation is stopped with a gentle dose of sulphur. The Saussignac, like their red wine, is aged in vat for eighteen months. I could not dispute that the wine is well made, but I could raise little enthusiasm for this rather insipid, slightly bland style. I much preferred M. Sadoux's red Côtes de Bergerac from 40 per cent Merlot with 30 per cent each of Cabernet Franc and Cabernet Sauvignon.

Montravel

Bernard Basset at Domaine de Gourgueil, near St-Michel-de-Montaigne on the western edge of the appellation, explained the intricacies of Montravel to me. Simple Montravel Blanc is a dry white wine, but in practice most producers in the fifteen villages of the appellation prefer to call their wine Bergerac. Côtes de Montravel is a *moelleux* wine and Haut-Montravel is even sweeter. For this the alcohol and sugar balance is usually about 12.5° plus 2.5°, depending on the quality of the vintage. Ideally it should be made from very ripe grapes and occasionally you get noble rot, but that is unusual. The wine is kept in vat for two years before bottling. The grape varieties are Sémillon, Muscadelle and Sauvignon. You can also have Ugni Blanc, provided it is balanced with the same amount of Sauvignon. The area of each appellation is defined so that Haut-Montravel comes from five villages, of which Fouqueyrolles is the centre. The Côtes de Montravel covers nine villages, of which St-Michel-de-Montaigne is the most important. Montaigne's château, where he shut himself up in a tower and wrote his *Essais*, is near by. Again most people prefer to sell their wine under the much better-known name of Bergerac and although Montravel covers a larger area than Saussignac, it suffers from the same identity problem.

M. Basset makes other wines as well as Montravel and we sampled his *bourrut*, the new wine that has barely finished fermenting, as we talked in the evening sunshine. He has 16 hectares of vines altogether and his dry wine is made from 60 per cent Sémillon, 20 per cent Muscadelle and only 20 per cent Sauvignon, as he does not want to emphasize the taste of Sauvignon too much. His methods of temperature control are not very sophisticated, but he manages to keep it at about 20°C for the white wine. Afterwards the wine is left on the fine lees, with no malolactic fermentation, and is bottled in January. His red wines are fermented at 30°C. The open vat looked like an enormous cauldron of blackcurrant jam, bubbling away gently. It will be aged in vat for two years. M. Basset would like some oak barrels, but that is a project for the future. He is a young man, full of infectious enthusiasm for his appellation: 'I love what I am doing and I want to do it properly.' He deserves to succeed. I thought he would, but with Bergerac, not with Montravel.

CÔTES DE DURAS

It is mainly administrative geography that defines the appellation of the Côtes de Duras. the vineyards cover fifteen villages in the north west corner of the department of Lot-et-Garonne. To the west they border the department of Gironde and the appellation of Entre-Deux-Mers; in the north they are limited by the department of the Dordogne and the vineyards of Bergerac; to the south they are bounded by the river Dropt.

Duras is an attractive country town. If you approach it from the south, your first glimpse is of the imposing château that dominates the valley. You climb the hill and find yourself in a bustling square, full of stalls of local produce on market-day. The château with its four magnificent towers was built in 1306 by Bertrand de Got, the cousin of Pope Clement V and Seneschal of Guyenne, and added to in the seventeenth century. Today it has a sad air of neglect. Attempts are being made to restore it and there is a small museum, but funds are obviously severely limited and an aura of decaying grandeur is inescapable. Nevertheless the views from the towers over the valley of the Dropt and the surrounding countryside are magnificent and in my version of the Michelin green guide Duras *vaudrait le détour*.

The vineyards of Duras go back to the Middle Ages. They were part of the vineyards of the Haut-Pays against which the Bordelais guarded their privileges so jealously, but there is little else of significance in their history. Côtes de Duras was one of the early appellations, created in 1937, but little was done to promote the wines and a considerable area of the vineyards was planted with hybrid grape varieties. At that time most of the production was white, similar to the neighbouring Entre-Deux-Mers. The Côtes de Duras are really a natural continuation of Entre-Deux-Mers and it is only the departmental boundary that divides the two appellations. The appellation of Côtes de Duras allows for both dry and *moelleux* white wines, pink (of which production is insignificant) and red, which has gained in importance over the last twenty years since the serious and successful efforts to revive the appellation in the 1960s.

The principal grape varieties are those of Bordeaux. White Côtes de Duras is made mainly from Sauvignon, Sémillon and Muscadelle although Mauzac, Chenin Blanc, Ugni Blanc and Ondenc are also permitted. Ugni Blanc is only allowed if there is an equivalent amount of Sauvignon to compensate for the lack of flavour. Ondenc is an old grape variety that has more or less disappeared because it is difficult to cultivate, being very susceptible to disease and rot. Red wines and the small amount of pink come from Cabernet Sauvignon, Cabernet Franc, Merlot and Malbec. They grow on soil that is varied in composition, but consists basically of a clay surface with limestone beneath. The red wine does better on clay while white grapes, which still account for 60 per cent of the appellation, thrive on chalk that is mixed with decomposed 'boulbènes', a regional name for a very fine siliceous soil that is easily compressed and hard to work. The climate is similar to that of Bordeaux, but tends to be warmer, and also a little drier, as the vineyards are further from the Atlantic.

The Cave Co-opérative de Duras is relatively new in co-operative terms, for it was only founded in 1960, with nine members. At first they concentrated on improving the composition of the vineyards and on eliminating the remaining hybrid varieties. The different grape varieties were all mixed up together in the vineyards, whereas today they are each in separate parcels, allowing for a different vinification for a specific variety. The cellars were built in 1965 and there are now ninety-two members who cultivate 400 hectares of a total area in production of 1,700 hectares. The older co-operative of Landerouat in the neighbouring Entre-Deux-Mers also produces a considerable quantity of Côtes de Duras, as its members often have vineyards in both appellations and it was well established as a producer of Côtes de Duras before the creation of the co-operative in Duras. Essentially this is a region of polyculture, for the gentle, undulating countryside allows for fruit trees, pasture and cereal crops as well as vines. It is also part of the large region of the *pruneaux d'Agen*, the famous prunes that are often preserved in Armagnac. Very few people live from vines alone.

The co-operative of Duras has worked hard to establish the reputation of the appellation. I was told how twenty-five years ago the wine of Duras was usually a rather neutral white wine made from Sémillon, whereas today there is much Sauvignon and the best Côtes de Duras Blanc is made from pure Sauvignon and has the crisp, pungent character of the grape. Usually the wine is dry, but the very ripest grapes are vinified for *moelleux* wine. The fermentation is stopped at 11°, leaving one or two grams of sugar. White-wine vinification at the co-operative is carefully controlled with a cool fermentation at 20°C lasting about eight days. The wine is bottled as

31

early as possible, when it is still fresh and fragrant, often at the beginning of December.

The co-operative's production of red wine has increased considerably over the last twenty years. In 1964 they made 5,000 hectolitres and in 1984 30,000 hectolitres. Cabernet Sauvignon is the dominant grape variety, accounting for 50 to 60 per cent of the blend, while Merlot provides about 30 per cent and the balance comes from Malbec and Cabernet Franc. The co-operative has introduced the process of carbonic maceration into the region for the vinification of Merlot. The objective is a fruity wine, with immediate appeal, for early drinking. It works, for the resulting wine is very perfumed and easy to drink, supple but with enough tannin to give some backbone. '*Gouleyant*' is the most apt description.

The other red grapes are vinified in the classic manner, with a fermentation at 30°C which lasts for eight to ten days, after which the wine spends eighteen months in vat. The co-operative has never had any wooden barrels. There are cement and stainless-steel vats, but they are not interested in giving their wines a taste of wood, for they are looking for lots of immediate fruit and flavour. A good Côtes de Duras will last five or six years but these wines are not intended to live too long. Nevertheless they can compete with many a *petit château* from the outlying vineyards of Bordeaux, with attractive blackcurrant fruit and some tannin.

Jean Fontviehl at Domaine Durand comes from one of the older-established wine-growing families of the appellation. In contrast to the new arrivals of recent years, Fontviehls have been here since the 1600s. As M. Fontviehl says, he was born into wine. He has never studied. It's all a question of practice and experience and it is the only thing he has ever done. His production from 20 hectares of vines breaks down into 60 per cent red and 40 per cent white and pink wine. The red comes from 60 per cent Merlot, 25 per cent Cabernet Franc and 15 per cent Cabernet Sauvignon. All his red wine is vinified in the classic way and he does not support the co-operative's work with carbonic maceration. His red wine is aged for two years in vat before bottling.

His white is predominantly pure Sauvignon, but in a good year he makes a *moelleux*, just from overripe Sémillon grapes. The grapes have a potential alcoholic degree of 14° but he stops the fermentation at 12.5° by the judicious use of sulphur dioxide. The wine then spends two years in vat and a year in bottle before it is sold. The tradition of sweet wine in the Côtes de Duras is as old as Monbazillac, while Sauvignon is an innovation; it was only introduced into the vineyards in the 1950s, when fashion was shifting from sweet to drier wines. I enjoyed a 1978 *moelleux* which had a gentle, mature, honeyed flavour. *Moelleux* ages well, prompting M. Fontviehl to comment: 'The older it is, the better it is, not like a man!' He also has some sparkling wine made for him from Sauyvignon and Mauzac. The co-operative is also enthusiastic about the area's potential for sparkling wine, even to the extent that they would like a new appellation, 'Crémant de l'Aquitaine'; but for the moment any sparkling wine from the Côtes de Duras remains anonymous.

Lucien Salesse at Domaine de Ferrant runs a traditional estate that dates back to the time of his grandfather. As well as vines he has orchards and cereal. There used to be animals too, but now the old ox-stables have been converted into an attractive tasting-room. For red wine he makes a blend of 60 per cent Cabernet Sauvignon with 20 per cent each of Cabernet Franc and Merlot. This gave a fuller, richer wine than that of Domaine Durand, which was a little more austere. The wine is aged for twelve to eighteen months and again there is no wood. A Côtes de Duras made from Sauvignon was crisp and fresh, with some attractive varietal character. He also has some Ugni Blanc, which can be used for Côtes de Duras Sec, provided there is the same amount of Sauvignon in the blend. Sometimes it goes into the sparkling wine which he has made for him elsewhere. The *moelleux* comes from Sémillon, Muscadelle and a little Sauvignon and the fermentation here is stopped at 11°, leaving 1.5° potential alcohol. It is usually bottled within a year of the vintage. A little pink is made, mainly from Cabernet Franc, by what the French commonly called the *saigné* method. A proportion of the fermenting juice is run off the vat once it has absorbed enough colour, usually after a few hours. More graphically one can speak of the vat being bled, hence the name of the process.

Although Domaine de Ferrant is quite an old estate, M. Salesse only began bottling his wine in 1978. Until then he used to sell it in bulk to the local *négociants*. He also makes some Vin de Pays de l'Agenais, from his young vines. The grape varieties are the same as for Côtes de Duras. This *vin de pays* covers most of the department of Lot-et-Garonne so that you can also find it in the Côtes du Marmandais.

Domaine La Grave-Béchade is the showcase of the appellation.

The estate was bought by David Amar who came from Morocco some twenty years ago, and no expense has been spared. The nineteenth-century château has been tastefully renovated and the cellars have been equipped with shining stainless-steel tanks, as well as some second-hand 225-litre barrels from Château Lafite. These were the only ones I encountered in the Côtes de Duras and they are still only used for experimental purposes. With 50 hectares of vines, this is the largest property of the appellation. I liked the wines. A pure Sauvignon was fresh and crisp, and a pink almost entirely from Cabernet Franc was attractively fruity, while the red was quite full and flavoursome. In 1983 they tried some carbonic maceration, but their vinifications generally follow the classic method. The blend for the red wine is usually 40 per cent each of Cabernet Sauvignon and Merlot with 20 per cent Cabernet Franc.

Finally, mention must be made of an enterprising idea which surely provides the answer to people who have ever dreamed of having their own vineyard. An English wine merchant called Andrew Gordon has created a scheme called 'Wineshare', based on the estate of Domaine du Grand-Mayne. You buy a row of vines and each year receive their production. The 25-hectare estate is planted with Cabernet Sauvignon, Cabernet Franc, Merlot, Sauvignon and Sémillon, so that both red and white wine is made by Michel Coutin, the full-time manager, who runs the property. Not all the vineyard is in production yet. I tasted the 1986 red wine, which was a pleasant, fruity glass of wine with some youthful stalkiness.

The Côtes de Duras feature among the several attractive wines of the south west. As such they may bear a similarity to the wines of Bordeaux, with red wines reminiscent of blackcurrants, and pungent whites from Sauvignon. However, they also have individuality. If you sip a glass of Sauvignon in the square, looking at the impressive entrance to the Château de Duras, in autumn sunshine, you cannot help feeling that all is right with the world.

CÔTES DU MARMANDAIS

In France Marmande is more famous for its tomatoes than for its wine, for the town of Marmande, in the fertile valley of the Garonne, is a centre for market gardening. Vines there are, to the north and south, but they are very much of secondary importance to fruit trees, vegetables and tobacco, and very few people make a living from vines alone. You see small patches of vineyards on well-exposed slopes, usually at an altitude of about 300 metres, with other crops on the valley floor.

The vineyards of Marmande are a natural continuation of those of the Gironde. They border Graves to the south of the Garonne and Entre-Deux-Mers to the north, while the lower edge of the vineyards is limited by the appellation of Buzet. In the Middle Ages wine was sent from the port of Marmande to Bordeaux; the wines of Marmande thus took their place amongst the wines of the Haut-Pays and their development is linked with that of Bordeaux. There are records that wine from Marmande reached London in 1306, while a town charter dated 1340 illustrates the importance attached to wine at the time. Until the Canal du Midi was built in the second half of the seventeenth century, the Garonne was the sole outlet for the wines of Marmande. Viticulture flourished in the eighteenth century and transport improved still further when the Bordeaux–Toulouse railway was opened in 1856; but then phylloxera struck in the mid-1870s.

The subsequent history is familiar. The vineyards were abandoned and mainly hybrid vines were planted until 1950, when a concentrated effort was made to improve the composition of the vineyards and the quality of the wine. The Côtes du Marmandais became a VDQS in 1955. The permitted grape varieties were a maximum of 50 per cent Bouchalès, Bouillet Noir, Abouriou, Merlot and Mérille and a minimum of 25 per cent of Cabernet Sauvignon, Fer Servadou, Syrah and Gamay. This was subsequently modified in 1983 to a maximum of 75 per cent Merlot, Cabernet Franc and Cabernet Sauvignon and a maximum of 50 per cent Cot, Fer Servadou, Gamay, Syrah and Abouriou. Bouillet Noir and Mérille have virtually disappeared from the vineyards of Marmande, while Bouchalès has been relegated to *vin ordinaire*, or Vin de Pays de l'Agenais.

It is Abouriou that gives the Côtes du Marmandais its individuality for this grape variety is not found in any other vineyards of France. Abouriou is an aromatic grape variety that ripens early and is resistant to disease, but does not age and needs to be blended with other varieties. The other more unusual grape of the vineyards of Marmande is the Fer, or Fer Servadou. This has a more distinctive flavour than the Abouriou, with a particular peppery taste and a hard finish, but it usually only represents 10 per cent in a blend as it is a late ripener.

Syrah has not adapted well to the south west. It was introduced to the area more recently, but the climate is too humid, rendering it very susceptible to rot. Nor does it ripen well. Gamay is an early ripener and is often used for *vin de primeur*. It is no surprise that it is the Bordeaux grape varieties that are the most successful. The growers do not want their wine to resemble a claret too closely, however, and so the local peculiarities of Abouriou and Fer are retained.

Although Côtes du Marmandais is predominantly a red wine, a little pink is made and also a small amount of white, from Sauvignon, Sémillon, Muscadelle and some Ugni Blanc. As in the Côtes de Duras, Ugni Blanc is allowed if there is an equivalent amount of Sauvignon. Even so, the best white wines contain a high proportion of Sauvignon and no Ugni Blanc.

The production of the Côtes du Marmandais is dominated by two co-operatives, at Cocumont to the south of Marmande and at Beaupuy to the north. The two co-operatives divide the area between them so that Beaupuy is responsible for seventeen villages and Cocumont for nine. Altogether the Côtes du Marmandais covers some 1,500 hectares. The co-operative at Beaupuy was founded in 1948, initially to make plain table wine, while the co-operative at Cocumont was born of the new status of Marmande and produced its first vintage in 1957. The co-operative of Beaupuy is the smaller and less dynamic of the two; it is hampered by its position, as much of the land on which its members have their vineyards is more valuable for building to accommodate the growing town of Marmande.

The co-operative of Cocumont is more modern in its outlook and methods. It has a small experimental vineyard, containing examples of the various grape varieties allowed in the appellation, as well as some new crossings such as Abouriou with Merlot. Work has been done on clonal selection, and since 1974 all new plantings have been with selected clones. The vines are planted in wide rows, 2.5 to 3 metres, to allow for the easy use of tractors and mechanical harvesters. There is usually a minimum of 3,000 vines per hectare, which are pruned in either single or double *guyot*. The soil in the Côtes du Marmandais is mainly clay and limestone and there is also some flint and gravel, for which SO4 and Riparia 3309 are the most suitable rootstocks.

The climate here is mild and maritime, similar to the Gironde. Frost can be a problem while hailstorms are very rare. With so many small valleys, however, there is considerable variation in microclimate.

The co-operative at Cocumont is well equipped for efficient vinification. There is nothing original in its methods. The red wines ferment for six to eight days on the skins and there are some new stainless-steel vats that can be programmed for automatic *remontage*. The red wine is centrifuged when the malolactic fermentation is finished; they consider this clarifies the wine more efficiently, as they do not want to leave it on the fine lees. Subsequently it spends sixteen months in vat before bottling, while the white and pink wines are bottled as early as possible.

A selection is made from the various *cuvées* and one property of 22 hectares, Château La Bastide, is vinified separately. The better grapes are used for the Cuvée du Président, with a high proportion of Merlot and Cabernet Sauvignon. The 1982 example that I tasted would be difficult to distinguish from everyday claret, demonstrating that it is the '*cépages d'appoint*', the secondary grape varieties such as Abouriou and Fer Servadou, that give Côtes du Marmandais any regional individuality.

I met one independent grower in the Côtes du Marmandais. M. Laugauzère at Beaupuy is a nursery gardener as well as a wine-grower. In his 20-hectare vineyard he has a little of everything, and makes white as well as red wine, but no *vin de pays*. His small cellar is delightfully rustic and has some magnificent spiders' webs. He still has an old open-topped stone vat in which all the different grapes are fermented together. He treads them with his feet to extract colour and has no means of controlling his fermentation temperatures. The press is the old-fashioned wooden vertical variety which these days is usually relegated to a museum. It all seemed rather contrary to modern oenology and I admit I experienced a certain trepidation before tasting his wine, but it was delicious. The white, containing 70 per cent Sauvignon, had an attractive pungency, while the red had a distinctive peppery flavour, with perfume and fruit; not a great deal of weight, but character and individuality.

The Côtes du Marmandais aspire to an appellation, and there has been a considerable programme of replanting in order to improve the content of the vineyards. The precise delimitation of the vineyards has been completed and an appellation would be a fitting reward for the growers' efforts. As yet, however, these are unrecognized by the Institut National des Appellations d'Origine.

BUZET

The vineyards of Buzet, in the heart of Gascony, lie in the shape of a half moon on the south bank of the Garonne, between Agen and Marmande. This is gentle countryside, where the little river Baise, a tributary of the Garonne, flows through the vineyards past the small village of Buzet. The Romans came here first, spreading viticulture through south west France. But the area is richer in vestiges of the Middle Ages, for the vineyards of Buzet were cultivated by the monks of the abbeys of Fontclaire, Buzet and St-Vincent. The area supported the English crown during the Hundred Years War and there are remains of medieval châteaux. Damazan was a fortified town and the village of Vienne still has its old walls intact, with four gateways, and four roads that meet at a crossroads in the centre.

The wines of Buzet were numbered amongst those of the Haut-Pays which the Bordelais refused to allow into the city until after St Martin's Day, 11 November. A list of prices dated 1284 mentions Nérac, a village in the appellation of Buzet, as one of the wine towns of the Haut-Pays, and a document from 1306 gives the exports of wine from various villages of today's appellation. Nérac was by far the most important with 281 *tonneaux*, followed by Villefranche du Queyran, with 71 *tonneaux*, Damazan with 62 *tonneaux* and Buzet with 45 *tonneaux*. Merchants in Agen helped to develop this trade, but the restrictions were not finally abolished until 1776. Wine from Buzet was then able to travel unimpeded to Holland, Prussia and even as far as New Orleans.

In the nineteenth century Cavoleau wrote that the wines of Nérac were sought after for their alcohol and weight. Indeed the nineteenth century was a period of prosperity for the area until phylloxera attacked in 1886. The vineyards were greatly reduced and any incentive to replant was finally removed in 1911 when a ministerial decree limited the wines of Bordeaux to those coming only from the department of the Gironde. Buzet was thus deprived of its chief market, for much of the area's production had found its way to Bordeaux to be blended as '*vin de médecin*' with lighter clarets. The rural depopulation following the First World War reduced the vineyards still further, so that when the Syndicat de la Défense des Vins des Côtes de Buzet was founded in 1946, there were very few vineyards on which to build the future appellation. Many were planted with hybrids but efforts were made to establish the appropriate grape varieties, which were rewarded by the creation of a Vin Délimité de Qualité Supérieure for the Côtes de Buzet in 1953.

The co-operative of Buzet at Buzet-sur-Baise was founded in 1955 in an attempt to develop the sales of the area. *Négociants* were reluctant to pay any more money for a VDQS than for an anonymous *vin ordinaire* and it is thanks to the efforts of the co-operative that the Côtes de Buzet became an appellation in 1973, with vineyards delimited in twenty-seven villages. With the 1988 vintage the name was changed to Buzet. It is undeniably one of the most efficient and dynamic of all the French wine co-operatives, and can justly claim credit for the revival of the wines of Buzet. It now accounts for most of the production of the appellation, although there are half a dozen independent producers who developed their estates following its success.

Although white and pink wines are allowed in the appellation, Buzet is essentially a red wine. The grape varieties are those of Bordeaux, with Cabernet Sauvignon, Cabernet Franc, Merlot and a drop of Malbec for the red and pink wine, and Sauvignon, Sémillon and Muscadelle for the tiny production of white wine. The soil of Buzet is mainly of clay and limestone, with *boulbènes*, a mixture of sand and clay, and a high proportion of gravel. The climate is similar to that of the Gironde, although the enormous forest of the Landes that lies to the south of Buzet has some influence on it. Spring frosts can be a problem, and also the occasional hailstorm. The grapes usually ripen a week later than in the Gironde, and although vintages generally follow those of Bordeaux, there are variations.

The vineyards are on gentle slopes. There is nothing particular about the viticulture of the region. The vines are pruned in the *guyot simple* manner and planted with a minimum of 4,000 vines per hectare, usually with 2 metres between the rows. About half the co-operative's vineyards are mechanically harvested.

The Vignerons Réunis des Côtes de Buzet, to give the co-operative its full name, now total 450 members, who between them cultivate 1,200 hectares of vines. Twelve to 15 hectares is the size of an average property and there are about 150 growers for whom vines are their principal source of income, while the others practise polyculture, growing melons, strawberries and wheat on the plain. There are fruit trees too. The growth of the appellation has been considerable, with a major shift from *vin ordinaire* to appellation wine. In 1976 *vin de table* accounted for two-thirds of the co-operative's total production of 60,000 hectolitres, while by 1983 production had increased to about 80,000 hectolitres, of which 55,000 to 60,000 hectolitres were appellation Côtes de Buzet. The total area delimited in the appellation amounts to 15,800 hectares, while the area actually planted is a mere 1,200-odd hectares and is unlikely to increase much more.

The most striking aspect of the vinification process at the co-operative is the ageing in 225-litre barrels to which all its wines are subjected. This must be the only co-operative in France with its own resident cooper, Yves St-Martin. His son is destined to succeed him when he retires and both went to the cooperage school in Beaune. A careful selection of grapes and *cuvées* is made so that wines are given the amount of wood ageing appropriate to their composition. The barrels, of Tronçais oak, are replaced every five years. The best wines spend six months in new oak, followed by six months in older wood. A wine is tasted after three months in wood, and then aged for a further six to nine months according to its development. Lighter wines may be given only three months' ageing in older barrels, and then blended with some wine that has only been kept in vat. The evolution of the wines is very carefully followed. Altogether they have nearly 4,000 barrels, kept in one large cellar. They are an impressive sight.

Vinification techniques are carefully controlled. An initial selection of the grapes is made, beginning even before the vintage, depending on their ripeness and the age of the vine. In a relatively young appellation, ten-year-old vines merit a bonus, while wine from young four- to six-year-old vines is also kept apart. The better-situated vineyards on the higher slopes also receive a bonus. The other important factors are the yield, which is set at a maximum of 45 hectolitres per hectare, and the condition and health of the grapes, which is rated on a scale of one to four. Any rotten or unripe grapes will be declassified into *vin de table*, which gives the growers an incentive to work well.

The grapes are destalked and the *cuvaison* can last from eight to twenty days, depending on the quality of the grapes. Temperature is maintained around 28–30°C. There are usually five or six *remontages* during the fermentation, but generally they prefer a longer *cuvaison* and fewer *remontages*. The best pressed juice is blended with the free-run juice, and the blending or *assemblage* of the different grape varieties takes place from December onwards after the malolactic fermentation. The wines are then subjected to cold treatment for the precipitation of tartrates before they are put into wood. As well as barrel ageing, the better wines are given bottle age before sale.

The co-operative has two estates, whose wines are vinified separately, Château de Bouchet is its flagship and the wine spends six months in one-year-old oak. You can taste the oak on the young wine, but there is some good blackcurrant fruit too, showing ageing potential. Château de Gueyze also spends six months in one-year-old wood and is a firmer, more closed style of wine, characteristic of the *terroir*, and with rather more ageing potential than Château du Bouchet. The château itself is one of those delightful French houses with two conical towers, reminiscent of dunces' caps. The building was begun in the sixteenth century, but bits have been added subsequently to create a hotchpotch of architectural styles. Then apart from the basic Buzet there is Cuvée Napoléon, which has spent six months in older barrels. I found hints of cedarwood on the nose, while the flavour is dry and firm, and again capable of two or three years' ageing. Even the simplest Buzet, of which half of each bottle has spent three months in wood, shows some potential for development along with youthful fruit and tannin. It is characteristic of the quality and potential of the whole appellation.

There is a handful of independent growers, not one of whom comes from Gascony. There is a *pied-noir* from Algeria, a Belgian and a Parisian. The most Gascon is Jean Ryckman at Domaine de Versailles. His parents moved here from Lille in 1937 when they bought a small plot of 4.5 hectares of land, so he has lived in Buzet since he was nine. He now has 25 hectares of land, 8 with vines, as well as chickens and wheat. He was a garage mechanic until he took over the family land. The vineyards were planted with vines like Alicante Bouschet and Bouchalès for *vin de table*, and there was also Chasselas for table grapes. He has replanted with the red grapes of the appellation, Cabernet and Merlot, but no Malbec.

The *lieu-dit* of his vineyard really is Versailles. But when he tried to register the name of the estate, the Institut National de la Propriété Industriale said that it was '*à nature de troubler l'ordre publique*'! M. Ryckman had to send a copy of the cadastral plan before the powers that be would agree to the name of Domaine de Versailles. The facilities were far from palatial, with plumbing reminiscent of the seventeenth century! We talked in the kitchen, with its lovely open fireplace. A door led directly into the old barn where M. Ryckman makes his wine.

He has replaced his father's old wooden vats with concrete ones. The *cuvaison* lasts for three or four weeks. The grapes are fermented as they are picked, with no precise blending, and the wine is left for two or three years in vat. It is usually bottled when he has an order. He has thought about buying some barrels, but thinks it might make the wine too heavy. It is tannic enough as it is, and he does not like the oxidation effect of wood ageing.

M. Ryckman gave me a very friendly welcome. I was invited to lunch and entertained to a tasting of recent vintages and to some amusing anecdotes of local gossip about his fellow wine-growers. He has adopted Gascony and pronounces Buzet in the Gascon way, as though it were Buzette. He had found a copy of Jules Verne's *Géographie de la France* when he repaired the roof of his house. This tattered volume told him that there were 70,000 hectares of vines in Lot-et-Garonne before the phylloxera and he himself has found the remains of vines in the nearby woodland. Apparently there was white wine, too – a sweet wine which was made from overripe grapes in the village of Clairac, now outside the appellation. The Côte St-Pierre, with its red, gravelly soil, gave the best grapes. That name has long disappeared; but for M. Ryckman it is still the red gravel that accounts for the quality of Buzet, for the colour of the soil gives colour to the wine.

The 1980 Domaine de Versailles, tasted in October 1985 and bottled only the previous July, had some attractive blackcurrant fruit along with the acidity characteristic of the vintage. 1979 was a better year and was described as 'an elegant old wine'. My favourite was the 1978, with its deep colour, and a mature, elegant flavour of blackcurrants. It was ageing well, but then you cannot drink a Buzet before the third winter. I was also introduced to the French country custom of the '*champereau*', whereby you pour a little wine into the dregs of your soup and drink them from the bowl. Lunch finished with a taste of marc d'Aquitaine and I drove off rather uncertainly along a narrow country lane to St-Colombe-en-Brulhois and my next appointment.

CAHORS

In the last century Cahors was famed for its black wine, from which a legend has developed of a wine that is sturdy, tannic and long-lasting. Today, although Cahors is more accessible, it remains one of the finer wines of the south west, with a taste that owes something to Bordeaux but also has a character of its own. Cahors is firmly red, for no white or pink wine in included in the appellation.

Like most of the vineyards of the south west its origins go back to the Romans. Domitian's edict of AD 92 halted the spread of viticulture throughout Roman Gaul so that wheat was planted instead, until the Emperor Probus authorized further plantings of vines in 276. The vineyards then grew steadily in importance. In the seventh century there was a record of St Didier, bishop of the city of Cahors, sending wine to his fellow cleric St Paul, bishop of Verdun, who thanked him enthusiastically and compared the wine to Falernian, the great Italian wine whose prestige dated back at least to the days of Virgil and Horace.

The marriage of Henry II of England to Eleanor of Aquitaine opened the way to the development of the vineyards not only of Bordeaux but also of the hinterland, the vineyards of the Haut-Pays that depended upon the river systems of the Garonne and the Dordogne to provide transport to their markets. Throughout the Middle Ages a struggle was waged against the Bordelais and their privileged position. However, there are records that Cahors was sold in London as early as 1225. From the early Middle Ages the black wines of Cahors were deemed to withstand travelling well, and even to improve with a journey. Taxes and privileges were negotiated over the years. At the beginning of the fourteenth century it was recorded that Bordeaux on average exported 82,710 *tonneaux* of wine per year, of which half came from Agen and Quercy. In 1365 the Black Prince, who had been given twenty-four pipes of Cahors wine, conferred a privilege which enabled a pipe of Cahors to enter the city of Bordeaux for five sous.

The ongoing events of the Hundred Years War intervened. The city of Cahors resisted Edward III, who in retaliation in 1373 forbade the wines of Cahors to enter Bordeaux until after Christmas. Previously, the wines of the Haut-Pays had been allowed into the port of Bordeaux on 11 November. Autumn was the crucial period, the moment of harvesting the grapes, making the wine and shipping the new vintage. Bordeaux could be avoided by sending the wine by land from St-Macaire to Bergerac on the Dordogne, which flows out into the Gironde below Bordeaux, but this was lengthy and

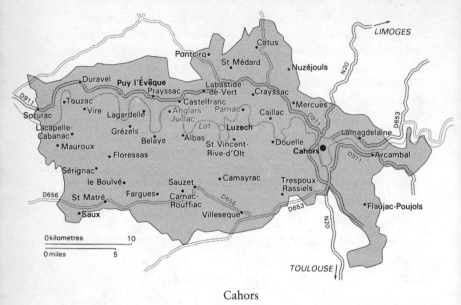

Cahors

impracticable in those days of atrocious roads. The Bordelais privileges were only finally abolished under Louis XVI in 1776.

François I contributed to the reputation of Cahors. He ordered vines from Quercy, the region around the city of Cahors, to be planted in the grounds of the château of Fontainebleau under the supervision of a wine-grower from Cahors. There is an account of a wine-grower called Rivals setting off for the royal court with thirty mules laden with vines and barrels. The prosperity of the area grew when the Lot was finally rendered navigable under Henri IV, with the construction of twenty-one locks. This was part of Sully's work of improving transport and communications throughout the country by the building of canals. Arthur Young, travelling in France during the years 1787 and 1788, wrote of the wine of Cahors. By the eighteenth century the fame of Cahors had spread to Russia, and Peter the Great is said to have drunk Cahors for his stomach ulcer. Cahors was also used by Russian Orthodox priests as their communion wine. In the nineteenth century it was a source of inspiration to the painter Ingres, who was born at nearby Montauban and insisted that a daily supply of Cahors was essential to his good health.

Writing in 1816, Jullien described three kinds of wine, black, red and pink. The black wine was usually only for blending, while the red was good table wine, and the pink was the customary drink of the local inhabitants. The black wines came from the Auxerrois grape and they were very dark, well-flavoured and high in alcohol; they were not suitable for everyday use, but were particularly good for giving colour, body and weight to weaker wines, and they also travelled very well. Their quality came from the manner of their vinification, rather than from the grape variety or the climate. Jullien considered that the Auxerrois resembled a *teinturier* variety, with coloured juice, and explained that either part of the crop was cooked in an oven or the whole vintage was boiled in large cauldrons before fermentation.

The red wine had less colour than the black wine, but was quite full-bodied, alcoholic and possessed of a good flavour. This is the wine that would resemble present-day Cahors, while Jullien's pink wine was a local drink made from water and the *marc* of the black wine.

In 1856 Rendu wrote of a long-lasting, full-bodied wine. The vintage usually took place during the first half of October, the date being determined by a *ban des vendanges* or public proclamation. Everyone destalked and crushed their grapes. Depending on the temperature of the year, the *cuvaison* lasted for a longer or shorter time, but usually for at least a month. Once the wine was in barrel it was topped up when necessary. The young wines were racked at least twice, in March and in November, and the old wines only once, usually in March. The wine was not bottled until it was ready, and only after six or eight years in barrel, when it was mature. It could be drunk after two years in bottle.

Five years later Dr Guyot enthused about the vineyards of Lot, saying that he had never seen any so picturesque, regular and well-maintained. He described the black wines, which were destined for blending. These wines were delivered in barrel to Bordeaux to give colour to other wines, and a few years previously they had been more expensive. He considered the table wines to be much better. When they had a little age, they were excellent and very healthy, without any excess of alcohol. He said he was surprised by the good effect of these wines on the digestion, on the strength of the body and on the spirit.

During the eighteenth century the vineyards of Cahors enjoyed a considerable expansion: in 1816 Jullien recorded that there were

40,000 hectares of vines in the department of the Lot, which compared with 33,000 in Aude, 73,000 in Hérault and 72,000 in Gard in the same year. This was a period of considerable prosperity for the region, but with the arrival of the railways, competition with Bordeaux was replaced by competition from the Midi. It was during this time that the Midi was transformed from a region of polyculture into one of monoculture, and the vine became the sole agricultural activity of the region. The facility of transport provided by the railways meant that cheap, easy-to-produce wines from the Midi became readily available all over France, and Cahors was one of the many vineyards that suffered from this transformation of the Languedoc.

Further misfortune was brought by the arrival of phylloxera in the Lot in 1887; the effects were as disastrous as elsewhere in France. An exchange of letters between a wine-grower in St-Vincent-Rive-d'Olt and his son who was doing his military service in Bordeaux described the fears and problems of the time. On 1 July 1879 the son wrote: 'It is with distress that I have learnt that phylloxera, this disease that is so terrible for the vine, has appeared all over our canton. As you say in your letter, if the disease continues, the country will be completely ruined for our principal resource is the vine.' In May 1881 his father wrote that 'the vines are not at all beautiful and we think that in two or three years we shall be without vines and forced to drink water'.

Vineyards were abandoned and people turned to cereals and livestock. Many left the region and entire villages were deserted, especially in areas where vines had been the only possible crop. Although the solution of grafting was soon discovered, the Auxerrois, which was the principal grape of the vineyards, did not adapt well to this process. Mildew also attacked, causing further damage, while the First World War aggravated the decline in population. The vineyards of the Lot lost their image of quality and could not compete in price with wines from the Midi or from Algeria. Hybrids were planted instead of the traditional vines of the region and the wines of the Lot merged with the lake of anonymous *vin de table*. However, this expedient at least ensured the survival of many of the area's vineyards and provided the basis for the revival of a vineyard of quality later in this century.

Cahors was recognized as one of the first VDQS in 1951. Nevertheless the remaining vineyards were depleted still further by the severe frosts of 1956 and it was not until the 1960s that the first efforts at a revival made themselves felt. The real impetus came with the recognition of the area as an appellation in 1971, and since then the area has undergone enormous growth and revitalization.

The appellation of Cahors covers a large area, with some 21,708 hectares delimited, of which in 1988 3,300 were in production, but that area is steadily increasing year by year. The western limit of the appellation is at Fumel, while the old town of Cahors is on the eastern edge. The Lot is crossed by Cahors' impressive medieval bridge, the Pont Valentré, with its three towers. There are forty-five villages in the appellation, mostly in the valley of the Lot, which stretches some 40 kilometres to the west of the town. Villages like Luzech, Puy-l'Évêque and Albas were once river ports that sent their wine by river to Bordeaux.

The view from above the village of Albas gives an insight into the geography of the area. Albas itself was a fortified village perched above the river, and was the summer residence of the bishop of Cahors. The river has cut out a narrow, meandering path, almost turning back on itself in a large loop, or *cingle*, which is the local word for this river formation. As the crow flies it is 25 kilometres from Puy-l'Évêque to the town of Cahors, but by the road which follows the river bank the distance is three times as long. The steep slopes of the valley, where once there were vines, are now covered with shrubs. Vines have been planted above the river on the more gentle lower slopes, or higher up on the arid plateaux, or *causses*, as they are known locally. In June the air is full of the scent of honeysuckle and wild roses in the warm sunshine. As this area was so much fought over during the Hundred Years War, it is crowded with medieval castles such as Grezels, Bonaguil and Mercuès.

Cahors is unique amongst the vineyards of the south west in that it does not allow any Cabernet Sauvignon or Cabernet Franc in the appellation. The regulations demand a minimum of 70 per cent Auxerrois, which is more commonly known as Cot or Malbec in other parts of France. No one is quite sure what the association is, if it exists at all, between this grape variety and the city of Auxerre in Yonne. Nor is there any link with the white Auxerrois grape. It is in Cahors that the Auxerrois is at its most characteristic, for there is no other appellation with such a high percentage of Auxerrois and it is indeed possible to find Cahors made from Auxerrois alone. The remaining 30 per cent may comprise Merlot, Tannat and Jurançon

Rouge. The recommended proportions are 70 per cent Auxerrois, with 15 per cent each of Merlot and Tannat. Merlot and Tannat were officially allowed in the area in 1966 as part of the effort to revive the quality of Cahors.

Jurançon Rouge, which is a member of the whimsically named Folle family of vines (*une folle* translates as 'a mad woman'), is an old Lotois grape variety that is now tending to disappear. It was once the principal variety for blending with Auxerrois, but with the search for better varieties in the late 1960s it has been gradually replaced, and by 1990 will no longer be permitted in the vineyards of Cahors. It is generally agreed that it has nothing to contribute to a fine Cahors for it has neither colour nor body and tends to make rather light, insipid wine. The occasional partisan will claim that it does well on the *causses*, but although it was once useful for diluting the tannin of the Auxerrois, that role is now performed better by the Merlot.

It is the Auxerrois that gives Cahors its tough, rugged quality, with a firm backbone of tannin. The chief problem of the Auxerrois is its susceptibility to *coulure*, so that yields can sometimes be very low – as little as 17 hectolitres per hectare in 1984. Work has been done with clonal selection, and with various rootstocks to find those most suitable for this sometimes temperamental grape. Certainly it was a courageous, if not obstinate, wine-grower who continued to grow Auxerrois in the immediate post-war years when its wine sold at the same price as that of the prolific hybrids with which most of the vineyards of Cahors were planted. Auxerrois on the *causses* is particularly tough and austere, while on soil with a higher proportion of clay it is more aromatic.

It is the Merlot that softens Cahors, giving it body and roundedness. It ripens before the Auxerrois but its yields can be small, as it too suffers from *coulure*. The maximum percentage of Merlot is 20 per cent and no more is permitted for fears of Cahors becoming too Bordelais in character. Opinions are divided over the qualities of the late-ripening Tannat. Some people like it for the extra tannin it gives, while others would say that it merely exaggerates the defects of the Auxerrois. It performs best on the arid land of the *causses*, while the Merlot prefers the vineyards of the valley with their more humid soil. Again 20 per cent is the maximum permitted percentage, a figure that relates to plantings in the vineyards rather than to precise proportions in the wine.

Other grape varieties were formerly allowed, such as Syrah, which proved unsatisfactory when an effort was made to introduce it in the mid-1960s. Cabernet also was eliminated in the course of these experiments, while the Abouriou of the Côtes du Marmandais disappeared with the granting of the appellation in 1971. Valdiguié, which is a relation of the Cot family but infinitely inferior, was abandoned with the change of regulations in 1966.

The climate partakes of both the Mediterranean and the Atlantic, Cahors being equidistant from Bordeaux, the Mediterranean and the Pyrenees. The topography of the vineyards also lends itself to a variety of different microclimates. Generally there is none of the Atlantic fog, and drying winds keep the vineyards free of rot; on the other hand the heat is not as great as on the Mediterranean. Frost can be a problem in spring, though land which is more vulnerable to frost, on the lower slopes, tends to be used for other crops. 1956, however, is remembered as the year of the great frost that virtually destroyed the remaining vineyards of Cahors. Hail can also be a problem and some growers are equipped with anti-hail rockets that attempt to minimize the danger. The aim is to change the temperature and thus prevent the formation of the hailstones.

The great debate of Cahors is over soil. The vineyards have grown considerably in the last twenty years or so, from 200 hectares at the beginning of the 1960s to over 3,000 hectares today. Now the expansion has been halted and planting is only permitted where remaining hybrid vines are replaced with noble varieties. A precise delimitation of the vineyards has been carried out by the INAO, with no controversy over their decision. Unlike in Chablis, the delimited area is undisputed; the appellation includes sites where vines flourished before the phylloxera crisis, and covers a variety of terrains with different soil characteristics that inevitably give different styles of wine. The debate centres on the merits or disadvantages of the valley slopes, or *coteaux*, as opposed to the *causses*.

The *causses* are the arid plateaux above the valley where the terrain is stony, with minimal topsoil. When Georges Vigouroux of Château Haute-Serre planted his vineyards, he spent three years breaking up the huge stones with bulldozers. The land had been planted with vines in the early nineteenth century, but had reverted to shrubland with the decline of Cahors. He is convinced of the merits of this dry, chalky soil, although he admits that he was considered 'the madman of Cahors' when he began planting his vines in what looked like a sea of stones. But with such limited topsoil weeds also have problems in growing, so there is no need for chemical weedkillers. In the old days they hardly needed to work the vineyards at all, only once a year. Nowadays during the summer they will not touch the vines from the end of June until the harvest. Drought can affect the quality of the wine, for if no rain falls during the summer, the roots need to go deep to seek out water; and sometimes the ripening of the grapes is blocked by drought, resulting in a more astringent wine.

Partisans of the *causses* believe that the wine from these vineyards is tougher, sturdier and generally longer-lasting, while the wines from the valley slopes are fuller and softer, with less astringency. However, as a local oenologist, Pascal Thiolet, pointed out, vinification methods also play their part. The practice of destalking the grapes affects the tannin levels in the wine. The growers of the valley had always tended to destalk their grapes, whereas those of the *causses* fermented their wine with the stalks. This has changed with the creation of the large estates and the arrival of the mechanical harvester, whose use is feasible on the flatter vineyards of the *causses*. Today most grapes are fermented without their stalks, automatically giving a less astringent wine.

The dominant soil of Cahors is clay and chalk, with some decomposed rocks for which the local name is *castines*. The proportions of clay and chalk vary from village to village. In some places there is a high iron content, giving a deeper red colour to the soil, while in other spots the soil is white and chalky. The river banks are alluvial and no vines grow there, as the land is much too fertile. In other sites there is flint mixed with clay. Those who favour the *causses* say that the tougher wine comes from these arid vineyards, while others prefer the wine from the gravel soil of the valley slopes, considering it to be more complete and rounded. The discussion is endless, especially as factors other than soil come into play in determining the taste of a wine.

In the last century the Auxerrois was always planted in the *gobelet* system of the Midi, where the vine looks like a small bush without any wires or supports. In fact it performed very badly in this way, and it was Dr Guyot who first attributed the low yields of the Lot, compared to those of Hérault, to the unsuitability of the Auxerrois to the short pruning of the *gobelet*. All the vines of Cahors are now trained on wires in the single *guyot* system. There is a permitted minimum of 4,000 plants of Auxerrois per hectare, while Merlot is usually more densely planted, as it gives a lower yield. You can see neat parcels of vines with rose bushes at the end of the row, as is common practice in the Médoc. In June they provide a welcome splash of colour as well as having the functional purpose of warning against an attack of oidium. In such a dry climate, however, rot is generally not a problem and the treatment of the vines is no different from anywhere else in the south west.

Vinification methods vary with the wine-maker. Usually, each grape variety is fermented separately and blended after the malolactic fermentation. Most people are equipped to a varying degree to control their fermentation temperatures and concrete is the most common material for vats. The use of wood is one of the points of discussion: virtually no one ferments in wood nowadays, but there is a growing use of 225-litre barrels, including some new ones, for ageing Cahors.

I was able to visit several of the principal growers of the appellation. What follows is a guideline to who does what. The largest producer is the co-operative, which accounts for 40 per cent of the appellation; there are also three *négociants* – Rigal, Reutnauer and Georges Vigouroux – and a growing number of independent producers. One of the encouraging aspects of Cahors is that the average age of the growers is relatively young. In some regions you feel that an appellation may die out as the men disappear, whereas in Cahors it is quite the contrary, with a youthful enthusiasm that is renewing the appellation.

The co-operative of Cahors is called Les Caves d'Olt, Olt being the old word for Lot. It was founded in 1947 as part of the early attempt to revive the reputation of Cahors. Today its 500 members have 1,500 hectares of vineyards. As well as Cahors it also makes Vin de Pays des Coteaux de Quercy, and is one of the largest producers of this wine. The co-operative went through the doldrums during the late 1970s, when the production of the new vineyards exceeded the demand for Cahors and the marketing expertise to remedy the commercial situation was lacking. The quality of the wine was indifferent, and insufficient to inspire a growth in sales. Happily things have changed: ten years on, Les Caves d'Olt have improved their methods and equipment and, with a greater emphasis on quality, are making wine that is more fitting to the reputation of Cahors.

New stainless-steel fermentation vats were installed in 1984 and they are equipped with cooling systems and pumps for *remontage* of the juice. The *cuvaison* usually lasts ten days. There is no separation of the different grape varieties as the makers believe that blending in the fermentation vat is better than in the finished wine. They are also developing the ageing of their better wines in new oak barrels. The first 225-litre barrels were bought for the 1983 vintage and a wine will usually spend three months in new wood. This treatment is reserved for their various châteaux and other estates, as well as for a new brand, Impernal. Everyday Cahors is aged in cement vats for twelve months.

You can find the wines of Les Caves d'Olt under a variety of names. Amongst their members there are five châteaux: Château Caix has associations with the Danish royal family, for its owner, Prince Henri de Laborde de Monpezat, is married to Queen Margrethe; Château Cayrou d'Albas is the property of his father, Comte André de Laborde de Monpezat, while Château Lagrezette belongs to the managing director of Cartier, Alain Perrin. There are also Château de Parnac, in the village where Les Caves d'Olt have their cellars, and Château des Bouysses. The several domaines include Labarrade, Landes, Léret-Monpezat, Dauliac and Massable; in addition there are several other brands, including Comte André de Monpezat, which is a selection of better wines, Clément Marot, named after a sixteenth-century poet from Cahors, Marquis d'Olt, and Oppidum. On two days during the vintage the members are encouraged to bring in what they consider to be their very best grapes, and it is from these that their better wines are made. The grapes from the châteaux and domaines are vinified separately and kept apart from the other wines.

Georges Vigouroux was a *négociant* before he became a vineyard owner. He inherited a family business that dealt not only in the wines of Cahors, but also in the other main appellations of the south west apart from Bordeaux. Then in 1970 he bought 60-odd hectares of shrubland and the ruined château of Haute-Serre on the *causses* outside the town of Cahors. He wanted to make the traditional wine of Cahors, 'as it was in the old days'. His first vintage was in 1976; since then he has purchased an adjoining property, the Clos du Pech de Jammes, and in 1983 he acquired the medieval Château de Mercuès. In the thirteenth century this was the palace of the counts of Cahors, and later belonged to the bishops of Cahors until the Revolution. M. Vigouroux plans to replant its once extensive vineyard, while the château is being transformed into a starred hotel and restaurant where I was treated to lunch. The subdued atmosphere of the elegant dining-room was disturbed by the arrival of the hotel Labrador, accompanied by a squeaking puppy that had been found abandoned on the doorstep of the hotel that morning. It was having immense difficulty in controlling its still unsteady paws on the highly polished floor!

Vinification methods at Haute-Serre are meticulous and no expense has been spared to equip the estate with efficient, streamlined cellars. The *cuvaison* lasts eighteen to twenty days in stainless-steel vats and the temperature is maintained at 27–28°C, with frequent *remontages*. Chaptalization is rarely necessary, as up on the *causses* the stones of the vineyards retain the heat of the day, which they radiate on to the grapes during the night. Haute-Serre is made from 75 per cent Auxerrois, 15 per cent Merlot and 10 per cent Tannat, which are blended together after the malolactic fermentation and before ageing in wood for at least eighteen months. The barrels are bought second-hand in Bordeaux and used for two or three years. New barrels are considered unnecessary as there is no need to supplement the tannin in the wine with extra wood tannin.

The wines of Haute-Serre are good and will undoubtedly improve as the vines become older. In 1985 the 1978 vintage was rather closed on the nose, with a slightly woody but still elegant flavour and a certain astringency on the finish. Vigouroux's best *négociant* wine is Les Comtes de Cahors; at two years of age the 1983 vintage of this was tough and youthful, with plenty of both tannin and fruit, showing considerable potential for the future.

The other important *négociant* company of the appellation is that of Rigal, which today is run by the twin brothers Franck and Jacques. The former is an oenologist and the latter, whom I met, deals with sales. The family have had vineyards in Cahors for 300 years and they were wine-growers long before they were *négociants*. It was only in 1945 that their father began to act as a broker for other merchants, and they did not begin bottling wine until the creation of the appellation in 1971. They own Château St-Didier, which was once a fortress and whose original eleventh-century cellars still exist. The 52-hectare estate is made up of four separate vineyards in the village of Parnac. They are planted with 80 per cent Auxerrois, 15 per cent Merlot and 5 per cent Tannat. The wine is aged in 225-litre barrels for eighteen months, while their *négociant* wine, sold as Carte Noire or Prince de Cahors, is kept in larger, older casks. They also have a more recent estate, Prieuré de Cénac, up on the *causses*. The land was bought in 1978 and two years were necessary to clear the scrub before the first vines could be planted. There are now 37 hectares in production, with another 8 planted. The blend varies slightly from that of Château St-Didier, with 10 per cent each of Merlot and Tannat and 80 per cent Auxerrois. A quarter of the production is aged for three to six months in new oak barrels, while a further quarter is kept in second-year barrels and another quarter spends a longer period in three-year-old wood. Both the 1985 and 1986 vintages have been enthusiastically received and are indicative of the new wave of wine-making in the appellation. A more recent acquisition is Château de Grezel. In addition to their own properties Rigal are responsible for various other estates, whose wine is bottled by them at the property with a mobile bottling machine.

They vinify each grape variety separately and also take into consideration the age of the vines, with different vats for vines aged from six to ten years, ten to twenty years, and over twenty years. Unusually, the final blending takes place after the ageing and before bottling and consequently we were able to taste some pure grape varieties. The Merlot was quite perfumed, noticeably the softest of the three with hints of blackcurrant. The Tannat was green and tough, with more acidity than the Auxerrois, while the Auxerrois had an almost cedarwood elegance and firm austerity. There was no doubt that a blend of all three was very much the better wine. At three years old the 1982 Château St-Didier was a pretty tough mouthful, with some cherry fruit and lots of tannin. We were told that it would develop like the 1969, which in 1985 was a rich meaty mouthful, with plenty of fruit and a good structure with balance and length.

The most important of the independent growers of Cahors is Jean Jouffreau. Fellow growers describe him as the patriach of Cahors. His family have owned Clos de Gamot for generations, since 1610, while the estate of Château du Cayrou is more recent, part of the new generation of vineyards that arose after the creation of the appellation. The château itself, however, is a fortified house of the twelfth century with later additions up to the seventeenth century. It is built of soft yellow stone, with creeper covering the walls and a cedar tree in the courtyard. The dovecot bears the emblem of the shell of Santiago de Compostela. In stark contrast, the cellars are new.

Monsieur Jouffreau's vinification methods are straightforward.

The grapes are destalked and the juice fermented at 27°C. In a good year the *cuvaison* will last twenty days, with regular *remontages* to extract the maximum colour, but if the grapes are unripe it will be shorter. The pressed juice is kept separate from the free-run juice and often used in the final blend. Each grape variety is fermented separately, too. The wine is aged in wood, in large casks averaging 104 hectolitres from Allier. M. Jouffreau is against new wood: 'Our friends from Bordeaux may need tannin from wood, but we do not.' The wood breathes and the thickness of the wood affects the evolution of the wine, hastening it or slowing it down. He makes wine to age and to last. A tasting of young wines at Clos de Gamot was therefore particularly difficult as the wines were all closed and unforthcoming.

More accessible were the *perpétuelles*. M. Jouffreau has maintained an old Cahors tradition founded on the belief that the wine keeps better in wood than in bottle. In the cellars at Clos de Gamot there are barrels of wine going back to the last century, the oldest from 1880. Great care is taken of them: the hessian around the bungs is washed every week when the barrels are topped up with wine of the same age, kept in a smaller barrel. First we tried the 1962, which had a warm raisiny nose, with very concentrated flavours and tannins. M. Jouffreau said this is the wine to drink with a *sauce aux truffes*, which is one of the great gastronomic specialities of the region. The 1949 was almost chocolaty, very rich with a dry finish, and the 1918 had undertones of roses and dried violets, as well as some velvety chocolate flavours. The 1904 was amber in colour, but showing no hints of oxidation, while the 1880 was beginning to fade a little. An allowance might be made, however, for it was after all 105 years old. When I asked M. Jouffreau about the black wine, he replied quite simply, 'That is what you have tasted today.'

The *perpétuelles* were made only from Auxerrois as they had never succumbed to the temptation of planting hybrid varieties at Clos de Gamot. M. Jouffreau reminisced. He left school at fifteen and learnt from experience in vineyard and cellar, as well as from his father and grandfather. He has visited all the wine regions of France except champagne, which he considers to be a fabrication. Wine is a passion for him: 'I have two faults, wine and football!' Clos de Gamot was the first to bottle its wine, before the Second World War. He had helped to achieve the VDQS for Cahors, being one of the few who had continued to make true Cahors when the area was going through the doldrums. He used to work with oxen and remembered that one was called Ravaillac, after the assassin of Henry IV! He looked back on the old days with a certain nostalgia, but he was also optimistic about the future of Cahors, firmly asserting that it had been born again after its fall.

With 41 hectares the Baldès family have one of the largest estates in Cahors, at Clos Triguedina. In the Languedoc *triguedina* means *il me tard de dîner* or *de boire*, in other words 'I need a drink'! The property has monastic origins, and was later a coaching house. Today you find an attractive old building, with cellars built round a courtyard. In June the roses are in flower. The functional modern cellars were built in 1976. Clos Triguedina is a wine that is made to last, and M. Baldès criticized some of his fellow growers for making wines for drinking too early. He considers that Cahors makes a vulgar young wine that can never be great, but a wonderful old wine.

The *cuvaison* at Clos Triguedina lasts two weeks. Each parcel of vines and each grape variety is fermented separately, and the pressed juice is only used if there is not enough tannin or colour in the free-run juice. The proportions are 70 per cent Auxerrois, 25 per cent Merlot and 5 per cent Tannat. This represents a high percentage of Merlot but M. Baldès was one of the first to plant Merlot in the area and he likes the supple quality it gives to the wine.

Since 1976 he has made a 'prestige wine' in the better years, called Prince Probus, after the Roman emperor who repealed Domitian's edict and allowed vines to be planted again in the area. The particularity of Prince Probus is that it comes from seventy-year-old vines and is aged in new wood for anything from nine to twelve months, using 225-litre barrels that are replaced after two wines. In contrast, Clos de Triguedina is aged in large casks for twelve to eighteen months. I don't think I was meant to, but I preferred Clos Triguedina. We sampled several vintages of Prince Probus, but they all left an underlying impression of new wood that had not blended with the fruit of the wine, while Clos Triguedina, to my taste, had better balance, with fruit and length.

Pierre Cantegrelle is characteristic of the new development in Cahors. He is part of the *négociant* company of Les Caves St-Antoine at Brive, and bought the run-down Château de Chambert, now his main activity, in 1973. The site was occupied by a medieval château which was destroyed by the English during the Hundred Years War; a second château was burnt at the Revolution and later rebuilt. The vineyards had turned into scrub. Fifteen years later there are 53 hectares of vines on the arid, stony land of the *causses* and the château has been restored to its former splendour. There are new cellars, as well as a small tasting-room built entirely from stones that were removed from the vineyards. The grapes are destalked and the fermentation, which lasts about twelve days, takes place in new stainless-steel vats, with the temperature maintained at 28°C. The juice is regularly run over the skins throughout the fermentation, and the wine then spends a year in vat, followed by a year in wood. Small barrels are bought from Château Margaux each year, used once and sold again.

We tasted the 1982 Château de Chambert. The ageing in wood had rounded the wine so that it was less rugged than some Cahors; it also contained 15 per cent Merlot, which has a softening effect. The vintage is late up on the *causses*; in 1984 they finished picking on 27 November. Chaptalization is rarely necessary. Several different *cuvées* are made, which are then all blended together, so that there is just one Cahors from Château de Chambert.

Robert Burc at Domaine de la Pineraie is a stocky man, with an earthy Lotois accent that was difficult to follow. But his welcome was friendly and he was happy to talk and taste. His family have been wine-makers in Cahors for over a hundred years and until the beginning of the Second World War they used to send their wine to Paris in barrel. They also grew maize and potatoes and kept chickens. Now they concentrate on vines. M. Burc has 20 hectares of Cahors, planted with 90 per cent Auxerrois and 10 per cent Merlot, as well as a few ares of Tannat, but he does not consider that it contributes anything to his wine. He makes two wines, Pierre Sèche and Domaine de Pineraie. The name Pierre Sèche, meaning dry stone, describes the soil of Cahors and was inspired by the vineyards surrounding his cellars outside the town of Puy l'Évêque. It is a lighter wine than Domaine de Pineraie, which is made from grapes grown on the *causses*.

At the moment Pierre Sèche is aged in large casks for six to twelve months while the Domaine de Pineraie spends twelve to eighteen months in small barrels, but the casks will disappear as more barrels are bought. Certainly the *domaine* wine, which accounts for three-quarters of his production, was a tough mouthful, with underlying fruit that needs time to develop and a noticeable oak influence in the young wine. M. Burc gives his wines six months' bottle age before sale and he hopes his customers will age them for even longer.

Jean Couture at Domaine Eugénie can trace his family back to 1470 in the archives of Cahors. He began working on the land in 1973 with 10 hectares, and with his brother Claude he now has 25 hectares. He makes the wine and his brother tends the vineyards, which are planted with 80 per cent Auxerrois, 18 per cent Merlot and 2 per cent Tannat. They make three different Cahors. The vinification methods are the same; it is the ageing process that changes. Each wine comes from a different part of their vineyards: Cahors Étiquette Crème comes from the slopes; the black label, Cuvée Réserve des Tsars, comes from the terraces near the river; and best of all is Cuvée Réserve de l'Aieul from the half-slopes at the foot of the hills. This is aged in 225-litre barrels for at least one and a half, if not two and a half years, while the other two wines spend one to two years in wood.

Each grape variety from each different vineyard is fermented separately and the *cuvaison* lasts for three weeks at 25–29°C, with a *remontage* every morning and evening. The blending of the different varieties is done in January before the wines are put into wood and there is a further blending of the different barrels before bottling. They buy their barrels from the better Bordeaux châteaux and use them for five or six years, and they also have a few new ones in which the wine would only stay three months. As well as small barrels there are larger casks, both new and old, which are easier to maintain, but the best wines are aged in small wood.

We were treated to a tasting of recent vintages and older wines in a welcoming tasting-room, with a large fireplace and a notice on the wall saying '*Un verre ouvre la voie: trois verres donnent la joie*'. The 1982 Cuvée Réserve de l'Aieul was delicious, a rich, concentrated glass of wine, with some blackcurrant fruit and a solid backbone of Tannin. 1982 was one of the best of recent vintages; 1981 and 1983 were also good, but slightly dwarfed by the stature of the 1982. Then to see how these wines can age, we tasted first the 1947 and then the 1929. The 1947 smelt of warm cedarwood, was elegant and long, and just beginning to lose its fruit in 1985. The 1929, which had been made by Jean Couture's grandfather, who died later in the same year, was the colour of mature burgundy and had a dry nutty nose, an example of faded glory, with a very long, drying-fruit finish.

At Clos de la Coutale in the riverside village of Vire we saw Mme Bernède; her husband's name is Valmy, after the first great Revolutionary victory, in which three Bernède brothers fought. Her son Philippe is taking over the running of the estate. This is another traditional property that is gradually being modernized. They bought a mechanical harvester in 1981 and have stainless-steel vats, equipped to control the fermentation temperatures. The wine is aged in large casks rather than smaller barrels, for they consider that there is already enough tannin in the wine without adding more from wood. The cellars are grouped round an attractive courtyard, where colourful creepers cling to the walls. The vines surround the property and the soil of the slopes opposite is too poor for anything but vines, so that yields are tiny, as little as 30 hectolitres per hectare. We tasted recent vintages, of which the 1983 was quite soft and rounded, with 20 per cent Merlot and 10 per cent Tannat in the blend, and the 1982 more concentrated. They have sold all their wine in bottle since 1973 and a great-great-grandfather won a medal for his wine in Paris in 1894.

You have to admire the energy and determination of Danielle Biesbrouck at Domaine des Savarines. You approach her estate along a 2-kilometre dirt track, along the top of a ridge, with views of rolling hills on either side. A Monsieur de Savary, a royal counsellor under Louis XVI, was once owner of this estate. There is an enormous chimneypiece with the date 1785, and views of the vineyards from the living-room windows. Mlle Biesbrouck bought the land and planted nearly 4 hectares of vines in 1970, 'without knowing anything about growing grapes or making wine'. She had been a riding-school teacher for ten years, but had always wanted to work on the land. Her parents helped her to buy a ruined house surrounded by scrub. She was also helped by M. Thiollet, the local oenologist, and she has read a lot but has had no formal training in wine.

Her first bottling was of the 1978 vintage, and for the first couple of years she sold her wine at the Saturday market in Cahors; now she deals with restaurants and private customers. Her cellar is under the house, and you are greeted by that wonderfully evocative smell of wine in wood. There is clean gravel on the floor and a carpet running between the two rows of barrels, so that I hardly liked to spit when we tasted. Dried flowers and an old plough provide an extra touch. Great attention is paid to detail. The Auxerrois and Merlot are fermented separately and the pressed wine is kept apart too, everything being blended during the winter. The wine then spends twelve to fifteen months in wood and is racked every three months. She buys a few new 225-litre barrels every year. The 1982 had masses of fruit with plenty of tannin, too, and was a rich, perfumed mouthful of flavours.

M. Durou at Domaine de Gaudou is a stocky, tanned farmer with a beret and a friendly smile. He is one of the characters of the village of Vire, and became mayor at the last election after thirty-two years as a municipal councillor. He has seen quite a few changes since he began working on his parents' land after leaving school in 1935 at the age of fourteen. He took over 7 hectares of land from his father; as well as vines they grew lavender, and kept their still to send oil to Grasse until 1970. They also had cows for dairy farming. The vineyards were worked with horses or oxen until they bought a tractor in 1955. There were few rewards, for the wine was sold to the *négociants* for a pittance – M. Durou remembered the price of 1.32 francs per litre in 1956. At that time the vineyards were on the slopes and it was only with the granting of the appellation that they began to spread down into the valley. He has gradually increased his vines year by year since the mid-1960s and now has 20 hectares of Cahors on what is generally considered to be one of the best sites of the appellation, some 30 metres above the valley. He also makes a little *vin ordinaire*, including some white wine, mainly from Sémillon but with some Sauvignon and Muscadelle, from very old vines that survived the frost of 1956.

His cellar was modernized in 1980, but this had not prevented a swallow from nesting in the rafters. Fermentation takes place in stainless-steel vats and lasts at least two weeks; the pressed juice is used for the *vin de table*. The wine is aged in old 225-litre barrels for twelve months, as well as being given a year in vat. M. Durou is against new wood as he considers it gives the wine too oaky a taste. His wines have an attractive rustic quality, with fruit, tannin and – as bottles from the 1960s demonstrated – good ageing potential. Since I visited the estate, the son René Gaudou has taken over and maybe things will change.

Cahors is an appellation in transition. Maybe the vineyards have grown too quickly, exceeding market demand for the wine. As in every appellation, there are people who care about the reputation of their wines and work hard to achieve the best, while others have a more haphazard approach. The growers' association, which attempts to control and promote the appellation, is viewed enthusiastically by some and dismissed by others. Efforts are being made by groups of growers to gain a greater recognition for their wines.

Franck Rigal has been responsible for the creation of a group or *collège* of some of the better names such as Clos Triguedina, Clos de la Coutale and Domaine Eugénie, who subscribe to a charter. They say that membership is 'open to all those who shall subscribe to its quality criteria'. The *Charte du Collège* lays down certain conditions: the maximum yield is limited to 50 hectolitres per hectare, herbicides are proscribed and the wines must reflect the *collège*'s criteria of quality. The wines are tasted regularly each year by a blind panel and a seal of quality is awarded.

Another select group, with some overlap of membership, calling themselves Les Seigneurs de Cahors, was founded in 1987 by Alain Perrin of Château Lagrezette in an attempt to promote the wines of Cahors more energetically. Membership depends upon standards of quality and so far there are ten estates: Château des Bouysses, Château Haute-Serre, Prieuré de Cénac, Château de Caix, Château Lagrezette, Château de Chambert, Domaine de Léret-Monpezat, Clos Triguedina, Domaine de Quattre and Château Treilles. The wines are identified by a red stamp on the label, applicable from the 1985 vintage. The members are undoubtedly those with broader, more international, horizons, including *négociants* and the co-operative, rather than the small farmers of the appellation. Their success remains to be seen.

There is no doubt that Cahors is an exciting area to visit. You cannot avoid the feeling that this is a wine that has come a long way in the last few years. There are numerous growers who are devoted to their appellation and working to make it succeed; their achievement is fully recognized in France and increasingly abroad. Vinification methods have improved, and after the reversion to the grape varieties necessary for the appellation, the most significant development has been the increasing use of new oak. Perversely, I find it difficult to say whether I prefer Cahors matured in new or old oak. I have enjoyed both, but on occasion have found the taste of new oak overwhelming. However, that will change as vines and wines mature, nor is it the only factor to affect the taste of a wine. The grape varieties, the soil and the talent of the wine-maker play their part, too. Cahors does age well, and at ten or fifteen years old, a wine from a good vintage like 1982 will provide a delicious bottle that can rival many a claret. Of all the wines of the south west, Cahors is the one with the most stature. The sturdy Auxerrois makes rugged wines with a firm tannic quality, wines that age gracefully rather than falling brutally. They may no longer be the black wines of Cahors, but then those were a legend that was unsubstantiated in the glass.

CÔTES DU BRULHOIS

The most recent newcomer to the appellations of the south west is the Côtes du Brulhois, which was promoted from a *vin de pays* to a VDQS in 1985 and covers two small areas that are divided by the Garonne. There are vineyards in the south east of the department of Lot-et-Garonne, and in the west of Tarn-et-Garonne. The river provides the departmental boundary. The city of Agen lies to the west and the town of Moissac, with its beautiful abbey, to the east. This is on the edge of Armagnac country and the name Brulhois originates from the French *brûler*, meaning to burn – a reference to the region's tradition of distillation. The name was originally given to a small area around the town of Layac.

The Côtes du Brulhois claim a reputation that dates back to the thirteenth century, for the wines were shipped from Bordeaux and even drunk at the English court by Edward III. In later centuries they were used, like Cahors, as *vin de médecin* to boost the lighter wines of the Bordelais. Before the phylloxera there was a large vineyard here, which was subsequently replanted with hybrid vines so that any reputation disappeared. Then in the 1960s a few growers decided that something should be done to retrieve the old renown of the Côtes du Brulhois. They began to plant the better grape varieties and their efforts were first rewarded with recognition as a *vin de pays*.

The co-operative at Donzac, in Tarn-et-Garonne, is responsible for 60 per cent of the production of the Côtes du Brulhois; and as well as a second co-operative, at Layac, there are about fifteen private producers, but none who bottle their wines themselves. There are now some 300 hectares in the appellation, planted principally with Cabernet Sauvignon, Cabernet Franc and Tannat, as well as Merlot, Malbec and Fer Servadou. As well as red wine they make a little pink, but no white.

Methods at Donzac are unsophisticated. This is the standard co-operative with cement vats. Their best wine comes from a single estate, the Château d'Agié near Donzac. I tasted the 1985 vintage, which was quite perfumed, and attractive in a jammy sort of way. The standard 1983 Côtes du Brulhois, tasted in April 1987, had quite a hard nose, and was a little rubbery and faintly reminiscent of young Bordeaux. The similarities came through on the palate, too. We were more enthusiastic about Château La Bastide, from a hotel wine list. A search for the estate took us through attractive countryside to a hilltop village near Valence and we found the château at the end of an alleyway of trees. The views were beautiful, but as for learning more of the wine, we were on a wild-goose chase: the château was firmly shuttered and the cellars locked.

For the moment it is difficult to predict the future of Côtes du Brulhois, for it rarely travels further than the nearby towns and has little more to recommend it than some of the better *vins de pays* of the south west. Time will tell.

LAVILLEDIEU

Lavilledieu is one of the lost appellations of the south west. It is a small vineyard to the west of the town of Montauban in the department of Tarn-et-Garonne. Its origins are Roman. Two rivers, the Tarn and the Garonne, meet nearby and in 150 BC the Romans built fortifications here to defend themselves against the Gauls. With the Romans inevitably came vines and the vineyards were further developed in the Middle Ages by monks from the surrounding abbeys. In 1254 Lavilledieu was the property of the local commandery of the Templars and its reputation grew under English rule during the Hundred Years War. Like so many of the wines of the south west, it experienced the same rivalry with Bordeaux and was mentioned amongst the wines of the Haut-Pays.

The rather gloomy village of La Ville-Dieu-du-Temple is the home of the regional co-operative, which for the moment is the only producer of this forgotten wine. The vintage began the day of my visit. I stood outside the standard co-operative building, waiting to see the director, watching the grapes arrive. There were two delivery points, marked respectively 'vinifera' and 'hybrid'. A docile-looking Alsatian was fast asleep next to a kennel marked '*chien méchant*' and a tortoiseshell cat basked in the sun.

The co-operative was founded in 1949 and helped the area to become a VDQS in 1952. There are thirteen villages in the VDQS, of which La Ville-Dieu-du-Temple is the most important. The co-operative now has 150 members, but in 1985 only eighteen of them were actually producing the required grapes for the VDQS. Much larger quantities are made of the various *vins de pays* of the area. Coteaux et Terrasses de Montauban covers, as the name implies, the terraces around Montauban and is limited by the particular type of soil, namely *boulbènes* of clay and chalk, which is the same for the vineyards of Lavilledieu. Then there is Coteaux de Quercy and the departmental *vin de pays* of Tarn-et-Garonne which goes under the name of Vin de Pays du Comté Tolosan.

The vineyards of the Vin de Lavilledieu, to give the VDQS its full name, suffered disastrously in the severe winter frosts of 1956. Many of the vines were destroyed. However, the co-operative, with the growers' association, has implemented an ambitious programme of replanting which began in 1975. By 1985 there were 19 hectares in production, but forty-five members of the co-operative have planted a further 80 hectares, which will come into production towards the end of the decade. The hybrid grape varieties are being replaced. But nobody lives from their vines alone, and there are fields of wheat and orchards of fruit trees too.

The regulations of the VDQS allow for a myriad different grape varieties. I was told that there used to be '*une mosaïque de vieux cépages*', all of which were included in the regulations, such as long-forgotten varieties like Mortérille, Chalosse and Milganet, as well as Négrette, Syrah, Tannat, Jurançon Noir and various Bordelais grape varieties. The climate here is both Mediterranean and Atlantic as the region is not far from either the ocean or the sea. In practice the grape varieties have been simplified to allow for Négrette, Gamay, Cabernet Franc, Syrah and Tannat. Twenty-five per cent is the maximum proportion of each, except Tannat, which is restricted to 15 per cent. Other grape varieties such as Abouriou, Jurançon and Cabernet Sauvignon are included in the *vins de pays*. There is no white Vin de Lavilledieu.

Vinification methods here are unsophisticated. Some selection of the grapes is made according to their potential alcohol, which must be a minimum of 10° for the VDQS. The fermentation usually lasts about six days, taking place in the standard cement vats. Fermentation temperatures are somewhat hit-and-miss in that there is equipment to heat the must, but not to cool it. The blending of the various vats takes place in the spring and bottling in July. For the moment most of the production is sold around Montauban, and Lavilledieu has little more than a local reputation. I tasted the 1983 vintage, which in September 1985 had quite a warm soft flavour, which was spoilt by some inky overtones. But it is not fair to judge an appellation on one tasting alone, and Lavilledieu features amongst those wines whose development will be intriguing to observe.

CÔTES DU FRONTONNAIS

The vineyards of the Côtes du Frontonnais lie on a plateau between the towns of Montauban and Toulouse and the rivers of the Tarn and the Garonne. There are two small towns, Fronton and Villaudric, which enjoy a centuries-old rivalry. During the Wars of Religion Villaudric was Catholic and Fronton was Protestant. Villaudric was destroyed, while Fronton survived. The rivalry continues today. The first vines were planted here during the Merovingian period, which lasted from AD 450 to 750. In the twelfth century the *vin de négret* found favour with Pope Calixtus II, and five centuries later Louis XIII and Richelieu were equally enthusiastic.

The individuality of the Côtes du Frontonnais comes from the Négrette grape, which is a member of the Cot family, and not found in any quantity in any other vineyard of the south west. There is a little in Lavilledieu and it features in the appellation regulations of Gaillac; it was also grown in Charente as the Petit Noir, with a few vines remaining on the Ile d'Oléron. Côtes du Frontonnais must consist of a minimum of 50 per cent Négrette – but Négrette is one of the most difficult grapes to cultivate. It is especially susceptible to disease and it dislikes humidity, so that it needs a hot dry climate. Nearby Toulouse is one of the hottest towns of France. In 1986, for instance, there was no rain between 17 May and 17 September, giving four dry summer months during which the Négrette flourished. It gives very little tannin, however, so that wine made from it oxidizes easily and ages quickly. It makes a supple fruity wine that is easy to drink, but really it needs to be blended with other grape varieties.

The appellation regulations allow for some flexibility of blending. Négrette must account for between 50 and 70 per cent while Cot and Mérille are limited to 25 per cent and are tending to disappear from the Côtes du Frontonnais, especially Mérille, which is a rather undistinguished variety. Cabernet Sauvignon, Cabernet Franc and Fer Servadou are also limited to 25 per cent and of these there seems to be a preference for Cabernet Franc. Then there are various *cépages d'appoint*, namely Syrah, Gamay, Cinsaut and (rather surprisingly) the white Mauzac, which can be used to tone down the deep colour of the wine.

Initially no precise regulations were laid down about the percentages of the different varieties. An opportunity for replanting came in 1956 when many vines were killed in the severe frost of 8 February, in which the temperature fell from 2°C to −26°C in the space of two hours. Some people wanted to copy Bordeaux, with more Cabernet, but fortunately those who favoured the originality of the Négrette won the support of the INAO when the appellation was created in 1975, so that at least half the wine is Négrette. As well as red wine a little pink is made, but no white. People with white grapes sell their wine as Vin de Pays du Comté Tolosan.

The vineyards of the Côtes du Frontonnais are confined to the plateau. About 1,800 hectares are in production, although the appellation allows for nearly three times as much and the vineyards are indeed increasing slowly. About 600 hectares of vines have been planted since the appellation was recognized, as its creation gave people an incentive. There are fruit trees too, peaches and nectarines, but little else will grow on this arid land. There is a monotonous quality about the countryside and the villages lack charm. The best soil of the plateau is gravel, which is red, with a high iron content. Locally it is called *rouget* and covers a crescent shape over the plateau where the vines give full fruity wines with a low yield. Fifty hectolitres per hectare is the maximum yield. Elsewhere on the plateau there are *boulbènes*, where the clay has decomposed to leave just sand, while the soil surrounding the plateau of the Côtes du Frontonnais is quite different.

Although Fronton was noted by popes and kings, it has really only enjoyed a local reputation. Before the days of strict delimitations of wine areas it was sent by river to Bordeaux, where it was blended with the wines of Gironde. In the 1850s wine was taken by horse and cart in barrels to Toulouse, which really remained its main market until the mid-1970s. The rivalry between the two villages of Fronton and Villaudric persisted. Mouillefert, writing at the beginning of the twentieth century, said of Villaudric that it had finesse and was delicate with a pleasant bouquet and a beautiful colour, while Fronton was more full-bodied and alcoholic, with a good flavour. The villages were given separate VDQSs within a couple of years of each other: Villaudric in 1945 and Fronton in

1947. It was only with the granting of the appellation that the two were combined, and even now there is nearly always the mention 'Fronton' or 'Villaudric' under the name Côtes du Frontonnais on the label. Partisans of Villaudric consider that their wine ages better than Fronton as traditionally their grapes were not destalked, which resulted in a tougher wine. Each village had its own co-operative, but in 1987 that of Villaudric went into liquidation. The co-operative of Fronton has the advantage of covering a larger area.

In fact the co-operative of Fronton is one of the biggest in France but a considerable percentage of its production is *vin de table*, while it also accounts for 70 per cent of the appellation of Côtes du Frontonnais. Each member must have in his vineyard the correct proportions of grape varieties for the appellation, the three families, so that if you only grow Négrette, your grapes will be used for *vin de table*. They make two qualities of Côtes du Frontonnais; the better wine contains more Cabernet and Gamay and has more colour and body. There are also two estates that are vinified separately, Château de Craussac and Château Marguerite.

The vintage date in Fronton tends to depend upon the amount of rain that falls during the summer, so that if there is virtually no rain, the harvest begins later, at the beginning of October. Usually, if the grapes ripen earlier, the vintage will start in the middle of September and lasts about four weeks. Sometimes the Négrette is picked when it is slightly unripe in order to retain a little acidity.

The estate that has done more than any other to bring the Côtes du Frontonnais to the attention of the outside world is Château Bellevue-la-Forêt. The land was bought in 1974 by Patrick Germain on his return from Algeria. There were orchards but no vines. He was tempted by the new appellation as his parents had been wine-growers in Algeria. He now has 103 hectares of vines from which three different styles of wine are made by his oenologist. There is a basic Côtes du Frontonnais, a special *cuvée* made from the best parcels of Négrette and Cabernet, and, very unusually, a pure Négrette, which is not entitled to the appellation and is made especially for the restaurateur André Daguin of the Hôtel de France at Auch. The bottle I tasted was soft and supple, with some attractive perfumed fruit, while the more conventional Côtes du Frontonnais was fuller-bodied but had the same attractive chewiness of the Négrette.

The vineyards are planted with 55 per cent Négrette, 20 per cent

Cabernet Franc, 5 per cent Cabernet Sauvignon, 15 per cent Syrah and 5 per cent Gamay. All the grapes are picked by hand, the Négrette being too susceptible to oxidation for a mechanical harvester.

The cellars are well equipped and modern, with a forest of red steel vats. Fermentation temperatures are efficiently controlled and the *cuvaison* lasts six or seven days, extending to fifteen days, space permitting. Each grape variety is vinified separately and blended after the malolactic fermentation. Both the red and pink are bottled in the spring. They are experimenting with some new oak barrels for Cabernet and Syrah. The Négrette has neither tannin nor acidity enough for wood ageing. They have just twelve barrels – four brand-new ones, four that have been used once and four twice; the wine is kept in wood for five months. The reaction of the other growers is that it is no longer Fronton. I am rather inclined to agree.

In contrast, Urbain Blancal, a friendly old man, was one of the original wine-growers of the appellation. His vineyards are five generations old. He was 'born in the vineyard' and studied some agriculture by correspondence course, but has really learnt by experience. He remembers his father working with horses and oxen, and he was thirteen when they bought a tractor back in the 1930s. It was such a novelty that everyone came to see it. He planted vines when he returned from the Second World War, during which he had been in the Resistance and then a prisoner of war. All his vines were destroyed in the frost of 1956 so that he had to replant completely, with Négrette, Gamay, Cabernet Franc, Syrah, Mérille, and some others like Mauzac and Cinsaut. He reckons that Syrah gives the wine more character, with good colour and alcohol, as well as bouquet. It has been encouraging over the last five or six years; both the Cabernets have been established a little longer, but he is not so enthusiastic about Cabernet Sauvignon.

His cellar is attractively traditional. He has an old-fashioned press alongside the cement fermentation vats, and also some old casks going back 200-odd years, where his wine spends two to four months, depending on how it develops. In accordance with the tradition of Villaudric most of his grapes are not destalked, so that his wine is tougher and more solid than others I tasted. However, I was uncertain how well it would age. The rivalry between Fronton and Villaudric also comes out in the bottle shape. Fronton chose the claret bottle, while the growers of Villaudric favour the burgundy bottle.

The attraction of Côtes du Frontonnais lies in its youthful fruitiness aided by the spicy flavour of the Négrette grape that gives it its individuality and character. The future of the appellation looks rosy, for there is a feeling of optimism about a wine that deserves a wider reputation than it has hitherto enjoyed.

GAILLAC

Gaillac is one of the oldest vineyards of the south west and perhaps even of all France, for the Romans planted vines here in the first century AD. The name, however, comes from the Celtic word *galad*, meaning a fertile land. The region suffered badly from barbarian invasions after the departure of the Romans and most of the vineyards were abandoned, so that it was the monks of the early Middle Ages who were really responsible for the development of the wines. There are records that the canons of Albi were given vines in 920, and that Benedictine monks established themselves at Gaillac on the banks of the Tarn and planted vineyards there during the tenth century.

Throughout the Middle Ages Gaillac enjoyed a flourishing trade in wine. The river supplied easy means of transport, with the Tarn flowing into the Garonne so that the wine could be taken to Bordeaux. The Bordelais energetically defended the privileges of their own wines so that wines from Gaillac and the other vineyards of the Haut-Pays were not allowed into the city until 11 November, St Martin's Day, and could not be sent to England until Christmas.

These measures did not prevent the wines of Gaillac from enjoying considerable popularity at the English court. King John is said to have been partial to them and willing to pay more than for any other wines. In 1253 Henry III appointed a certain Arnaud, a merchant in Gaillac, as purveyor of the wines of his table and ordered a barrel of wine from him to be sent as a present to the Earl of Southampton. Records show that wines were imported to England in 1308 from Gaillac, Rabastens and Albi, and wine from Gaillac also went to the Low Countries. The barrels were branded with a cockerel, from the arms of the town, as a guarantee of their authenticity.

Gaillac suffered during the wars of the Middle Ages, for it was under the control of the counts of Toulouse, whose territories were the theatre of the Albigensian Crusade. The Hundred Years War also left its mark on the prosperity of the region, and at the end of the

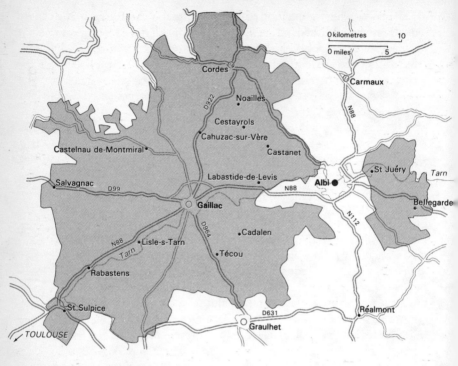

Gaillac

fourteenth century plague outbreaks reduced the population to 303 inhabitants in 1374 and only sixty-four in 1388.

The situation had improved by the sixteenth century. Henry VIII of England brought wine from Gaillac and in 1535 François I received ten barrels of white wine and thirty barrels of red. A document of 1509 refers to the full and powerful nature of these wines, saying that they were improved appreciably by transport over land and sea. Catel, in his *Mémoires du Languedoc* of 1633 wrote: 'I learnt on passing through Gailhac, from the inhabitants of the town, that this wine has the characteristic that if someone drinks too much of it, nevertheless he has a good hour or an hour and a half to retire, before it disturbs his brain.' In 1680 Duval, geographer to Louis XIV, commented on the sparkling wine of Gailhac and Limouth, a fact which may lend support to an argument that the sparkling wines of these regions are older than those of Champagne.

Gaillac merited a mention in Boyer's *Royal Dictionary: English and French*, published in London in 1753, that defined Gaillac wine as 'a sort of French wine, so called from Gaillac, a town in the Languedoc, where it grows'. But English enthusiasm for Gaillac had waned after the loss of Aquitaine; it revived fitfully in the eighteenth century only to fade again after the Methuen Treaty and even more as a consequence of the Continental Blockade of 1806–9. The wines of Gaillac tended to lose their separate identity and they began to feature amongst the black wines or the *vins de médecin* which were used to boost some of the more feeble wines of the Gironde.

Writing at the beginning of the nineteenth century, Jullien said that vines were the principal source of income of the region. The red wines were thick, with a very deep colour, and at the same time quite alcoholic. They withstood long sea journeys and only improved with them, while the whites were esteemed in the area for their body and alcohol and travelled well, but were rarely exported.

In 1852 the vineyard of Gaillac produced 12,500 hectolitres of white wine and 4.48 million hectolitres of red. Before the phylloxera, Gaillac was above all a red wine. White wine only became important in the region with the subsequent replanting. There had always been some white wine in Gaillac, however, and in the Middle Ages sweet wine made from the Muscat grape was more highly rated than the dry white wine. The white wine that was produced at the beginning of this century was often sweet and also sparkling, and it sold very well until the Second World War when tastes shifted to drier white and red wines. The vineyard area declined as white wine fell from favour and far-sighted growers saw the need to resurrect the red wines of the region. Consequently Gaillac was given its appellation in two stages, for white wine in 1938 and for red wine only in 1970.

The vineyards of Gaillac cover an extensive area north west of Toulouse. Originally the appellation for white wine was for the vineyards of the town of Gaillac. With the addition of red and pink wine, the appellation was extended to cover seventy-three villages. The town of Gaillac is their centre, while the city of Albi divides the appellation in two, with a smaller group of vineyards to the east of the city. The hilltop village of Cordes is one of the more northern vineyards of the appellation. Many of the vineyards are on either side of the frighteningly fast N88 that leads to Albi, past Rabastens, Lisle-sur-Tarn and Gaillac itself.

Gaillac is a rather gloomy town. The monastery of St-Michel has an air of delapidation and even the main square seems to lack animation. In contrast the appeal of Albi is immediate. It was the home of Toulouse-Lautrec and the museum houses a fine collection of his paintings and drawings. The red-brick cathedral has the air of a medieval fortress, and indeed played its part in the Albigensian Crusade. You can wander round narrow streets and there is even a wine bar, Le Petit Zinc, in the market square, where you can sample local wines by the glass with some *charcuterie* or cheese. Cordes is a picturesque hilltop town, beloved of tourists and well worth the steep climb up narrow cobbled streets. The countryside of Gaillac is pleasing, with gentle hills of attractive farmland dotted with little villages, and sloping down towards the banks of the Tarn. It is a rich area, sometimes known as the Pays de Cocagne, which the Harraps dictionary translates as 'a land of milk and honey'. In this instance the wealth came from the plant that provided the pastel-blue dye throughout Europe in the Middle Ages.

The appellation of Gaillac allows for a large and at first glance confusing variety of different grapes, which in turn make a diverse number of wines. White Gaillac can be dry, sweet, or *moelleux*; sparkling or *perlé*. As for red wine, there is Gaillac Nouveau, as well as longer-lasting reds, and also a little pink. In addition a handful of villages are entitled to the extra classification of Gaillac Premières Côtes, namely Broze, Cahuzac-sur-Vère, Castanet, Cestayrols, Fayssac, Lisle-sur-Tarn, Montels and Senouillac. Their yield is restricted to 40 hectolitres per hectare as opposed to 45 hl/ha for the rest of the appellation, but in practice few people make use of this distinction on their label.

The grapes for white Gaillac include some Bordelais varieties and some that are rarely found elsewhere. The most traditional variety is the Mauzac, which is also grown in Limoux for sparkling wine. Gaillac is virtually the only example of still Mauzac. It gives rounded wines, which sometimes can be a little too soft. Often, especially for Gaillac *perlé*, it is blended with Loin de l'Œil, called Len de l'El (or l'Elh) in Occitan. The name Loin del'Œil apparently comes quite literally from the fact that the bunch of grapes develops a long way from the original eye. Loin de l'Œil must be fully ripe, otherwise its juice is like water, so for the grapes to develop their aroma you must wait until they are almost overripe and even a little rotten. Then there are Sauvignon, Sémillon, Muscadelle and Ondenc, a variety which is disappearing. Ondenc was once planted quite extensively in Gaillac and other appellations of the south west, but its popularity has waned as it suffers badly from oidium and grey rot. Muscadelle is sensitive to rot, but it performs well on the plain where there is good drainage and the sandy, pebbly soil does not retain the humidity.

The grape varieties for red and pink wine include Duras, Fer Servadou, which is also called Braucol or simply Fer, Syrah, Gamay and Négrette. These must form a minimum of 60 per cent of the finished wine. The complementary 40 per cent can come from Cabernet Franc, Cabernet Sauvignon, and Merlot. It seems that there is nothing new in this diversity of grape varieties. Guyot, writing a hundred years ago, regretted that there were so many different varieties and advised that there was considerable elimination to be made. For reds he mentioned Pignol, Brocol, Prunelat, Négret and Duraze, and for whites, Mozac, Ondenc, Endelel and Sécal.

Duras is a peculiarly Gaillacois grape variety. It bears no relationship to the Côtes de Duras and is found almost exclusively in the department of Tarn. It can be susceptible to spring frost as it has an early budbreak, and it also suffers from oidium and black rot. Fer is grown in other vineyards of the south west, and in particular gives the wines of Aveyron their individuality. In practice Négrette is rarely found in Gaillac and is confined to the Côtes du Frontonnais, while Gamay is used mainly for *vin nouveau*. As for the other varieties, a pattern emerges. Jean Cros, from one of the leading estates, explained that you find two types of red Gaillac, both based on Duras, which is the grape that gives Gaillac its distinctiveness. The first, for which M. Cros would like to see the name Gaillac Paroisse (like 'Villages' in other appellations), comes from Duras blended with Fer Servadou and Syrah. Fer gives the Duras structure and Syrah adds colour. The second style brings out the affinities with Bordeaux, allowing Duras to be blended with Merlot and Cabernet. Even so, the variety is enormous and it is sometimes difficult to see any uniformity in red Gaillac, especially as there are growers who are unwilling to conform to the pattern.

Altogether 40,000 hectares have been delimited in the appellation, but as of 1986 only 15,000 are actually planted with vines. Of those only 8,000 hectares are planted with the correct grape varieties for the appellation, and in practice commercial and economic demands dictate that only the production of 1,500 hectares is actually declared as appellation Gaillac. If the market demand were present, the production of Gaillac could treble from one vintage to the next.

Unfortunately little is being done to develop that demand, for the local Comité Interprofessionnel (the body responsible for the general promotion of the appellation) seems to be resting on its laurels and is failing to provide any direction. Consequently the wine from the other 13,500 hectares is sold as Vin de Pays du Tarn, which includes grape varieties that are unsuitable for the appellation such as Jurançon Rouge, Portugais and a considerable quantity of Mauzac that does not reach the required quality for the *labelle* tastings that grant individual wines their appellations.

The 700 hectares of white grape varieties break down into 150 of Mauzac, 50 of Sauvignon, 350 Loin de l'Œil and 150 of Muscadelle, with a very little Sémillon and a minute amount of Ondenc. The 800 hectares of red varieties consist of 250 of Duras, 100 of Fer Servadou, 210 of Syrah, 30 of Merlot, 150 of Gamay and 60 of Cabernet Sauvignon and Cabernet Franc. Cabernet Sauvignon is the more successful, as Cabernet Franc has a tendency to overripen.

My first visit in Gaillac was to the Domaine Jean Cros and its second estate, Château Larroze. This is very much a family concern. Jean Cros is the Grand Chancellier of the Gaillac *confrérie*, L'Ordre de la Dive Bouteille de Gaillac, and is one of the personalities of the appellation. His two sons Jean-François and Jean-Étienne are responsible for viticulture and vinification respectively, and his English son-in-law Lance Edynbry is busy putting Gaillac in general and Château Larroze in particular on the export map.

With two estates and different grape varieties grown on each, they make quite a range of different Gaillacs. Château Larroze Blanc Sec is pure Mauzac, while Gaillac Perlé is composed of one-third Loin de l'Œil with Mauzac. *Perlé* wines are traditional to Gaillac and the authentic way to make them is to retain a little of the carbon dioxide from the malolactic fermentation when they are bottled. This requires very careful handling of the wine, and a true Gaillac *perlé* has a very individual taste. The bubbles in the glass should look like tiny pearls, hence the name. Less scrupulous producers have been known to add carbon dioxide at the bottling. As for Sauvignon, they are not convinced of its future.

Jean Cros make their sparkling wine according to the *méthode gaillacoise*, which in other parts of France can be called the *méthode rurale*. The original way to stop the first fermentation was to immerse the barrels in ice-cold water. Nowadays they centrifuge to remove the remaining yeast. They prefer to remove the sediment of the second fermentation, so they have *pupitres* for *remuage* and after two years ageing on the lees the bottles are disgorged *à la volée*, without freezing the necks. No *dosage* is added at any time. Some people use the champagne method, but Jean Cros is against it, considering that it gives a poor imitation of a bad champagne, rather than a wine with true regional character.

As for red wines, they have Gamay for a *vin nouveau* made by carbonic maceration. The red wine of Château Larroze comes from two-thirds Duras, one-sixth Merlot and one-sixth Cabernet Sauvignon, while the red wine of Domaine Jean Cros is made from two-thirds Duras with one-sixth Syrah and one-sixth Fer Servadou. Even though Duras is the principal grape variety of both wines, the complementary grapes are completely different, giving quite contrasting styles of wine. The first had a rounded, substantial flavour reminiscent of Bordeaux and the second was lighter, with some peppery fruit. It is Duras that should give red Gaillac its individuality, but it must be blended with other grapes for although it has a distinctive peppery taste, with good acidity and balance, it lacks colour.

It is the diversity of soils within the appellation that allows for so many different types of grape. Soil determines what you plant where, and the geological complexity provides variety in the vineyard. Distinct areas can be defined. The seven villages around Cunac to the east of Albi bear no resemblance to the rest of the appellation. The vineyards here are on the edge of the Massif Central and the soil is a mixture of clay and gravel. On the right bank of the Tarn are the slopes of the villages of the Premières Côtes, whose soil is a mixture of limestone and clay which makes wine suitable for ageing. The land rises in terraces from the river, so that the vineyards around Cordes in the north are higher, with more limestone, which makes for a tougher wine. In contrast, on the left bank of the Tarn the soil is more alluvial, with sand and gravel.

Climate varies also, for Gaillac is not too far from either the Mediterranean or the Atlantic. They have rain from the ocean and spring and autumn showers from the Massif Central. The hot summer comes from the Mediterranean, and drying winds from the south and south west. The Massif Central also gives them cold winters and spring frosts.

Co-operatives play an important part in the appellation. The largest is the Co-opérative de Labastide-de-Levis which accounts for

about a third of the production of all Gaillac. With the arrival of a
new director, M. Pomier, it is undergoing a considerable improvement both in the quality of its wines and in its commercial efforts.
They have invested in new presses and equipment for cooling their
must, and the bottling line has also been improved. Their wines have
been given a new presentation, all in an effort to enhance their image.
As well as Gaillac they also make a considerable quantity of Vin de
Pays des Côtes de Tarn. Nevertheless they see Gaillac Perlé as their
flagship wine.

The Cave Co-opérative de Técou is generally considered to be
the best of the three co-operatives, while the other at Rabastens
concentrates on sparkling wine. At Técou the members have between
them most of the grape varieties allowed in Gaillac; the only omissions
are Cabernet, which does not grow well south of the Tarn, and
Sémillon. Vinification methods are standard and well controlled.
They make two red wines, Gaillac Tradition from Syrah, Duras and
Gamay, and Gaillac St-Vincent from Merlot, Fer Servadou and
Syrah. Both have some attractive peppery fruit. With the 1986 vintage
they have made their first tentative experiment with oak ageing, using
new 225-litre Bordeaux barrels. Their white wine is a blend of
Sauvignon and Loin de l'Œil. Mauzac is used for sparkling wine
made by the *charmat* method, while Loin de l'Œil is used for the
champagne method; they have completely given up the *méthode
gaillacoise*.

Although the appellation lays down general guidelines for the
composition of the various wines of Gaillac, it still allows considerable flexibility and a determined grower can apparently do what he
likes with the grape varieties in his vineyard. Each has his own
personal view of the appellation. One grower I met made as many as
seven different wines from just 13 hectares of vines. That was Robert
Plageoles at Domaine des Trois Cantous. He is quite the most
unconventional member of the Gaillac fraternity, with opinions and
ideas that upset his colleagues. As he said himself, 'I am going against
the mainstream,' and you can see that he delights in doing so. The
vineyard of Gaillac is moving towards red wines made from a blend
of grape varieties; he, on the other hand, is concentrating on white
wines made from a single variety. For him the blending of different
varieties is a means of hiding the defects of a grape, in the same way
that you can dress up a man to hide his imperfections.

He is an enthusiast who exudes energy and ideas. His cellar is a picture of organized chaos, with fermentation vats outside and wooden barrels inside. He is adamant that he does not make modern wines. He uses his cooling equipment as little as possible and does not look for particularly low fermentation temperatures. 'Wine is not manufactured, but is carefully nurtured.' He uses the simplest physical methods, stating firmly that the true wine-maker knows how to work with the least complicated equipment. 'The fact that I have not got stainless-steel vats does not mean that I do not make good wine, just as the fact that I may own a fast sports car does not necessarily mean that I am a good driver. It is men who make wine.'

He makes two red wines, one from Gamay and one from Duras. He has no Bordelais grape varieties as he does not want to be 'a cousin of the Bordelais'. Duras, which is the original grape of Gaillac, makes a solid wine with rich fruit and quite high acidity. Normally his red wine is not aged in wood, but he is considering some new 225-litre barrels for the Duras, made of oak from a local forest. Gamay is made by a traditional vinification; there is no carbonic maceration here and the sample I tasted had quite a tough, earthy flavour.

As for white wines, there is a dry Sauvignon, with good varietal character. Mauzac is vinified dry without the addition of any Loin de l'œil, which M. Plageoles described as 'a sentimental wine, playing its part in the nostalgia of the region'. It is well made, with some nutty flavour but without the bitterness that can characterize the Mauzac. I preferred the Sauvignon, however, and better still was the Mauzac *moelleux*. Mauzac has a thick skin which enables it to withstand the September rains, so that it produces overripe grapes without too many problems with rot. The wine was not very sweet, but lightly honeyed, with a gentle, elegant flavour. We later enjoyed it with our picnic in the vineyards.

A sparkling wine is made by the traditional *gaillacoise* method. The juice is fermented in wood, and when there are equal amounts of sugar and alcohol it is filtered and bottled. It spends the winter in bottle and in the spring begins to ferment again. M. Plageoles carries authenticity and lack of sophistication to the extent of keeping the lees from the second fermentation in the bottle, with a discreet back label explaining their presence. The wine is rich, with quite a heavy nose and a full, yeasty flavour with a hint of sweetness.

There are numerous small producers of Gaillac who are worth a visit. I saw a handful. First was Jean Albert at Domaine de Labarthe who has 22 hectares. There have been vines on his land since the sixteenth century, and a lawyer's document records the exchange of land on the estate at that time. Once again he makes a considerable variety of wines, each with an element of individuality. There is a fruity Gamay *primeur*, which has more taste than many a Beaujolais Nouveau, while his standard red wine comes predominantly from Fer Servadou, with dollops of Duras, Merlot, Cabernet Sauvignon and Cabernet Franc. His Syrah does not ripen well enough, so it is only used for pink. As for white wine, there is a dry white with a high percentage of Sauvignon and a *moelleux* is made from Mauzac.

These are the last grapes to be picked, when they are very ripe, but not dried as in Jurançon. They ferment slowly, and then in November he leaves the cellar doors open and the fermentation gently stops. The wine is filtered and lightly sulphured. Gaillac *doux* must contain 70 grams of sugar, while *moelleux* depends upon the grower's taste. M. Albert's is lightly honeyed. His sparkling wine also is made from pure Mauzac and, like many of the producers of sparkling Gaillac, he is part of a group who share the same equipment, kept in the old abbey of St-Michel. Each grower makes his own base wine and bottles the wine himself, sharing the necessary equipment for the intermediary stages.

You approach Château Lastours along a pleasant alley of plane trees. The property has belonged to the de Faramond family for 400 years. Most of the present-day château was built just before the Revolution, but incorporates a hunting lodge dating back to Henri IV, and a Carolingian chapel that is one of the oldest historical monuments of the department. From the terrace you look over an attractive garden *à la française* and the banks of the Tarn.

Unusually, M. de Faramond has no Mauzac in his vineyards as he does not like it; he considers that it performs better on the clay soil of the hills, whereas the soil of his vineyards on the plain is gravel. His white wine is made from Sémillon, Muscadelle and Sauvignon – he is one of the few growers to have Sémillon. He makes a dry white, but no *moelleux*. As for sparkling wine, he belongs to the group of the abbey of St-Michel. For his red wine he has Duras, Braucol, Syrah and Cabernet Franc, and has planted some Merlot and Cabernet Sauvignon. He does not like what he considers to be the fad for Gamay *primeur*, so he makes just one red wine, which he leaves 'to reflect' for eighteen months in wood. He generally tries to treat his

78

wine as little as possible, and the result here is a wine of some character, with an attractive peppery nose and some good fruit.

My favourite dry white Gaillac came from Mas Pignou, that belongs to the friendly Auque family. Their vineyards are on a steep hill outside the town of Gaillac. The white wine is made from equal parts of Loin de l'Œil and Sauvignon; they have some Mauzac, but do not consider it to be any good for dry white wine as it does not have enough acidity or freshness. They were amongst the first to plant Sauvignon about twenty years ago and find that it complements the Loin de l'Œil, that does not age well, and gives the wine an attractive, lively character. Their red wine comes from Duras, Fer Servadou, Merlot and Cabernet Franc, of which Fer Servadou is the most important, though the exact proportions depend upon the year. Each grape variety is vinified separately and the final blend is made after the malolactic fermentation. They are more enthusiastic about Fer Servadou than Duras; they do not find that the latter ages well, so they are planting more of the former and also of Merlot. The red wine usually spends between four and seven months in wood and is bottled after about eighteen months. The 1985 made an attractive, fruity glass of wine, with a little ageing potential. The Auque family are remarkable for not having the plethora of wines of most estates, and I could not help thinking that perhaps their wines were the better for that.

I left Gaillac with mixed feelings. It is undoubtedly an area of immense viticultural richness and there are few other regions that provide such a range of flavours and tastes within one small appellation. But despite the efforts of people like Jean Cros the area seemed to lack cohesion, and a bottle labelled Gaillac Rouge can vary enormously in taste. However, there is no doubt that it is an appellation of considerable potential, especially as a new generation of wine-makers is making its mark on the appellation. It is with them that the future lies.

VINS DE PAYS OF THE SOUTH WEST

Vin de Pays Charentais

All over France the most important vins de pays are those where there is no competing appellation – where the vin de pays is the grower's best wine, rather than second string to his appellation wine, so that the best grapes are used, rather than rejects from the appellation wine.

In south-western France the fall in the consumption of spirits has had a marked effect on the viticultural activity of the regions that are better known for Cognac and Armagnac, resulting in the creation of Vin de Pays Charentais and Vin de Pays des Côtes de Gascogne.

Vin de Pays Charentais covers the two departments of Charente and Charente-Maritime, so in fact it is larger than the production area of Cognac. Although the region is known above all for Cognac, it has a long tradition of wine-making that goes back to the Middle Ages, when there were references to the vineyards of the Ile de Ré. They merited some praise in 1475, but quality must have declined subsequently, for in 1633 the wines of nearby La Rochelle were rated in England as 'small and thin'. The Dutch were no more enthusiastic.

In the early nineteenth century Jullien described the wines of Charente and of what was then called Charente-Inférieure. Of the reds of Saintes, St-Jean d'Angély, La Rochelle, the Ile d'Oléron and the Ile de Ré, he wrote that they were not highly considered, nor were those of Charente, and most were consumed locally or, of course, distilled.

The first vintage of the Vin de Pays Charentais was in 1981. Wine has always been made here, especially on the periphery of the Cognac area, but it had no identity above that of anonymous *vin de table*; the creation of the Vin de Pays Charentais was designed to rectify this. Production has increased rapidly. In 1981 just 5,000 hectolitres were accepted by the official tasting panel, in 1982 10,000 hectolitres, and in 1984 there was a dramatic increase to 25,000 hectolitres. The vineyards were already planted. What was needed was a radical improvement in vinification methods, since producing wine for distillation requires no attention to hygiene or vinification details. The output of Vin de Pays Charentais has grown as this change in approach has occurred. Most of the wine is white, made from grape varieties that were originally planted for Cognac. There are Folle Blanche, Colombard and Ugni Blanc, while more enterprising growers are considering Sauvignon. Chenin Blanc, Sémillon and Muscadelle are also allowed, as is Chardonnay since 1985.

More red grapes are being planted, too, often for pink rather than red wine. We went to see a young independent grower, Jean Mellinger near the village of Moulidars, not far from Cognac. He has just begun to make pink wine from Merlot, Cabernet Sauvignon and Cabernet Franc, planted on soil that is a mixture of clay, sand and chalk. It is also very pebbly, so that the stones absorb the heat during the day and radiate it back on to the grapes at night. As for his white wine, it comes from Ugni Blanc and Colombard. Colombard on its own is too acidic here, so it needs to be blended with Ugni Blanc, which has tended to replace the Folle Blanche that is also very acid.

Ugni Blanc is the main variety for distillation. It produces large bunches of juicy grapes and is not sensitive to disease, but its principal disadvantage is that it adapts badly to a mechanical harvester. The wines that we tried, both white and pink, were well made, fresh and crisp, with a high level of acidity. They would compete quite adequately with a Gros Plant from Nantes and went well with the *grillons charentais*, the local version of *rillettes*, as we tasted outside in a geranium-filled courtyard.

A grower in the heart of Charente is presented with several choices. He can make Cognac (as M. Mellinger does, just a little), he can make Pineau de Charente (the regional aperitif that is produced in the same way as ratafia, with Cognac added to grape juice to prevent the fermentation), and he can also make wine. In the outlying areas of Cognac, such as the Bon Bois, it is as profitable to grow grapes for wine as for distillation.

Vin de Pays des Côtes de Gascogne

There is no doubt that the more successful *vin de pays* is that of the Côtes de Gascogne, which has the immediate advantage of more generous climatic conditions. It covers the whole department of Gers, while the area of Armagnac spreads into Lot-et-Garonne and Landes. Like Vin de Pays Charentais, Vin de Pays des Côtes de Gascogne was born of the fall in sales of brandy, but this time of Armagnac; and as with Armagnac, the heart of the vineyards is around the town of Condom.

Producers in the parish of Condom itself may also choose to call their wine Vin de Pays des Côtes du Condomois, a name designed more for red than white wine. While Vin de Pays des Côtes de Gascogne is still two-thirds white, with a growing amount of red, Vin de Pays des Côtes Condomois is the reverse. This is an aspiring VDQS; but another neighbouring wine, Vin de Pays des Côtes de Montestruc, that was produced solely by the co-operative of

Montestruc, is likely to disappear altogether as the co-operative is closing down.

The Vin de Pays des Côtes de Gascogne was recognized in 1982. The white wine comes from grapes that were originally destined for Armagnac, namely Ugni Blanc and Colombard; Folle Blanche can also be included, but tends to be used only for Armagnac as its flavour is too neutral. More adventurous growers have also planted the Gros Manseng of Jurançon, as well as Sauvignon and Chardonnay. Red grape varieties are a more recent innovation, with plantings of Merlot, Cabernet Sauvignon, Cabernet Franc and Tannat.

The Union de Plaimont, with co-operatives at St-Mont, Plaisance and Aignan, all in Gers, is one of the largest producers of Vin de Pays des Côtes de Gascogne and demonstrates admirably how much vinification methods have improved in the region. The more interesting wines, however, come from the independent growers. This is a delightful region to visit, with its gently undulating landscape interrupted by old towns and fortified villages. Montréal has an arcaded square, while Fourcas is another picturesque spot, and Larresingle an enchanting fortified hilltop village.

Our first visit was to Domaine de Tarriquet, which is owned by the Grassa family, along with three other estates – Domaine de Rieux, Domaine de la Jalousie and Domaine de Plantérieu. The château de Tarriquet was built in 1683. The wine is made in the outbuildings, with stainless-steel vats outside, while the original bakery of the château has been converted into a small tasting-room. Altogether the Grassa family have 67 hectares of vines, planted with Ugni Blanc, Colombard, Gros Manseng, Folle Blanche and Baco. The last two are used only for Armagnac. They began making wine seriously about 1980 when sales of Armagnac had declined dramatically.

The base of their white wine is Ugni Blanc, with some Colombard. Gros Manseng is just coming into production and will give the wine more body, which is particularly desirable for their experiments with oak ageing. They also have plans to plant some Chardonnay. Yves Grassa is very keen on trying out different techniques and he has some new 225-litre barrels of Tronçais oak. They are only used three times, and only for three months at a time. The first vintage of their *cuvée bois* to go on the market was the 1985. The taste of oak is quite strong, but does not entirely overwhelm the fruit. Certainly it shows potential. They are also experimenting with skin contact to give the wine more aroma, but only with the best grapes. Otherwise their methods are those of a classic white-wine vinification, with a cool, slow fermentation, and their wines demonstrate the enormous potential of the area. I liked the fragrant nose, fresh acidity and rather smoky flavour of their wine.

Patrick Aurin at Domaine Meste Duran outside Condom is a friendly, enthusiastic man who clearly enjoys what he does. His grandfather made red wine from inferior varieties like Alicante Bouschet and Jurançon Noir. His father, however, began planting better varieties and was one of the first to introduce Merlot to the area some thirty years ago. M. Aurin now has 55 hectares of vines, and with the boom in *vin de pays* has given up Armagnac completely. His white wine is made from Ugni Blanc and Colombard and he has just planted some Chardonnay. His white grape varieties grow on clay and limestone soil, while the reds are on gravel.

His red wine comes mainly from Merlot, Cabernet Franc and Cabernet Sauvignon, though he also has some Jurançon Noir, which is usually low in alcohol, for reducing alcohol content in hot years. His red wine is usually sold as Vin de Pays des Côtes du Condomois, for which the permitted yield is lower (70 hectolitres per hectare as opposed to 80 hl/ha), but otherwise the two wines are the same. He said *'des histoires politiques'* are standing between the Côtes du Condomois and the status of VDQS.

M. Aurin has tried skin contact, too, but considers that sometimes the results can be too perfumed. He has an open-minded view of his vinification methods, cheerfully stating that he has 'tried everything'. He is well equipped to control his fermentation temperatures and he uses cultured yeast from Alsace for white wine. His red wines generally spend a year in vat and some a few months in wood, for which he has just bought some second-hand 225-litre barrels. What he would really love is some new ones. His enthusiasm has wider horizons than Gascony: he declared himself a fanatic of Bordeaux, proclaiming it the greatest wine ever.

The Vin de Pays des Côtes de Gascogne is attracting attention, and with reason. It shows enormous potential, producing dry white wines that are eminently drinkable and refreshing, and light fruity reds. Of all the *vins de pays* of the south west they best merit upgrading to VDQS.

3

The Lost Vineyards of the Lot, Aveyron and the Landes

GLANES

All over France you can find remnants of a lost viticultural tradition, often in unexpected villages. The department of the Lot is known above all for Cahors, but in the region of Haut-Quercy, around the town of St-Céré, there are wines to be discovered. Sometimes you need detective powers to lead you there, and also good luck, as my day in Haut-Quercy illustrates.

I had noticed a passing reference to Vin de Pays des Coteaux de Glanes in the ONIVIT handbook on *vins de pays* (ONIVIT is the equivalent of the INAO for *vins de pays* and *vins de table*). On the map it was some distance from any of the other *vins de pays* of the region, a tiny island of wine in the northern corner of the department of the Lot. Curiosity was aroused and we set out to explore. Glanes was a small dot on the Michelin map, in the hills above St-Céré near the imposing fortress of Bretenoux. We had no contact name but we were confident that there would be a café or a village shop where we could ask. Glanes has neither and the village was deserted, apart from a lad mixing cement in what passed for the main square. This did not augur well, but you never can tell. When I said I was looking for a producer of Vin de Pays des Coteaux de Glanes, the immediate reply was 'Yes, I make some.' He turned out to be a member of the GAEC des Vignerons du Haut-Quercy and was only to eager to give up mixing his cement in order to show us their cellar.

There are eight members of the group, which was founded in 1976. This is above all a region of fruit trees, especially walnut trees, but before the phylloxera crisis most of the hillsides around the village had been covered with vines. The hybrid varieties had remained, but traces of old plants of Merlot, Gamay, Abouriou and Cot had also been found, so they had elected, with the guidance of M. Pelissié, the oenologist for Cahors, to plant Merlot and Gamay. There is also talk of a new variety, called Ségalin, that is a cross between Jurançon Noir and Portugais Bleu, which ripens early and suffers from neither rot nor *coulure*. For the moment, however, they have 15 hectares of vines planted half in Merlot and half in Gamay. The Gamay ripens early, but as it does not give enough colour it needs to be supplemented with the body and colour of the Merlot. Unfortunately the Merlot is very susceptible to *coulure*, and in 1984 they hardly made any wine at all for that reason.

Each grower cultivates his own vines and the grapes are all vinified together in a modern functional cellar. They ferment in stainless-steel vats, with water to cool the must if necessary. The grapes are destalked and fermentation takes about six days. The wine is bottled at the beginning of May. We were given the 1983 to taste (this was in September 1985) by the president of the group, Georges Vidal. It was really rather good, with some fruit, a rounded flavour and soft tannin – a nice glass of wine.

M. Vidal explained over a glass of ratafia how his grandparents lived mainly from wine, which they sold in the Auvergne where very little wine was produced. People gave up their vines with the rural exodus and turned to walnut trees. But walnut trees are for old people, as they take so long to bear fruit. There is now a revival of interest in vines. At first they were called Vin de Pays du Lot, but they wanted a more individual definition. Consequently the Vin de Pays des Coteaux de Glanes was delimited in 1981, according to the limestone soil of the vineyards, which are on west-facing hillsides. Six villages make up the area, but for the moment the vineyards are concentrated on Glanes.

The production is still small – 76,000 bottles in 1983 – but there is an interested demand and they have even sent some wine to Holland. They are optimistic for the future and deserve well. The main problem is the tiny quantity, so for the moment the Vin de Pays des Coteaux de Glanes is sadly condemned to remain an unknown local wine.

QUEYSSAC-LES-VIGNES

I had read that the nearby village of Queyssac-les-Vignes had a tradition of making *vin de paille*, and that one or two dedicated people were struggling to maintain it. 'Let's go and find some,' we said. Queyssac-les-Vignes is an attractive village, split into two. At the top of the hill we found a restaurant called Le Vin de Paille and a tower that you can climb for wonderful views over the valley below. But the café failed to live up to its name. They did not serve *vin de paille* and they did not know who made it, or indeed even if it was still made. The bored waitress suggested that we might ask in the village below. The lower village was a cluster of houses, and two lads were chatting at the entrance to a farmyard. We were lucky. The English translation of the reply to my question would have been: 'Hang on a minute, love, I'll just go and fetch my mum.' We parked the car, accidentally disturbing a nesting chicken, and Mum appeared. Mme Soursac was a sturdy woman whose most notable feature was her silvery moustache.

This valiant lady rears lambs, but she also has a hectare of vines scattered around the village. Before the phylloxera all the hillsides round about were covered in terraces of vines. Her family have continued the local rural tradition of wine-making, in the way that growers in other parts of France make ratafia. Mum explained that she picks the ripest and healthiest grapes, taking care that none has any rot, and leaves them to dry on straw in a draughty barn. They are pressed at the end of January when they are nicely shrivelled. The wine is then put in small barrels and the fermentation is very slow, lasting into the summer. The wine is racked when the fermentation is finished and kept for another two years in barrels, which are occasionally topped up. Asked what grape varieties she had, Mum said a bit of everything; she didn't really know – 'numbers' (meaning the numbered hybrids).

We tasted her *vin de paille* from the barrel in the old barn. It was dark brown in colour, very rich and raisiny, sweet with a good bite of balancing acidity and quite delicious. The alcohol level is about 15–16°. We bought a bottle which was filled from the barrel. There was a pile of empty bottles which were being recycled. Our wine came in a claret bottle and the cork was inserted with a piece of equipment that would be more at home in a wine museum. There was no label, and the finishing touch was a sheet of month-old newspaper to wrap our bottle. From there the road took us further along the Lot valley into Aveyron.

ENTRAYGUES ET DU FEL

North of Decazeville the river and the road narrow. The river twists and turns, with the road carefully following every bend on its way to the little town of Entraygues-sur-Truyère. The river valley is steep and tree-covered, so that in autumn it is a glorious sight of brilliant red and russet. Entraygues is the point where the Truyère, which rises in the heart of the Massif Central, joins the river Lot. A thirteenth-century bridge spans the river with pointed arches. In *occitan* Entraygues means *entre eaux*, between the waters, i.e. rivers. It is an attractive town with an old castle.

The earliest references to viticulture in this area go back over a thousand years. In the archives of the nearby abbey of Conques there are records that local wine-growers made donations of vines to the abbey in AD 902, and again in 997. During the Middle Ages the monks from Conques did much to establish viticulture in the area. The Lot is navigable as far as Entraygues, providing easy transport for the wine by river. In later centuries wine from Entraygues was sent to Aurillac in the Auvergne. It was also drunk by the thirsty mining community of Decazeville and even found its way to Paris, for the Auvergnats are the traditional café-owners of Paris and naturally bought the wine from their friends and relations.

Before the phylloxera the hillsides of the Lot valley were covered with terraces of vines interspersed with chestnut trees, and you can still see the crumbling remains of these terraces today. Entraygues never really recovered from the phylloxera crisis, for the traditional markets for its wines were disappearing and the effects of the First World War and the rural exodus hastened the decline. Where once there were 1,000 hectares of vines around Entraygues there are now barely 15, with only two producers of any importance for this VDQS of Entraygues et du Fel, to give its full name. Le Fel is a village of just a few houses and a tiny church. It had a reputation for its red wine, while Entraygues was known for white. Today the VDQS covers all three colours.

The soil here is a mixture of schist and sand which allows for a veritable hotch-potch of different grape varieties. I went to see M. Viguier, who with 7.5 hectares is the largest producer. He is an old man, whose son now does most of the work in the cellar. Nevertheless he is still very attached to his vines and I was taken to see the vineyard. He shuffled along in his slippers, pointing out the different varieties and their characteristics. It was rather like an elderly uncle discussing the merits and defects of his favourite nieces and nephews.

There was Fer Servadou which is a late ripener and resistant to rot, but not a big producer. Négret, I was told, was not the same as the Négrette of Fronton, but part of the same family as Fer Servadou. He has introduced some Gamay which is an earlier ripener and gives some body and alcohol to the wine. He also has Cabernet Franc and Cabernet Sauvignon – the latter being another recent introduction which he likes for its finesse, and which, with its loose berries, is also rot-resistant. Finally there is a little Jurançon, which will be eliminated, as it does not give very good results. White wine comes from Chenin Blanc and he has tried some Mauzac and Baroque, but they are not very satisfactory.

The Viguier family have been wine-growers for generations. There is a sixteenth-century lawyer's document referring to an ancestor renting vines from the Seigneur d'Entraygues. Today the family still concentrate on vines, but also have a herd of goats. They began bottling their wines in 1950, before which they were sold in barrel to local cafés. Methods are rustic and they did not have a tractor until 1975. The cellars are primitive, with cobwebs galore, despite evidence of the son's attempt to introduce an element of the twentieth century into the procedures.

The red grapes are not destalked and are fermented in an open-top cement vat for five or six days and bottled in the late spring. We tasted the 1948 which was quite astringent, with some raspberry fruit. The pink is a *vin de saigné*, mainly from Jurançon, which does not give very exciting results. I liked the white best, which is fermented in wood, although there is a stainless-steel vat outside to encourage the precipitation of tartrates during the cold winter months. It was quite acidic, with a little honey, characteristic of the grape.

ESTAING

Further up the Lot valley is the town of Estaing. The difference between Entraygues and Estaing lies in the soil, which here is a mixture of schist and chalk. The vineyards are also a little higher in altitude and the climate a little cooler. The vintage is usually in October. Again red, white and pink are made. Pink wine was once the most important, perhaps because the grapes did not ripen sufficiently for red wine, and there are not many vines for white wine. The grape varieties are the same as at Entraygues: mainly Gamay, Cabernet Franc, Fer Servadou, Mauzac and Chenin Blanc.

Estaing is another old vineyard. The earliest reference comes in 1399 in a document from the nearby monastery of Cabrespines. Today it is an attractive small town. A bridge spans the river and houses cluster around the foot of the château. Estaing prides itself on being the very smallest VDQS of France, with just 6 hectares of vines and only one producer of any note, who has just 1.5 hectares.

We tracked down the Rieu family in the hamlet of Le Viala. Pierre Rieu was at a meeting to discuss plans for the construction of a communal cellar for the eight producers. Mme Rieu was busy with her daughter, baking some delicious-smelling cakes for a friend's wedding the next day, but she was quite happy to take time off from the kitchen to show us the family cellar, which had been built in 1905 by a great-grandfather. He used to send his wine to his brother who owned a café in Paris.

Again the methods were more those of the great-grandfather's time. The fermentation takes place in open barrels for red wine, and closed barrels for white. The press is the old-fashioned kind and the wine is stored in oak or chestnut barrels of uncertain age. In *occitan* they call them *tines*.

The white wine from Chenin Blanc, softened with a little Mauzac, proved remarkably drinkable in the congenial atmosphere of the large farmhouse kitchen. It survived the journey back to London, too. The pink was fruity without too much acidity, and the red quite tough and astringent, with some body and fruit.

MARCILLAC

More exciting are the red wines of Marcillac. This is the most flourishing of the three wines of Aveyron thanks to the creation of a *cave co-opérative* in 1965, the year after Marcillac was recognized as a VDQS. The co-operative was able to group together all the farmers, some seventy people; between them they have only about 85 hectares of vines, while the total area of the VDQS comes to just 110 hectares. These are people with a few ares, or maybe a hectare of vines. Viticulture is just one of their activities as they may have other crops or livestock, or even an office job. The town of Marcillac itself is unprepossessing and does not merit a detour. The surrounding countryside, however, is hilly and breathtaking. The vines are on steep slopes at an altitude of 300 to 600 metres, so that the growers sometimes need pulleys to manoeuvre their equipment.

The climate here is quite mild. Usually they have cold winters, wet springs and fine summers with the occasional storm. Autumns are generally dry. During the summer the prevailing wind from the Midi keeps everything dry and prevents any problems with rot. Frost in the spring can be a problem and you never see vines on the lower slopes.

There were 3,000 hectares of vines around Marcillac before the phylloxera crisis. Many of them actually survived until the First World War and then disappeared as the traditional markets for Marcillac were lost. Now new vineyards are being planted. Some of the old terraces are being restored and new ones constructed. The soil here is red sandstone and some of the vines are planted according to the '*système suisse*', with the rows across the hillsides rather down the slopes. The new plantings have about 5,000 vines per hectare, trained on wires, while the old vineyards have 8,000 to 9,000 plants per hectare, closely spaced and without wires, so that in high summer the branches tend to sprawl over the ground.

One or two of the younger growers are investing in new cellars; Philippe Teulier of the Domaine Laurens-Teulier is one of them. His cellars are built into the hillside, the new cellar alongside the old one that was constructed by a great-great-grandfather in 1827, and they function by gravity: the grapes arrive at the highest level, are pressed and fermented in vats at the next level, and the wine is aged on the lowest level.

The wine is fermented in open-top vats of wood or cement.

Although M. Teulier carries out a mechanical *remontage* every evening, he still believes in the value of submerging the cap of grape skins in the morning by the time-honoured method of pressing it down with the feet, for he considers that this gives the wine a better aroma. All his wine is kept in wood, in oak or chestnut barrels that may be as much as 200 years old. It is fined with real egg whites, not a powder product, and is never filtered. We tasted the 1984, which has some delicious *cassis* fruit and some acidity and went very well with Cantal cheese.

The two principal villages of Marcillac are Clairvaux and Brue-jouls, which is an attractive redstone village. There we saw Jean-Louis Matha, who in a gesture of independence withdrew from the co-operative so that he could make and sell his own wine. His grandfather had had vines, but his father had preferred fruit trees. M. Matha has bought unplanted land and built terraces. He now has 7 hectares of vines on south-facing slopes around the village, planted mainly with Fer Servadou as well as a little Gamay, and with a few vines for a drop of white wine, namely Mauzac, Chenin Blanc and Muscadelle.

His red wine is fuller than that of M. Teulier. The difference comes from the vinification methods. He gives it a longer *cuvaison* of fifteen days, but destalks a percentage of the grapes, otherwise he would have too much tannin. He does a *remontage* every other day. His cellar was set up in 1982, when he left the co-operative. We were escorted on our visit by a friendly black spaniel who answered to the name of Reagan, 'like the President'. Everything is very traditional and methods have not changed much since his grandparents made wine. His red wine spends a year in wood. The 1983 had a rich blackcurrant nose and plenty of fruit. It should age well for a few years. Certainly, an anonymous bottle from the co-operative's 1975 or 1976 vintage, on the hotel wine list in Entraygues, provided a lovely glass of mature wine with flavours of blackcurrants and herbal undertones. It was not unlike a mature Beaujolais.

These lost wines of Aveyron are unlikely ever to be of much more than regional interest. They are mainly drunk in local restaurants or may perhaps travel as far as Paris. It would be sad to see them disappear, and happily it looks as though a revival in their fortunes is assured. Entraygues and Estaing will remain tiny wine islands, but Marcillac has the promise of a more flourishing future, especially as it is now in line for an appellation.

TURSAN

Tursan is one of the last remaining vineyards of the *vins des sables* that were scattered all over the Landes in the last century. Today there are still a few vines in the sand dunes near Messanges, called Vin de Pays des Landes, but the vast area of the Landes to the south of Bordeaux is now given over almost exclusively to pine forests; you drive for miles on long straight roads which seem to form endless alleys of pine trees. In the summer heat the scent of pine is intoxicating.

The traditional *vin du sable*, which is now little more than a memory, came from grapes grown in the sand dunes of the Landes. The vines had very deep roots going through the sand and were trained so low that the grapes almost rested on the sand and absorbed warmth from it, so that they ripened easily and produced rich, heady wines, with a tang of the sea.

The vineyards of Tursan are on the south east edge of the Landes. The little town of Geaune is the centre of the region. I arrived at lunchtime as the market in the main square was closing. There are the remains of a ruined medieval tower. The village of Vieille-Tursan is the most important of the twenty-seven villages in the VDQS, but no doubt the most famous is Eugénie-les-Bains, known not for its wine but for one of the leading restaurants of France. It proudly calls itself '*le premier village minceur de France*'. The thermal baths became fashionable when the Empress Eugénie, the wife of Napoleon III, came here to take the waters, and their popularity was revived with the arrival of the talented chef Michel Guérard.

Tursan was one of the many wines enjoyed in the Middle Ages during the English occupation of Aquitaine. The wines were sent all over Europe from the port of Bayonne and there are records of Tursan being drunk in London, Seville, Rotterdam and Hamburg. Today its importance has declined to the extent that the co-operative of Geaune is by far the largest producer, accounting for 400 out of the 420 hectares of vines in production. There is just one courageous independent grower at Domaine de Perchade-Pourruchet.

The co-operative was founded in 1957 and the wine was recognized as a VDQS in 1958; it is now aspiring to become an appellation. Few of the co-operative members make their living from vines alone, for this is a region of polyculture: vines grow on the hillsides, but there is maize on the valley floor and fields of grazing cattle. Ducks for the regional speciality of *foie gras* are also important. M. Paraillous, the dynamic young director of the co-operative, explained that the vineyard area is likely to increase; vines had been competing against maize and ducks, but French maize is too expensive by comparison with American imports, while *foie gras*, as a luxury item, cannot assure a living.

The reputation of Tursan was based on white wine, while red is a recent introduction of the 1960s. White Tursan is made from a singularly uninspiring grape, the Baroque, which can also feature in the white wine of Béarn and is also found in small quantities in Aveyron. However Tursan is the only wine to attribute so much importance to Baroque. No one is sure of its origins. Jancis Robinson, in her authoritative book *Vines, Grapes, Wines*, puts forward several theories. Pilgrims returning from Santiago de Compostela in Galicia may have brought it with them. Perhaps it has more than just a similarity of name with the white version of Portugal's Tinta Barroca; or maybe it is firmly native to this corner of south west France.

At present white Tursan is made only from Baroque, although other grape varieties could be included such as Manseng, Raffiat, and even Sauvignon, which would give the wine a little vitality. So far there is just one hectare of Sauvignon, not yet in production, at Domaine de Perchade-Pourruchet. The Baroque is a sturdy vine that produces large grapes with a lot of juice. It adapted well to grafting after the phylloxera and is not too susceptible to rot. However, it does require careful vinification as it can oxidize very quickly.

Red wines only appeared in the 1960s. They are made from the grape varieties typical of the south west: Tannat, Cabernet Sauvignon and Cabernet Franc. There is about 20 per cent Tannat and a drop of Cabernet Sauvignon, but Cabernet Franc is by far the most important grape.

The Tannat and the Cabernets are fermented separately. The Tannat usually spends a little less time on the skins and the juice of the Cabernet is run over more often. The grapes are all destalked and about 10 per cent are in any case picked by mechanical harvester. The final blending is done a year or so after the vintage, usually when the wine is needed for bottling. Two qualities of each colour are made, as well as Vin de Pays des Landes from any wine not suitable for the VDQS. One individual property, Domaine de Castèle at Vieille-Tursan, is vinified separately. Cuvée Paysage is the basic quality, while Cuvée Carte Noire is the better wine; vintages appear to be irrelevant and do not feature on the label.

I tasted most of their wines, which seemed fairly well made but failed to excite me. The whites are rather solid and dry, without much real fruit, which is probably the fault of the grape variety rather than the vinification. The pink had a hint of raspberries, while the two reds were both a little astringent without much real fruit.

From Tursan it was only a short drive to Pau, to discover the delights of Jurançon and the other wines of the Pyrenees.

4

The Foothills of the Pyrenees

———

JURANÇON

Henri IV made Jurançon famous. Everyone knows the story of his christening at the Château de Pau when his grandfather Henri d'Albret rubbed the baby's lips with garlic and moistened them with Jurançon, thus beginning a French royal tradition. Louis XVIII did the same for his nephew the Duke of Bordeaux in 1820.

It was Colette who made Jurançon notorious. Other writers and poets have written of Jurançon, but none more dramatically than with the words, 'I was a girl when I met this prince; aroused, imperious, treacherous as all great seducers are – Jurançon.'

The Romans were the first to plant vines here, but no precise date is known. The first written document referring to vineyards in the area, according to Hubrecht Duyker in his excellent *Grands Vins du Rhône and du Midi*, which in fact covers much more than those two areas, was in the fourteenth century when a monastery recorded the renting of a vineyard to a farmer on the condition that he cultivated the vines according to the prescribed regulations. The Albret family, kings of Navarre, planted a vineyard at Nérac which enjoyed a considerable reputation in the sixteenth century and it is probable that they also encouraged viticulture around the town of Pau. Certainly it was recorded that in 1564 Jeanne d'Albret gave a vineyard to one of the ladies of her court. At that time Jurançon had a reputation for red as well as white wine and it was not until the seventeenth century that white wine gained its pre-eminence. During the seventeenth and eighteenth centuries wine was shipped from the port of Bayonne by the Dutch and the English. Jurançon drunk at the court of Charles II was described as very white, very sweet and

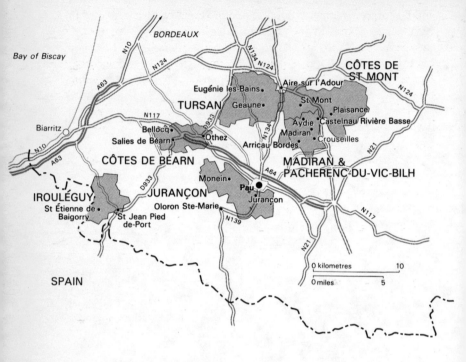

The Pyrenees

very good. The Dutch fortified their wine slightly to enable it to withstand the sea voyage across the Bay of Biscay.

The eminent nineteenth-century authority Jullien described white Jurançon as being distinguished by a taste and a perfume approaching that of a truffle, and said that it gained flavour with age. He also mentioned red Jurançon as having body, alcohol, a beautiful colour and an attractive bouquet. Today Jurançon is firmly white. In addition, Jullien described *vins paillets* as also enjoying a good reputation. These wines were made from a mixture of red and white grapes and were very light, fine and delicate, with a very pleasant taste. Curiously there was no mention that Jurançon is a sweet wine.

Guyot, a few decades later, described white Jurançon as resembling the wines of the Rhine, but with more body and less sweetness. He enthused about red Jurançon as being deep in colour, full-bodied, with a bouquet and flavour that were clean but delicious. Both Rendu and Cavoleau, writing within a few years of each other, referred to various *crus*, some of which reflect names known today, but most of which have sunk into insignificance. Rendu's list included Jolys, and today Château Jolys is one of the better producers of the appellation. He mentioned Petit Manseng as the best grape variety, which is still true today. Cavoleau described the best wines as being distinguished by an aroma of truffle. By 1900, in *Les Vins de France* Adrien Berger was saying that Jurançon was heady and sweet, and when aged acquired a bouquet similar to the taste of quince.

After the phylloxera crisis the area went into decline, and two world wars added to the economic crisis. By 1949, despite the creation of the appellation in 1936, quality had plummeted as producers were tempted to add sugar to their wines to boost the level of sweetness. Yields were tiny, 12 to 15 hectolitres per hectare, with holdings averaging 1.5 hectares per grower. Hubrecht Duyker attributes the salvation of the appellation to the founder of the Cave Co-opérative de Gan, Henri Meyer, an eminent oenologist, biologist and agronomist who has done much for the viticultural life of the Pyrenees. Today Jurançon is once again a flourishing appellation, with a reputation for both sweet and dry wines – or rather, to quote Jean Chigé, one of the leading producers, 'dry wines that are not really dry and sweet wines that are not very sweet'.

The vineyards of Jurançon are set amongst one of the most beautiful landscapes of France. They are on the first hills of the Pyrenees to the south of Pau, the capital of Béarn, with its imposing château. In the early nineteenth century Pau was fashionable with the English upper middle classes, and an English colony played golf and hunted foxes from their elegant villas in the foothills of the mountains. The English cemetery in Pau is full of names like Cartwright and Jenkins, and there is even a *jardin anglais*. The view from the Boulevard des Pyrénées, with snow-capped mountains in the distance, is magnificent.

The appellation of Jurançon now covers twenty-five villages to the south and west of Pau in the department of Pyrénées-Atlantiques. The village of Jurançon itself is almost a suburb of Pau and does not even feature in the Michelin Green Guide. Two rivers, the Gave d'Oloron and the Gave de Pau, limit the area to the north and the south, and once provided transport to the port of Bayonne. It is an area of tiny villages perched on the foothills of the Pyrenees. The hills create a multitude of microclimates. There are small parcels of vines, usually on steep slopes, facing south west or south east, mixed with sunflowers and maize and pale cattle grazing in gentle fields. I have a French aunt in Pau, who is proud of her Béarnaise origins and knows the area like the back of her hand. Tante Colette was a welcome guide around the narrow, winding country lanes, helping me to track down obscure addresses without many deviations.

Jurançon is produced from three principal grape varieties, Gros Manseng, Petit Manseng and Courbu. Two unknown varieties, Lauzet and Camaralet, are also permitted but have virtually disappeared. These varieties are occasionally found in other nearby white wines such as Pacherenc de Vic-Bihl and Vin de Pays des Côtes de Gascogne, but otherwise it is very unusual to find them elsewhere. Aimé Guibert grows Petit Manseng at Mas de Daumas Gassac in Hérault, but that is a unique example. One of Jurançon's oldest growers, Mme Migné at Clos Joliette, said of them: 'Petit Manseng, he is the king and the Gros Manseng is his page boy.' It is Petit Manseng that gives sweet Jurançon its quality; it is also more difficult to grow as it produces little grapes in loose bunches, but in small quantity. It has more sugar and thus more alcohol, and is therefore more suitable for the *moelleux* wines. Petit Manseng does not really resemble Gros Manseng, though it may originally have derived from it. Thirty hectolitres per hectare is its maximum yield, but it gives a wine with a much richer bouquet. It is also sensitive to *coulure*.

In contrast Gros Manseng provides quantity, especially for Jurançon Sec. It does not ripen early, but it gives regular yields and is generally resistant to *coulure* and the ravages of bad weather. Courbu, which like Gewurztraminer has a slightly pink skin, only represents 5 per cent of the vineyards. It tends to be rather sensitive to *coulure* and to rot, with its very tight bunches, and also ages less successfully. It takes away the character of the Manseng grapes, is not very acid, and tends to give quantity rather than quality. It is less perfumed and ripens a little earlier. Some people have no Courbu at all in their vineyards and the percentage of Gros and Petit Manseng varies from grower to grower. A general belief in two-thirds Gros Manseng to one-third Petit Manseng is sometimes rejected. M. Latrille at Château Jolys favours half and half. He described Petit Manseng as being the size of hard *petits pois anglais*, and those of Gros Manseng as being the size of a small cherry.

Some work is being done on clonal selection. The Lauzet is very fragile, with large grapes in small bunches; it rots easily, but could have some future potential if successful anti-rot treatments can be developed.

Henri Ramonteu at Domaine Cauhapé explained how he makes his Jurançon *moelleux*. The concentration of the grapes comes only very rarely from noble rot, but much more commonly from a process called *passerillage* whereby the grapes are left on the vines until well into the autumn. In 1982, for instance, he finished the vintage on 9 November. This is a region of long sunny autumns; the prevailing wind from the Pyrenees, locally called the *Froin*, a drying wind from the warm plains of Spain, combines with freezing temperatures at night to shrivel the grapes and make their juice rich and concentrated. Purists practise *triage*, a careful selection of the grapes by several pickings. Economic reality and practical considerations mean that there are usually two pickings, one for the grapes for Jurançon Sec in early October and a second picking a few weeks later for the *moelleux*. M. Ramonteu makes his *moelleux* from one-quarter Petit Manseng to three-quarters Gros Manseng. The wine ferments for up to a month, compared with only twenty days for the Jurançon Sec which is a blend of Gros Manseng and Courbu. Whereas dry Jurançon is bottled in the spring following the vintage, *moelleux* is aged, usually in wood, for several months. Jurançon Sec is a wine to drink in its relative youth, while Jurançon *moelleux* merits some considerable bottle age and in the best vintages can be treated like a good Sauternes.

The Cave Co-opérative de Gan is by far the largest producer of Jurançon, for of the 500 hectares of the appellation 60 per cent belongs to the 350 members of the co-operative. It was founded in 1950 at a time when the appellation was badly in need of resuscitation. It did a good job in the initial years of its activity, but then declined and has now been revived by new management in recent years. Their wine-maker, M. Leprun, who arrived there fresh from oenology school, should go far. He has introduced new, improved methods of vinification so that they now have stainless-steel fermentation vats and can control the fermentation temperature at 18°C. A careful selection of the grapes is made, as they produce three qualities of dry wine and three of sweet wine.

The dry Grains Sauvages and sweet Apéritif Henri IV are both bottled between December and February in order to retain their youthful fruitiness. The Grains Sauvages has hints of grapefruit or passion fruit, with good, fresh acidity, while the Apéritif Henri IV is light and honeyed, and is usually made from the first pickings for *moelleux*. The next category is Peyre d'Or for dry wine and Prestige d'Automne for *moelleux* – the latter being made only from Petit Manseng and aged for eighteen to twenty-four months in vat. As yet they do not have any oak barrels. The wine could benefit from ageing in wood, but the expense of buying new oak barrels and the necessary maintenance and so on would increase the price of the wine by as much as ten francs a bottle, which would be unacceptable. They make two wines that are a blend of vintages, a dry Brut Océan and a sweet Cuvée Quatrième Centenaire, which commemorates the 400th anniversary of Henri IV's christening. In addition they have taken over the vineyards of Château les Astous, an impressive but dilapidated, and at present uninhabited, edifice overlooking the road between Pau and Gan. It belonged to a Pau family who employed someone else to make their wine. He has now retired and in any case was never a good wine-maker. The co-operative is intending to resurrect the property's previous reputation and use the wine, which they will vinify separately, as their flagship.

The co-operative at Gan represents a sound standard of wine-making, with well-controlled, up-to-date methods. Its wines are representative of the appellation, but as yet not very exciting. The standard of expertise in the region varies enormously. There is the very good and the very bad. There are the traditional ill-equipped and rather rustic cellars, where hygiene seems unimportant and where they are somewhat heavy-handed with the sulphur and sugar. In contrast there are some new young wine-makers who are questioning their parents' methods and approaching the wines of Jurançon with an open, inquiring mind.

Henri Ramonteu at Domaine Cauhapé is one such grower, who does make wines that excite. His wines were indeed a revelation that quite upset any preconceived ideas I had about Jurançon before my visit. We tracked him down outside the village of Monein in the heart of the appellation. You approach his property through an alley of maize. He is a farmer, with cows as well as maize, with just 7.5 hectares of vines, only six of which are for Jurançon. From the rest he makes Rouge de Béarn. He has 2 hectares of Petit Manseng and 4 of Gros Manseng, and a little Courbu. Most of his vines are just by the farmyard, on a steep south east-facing slope, and have been given the traditional high pruning of the area. Henri Ramonteu says he knew nothing about wine-making when he was twenty and he is now in his late thirties. He is self-taught, has read books and done short courses, but has had no formal training, which seems to make his approach more questioning. Until 1980 he sold all his wine to the local *négociants*, but now bottles all himself and is constantly experimenting with his vinification methods. When I visited him, he had just bought twenty new oak barrels in which to age his *moelleux* wine. His intention was that each wine should spend six months in barrels, which could be used four times. He wants his wine to breathe and benefit from the oxygen exchange, and is convinced that 'it makes the wine more noble'. Even more interesting is the skin contact he is giving the juice for his Jurançon Sec. Half the crop is left on the skins for a few hours and then blended with the free-run and pressed juice, for otherwise the aromas are too strong. He was also intending to try this for his sweet wine. Another project is to experiment with fermentation in oak. At the moment he has brand-new stainless-steel barrels which are hidden in an old farm building with the date 1781 on the outside wall. Henri Ramonteu is convinced of the future of Jurançon. He is sad that there are people who continue to make Jurançon badly and that there are not enough young growers in the area. He described the French as a nation of good-for-nothings.

Charles Hours at Clos Uroulat, an isolated property also near Monein, is a man after M. Ramonteu's own heart. When I went to see him, he had only been making Jurançon for two years, after studying oenology at Bordeaux University. His 9 hectares of vine-yards are in an amphitheatre of hills which provides a magnificent microclimate, allowing the vines to soak up the heat and sunshine. He too is experimenting with ageing his *moelleux* wines in new oak and they will not be bottled until after the second winter. In contrast his dry wine is bottled young. For M. Hours sweet Jurançon is a *vin de garde*, but to make that you must have wood, and not just any old wood. He wants to develop a stock of old bottles, but it is still early days for that. His 1985 *moelleux*, drunk in April 1987 at Eugénie-les-Bains with *foie gras*, can only be described as delicious. It was elegantly honeyed on nose and palate, with a long, lingering finish, but without the weight of a Sauternes.

So often it is people coming fresh to an area who see their appellation with the most objectivity and clear-sightedness. One such person is Robert Latrille at Château Jolys. His family were Bordeaux *négociants* who settled in Algeria in 1920. He bought Château Jolys in 1958. The last vines had been pulled up in 1957 and he spent the following six years reorganizing the terrain and replanting the vineyards. He has only been making his own wine since 1983 and until then sold his grapes to Menjucq, the *négociant* house outside Pau. M. Latrille has championed a cause: 'I believe in Jurançon and I will fight for Jurançon to become known and appreciated.' His enthusiasm and determination are infectious. He also admits that 'wine is my vice!' His cellars represent a considerable investment in equipment. But it was in the elegant Louis XV salon that he explained his vinification methods in exact detail. The grapes are gently crushed and the juice is chilled for *débourbage*, which takes twenty-four hours. His Jurançon Sec is made according to modern vinification principles. If the fermentation does not start within forty-eight hours, he seeds it with yeasts from Alsace and it takes about ten to twelve days at a temperature of 15–18°C. Like everyone else he selects the grapes for the dry and the *moelleux* according to their ripeness, and ferments all the grape varieties together rather than blending afterwards. However, unlike most growers in Jurançon, he encourages the malolactic fermentation, which reduces the total acidity and gives a more stable wine. He is meticulous about hygiene ('for 1 hecto of wine, you need 100 hectolitres of water') and he is adamantly against chaptalization, which he rightly considers to be unnecessary and detrimental to the quality of his wine. His dry wine is bottled in the spring as and when it is needed.

As for his *moelleux*, the juice must have potential alcohol of between 13° and 16°; 16° is ideal, as the perfect balance of alcohol and sugar is 13° plus 3°, while one degree of chaptalization is allowed. Again the fermentation is carefully controlled, and stopped by the addition of 200 milligrams per litre of sulphur dioxide when the right balance of sugar and alcohol has been reached. This may sound quite high, but in fact the legal maximum of sulphur in Jurançon *moelleux* is 400 mg/l. Sulphur of course prevents any malolactic fermentation. He would like to have barrels in order to age his sweet wine in wood for six to twelve months, but as yet that is an experimental project. At the moment his cellars are equipped with stainless-steel vats. His wines are improving with experience and his 1984 *sec* was very much better than the 1983, which lacked character. The 1984 *moelleux*, not a good year for Jurançon, suffers from lack of sunshine but has a hint of concentrated apricots, with a good acidity balance. His vineyards adjoin the château in another amphitheatre of hillsides, with the vines in rows like a fan, and roses in flower at the ends of the rows. Then we sat and drank tea in the sunshine, with two large sheep-dogs, Crocus and Berlioz, and a little dog called Atchoum, which is how the French spell the noise you make when you sneeze! Asked of the future, M. Latrille's prompt reply was '*Un soleil fantastique!*'

Roman Guirardel is an old man who has almost given up making wine. He has just 2.5 hectares of vines; once he had eleven, but sadly his family were not interested in keeping them. He lives on a farm in the middle of nowhere, or so it seemed. We sat in the garden in the September sunshine and talked. There were chickens running round the courtyard. Tante Colette encouraged him to reminisce. He has been making wines for seventy years. He had oxen and took the change to tractors very slowly, as you cannot use them easily on the steep slopes. He remembered treading the grapes and sometimes you had to warm your feet with hot water, as the grapes were almost frozen if they were picked in November after the first snows had fallen. The wine was put in large wooden vats and left to ferment gently until March. They never chaptalized their wine and it was racked four times during the year: after the fermentation had finished, at the flowering, at the *véraison*, when the grapes turn colour, and at the vintage. Very few people bottled their wine and it was mostly sold to the local cafés in barrels. He would take it into Pau by ox-cart, a journey which took seven hours. At that time the wine was called Vin de Monein, rather than Jurançon. There were very few vines in Jurançon between the two world wars, and the town was better known for the tuberculosis cures effected by its fresh mountain air. Oidium did much more damage than phylloxera. M. Guirardel remembered one year when he made just 300 litres of wine from his 11 hectares. His vines are at the bottom of the garden, beyond the vegetable patch. He has an old stone vat for treading the grapes and old barrels for fermenting and ageing his wine. Once people used to pick five or six times, making for a very prolonged vintage, but now there is much less *triage*, just a selection of small parcels of vines. He reckons his family is as old as Henri IV. The name has changed as the female line can inherit in Béarn, but the family is the same. We tasted his 1983, which was mature and nutty and rather rustic.

Mme Migné of Clos Joliette, an old lady in her seventies, has a reputation for her fine old vintages of Jurançon. Sadly, the day we went to see her she was out of sorts. Even Tante Colette's Béarnaise charm could not persuade her to allow us to see her cellar or buy any wine. It was a pity, for she has been making wine for fifty-five years. She has just 1.6 hectares now, south-facing vines on a steep slope, planted only with Petit Manseng and giving just 25 hectolitres per hectare. She makes only *moelleux* and her wine is aged in wood for three and a half years. She is one of the great traditionalists of Jurançon, and everyone speaks of her with respect.

MADIRAN AND PACHERENC DE VIC-BIHL

Pacherenc de Vic-Bihl is to Madiran what Condrieu is to Côte Rôtie – a delicate, oily white wine to accompany a sturdy, tannic red. Unlike the two Rhône appellations, however, their delimited area is identical; so that if a grower makes red wine it is Madiran, while the white will be the mouthful of a name Pacherenc de Vic-Bihl. Vic-Bihl means *vieux pays* in Gascon, and Pacherenc is a distortion of *pachet en renc*, or in French *piquets en rangs*, implying that the vines must once have been grown in a row, supported by posts. As for the pronunciation, it sounds something like 'pash er rank de vick beel'. Madiran takes its name from a sleepy village. On a hot September afternoon, hardly a fly stirred. There is an old church and an attractive market square.

The two wines share a history. Roman mosaics depicting vines have been found at Taron. However, it was the monks that gave real impetus to Madiran when a priory was founded in the village towards 1030. Further growth came in the twelfth century with the foundation of the abbey of Madiran by Benedictine monks. Throughout the Middle Ages Madiran was described as *un vin de curé*, as it was used in neighbouring dioceses for the mass. It also enjoyed a reputation with the pilgrims making their way over the Pyrenees to Santiago de Compostela.

Madiran is a relatively recent name for the wine. Sometimes it was referred to as Vin de Vic-Bihl and in the eighteenth century as Vin de Rivière Basse. The wine travelled by river to the port of Bayonne and then on to London, Holland and (in the eighteenth century) even as far as Finland and Russia. Local transport, however, was not always so easy. In 1820 the abbé Robin of St-Pé wrote to the *négociant* Monsieur Laplante at Castelnau: 'The old white wine that you should have sent me at least ten months ago has still not arrived. I hope I will be pleased with it, as I wanted an old wine, and that it will certainly be. If you had let me know the way you would send it, I could have sent my men to fetch it.'

Jullien rated Madiran as the best wine of the Hautes-Pyrénées, and described wines that were rich in colour and had a sweet taste during the first two years. They kept for eight to ten years in cask without declining, and could be bottled after five or six years when they had a lighter colour; they had body and alcohol and a pleasant taste. From a good year and aged in bottle, they could be offered at the best tables in the country. Guyot also praised the excellent red wines of Madiran, that were made from Bouchy, Mansenc and Tannat. The first two varieties used to dominate, but by the mid-nineteenth century it was the Tannat that was the most important, giving the desired colour and alcohol. By 1900 Berger described the wines of Madiran as harsh and full-bodied, saying that they only developed their qualities after several years' maturation.

Phylloxera wrought its customary havoc on the vineyards. The development of the railways alleviated the difficulties of transport, however, and the growers were encouraged to replant their vineyards with American rootstock; but the lack of resources made it a long, hard struggle. Those who were tenacious and serious planted the traditional grape varieties of the area, rather than succumbing to the temptation of easy hybrids. In 1906 a number of growers formed a voluntary organization, the first growers' association of Madiran, with the aim of maintaining the quality of their wine. In 1910 they achieved an official delimitation of the area covering villages in three departments, Gers, Pyrénées-Atlantiques and Hautes-Pyrénées. In 1936, as the Syndicat du Vic-Bihl, they began to work for the creation of the appellation of Madiran, which was finally achieved in 1948. Since then the decree has been revised several times. The last occasion was in 1975.

The appellation now covers a total of thirty-seven villages, with three in Gers, six including Madiran itself in Hautes-Pyrénées and twenty-eight in Pyrénées-Atlantiques. The actual area of the appellation under vines is still relatively small, only 1,100 hectares, although it underwent a considerable increase during the 1970s as more independent growers took an interest in the region and extended their estates. The *délimitation parcellaire*, the official definition of the precise parcels of land included in the appellation, irrespective of whether they are planted with vines, has been done and allows for an excessive 15,000 hectares. Most of these will never come under vines, and with a gentle increase the area is likely to stabilize at about 1,400 hectares.

The characteristic grape of Madiran is the Tannat, and earlier this century it was not uncommon to find Madiran made from Tannat alone. As its name implies, it is a very tannic, tough-skinned grape giving a solid mouthful of wine, and it needs to be toned down with other varieties and aged in wood for several months. The appellation regulations dictate between 40 and 60 per cent in a blend, to be supplemented with Cabernet Franc, also called Bouchy, and Cabernet Sauvignon. There is more Cabernet Franc than Cabernet Sauvignon as it makes the wine more supple, and both have developed in the region over the last twenty years or so. A drop of Fer Servadou, or Pinenc as it is known locally, can also be included.

The vineyards are on the last foothills of the Pyrenees, about 40 kilometres north of the towns of Pau and Tarbes. The soil is very varied, lending itself to a mixture of different grapes; Pacherenc de Vic-Bihl is also made from a blend of several varieties. The hotter south west-facing slopes are best for red wines, while white grapes are grown on the cooler south east slopes. It is a region of polyculture, with maize, cereal and cattle as well as vines. Spring frost is an occasional hazard and rain, or sometimes lack of it, can be a more severe problem. Heavy rain can fall in the spring while the summer months can remain without a drop of water, as in 1985, when by September parts of the region were suffering from drought and declared disaster areas. The vines survived, just, but the maize was wilting in the fields.

The co-operatives, of which there are three, are the most important producers of the region. There is a tiny one at Castelnau-Rivière-Basse which is insignificant, another one at St-Mont which is part of the larger Plaimont group, and the largest is at Crouseilles. At one time, soon after its foundation in 1950, the co-operative at Crouseilles accounted for over 90 per cent of the production of Madiran. Today that percentage has shrunk to 40 as the independent growers have enlarged their vineyards and gained in importance. The co-operative now has 350 members, of whom 200 have vineyards only in the appellation of Madiran, while the others also grow grapes for the appellations of the Côtes du St-Mont and Pacherenc de Vic-Bilh, as well as Vins de Pays des Pyrénées-Atlantiques.

However, it cannot be denied that the more interesting and distinctive wines come from the individual growers. Jean-Marc

Laffitte at Domaine de Teston is a name to look out for. He had just taken delivery of his first new 225-litre barrels, which he was busy filling when I arrived. The final topping-up, to ensure that the barrel was absolutely full, was being done with a watering-can! He is planning to age his wine in wood for six to eight months; he has bought thirty new barrels to begin with and intends to change them every three years. Philosophically he reflected: 'Wooden barrels, you have to take care of them every day, like your mistress!'

Altogether he has 20 hectares of vines including one of Pacherenc de Vic-Bilh, and his vines are between four and seventy years old. He runs a family property with maize and cereal too, but wine is most important to him. That is what he loves. He explained his vinification methods to me in his thick Pyrenean accent. His wine consists of 60 per cent Tannat with 40 per cent Cabernet, including quite a lot of Cabernet Sauvignon as it balances the astringency of the Tannat to give a more rounded wine.

He vinifies each grape variety separately and blends them in March. The fermentation takes about eight days at 25–30°C in stainless-steel vats which he can cool with running water. The vintage generally takes place in October, when the days are warm but the nights are cool, so he does not usually have to resort to cooling his vats. There is rarely any need to chaptalize. I liked his wine as it was rich and firm, with fruit and tannin, but not hard, lacking as it did the aggressive, puckering dryness of some Madiran.

One of the leading and most experimental growers of the appellation is Alain Brumont at Château Boucassé. Boucassé is the family property, and five years ago M. Brumont bought the nearby Château Montus to make a total of 60 hectares. This is a property very much in transition. A lot of the vineyards have been replanted and enlarged. When I was there, the vinification installations were being modernized and resembled a building site more than a cellar; brand-new stainless-steel fermentation vats were housed in the old barn. The vinification of both vineyards is done at Boucassé, but there are plans to create a real *chai d'élevage* at Montus that will house 1,000 oak barrels. So far there are 250 new 225-litre barrels and some cast-offs from Château Margaux. Château Montus is aged in new barrels, and Boucassé in the one-year-old barrels from Bordeaux. The investment is showing results and the products of both estates rank amongst the leading wines of Madiran. Perhaps Montus has the edge on Boucassé, but it is a debatable point. The 1982 Montus, tasted in

1985, had the concentration of flavour and fruit and the firm structure commonly associated with fine Madiran. These are wines to age for several years, and will be drinking well in ten years' time.

The creation of one of the more obscure *vins de pays* of the south west was thanks to Monsieur Brumont's efforts. Vin de Pays de Bigorre covers three villages in the Hautes-Pyrénées – Castelnau, Maubourget and Vic-Bigorre – and its object is to give the wine from vines not yet old enough to make Madiran some identity other than *vin ordinaire*. The first vintage was 1985 and Brumont was the sole producer, though the co-operative at Crouseilles is following his example.

A more traditional grower is Pierre Laplace at Château d'Aydie in the heart of the Madiran vineyards. He is an older man, with the typical navy beret of the French farmer and a smiling sun-tanned face. In his small tasting-room there is a verse which runs '*Dieu fit l'eau; L'Homme fit le vin; Respectons l'eau; Buvons le vin*'. There are 25 hectares of vines at Château d'Aydie, including a small parcel of pre-phylloxera vines. The Laplace family have been there since 1759. Pierre Laplace works with his father and his three sons, and they make Pacherenc de Vic-Bihl as well as Madiran. He remembers some of the changes that have taken place over the thirty years that he has been making Madiran. He worked with oxen until the arrival of tractors as late as about 1960. They went in pairs: there were Martin and Bouet, Mascarette and Imoulette. Originally they never bottled any of their wine, so that it went to the *négociant* and was not even sold as Madiran. His first bottling was in 1961. The wines needed to be softer than the robust traditional style of the region, so in the mid-1960s they began to destalk the grapes to make lighter, less tannic wines. Now this is common practice.

Pierre Laplace invested in a new cellar in 1980, so that now all his vinification is done in stainless-steel vats. His Madiran is made up of 50 per cent Tannat with 25 per cent each of Cabernet Sauvignon and Cabernet Franc. Each grape is vinified separately with the fermentation taking eight to ten days at 25–28°C. The juice from the first pressing is blended with the free-run juice and the final blend is done in June or July. The Tannat spends three or four months in large casks that are two generations old, while the Cabernet does not go into wood at all, and after blending the final wine spends up to three years in vat before bottling.

We sat in the courtyard outside the cellars, with a view of the vineyards in the September sunshine, and compared the 1982 and 1983 vintages. 1982 was the better year in Madiran and the wine had more elegance and length, with a little more subtlety and very good fruit. The 1983, which had recently been bottled (in September 1985), had a rather closed nose, but was a very solid mouthful of wine, with plenty of fruit to balance the tannin. We also tasted the 1979, which was a good, large vintage, as in Bordeaux, with wines which have developed well. It had a lightly herbal flavour, with some elegant fruit and considerable length.

Château Arricau-Boudes is a new estate with a long history. Tante Colette remembered the old château in ruins, but it has now been beautifully restored and was very imposing overlooking the valley in the evening sunshine. It dates back to the twelfth century, and the nearby farm, which has been transformed into a vinification plant, belonged to the d'Artagnan family of *Three Musketeers* fame. The farm is a little later than the château and is built of soft stone and solid oak beams; inside is a streamlined modern cellar, with stainless-steel vats. The present owners bought the property twenty years ago when there were vines on the land, but no wine was made. The cellars were created in 1980, and the area of vines has been slowly increased from 5 to 13 hectares, on nearby south west-facing slopes. The soil is difficult to work, with large pebbles and a clay and gravel base.

They have half Tannat and a quarter each of Cabernet Sauvignon and Cabernet Franc, which are vinified separately and blended after the malolactic fermentation. They find the Cabernet Franc more fragile, while Cabernet Sauvignon gives more perfume. As the Tannat is a more productive grape than Cabernet, there is usually 60 per cent Tannat in the wine. The pressed wine is also vinified separately, and may or may not be used, depending on the character of the vintage. The wine is aged in stainless-steel vats for two years and they are considering experimenting with some new oak. Good wine is being made here too, with perhaps not quite the richness of Château d'Aydie – but that will probably come with time and experience. Certainly I would use these and others to argue my view that Madiran is the most exciting red wine of the south west, with an individuality that does not relate as closely as others to Bordeaux.

From Madiran it is an easy step to Pacherenc de Vic-Bilh, which has enjoyed something of a revival in the last decade or so. The wine had virtually disappeared in consequence of the French lack of interest in white wine, but has now fortunately been resuscitated. It shares its early history with Madiran, benefiting from monastic interest in the Middle Ages but lacking a Henri IV to give it the prestige of Jurançon. In the early nineteenth century Jullien described the sweet wines of this area as being sweet without being thick in substance and as having more body, spirit, unctuousness and sap than those of Jurançon. Bottled after four years in cask, they became excellent and were often preferred to Jurançon.

For Guyot, the wines of 'Vicbille' were sweeter and richer than those of Jurançon, less alcoholic and of lower quality. Cavoleau described how they could be kept for a very long time and were made from several pickings, even up to the end of December. The grapes were left on the vines until they were almost rotten. Berger described them as similar but more common than Jurançon.

Today the annual production of Pacherenc de Vic-Bilh is less than 1,000 hectolitres. A few producers of Madiran also have a hectare or two of vines for this complementary white wine. Lucien Oulié at Domaine de Crampilh makes quite the best Pacherenc de Vic-Bilh that I have tasted. While we talked, we drank his 1984; it had a perfumed nose which reminded me of the Viognier of Condrieu, with a similar flavour on the palate and a certain roundedness – a delicately flavoured wine, with hints of unctuousness.

M. Oulié has 2 hectares for Pacherenc de Vic-Bilh, planted with Gros Manseng, Petit Manseng and Courbu (which are the grapes of Jurançon), as well as with a local peculiarity, Arrufiat or Ruffiac, which gives Pacherenc its distinctive taste. Gros Manseng represents 40 per cent of the blend and the other three 20 per cent each, but there are no precise percentages laid down in the appellation regulations. The vineyards are on south east-facing slopes, with clay-based soil containing large pebbles. If the grapes are ripe enough, M. Oulié makes a *moelleux* or *demi-sec*, as in Jurançon. He also produces a good Madiran. For him Madiran has a good future as there are young people who believe in it – as for the old folk, 'They are fast asleep, these people in Madiran.'

Traditional Pacherenc de Vic-Bilh, like Jurançon, is *moelleux*. The grapes are left on the vines until the end of October, so that they are rich in sugar. The ideal balance is 13° of alcohol to 3° of sugar. Chaptalization is permissible if necessary.

The Arrufiat grape, which distinguishes Pacherenc from Jurançon, is sensitive to adverse conditions and particularly difficult to grow.

Some work is being done on clonal selection, and this is encouraging people to plant it again, so that the area of Pacherenc de Vic-Bilh is slowly increasing. Enthusiasts like M. Oulié are keen to plant more. Like Jurançon *moelleux* it benefits from a few years' bottle age and it is certainly one of the most individual white wines of the south west.

Pierre Laplace makes his Pacherenc de Vic-Bihl from the four traditional grape varieties and is planning to increase his 2 hectares, but not with any Sauvignon or Sémillon. His wine is not as high in alcohol, 11.5° plus 1.5° sugar, with a more gentle flavour – it is not really *moelleux*. Another variation comes from Jean-Marc Laffitte who makes only dry Pacherenc de Vic-Bihl, and only from Gros and Petit Manseng. Altogether only ten of the forty-eight independent growers of Madiran make Pacherenc de Vic-Bihl, but those who do feel that it is 'a wine to be defended', and they would be sad to see it disappear.

CÔTES DE ST-MONT

Pierre Casamayor, in his survey *Vins du Sud-Ouest et des Pyrénées*, describes the Côtes de St-Mont as '*la petite dernière des appellations gasconnes*'. This little-known wine became a *vin de pays* in 1974 and was promoted to VDQS in 1981. Already it has justifiable aspirations to appellation status. There were vineyards at St-Mont in Roman times, and the arrival of monks from Cluny to found the abbey of St-Mont in 1050 gave viticulture a fresh impetus. During the Middle Ages the wines of St-Mont travelled by river, like those of Madiran and Béarn, to the port of Bayonne. Jullien wrote that the red wines were appreciated and compared to the best of Gascony. In the nineteenth century viticulture was the exclusive farming activity of the area, and the hillsides were covered with vines until phylloxera struck.

The vineyards of the Côtes de St-Mont are on the slopes of the hills rising from the banks of the River Adour, to the north of Madiran and to the east of Aire-sur-Adour. St-Mont may be one of the main villages of the vineyard, but it is very much off the beaten track, away from fast motorways or railway lines. You approach it by narrow country lanes and there is not much there but the co-operative, not even a village café. We picnicked near the churchyard and the closed remains of the dilapidated twelfth-century church.

Today the leading producer of the appellation is the Cave Co-opérative de St-Mont, which was founded in 1948. It now has 480 members and not only makes, red, white and pink Côtes de St-Mont, but also Madiran, Pacherenc de Vic-Bihl and Vin de Pays des Côtes de Gascogne. Nevertheless it does account for 98 per cent of the production of Côtes de St-Mont, and I was told that there was no independent wine-maker producing wines of sufficiently consistent quality to be *labelisé* regularly each year. It is really this co-operative that has put St-Mont on the map. It is part of the Union de Plaimont, being linked to the two other co-operatives of Aignan and Plaisance for bottling and sales activities.

As the area of the Côtes de St-Mont is a natural continuation of the vineyards of Madiran and Pacherenc de Vic-Bihl, it is no surprise that the grape varieties are the same. Red Côtes de St-Mont is made from Tannat, Cabernet Sauvignon, Cabernet Franc and Fer Servadou. At the co-operative Tannat dominates with 70 per cent, and there is 15 per cent Cabernet Franc, 10 per cent Cabernet Sauvignon and a 5 per cent drop of Fer Servadou. White Côtes de St-Mont consists of Gros and Petit Manseng, Petit Courbu and Ruffiac. The precise percentages are in a state of flux.

It is only in the last ten years or less that the co-operative has concentrated its energy on improving and promoting the wines of St-Mont. It invested in new vinification equipment and a bottling plant in the 1970s and is now one of the more impressive co-operatives of the south west. Everything at the vintage is carefully controlled. The grapes are checked for sugar and their *état sanitaire*, and the amount of grapes brought each day is limited so that the facilities are not overloaded. Mechanical harvesters are forbidden, as they feel they damage the grapes, and for members who are an hour or more away, the oxidation risks are too high. They are well equipped to control their fermentations, with stainless-steel vats, cooling equipment (using water), and modern presses and centrifuges for the pressed juice. The fermentation vats are outside so that they benefit from the cool nights.

The white Côtes de St-Mont was clean and fresh with some acidity; quite short, with light fruit. At present it is always dry, but they may try making a sweet version. The pink is made by leaving the juice on the skins for a few hours, but along with the white it represents a very small part of the production. The more interesting wines are red. The co-operative produces two qualities. The basic wine has a short maceration and is light and fruity, with the stalkiness associated with Cabernet Franc. It is best drunk within five years. The wine sold under their Collection label has spent some months in wood and was a much tougher wine, with a rather closed, hard nose, and quite a high amount of tannin, with perhaps not quite enough fruit to balance the tannin. However, the co-operative of St-Mont is optimistic for its wines. It is looking to the future, expanding its facilities and extending its vineyards. At present the Côtes de St-Mont represents about 800 hectares, but they hope to plant more than double this eventually. Red accounts for three-quarters of the appellation, but ideally they would like the same amount of white wine.

IROULÉGUY

Irouléguy is one of those unexpected islands of vineyards with which deepest France abounds. The village of Irouléguy nestles in a valley in the heart of the Pyrenees not far from the Spanish border. White-painted houses with russet roofs cluster round the church and the *pelote* court, for we are in the Basque country where *pelote* is the national sport. There were a couple of sleepy dogs and a few chickens scratching for sustenance, but otherwise little sign of activity.

The vineyards of the Basque country developed on both sides of the Pyrenees with the foundation of abbeys in the eleventh century. In 1080 a lawyer's document referred to apple orchards, meadows and vineyards, and in the Middle Ages wines from this area were enjoyed in Bayonne. In the fifteenth century monks from the abbey of Roncevaux, which was too high in altitude for viticulture, came to Irouléguy and Anhaux to plant vines.

Phylloxera arrived here later than other parts of France. In 1900 there were 500 hectares of vines, which were virtually destroyed by the parasite between 1910 and 1912. The First World War and the ensuing economic crisis prevented any replanting of vines until the mid-1830s. The vineyard of a M. d'Etcheberry had a certain reputation before the Second World War and provided the foundation for the VDQS in 1952. It took another eighteen years to reach appellation status in 1970.

In 1985 the sole producer was the co-operative at St-Étienne-de-

Baigorry, with just 87 hectares in production, but they envisage 180 by 1990. The vineyards cover nine villages to the north of St-Étienne and towards St-Jean-Pied-de-Port, including St-Étienne itself, Irouléguy and Anhaux. The countryside is hilly, if not mountainous. The vineyards are on steep slopes, often terraced, facing east, south and south west at an altitude of between 200 and 400 metres. The terraces vary in width. Government subsidies can be obtained to help with their construction. Some are wide, 3.5 metres, where you can use a tractor, while others are narrow, following the Swiss system, and only 2 metres wide. Terraces generally give the vines more sunshine and better aeration.

The grape varieties of Irouléguy are Tannat, Cabernet Sauvignon and Cabernet Franc. Tannat is the typical grape of the Pyrenees. Cabernet Franc has long been established in the area and is called Acheria in Basque. Cabernet Sauvignon has been introduced with the new plantings. The blend varies so that sometimes the Cabernets dominate and sometimes Tannat is more important.

The co-operative was created in 1956, initially to protect the price of Irouléguy, and now has sixty-six members. Previously the wine was sold to *négociants*, who 'did what they wanted with it'. Vinification methods are traditional. The grapes are destalked and they run the juice over the skins two or three times a day during the eight-day fermentation. There are enamelled iron fermentation vats and the wine is stored in the typical cement vats. They intend to age the Tannat for a few months, but usually the wines are bottled fairly young. They make pink as well as red, by running off the juice before it has taken too much colour. The region used to produce some white wine which has long since disappeared, but there is talk of replanting white grape varieties again.

Viticulture in this mountainous region competes with cattle and sheep. The sheep's milk used to go to Roquefort for cheese, but no longer. Some people continue to make their own cheese, while others have turned to viticulture – though you can buy locally produced sheep's cheese as well as wine in the busy co-operative shop.

They make two qualities of red and pink Irouléguy, as well as some Vin de Pays des Pyrénées-Atlantiques. The better-quality red, under the Maître des Vignerons label, is a delicious glass of wine without the astringency you might expect from Tannat. With a couple of years' bottle age it was peppery and perfumed, with quite a dry finish, but not a wine to age like Madiran.

BÉARN

The appellation of Béarn covers three distinct parts of the Pyrenees. It can be considered the second wine of both Jurançon and Madiran, for growers with red grapes in Jurançon will make Béarn, while pink wine made in the area of Madiran will also be Béarn.

The most individual and important part of the appellation, however, producing nothing but Béarn, is centred on the village of Bellocq and the attractive Pyrenean town of Salies-de-Béarn, which is better known (as the name implies) for its salt springs than for its wine. The region is hoping to distinguish itself from the other parts of the appellation by means of a special 'Béarn Salies–Bellocq' mention on the label. As yet this decision is still in the hands of bureaucracy.

Bellocq has the remains of a medieval château and ramparts and was a fortified village in the Middle Ages, owing allegiance to the count of Béarn. It survived the Hundred Years War unscathed and for centuries sent its wine along the Gave de Pau to Bayonne and from there on to England and Holland. A report by the Intendant Pinon in 1691 gave an indication of the quality of the wines of Béarn, stating that on the slopes there were many vines that made excellent wine and that few places produced wine as good as that of Jurançon, Bellocq and Puyoo.

Phylloxera nearly destroyed the vineyards. Hybrids were planted and it was only after the Second World War that some effort was made to revive the quality of the wines by renewing the vineyards, and also by creating the Cave Co-opérative de Salies-de-Béarn–Bellocq. Henri Meyer was the leading light of this struggling wine. He founded the co-operative in 1947 and created a new wine, Rosé de Béarn, which had an instant success in Paris because it conformed to the current fashion for pretty pink wines. Béarn was recognized as a VDQS in 1951 and became an appellation in 1975, for all three colours.

There are 200 hectares of vines around Bellocq and Salies-de-Béarn, and the co-operative is responsible for all except one small estate. About 70 per cent of the wine is red, made from Tannat, Cabernet Franc and Cabernet Sauvignon. Pink has long since declined in popularity. At the co-operative it is made either from pure Tannat or from pure Cabernet Franc. White wine is made from Raffiat de Moncade, a peculiarly local variety permitted only in this part of Béarn. The other white grapes of the Pyrenees, Manseng and Courbu, are also allowed and are used in the other areas. Before the war Baroque was planted in large quantities here, but happily has disappeared and is no longer used for the appellation.

We drove through the vineyards along a ridge offering views of beautiful scenery, with fields of maize as well as vines. Traditionally the vines are trained '*en hautain*', on high wires on a kind of grid system, with wires in squares along and across the rows. These high vines offer greater protection from frost, which can be a problem in this mountainous region. Some of the new plantings, however, tend to be lower than the traditional 1.5 metres.

Equipment and technology at the co-operative at Bellocq tends to be pretty unsophisticated. But they have a centrifuge and some cooling equipment, so the juice is clean and the fermentations well controlled. The red wines are kept in vat for a year and a half before bottling. There are no oak barrels.

They make several wines: a fresh white wine from Raffiat de Moncade, and two pinks from Cabernet and Tannat. I marginally preferred the Tannat version, but was not enthusiastic about either. Their basic red wine is a Vin de Pays des Pyrénées-Atlantiques, which was quite full and inky. Next came a Cuvée des Vignerons from 15 per cent Cabernet Sauvignon, 35 per cent Cabernet Franc and 50 per cent Tannat, which was a meaty, chewy wine, with a hint of raspberries. They have named their best wine after Henri de Navarre. It is made from 60 per cent Tannat and 40 per cent Cabernet Sauvignon and is rather tough and harder than the Cuvée des Vignerons and needs some bottle age.

More Rouge de Béarn is produced in the Jurançon areas, as virtually everyone has some red grapes. Usually they are Tannat, Cabernet Sauvignon and Cabernet Franc. Henri Ramonteu also includes 10 per cent Manseng Noir in his blend, as it gives the wine colour and acidity and provides a generous yield. He ferments all four varieties together in stainless steel for twenty days and then ages the wine in barrel for six months before bottling. In these two areas, however, Béarn is a rather secondary consideration; the most individual, though not necessarily the best, Béarn comes from Bellocq and Salies-de-Béarn.

5
Wines of the Midi

The Midi, that vast vineyard of Languedoc–Roussillon, is full of contrasts and contradictions. Altogether it covers the four departments of Pyrénées-Orientales, Aude, Hérault and Gard. The production of '*le gros rouge*', the everyday '*pinard*' or plonk, is still the principal activity of many a conservative wine-grower, but over the last ten years the winds of change have swept through the region at near gale force. The Midi is the vineyard of the future, for the potential is tremendous; it has even been described as 'a true California', such is the quest for quality and technology.

It is the oldest vineyard of France, for viticulture was brought here by the Greeks when they settled around Agde in the fifth century BC. They prepared the way for the Romans who came to Narbonne some 2,000 years ago. Since then viticulture has been a vital part of the activity and economy of the region, apart from a short period of Arab rule which was ended by the efforts of Charles Martel and Pépin le Bref in the eighth century. During the Middle Ages the successful continuation and expansion of viticulture was assured by the region's abbeys, such as Lagrasse and Fontfroide in the Corbières, Caunes in the Minervois, and St-Guilhem-le-Desert in the foothills of the Massif Central.

The region remained relatively isolated from the rest of the country until the building of the Canal du Midi under Colbert in the seventeenth century. The reputation of virtually every wine has depended upon ease of transport; most great vineyards are close to river systems, which were vital in the days of unpassable roads, before the invention of the railways. The Canal du Midi linked the Mediterranean and the Atlantic, joining Sète with Bordeaux and opening up the Midi as never before.

The terrible winter of 1708–9, with severe cold that lasted from

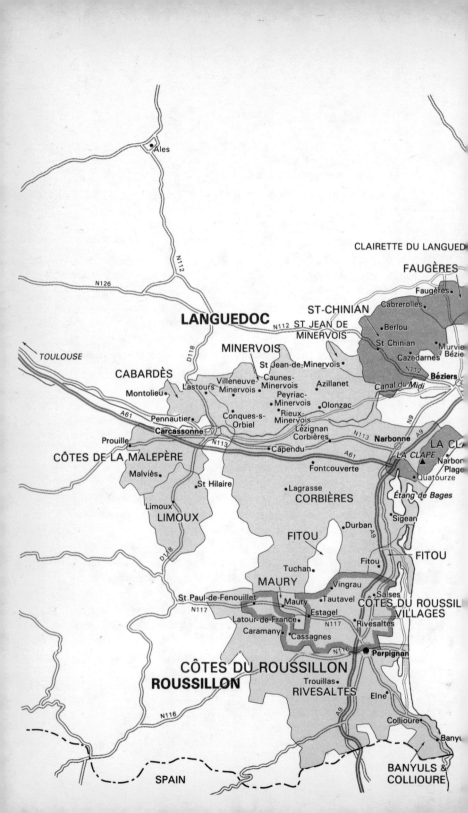

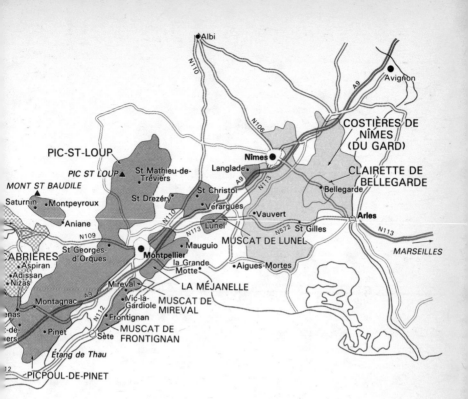

PIC-ST-LOUP

MONT ST BAUDILE

• Albi

N110

N106

COSTIÈRES DE
NÎMES
(DU GARD)

PIC ST LOUP

St Mathieu-de-
Tréviers

Nîmes ●

Langlade

CLAIRETTE DE
BELLEGARDE

Saturnin • Montpeyroux

St Drezéry

St Christol

• Aniane

Véargués

N109

St Georges-
d'Orques

ABRIÈRES

• Aspiran

• Adissan

• Nizas

Montagnac

enas

• Pinet

• Montpellier

Mireval •

Frontignan

Sète

N112

Étang de Thau

PICPOUL-DE-PINET

Vic-la-
Gardiole

N110

N113

Lunel

Mauguio

la Grande
Motte

• Bellegarde

• Vauvert

St Gilles

N572

Arles

N113

MARSEILLES

MUSCAT DE LUNEL

• Aigues-Mortes

LA MÉJANELLE

MUSCAT DE
MIREVAL

MUSCAT DE
FRONTIGNAN

A9

A9

12

N113

Avignon ●

MEDITERRANEAN SEA

COTEAUX DU LANGEUDOC

CÔTES DU ROUSSILLON VILLAGES

0 kilometres   40

0 miles   25

The Midi

the middle of October 1708 until the end of February 1709, caused untold damage to agriculture, including vineyards, especially in the more northern parts of France. Many vineyards were devastated by frost; only those near the sea in the south, with their more equable climate, survived – notably those of Languedoc, which enjoyed a considerable demand in the years that followed. A royal edict of 1710 facilitated their transport and sale to Paris, causing friction with the Bordelais who struggled to maintain their privileges. But it was during the nineteenth century that the vineyards of the Midi embarked upon a period of truly immense prosperity.

The period of industrialization after Napoleon brought an untold demand for the wines of the Midi. With the Industrial Revolution came a new clientele, the factory workers and miners of the north who wanted a cheap, energy-inducing drink, namely wine. The Midi adapted itself to this demand and created an industrial vineyard for producing 7° or 8° 'pinard', a thin, acidic drink that would be watered down by its consumers – a product that we would consider quite undrinkable today. The economic and agricultural success of the Midi at this time was extraordinary, for this was the period that saw the building of many fine châteaux and of their immense cellars. Any technical progress in wine-making at that time came from the Midi, not from Bordeaux or Burgundy. The continuous press was invented in the Midi in the nineteenth century. In a vineyard near Mauguio in Hérault, Henri Bouschet created a new grape variety, the Alicante Bouschet, by crossing Grenache with a hybrid of Aramon and Teinturier du Cher, which had been developed by his father Louis. Later, enormous energy was devoted to finding the remedy for phylloxera.

The nineteenth-century authorities wrote of the wines of Languedoc with varying degrees of enthusiasm, sometimes singling out specific crus for particular note. Jullien said that the red wines of Languedoc generally had body and alcohol and some were very good. He designated three categories, plus the vins de chaudière, i.e. those for distillation. By 1862 Rendu was more precise. He classified the wines of Languedoc into three categories: the wines of the hills or the garrigues (a regional name for the wild scrub of the foothills of the Massif Central) provided wines for export; the vines on the terraces, where the soil consisted of pebbles mixed with iron, gave suitable wines for commerce; and finally the vineyards of the plains, planted with Aramon and Terret Bouret, produced wines for distillation.

In the 1860s Doctor Guyot undertook a very detailed report of the vineyards of France for Napoleon III. He enthused about the quality of the Mourvèdre, called Espar in the Midi, and regretted the development of what he called the common grape varieties. In Hérault he found wines for distillation, ordinary wines and great wines, as well as fortified wines and brandy. Even in the 1860s the surplus wine production was destined for distillation. He also mentioned that some eminent wine-growers of Hérault were experimenting with Pinots, Cabernet, Syrah, Cot, Sauvignon, Sémillon, as well as Spirans, Espar, Carignan, Grenache, Morastel, Clairette, which gave some very superior wines and drinks that were much in demand.

Yields increased enormously in this period. In the six years that Guyot was preparing his report, between 1861 and 1867, the production in Hérault rose from 9 to 14 million hectolitres. The all-time record in Hérault was 15,236,000 hectolitres (from 226,000 hectares of vines) in 1869, while the year 1875 saw a record total harvest in France of 84 million hectolitres.

The development of the railways which coincided with the period of industrialization encouraged the growth of the Languedoc vineyards, for an easy means of transport to the capital and the industrial north was provided by the railway links with Sète, Montpellier, Béziers and Narbonne. A severe attack of oidium in the 1850s changed the composition of the vineyards so that Carignan and Aramon became the principal grape varieties when replanting took place. Then the phylloxera louse was discovered in Gard, in the village of Pujaut, in 1863, in the vineyards of a wine-grower who had imported some American vines. The devastating effects of this louse were not really noticed until the end of the decade. Montpellier pioneered the remedy of grafting European vines on to American rootstock, which subsequently proved to be the only viable solution. By 1879 there were 450 hectares of grafted vines in the region. Meanwhile other solutions were explored: for instance, vines on the coastal plains were flooded – and so the better vineyards of the Midi, those on slopes, were gradually abandoned in favour of those of the plain, which could be flooded. It was also found that the vines adapted to grafting more easily in the more fertile, less chalky soil of the plains.

The vineyards of the Midi were reconstituted during the last decades of the century. In 1900 there were 200,000 hectares of vines in Hérault, while together the three departments of Languedoc –

Aude, Hérault and Gard – produced 21,346,000 hectolitres from 384,560 hectares of vines. The average yield of the particularly prolific vineyards of Hérault was 66 hl/ha, which was enormous for the period, when the national average was only 29 hl/ha. In 1899 these three departments, with 23 per cent of the country's vineyards, accounted for 44 per cent of total French production. The Midi had become a region of monoculture.

At the same time the vineyards of Algeria were being developed, with a phenomenal increase in production from 338,000 hectolitres in 1878 to 22,762,000 ten years later. Wine-growers from Gard, Hérault and Aude, as well as from Spain and Italy, settled in Algeria and planted the grape varieties of the Midi – Grenache, Cinsaut, Carignan and Aramon. The wines of Algeria soon became known as '*vins de médecin*', and the port of Sète did a lively trade with Oran. The rich, full-bodied wines of Algeria had low acidity and deep colour to complement the pale, thin wines of the Midi. This is when Sète (or Cette, as English writers of the time called it) developed a flourishing trade in all kinds of spurious wines. A multitude of different flavours could be produced on demand – sherry and Chablis were two popular lines – and fraud was rife. The wines of Languedoc became synonymous with all that was bad in wine.

1907 brought the first economic crisis in the vineyards of the Midi. The enormous over-production of wine was having social and political repercussions, including riots in Béziers and Narbonne. There were protests about fraudulent practices. '*Halte à la fraude!*' was the cry of the protesting wine-growers, and indeed the Répression des Fraudes first came into being at this time.

Nevertheless the period of prosperous monoculture continued in the Midi until the first warning signs of change in 1956. Superficially 1956 was a year like any other, but a turning-point had been reached: the national consumption of wine fell for the very first time. In 1956 France was emerging from the austerity of the post-war years, and barely perceptible changes in social habits were occurring. The French were beginning to drink less but better, and so the demand for the wines of the Midi, which was purely national, began to fall sharply.

The Midi had enjoyed tremendous prosperity since the 1820s and it was completely unprepared for such a change. The longer the period of prosperity, the greater the decline, and after 130 years of affluence the region was resting on its laurels. The wine industry was out of date at all levels, both in its co-operative systems of production and in its methods of distribution through *négociants*. There had been no incentive to improve techniques and methods, and so complacency was rife. The Midi has taken thirty years to come to terms with the situation, and some dramatic changes have taken place in that time as the area has sought to adjust to the modern world.

Probably the first to suffer were the *négociants*, for their systems of production and distribution had been established to meet the demands of the nineteenth century. In 1962 there were seventy *négociants* concentrated in the attractive port of Sète, which had been an important centre for trade throughout the long period of prosperity; today there are only fifteen. Jean-Pierre Bonfils explained as we sat in his office overlooking the port, with its colourful fishing-boats and noisy seagulls waiting for the catch. M. Bonfils, who is the president of the *négociants*' association, sees the *négociants* as the actors on the market-place. They have been more affected than the producers. His company took a decision twenty-five years ago to modify its activity; if it had failed to do so, it would have disappeared like so many others. The decision was provoked in part by the effects of Algerian independence in 1963, which meant that the medicinal wine from North Africa was no longer available to bolster the insipid wine of the Midi (southern Italy has now replaced Algeria).

The company realized that it would only survive if it played the card of quality. Twenty-five years ago it dealt only in *vin de table*, sold in bulk, but since then it has turned to appellation wines in bottle. *Vin de table* still remains an important part of its business, but it is either *vin de pays* or *vin de table* of the better quality. Quality in *vin de table* is still measured by alcoholic degree, the higher the better, the price being fixed per degree hecto (hectolitre). Since 1980 it has developed its bottling facilities which, M. Bonfils admitted, were quite unsophisticated till then. He sees the modern role of the *négociant* as one of promoting quality in his region, as in Bordeaux or Burgundy, though it has come about much later in Languedoc. Like other *négociants* they also have close, exclusive relationships with various châteaux in the region.

The *négociants* are threatened by the *groupements de producteurs* or producers' associations, which are a relatively new phenomenon in the Midi. They were born out of the need to do something for the future, and out of the urgent problem of the fall in sales of the region's wines. They have their supporters and their critics. The most important is the group of Producteurs du Val d'Orbieu. The group was founded in 1967 by five particularly dynamic wine-growers based in the valley of the Orbieu, outside Narbonne. The leading light, M. Barsalou, is now the president of the Crédit Agricole. Their objective was to give a new importance to their vineyards and to recover their prosperity. Today the members of the group include thirteen co-operatives in Corbières, Minervois, St-Chinian and the Coteaux du Languedoc. The most recent members are the co-operatives at Lesquerde and St-Jean-d-Minervois. In addition there are 200 independent producers in Aude, Hérault and Pyrénées-Orientales, from all the appellations of the region. They also own the Château de Jonquières outside Narbonne, in Corbières, which they are using as an experimental vineyard.

The role of the Producteurs du Val d'Orbieu is essentially a commercial one. Their members make and age their own wine, while the group is responsible for any blending, as well as for the bottling and sale of the wine. In the autumn of 1987 they were installing an absolutely up-to-date bottling line at their plant on the industrial estate outside Narbonne. Sophisticated technology is the order of the day. Although the vinification of their members' wine is not their responsibility, they still play an important role as advisers and consultants and have instigated changes in the vineyards and improvements in equipment and techniques. The Midi's leading oenologist, Marc Dubernet, is responsible for their wines.

The producers' associations were born of the inability of the co-operatives to market their own wine. All are based on co-operatives, but co-operatives on their own were not able to satisfy the requirements of large-scale distribution and the needs of hypermarkets such as Auchan and Casino. In many respects these associations of producers have replaced the regional *négociants*.

One important advantage of these groups is that they have been able to receive the government and EEC subsidies that are available for what is called the *restructuration* of the vineyard. This was explained to me by Patrick Shea from UCOVIP (another association, the Union Co-operative Vinicole du Pic St-Loup, which includes eleven co-operatives in the Coteaux du Languedoc and some 200 individual growers). When the French government finally recognized the need to change the wine economy of Languedoc–Roussillon in the mid-1970s, it chose the producers' associations, rather than individual co-operatives, as the main vehicles for the transformation.

Many of the new plantings are linked to producers' associations. A group of producers will submit a planting schedule to the government for approval and subsidy, and one has to be a member of a group in order to obtain a subsidy for replanting. Only very large private companies such as Les Salins du Midi and Bonfils were able to benefit from such subsidies. The producers' associations are also able to offer guidance with vinification methods and with marketing strategies. In theory they are able to ascertain market demand and plan accordingly in vineyard and cellar.

This may all sound a little too idealistic. It is certain that the producers' associations have provided outlets and sales where none existed before, but they are also criticized for the effect that they have had on the region. They have been accused of keeping prices unnaturally low, and rumours abound about government subsidies to save them from bankruptcy. But those that I visited – namely the Vignerons Catalans in Perpignan, the Producteurs de Val d'Orbieu and the UCOVIP – exuded an atmosphere of healthy commercial success and technical competence. Altogether there are about fifty-six groups in Languedoc–Roussillon, but only about twenty do any serious marketing and the others are more concerned with planting vineyards and with vinification. Some will probably disappear in the next few years.

It is generally agreed that the only solution to the problems of the Midi lies in dedication to quality; and quality begins in the vineyard, for you cannot make good wine from bad grapes. Over the last ten years the move away from Carignan and Aramon has gathered momentum. Grenache, Syrah and Mourvèdre are now all an essential part of the appellations of the Midi and some growers would like to be able to include Cabernet Sauvignon and Merlot as well. They are resentful of the iron grip that the Bordelais have on the INAO, enabling them to retain a monopoly of these grape varieties. People may have turned to Bordeaux varieties first as they are the classics of proven quality in other parts of the world outside Bordeaux; why not the Midi, too?

Marc Dubernet told me, however, that before 1900 there were as many as 150 different grape varieties in the Midi, most of which disappeared with oidium and phylloxera and the industrialization of the vineyards; the result was a concentration on Carignan and Aramon. Today the choice is not much greater: Carignan is still the base, with some Cinsaut, some Grenache and a smattering of Syrah and Mourvèdre. This is quite insufficient, and M. Dubernet would like to see a possible choice of twenty-five or thirty different varieties. Research is being done and they are looking to Provence, Spain, even Italy and Greece. There are experimental plantings of Counoise, Calitor, Muscardin and Monastrell, which used to be grown here before the phylloxera. Cinsaut is improving with clonal selection, while Aramon will disappear and Carignan diminish. The percentage of Cabernet Sauvignon planted in Languedoc–Roussillon at the moment is still only a minute 0.02 per cent. Its progress will be slow and something else may well supersede it, but in the absence of serious research on indigenous varieties it was considered to be 'the least bad solution'. The potential is enormous.

Two organizations have made considerable contributions to research into the performance of grape varieties in the Midi. The first is ANTAV, L'Association Nationale Technique pour l'Amélioration de la Viticulture, which was founded in 1963 and is still in existence with an experimental vineyard of 114 hectares at Domaine de l'Espiguette at Grau du Roi in the department of Gard. Its name explains its function, and it carries out work on the health of vines and on the viruses that attack them, as well as research on clones and rootstocks.

The second organization was SICAREX, as the Société d'Intérêt Collectif Agricole des Recherches Expérimentales was commonly called. During the fourteen years it was in existence between 1969 and 1982, it operated as a research station conducting experiments in vineyard and cellar. It demonstrated the potential of grape varieties like Syrah, Mourvèdre, Cabernet Sauvignon and Cabernet Franc. It also showed what was possible with the traditional varieties of the Midi and how they could be improved. In the cellar its work covered every aspect of vinification, including ageing and conditioning. A sad combination of circumstances led to its closure in 1982 while it was still in the middle of its work.

New vineyards are being planted in the Midi, on land where there were vines a hundred years ago, but which was abandoned with the shift from hillsides to the plain. We went to a *chantier de défrichement* outside the village of Villeveyrac in the Coteaux du Languedoc. One hundred hectares of scrub have been cleared with the help of bulldozers, leaving stony, arid soil that will be planted with Syrah, Grenache and Mourvèdre. Nothing else can be cultivated here but vines. There were even the remains of a centuries-old shepherd's shelter, a pile of stones looking rather like an igloo. The soil here is clay and limestone and the altitude is only 60 metres. The co-operative at Villeveyrac is the force behind the project but it has been assisted by the SAFER, the body that controls agricultural holdings including vineyards. Various official organizations have also helped with the funding of the exercise. There are some twenty sites like this in the Coteaux du Languedoc, a sign of the willingness of a small minority to adapt their vineyards to the future. The first such 'reconversion' was done about ten years ago in Faugères near Cabrerolles. Success depends upon a dramatic change in people's attitudes.

The opposite side of this coin is the policy of *arrachage*, of pulling up vineyards that can never produce anything but inferior *vin ordinaire*. While there is a gentle shift back towards the vineyards of the hills, the vineyards of the plains will gradually disappear. *Primes d'arrachage* have encouraged some pulling-up of vines, but they are not high enough to be a big incentive while more money can be earned by sending wine to the distillery. If the vines are pulled up, what will the land be used for instead? Cereals are a possibility, except that you need more hectares to make a living from wheat or maize than you do from vines. However, there is no doubt that a considerable area of the vineyards of the Midi will disappear simply with the passage of time, for the average age of the co-operative member is over fifty; gradually the old people will give up their vines which, as the succeeding generation often has no interest in them, will inevitably be abandoned and pulled up.

The wine lake is the notorious result of the overproduction of *vin de table* or *vino da tavola* in the EEC. France and the Midi must take some responsibility, but by no means all. Italian wine must take a share of the blame, for much has been used to boost the quality of French *vin ordinaire*. There were dramatic incidents a few years ago, with French wine-growers protesting on motorways and railway lines. French wine imports from Italy have fallen by 25 per cent between 1982 and 1986. Distillation seemed one answer to the problem of the wine lake, but now we have an alcohol lake as well. In the early 1980s a sliding scale, based on your yield, was instituted to determine how much of your production you had to send to the distillery. If your vines only produced a very modest 45 hectolitres per hectare, 2 per cent of your production (which could be accounted for by lees and some pressed wine) went to the distillery. If your yield reached 90 hl/ha, which is considered very reasonable for the Midi, you sent 11.5 per cent of your production. However, once you exceeded 90 hl/ha (the standard yield for a *vin de pays*), you were penalized. The short-sighted grower who still thought it was worthwhile to '*faire pisser*' his vine, as that would still earn him money, was severely discouraged. If you produce more than 135 hl/ha nowadays, you do not get enough money to make it remunerative; consequently the use of fertilizers has declined considerably. The more you produce in excess of 90 hl/ha, the less wine you can sell, and what you receive for distillation is less than the price of *vin de table*. Even so, there is still a frightening amount of wine finding its way to the distillery from the co-operatives of the Midi. The problem arises largely from the attitude of the average wine-grower of the Midi. There are still countless conservatives who follow the philosophy of le père Séchard in Balzac's *Les Illusions Perdues*, for whom, quite simply, quality equals money in the bank: the more wine they produce, the more money they make.

A contemporary account of the viewpoint of the twentieth-century wine-grower comes from Emmanuel Maffre-Baugé, who was president of the Fédération Nationale des Producteurs de Vins de Table et de Vins de Pays for many years. In his book *Vendanges Amères* he relates the changes in the vineyards of Languedoc over those years, describing the problems, the confusion and lack of understanding of the growers, and the inability of the government to improve the situation.

It is not an exaggeration to say that more changes and improvements have taken place in the last five years than in the preceding fifty. Today in the Midi you cannot help but sense the wind of change. Dramatic improvements have also been made in vinification methods. The most striking evolution, in the opinion of Marc Dubernet, is the development of carbonic maceration: this considerably improves the ubiquitous Carignan, and helps to mask its defects while giving some character to the wine. The vinification of white wine has also been mastered with the extensive use of cooling equipment, most of which is new within the last five years.

Marc Dubernet has worked as an oenologist in the Midi for twenty years and I asked him to look back over this period. At the beginning it was very difficult to gain access to a grower's cellar; to ask him to show you where he made his wine was almost as dramatic as committing rape and was seen as a gross infringement of privacy.

Today confidence has been established and the producers ask for advice – in fact some will hardly treat their wine without the guidance of the oenologist. Waiting to see M. Dubernet at his laboratory, I had the impression that I was sitting in an eminent doctor's waiting-room. The vintage was nearing its end and samples of wine were awaiting the pronouncement of the oenologist. Their lives were in his hands; he was responsible for their future well-being.

Marc Dubernet now runs the most advanced laboratory in Europe. Everything is fully computerized and automatic, so that some 600 wines a day are analysed, with each wine receiving on average six analyses. But M. Dubernet is insistent that good wine is made in the cellar, not in the laboratory. It is a work of sensibility. Of artistry? No, not to that point. You need what he called 'solid technical luggage' as well. The real problem is that there are no two vineyards, no two cellars, no two wine-makers that are the same. The good oenologist must bring out the quality and character of the product, and that is what M. Dubernet does for 250 estates from Maury in Pyrénées-Orientales to Sète in Hérault.

The key, what he referred to as the master card, is provided by the appellations, notably the numerous *crus* of the Coteaux du Languedoc, as well as Fitou, Corbières and Minervois. These are the areas with the crucial advantage of good soil and terrain. Until recent years they have been submerged by the industrial vineyards and their recognition is only recent. The Coteaux du Languedoc are fortunate to have an energetic and vocal advocate, Jean Clavel. He is the secretary of the association of the Coteaux du Languedoc and the leading exponent of the concept of an umbrella appellation for the Midi, namely Coteaux du Languedoc, with the various *crus* representing the top quality of the appellation. He would like to include Minervois, Corbières and Fitou in his scheme of things, but whether he will succeed remains to be seen. Local jealousies and rivalries abound and the French wine-grower is an individualist who is often reluctant to join up with a large group, even if it may help him in the long run.

There is a financial advantage to membership of the large appel-lation, in that growers will be in a much stronger position to organize promotions of their wine, to market it and create an image for it. Some growers concede the benefits, while others remain strongly independent. For the moment Coteaux du Languedoc has little consumer recognition, and no strong identity. Some of the individual *crus* or appellations are better known, but the idea is that it should be the basic appellation of the Midi, as Bordeaux is for the Gironde, with various villages singled out for recognition, so that Faugères or La Clape would be to the Coteaux du Languedoc what Margaux or St-Émilion are to Bordeaux. The delimitation of the vineyards of the Coteaux du Languedoc has been done, and the actual area of the appellation under vines is increasing as more vineyards are planted with the right grape varieties. As yet many of these vineyards are making wine that is only fit to be *vin de table* or possibly *vin de pays*, but the production of Coteaux du Languedoc is increasing: in the seven years between 1979 and 1986 it rose from 200,000 to 325,000 hectolitres.

The shop-front of Jean Clavel's efforts at promoting the Coteaux du Languedoc is the Hôtel Montpellierain des Vins du Languedoc. It is a cross between a wine bar and a restaurant, established in the cellars of a thirteenth-century town house in the centre of Montpellier. There is an extensive choice of the better wines of the appellation and it is a friendly place to taste and drink.

There is no doubt that the Midi is coming out of the wilderness. Jean Clavel is convinced that viticulture will be an essential part of the economic renaissance of the region. Marc Dubernet used the image of a virgin forest, with beautiful flowers, but you have to look for them. What follows is what I found, but first some more introductory comments on the *vins de pays* are necessary.

INTRODUCTION TO *VINS DE PAYS*

In the Midi the *vins de pays* were born of an urgent need to give the hundreds of thousands of hectolitres of anonymous wine some identity and to encourage a move towards an image of quality. Something had to be done to solve the pressing viticultural crisis of the south. The first tentative steps towards the creation of *vins de pays* were taken in 1973 when Jacques Chirac was Minister of Agriculture. Six years later in 1979 the *vins de pays* were defined by an official government decree.

Essentially they are superior *vins de table*: they are not considered by the Common Market to be quality wines from a specified region, but *vins de table* with some individual character. The criteria of production are much stricter than for basic *vin de table* and much more flexible than for an appellation or a VDQS. For *vin de pays*, yields are limited to 90 hl/ha. If you are a producer of both *vin de pays* and *vin de table*, however, you are not allowed to make more than 100 hl/ha over your whole property. This means that you may make less for *vin de pays* and quite a lot more for *vin de table*, but in the long run you are firmly discouraged from excessive production. Yields of 200 hl/ha were commonplace in the Midi in the early 1970s. Alcohol is another criterion. For *vin de table* a natural degree of 8.5° must be reached, while for *vin de pays* the minimum is 10°. *Vin de pays* has to pass analytical and organoleptic tests, so that levels of sulphur and volatile acidity are also controlled. In the Midi chaptalization is permitted for *vin de pays*, but not for appellation wines.

Vins de pays allow for an imaginative flexibility as to what grape varieties may or may not be planted. There are two lists for each department, of grape varieties that are recommended and those that are authorized. Authorized varieties are not as good as recommended ones, but they are not bad enough to be forbidden altogether. You may not have more than 50 per cent of authorized varieties in your vineyard and they should only be used for *vin de table*. If a grape variety is mentioned on the label, the wine must be made from that variety alone, a regulation that is stricter than under the Common Market rules. The flexibility over grape varieties has allowed more adventurous growers to plant unusual varieties under the guise of experimentation, with exciting results. The Salins du Midi had Bordelais grape varieties in their vineyards soon after the Second World War, but it was only in 1973 that they could openly make a wine from Sauvignon Blanc or Cabernet Sauvignon.

Vins de pays are demarcated from each other by political geography rather than by geology; the single exception is the Vin de Pays des Sables du Golfe du Lion, where the sand is the decisive factor. Otherwise there are two main types of *vin de pays*: one that covers a department, such as Vin de Pays de l'Hérault or de l'Aude, and one that covers a zone within a department, which usually has more restrictive regulations, with a lower yield of 80 hl/ha and a higher minimum alcoholic content of 11°, such as Vin de Pays des Coteaux de Bessilles (which is one of the newer *vins de pays*, from around Montagnac in Hérault). In addition there are a couple of larger regional *vins de pays*, namely Vin de Pays d'Oc and Vin de Pays du Jardin de la France. The latter covers the Loire valley, the former the whole of Languedoc–Roussillon. To be sold as a Vin de Pays d'Oc, however, the wine must already meet the criteria of another smaller *vin de pays*. The regional name allows for blending between *vins de pays*, and producers sometimes prefer to use the better-known name rather than one of which no one has ever heard.

That is one of the problems of the *vins de pays*, that in the last few years they have proliferated. Most of them are concentrated in the Midi, but you find them all over the wine regions of France. There are very few vineyards without a *vin de pays*. In the Midi especially, a grower may make two wines, an appellation and a *vin de pays*; and depending on his approach, the *vin de pays* can be very much better or worse than his appellation wine. Many of these small *vins de pays* will remain unknown for they have often been created to satisfy one or two growers who have known how to pull strings in high places. Vin de Pays de Bigorre near Madiran is an example, where a grower who had planted extensively wanted to be able to sell the production of his young Madiran vines as something better than *vin de table*. Some *vins de pays* will become known as there are dynamic producers who create a reputation for themselves and their wine. An obvious case in point is Les Salins du Midi and their Vin de Pays des Sables du Golfe du Lion; another is Domaine de l'Arjolle and its Vin de Pays des Côtes de Thongue. Others will never progress beyond the official decree that created them and will remain shrouded in obscurity until they ultimately disappear.

Nevertheless, even though there is still a long way to go, there is no doubt that the creation of the *vins de pays* has contributed towards solving the problem of the anonymity of most wine production in the Midi.

ROUSSILLON

The vineyards of Roussillon cover a substantial part of the department of Pyrénées-Orientales. They are limited by the Pyrenees in the south and the mountains of Corbières to the north, so that the hills of Roussillon seem to form an enormous amphitheatre around the fertile plain surrounding Perpignan. Further inland the scenery is wild and dramatic, with rugged, arid hillsides. River valleys break up the countryside as the Agly and its tributaries twist and turn, meandering their way to the Mediterranean. The Canigou, the highest peak of the Pyrenees, dominates the horizon. Little will grow here apart from vines and olive trees, and viticulture is and always has been a vital part of the region's economy.

Present-day Roussillon is synonymous with the department of Pyrénées-Orientales. The principal appellations for table wine are Côtes du Roussillon and Côtes du Roussillon-Villages, while Rivesaltes is the largest appellation in the area for *vin doux naturel*. The *vin doux naturel* of Maury, with its stricter production regulations, forms an enclave within Rivesaltes, while to the south towards the Spanish frontier there are the twin appellations of Banyuls and Collioure: Banyuls is the *vin doux naturel*, while Collioure is the table wine. Their areas of production are coterminous.

The wines of Roussillon have a long history, as does the entire region. The remains of the first European man, dated between 400,000 and 500,000 years ago, were discovered near the village of Tautavel in the heart of Roussillon. In the eighth and seventh centuries BC Greeks came here to mine iron ore, and there is a claim – certainly apocryphal, as Hannibal was not born until 247 BC – that some of Hannibal's warriors settled at Maury in 277 BC and became the first wine-growers of the region. Certainly the wines of Roussillon were praised by Pliny the Elder, who eulogized the Muscats and mellow sweet wines that were gathered on the hillsides and in the gorges of the area, producing a wine comparable to Falernian or Caecuban, or the best *crus* celebrated by Horace.

After the Romans came the Saracens, until Roussillon was joined to Aquitaine by Pépin le Bref in 759. In the thirteenth century it became part of the kingdom of Majorca which in turn passed to the kings of Aragon, and so the province remained under Spanish rule until it returned to France with the Treaty of the Pyrenees in 1659. The Spanish influence has remained and the local dialect is Catalan. The area's greatest contribution to wine-making was the development of the discovery at the end of the thirteenth century that the addition of alcohol stops a wine fermenting. The process of distillation had already been brought there by the Knights Templars returning from the Crusades.

Table wines and *vin doux naturel* flourished together. Viticulture was the dominant agricultural activity. By 1868 Guyot recorded 60,000 hectares of vines in the department. He said that the hotter climate, where the land was more sheltered from wind than in Hérault, gave wines that were richer, sweeter, more solid and with more colour than those of Hérault. The vines were planted on terraces and mixed with olive trees. The main grape varieties were Grenache, Carignan, Picpoule Noir, Mataro (which is the Spanish name for Mourvèdre), Malvoisie, Clairette and Pampanal. He particularly praised Banyuls and the Muscats of Rivesaltes, while the ordinary wines had a very deep colour and the fine wines body, spirit, weight and vinosity. They travelled well and were worth as much as the best wine of Porto, either as a fortified wine or mixed with lighter wines.

Rendu described the wines of Roussillon, saying that the best-known vineyards were Banyuls-sur-Mer, Collioure, Port-Vendres, Rivesaltes and Perpignan. The *vin doux naturel* received the most comment while the table wines merited little distinction, for it seems their role was one of blending. Favoured for their high alcohol and deep colour, they were destined to be mixed with lighter wines that were deficient in these qualities. Earlier in this century Morton Shand described them in much the same way, and it is only in the past twenty-odd years that the table wines of Roussillon have acquired some separate, distinctive identity.

Côtes du Roussillon and other table wines

Although Roussillon is often grouped with Languedoc in one all-embracing term covering the Midi, it is in fact proud of its separate identity. The wines are different from those of Languedoc; the climate is generally hotter and if the vines are not scorched by sunshine, they are burnt by the drying winds of the *tramontana* which blows hard one day in three. Roussillon also began its first tentative steps towards an image of quality a few years earlier than Aude and Hérault. The first moves away from production of '*le gros rouge*' were made in the early 1960s; by 1970 three VDQS were recognized – Corbières du Roussillon, Corbières Supérieures du Roussillon and Roussillon des Aspres. In 1973 these were regrouped into one VDQS, Coteaux du Roussillon, to which a village name could be added. Then in 1977 the two appellations of Côtes du Roussillon and Côtes du Roussillon-Villages were created, together with two named villages, Caramany and Latour-de-France.

Côtes du Roussillon is made up of the former Corbières du Roussillon and Corbières Supérieures du Roussillon and consists of twenty-five villages in the northern part of the department, adjoining the appellation of Corbières; Côtes du Roussillon covers 117 villages in the former Roussillon des Aspres. Côtes du Roussillon-Villages can only ever be red, while simple Côtes du Roussillon allows for white and pink wine in the appellation. There are also differences in the production regulations, with a maximum yield of 45 hectolitres per hectare for the Villages wine, as opposed to 50 hl/ha for the basic appellation. From 1977 Côtes du Roussillon-Villages has always had to be made from three grape varieties, while this improving regulation has only applied to Côtes du Roussillon since 1985.

At first not everyone had three grape varieties in his vineyard. The area was and still is dominated by Carignan. The planting of *cépages améliorateurs*, notably Syrah and Mourvèdre, has been encouraged so that the proportion of Carignan has decreased considerably and is restricted to a maximum of 70 per cent. Grenache Noir, Lladoner Pelut (which is very similar to Grenache) and Cinsaut are used, as well as Syrah and to a lesser extent Mourvèdre. The first plantings of Syrah were in 1970 and it is now well established in the area, contributing as much as 30 per cent to some wines. Mourvèdre is a late ripener, and with as much as a month's difference between the ripening time on the plains and that in the hills, is not planted in the Roussillon-Villages vineyards. Carignan has its supporters here, who argue that the Carignan is at its best in Roussillon, better than anywhere else in the Midi, for on these arid, sun-soaked hillsides it ripens well and gives low yields of ripe grapes to make warm red wine with soft tannin. The average age of the vines tends to be greater here, too.

It seems perhaps a little surprising that Caramany and Latour-de-France should have been singled out within the appellation of Côtes du Roussillon-Villages; other villages such as Lesquerde, Rasiguères, Cassagnes, Vingrau and Planèz would also like to be able to mention their names on the label. The appropriate *dossiers* have been submitted to the INAO, but as yet no decision has been taken. When the appellation was created in 1977, the wine from the co-operative of Latour-de-France was bought and bottled in quantity by the large wine merchants Nicolas, so that the name, with its memorable ring, already had a wide following. Caramany may possibly owe its status to a more qualitative decision, in that back in 1964 it was one of the very first co-operatives to use the technique of carbonic maceration. The co-operative was already well organized for this purpose as the cellars are built on a slope, enabling the vats to be filled easily from above by gravity, without the need to pump the grapes. As a comparative tasting demonstrated, the various villages do have quite different characteristics, determined partly by microclimate and partly by the blend of grape varieties.

The production of the Côtes du Roussillon is dominated by the co-operatives. Nearly every village has its co-operative, and the majority of them belong, in turn, to a *groupement de producteurs*, the Vignerons Catalans, who are responsible for a considerable proportion of the wines of Roussillon–Rivesaltes and *vins de pays* as well as Côtes du Roussillon and Côtes du Roussillon-Villages. Their production in 1986 totalled some 14 million bottles, while their membership consists of fifty-one co-operatives out of the ninety in Roussillon, as well as seventy-four private estates. Above all they are a sales and marketing organization, but since their foundation in 1964 they have also encouraged innovation and experimentation in the area; they help their members with the conversion of their vineyards to better grape varieties and with improving vinification methods and ageing techniques. They are one of the several producers' associations who have considerable weight and influence in the Midi, and are often the force behind plans for replanting vineyards and building new vinification plants.

One of the leading private producers of the Côtes du Roussillon is the Château de Corneilla, in the village of Corneilla, south of Perpignan on the road to Elme. It is owned by Philippe Jeanquères d'Oriola and has been in his family since the late fifteenth century. It is an imposing building in red brick, with an attractive courtyard, full of flowers in May, with views over the valley below. The family came originally from Spain, from the village of La Jonquère on the Spanish frontier; they still own land in Spain, and at Château de Corneilla have 60 hectares of vines as well as extensive grazing land for horses, which is their other passion. They breed horses for show-jumping, and Philippe d'Oriola's grandfather was a world horse-jumping champion in the 1930s while his uncle was twice Olympic champion.

Their vineyards are in the Côtes du Roussillon, in the foothills of the Pyrenees on what is called the Terrain des Aspres, below the mountain of the Canigou. The soil there is a mixture of clay and limestone, with large stones. They make all three colours of Côtes du Roussillon as well as Rivesaltes and Muscat de Rivesaltes and Vin de Pays Catalan. Their appellation red wine is made of 50 per cent Carignan with 35 per cent Grenache Noir and 15 per cent Syrah. M. d'Oriola prefers the classic method of vinification to that of carbonic maceration, although he agrees that it improves the character of

Carignan; but he wants to make wine to last, and would prefer to replace his Carignan. A little of his wine is aged in wood, about a third of it, for about six months. You need a well-insulated cellar for wood ageing in this hot climate, and this is not normally a viable economic proposition. But as his cellars are almost underground, with an insulated roof, he allows himself a little wood ageing, though not as much as to alter the character of his wine completely.

His *vin de pays*, which is sold mainly in bulk, includes some Cabernet Sauvignon with Grenache and Syrah, and he also grows some Merlot, which he uses for a *vin nouveau*. There are no specific restrictions relating to *vin nouveau* as a *vin de table* and so it can be sold as soon as it is ready, at the end of September, while for a *vin de pays* you must wait until mid-October, and until November for an appellation wine. M. d'Oriola finds that Cabernet Sauvignon, which he has grown for seventeen years, gives good results here and he would like to be able to include up to about 15 per cent in his Côtes du Roussillon.

His pink wine is made from Cinsaut and Grenache, and his white Côtes du Roussillon from 90 per cent Macabeo and 10 per cent Malvoisie. He is well equipped with cooling equipment for his fermentations, so that the red is controlled at 28°C and lasts eight days, the pink at 22°C for fifteen days and the white at 18°C for three weeks.

M. d'Oriola has been managing the family estate since 1970 and he soon realized that the only future lay in selling his own wine in bottle, which he began to do about ten years ago. His view of the economics of the region's viticulture is brutally realistic. You simply do not make money from cultivating vines, and he believes that of the 85,000 hectares of vines in the department in 1987, 22,000 will have been abandoned by 1990. The big problem is the attitude of the old people who dominate the co-operatives. Many of the co-operatives do not want to change their policies, for 80 per cent of the co-operative members in the department are over the age of fifty, and beyond the age for considering change. Most of the co-operatives sell their wines at little more than cost price to large groups of producers, who have replaced the traditional but now mostly bankrupt *négociants*. Most of the *groupements* are not financially viable either, but their presence is necessary in the vicious circle, from which it is very difficult to escape. M. d'Oriola *has* escaped, for he is one of about twenty private producers in the whole of Roussillon who bottle their own wine. Altogether there are only about 150 private estates, most of whose owners are content to sell their wine in bulk to *négociants* or to belong to a group. He feels he has come a long way in ten years or so; his father used to make just a red wine and a sweet wine, while he himself now produces eight different wines. But although Côtes du Roussillon is an appellation, he fears for its reputation. It sells at an unrealistically low price in French supermarkets, which only serves to degrade its image, so it is not surprising that some people prefer to concentrate their efforts on *vins de pays*.

One of the most important individual estates of the Côtes du Roussillon is the Château de Jau, in the valley of the Agly near Estagel. Altogether they own 102 hectares of vines, of which 30 hectares of Grenache and Carignan were planted in 1982 on the rocky slopes behind the château at an altitude of 200 metres. These varieties do not need wire supports and will resist the strong winds that are prevalent, particularly at high altitudes. The soil is very poor and there is little of it. They first had to clear the *garrigues*, which was a long and arduous task. Their neighbours thought they were mad! But they are confident that the quality of their wine will be improved. They imposed strict controls to ascertain conditions on the *garrigues*. The most significant factor is that the level of humidity is much higher on the hills than in the valley, as the sea wind brings moisture and the vines can feed from this through their leaves so that they do not suffer from drought.

Château de Jau was bought by Bernard Daurée in 1974, which is when the first Syrah and Mourvèdre were planted. The origins of the property are monastic and the château itself is an imposing red-brick building. When I visited it, the cellars were being enlarged to allow for the installation of some new stainless-steel vats. They are equipped with rotating fermentation vats, which remove the need to pump the juice over the cap of grape skins, and allow for a shorter *cuvaison*. Their wine is not aged in wood as they consider that sufficient tannin comes from the grapes and that the taste of wood is foreign to wine. The wine is good enough 'without sending it to school to be trained'.

Château de Jau is an estate to visit, for Bernard Daurée and his wife are enthusiastic lovers of modern art; they fervently believe in the relationship of art and wine and accordingly organize summer exhibitions at the château. There is a restaurant which specializes in *grillades aux sarments*, using the vine-cuttings of Carignan, and in the courtyard there is a 300-year-old mulberry tree, which curiously has a small fig tree growing from its trunk.

Although the vineyards of Château de Jau are within the area of Côtes du Roussillon-Villages, they prefer to label their wine as Côtes du Roussillon as they do not consider the quality to be good enough yet for the full appellation. As well as red wine, they also make some Rivesaltes and a little white Côtes du Roussillon, and a *vin de table* (poetically labelled *vin de l'été*) made from old Aramon vines. It was rather reminiscent of cherryade!

The principal grape varieties for Côtes du Roussillon Blanc are Macabeo and Malvoisie de Roussillon, which is said to be related to the Torbato of Sardinia. Indeed a local name for it is Torbat. At Château de Jau they are trying to revive this old Catalan variety for their white wine as they consider the Macabeo to lack acidity and aroma. The Vignerons Catalans are also experimenting with white grapes for Côtes du Roussillon as they themselves are not happy with Macabeo; but so far they are disappointed with Malvoisie, which makes attractive wine in small experimental vinifications, but somehow not on a large scale. They would like to see changes in the INAO directives on grape varieties, and are working on other varieties in the context of *vins de pays*.

Bernard and André Cazes are the men behind Cazes Frères, a successful producer and *négociant* company, based in Rivesaltes and making a range of wines from Roussillon. André Cazes was a little reticent at the beginning of our meeting, but soon thawed and was willing to voice his view of the region and its wines. He has a healthy disrespect for authority and is not alone in resenting the INAO's iron grip on the control of grape varieties. The INAO exercises protectionism on a national scale, but can do nothing internationally. As a result Cabernet Sauvignon is grown all over the world, but in France the Bordelais, and neighbouring vineyards, have the monopoly in their appellations.

His view of the permitted grape varieties of Côtes du Roussillon was thought-provoking, too. He considers Syrah to be good, while Cinsaut is too light and Carignan should be dismissed completely. The quality of Mourvèdre in the area is debatable and Grenache does not last. He feels strongly, and he is not alone, that another grape variety, such as Cabernet Sauvignon or Merlot, is needed. If the regional character of a wine is no good to begin with, you need to modify it, for it should only be kept if it is good; and so he wants to improve the taste and aroma of his Côtes du Roussillon. Certainly he is working on the quality of his appellation wine. His best wine is aged in wood for six to nine months, in 600-litre *demi-muids* of Limousin oak which are changed every three or four years. His Côtes du Roussillon-Villages is a wine to age, so the vinification is classic; in contrast the Côtes du Roussillon, destined for earlier drinking, is made partly by carbonic maceration and blended with wine of a traditional vinification to give some tannin. Cazes Frères are in fact one of the few producers to age their Côtes du Roussillon-Villages in wood.

Although they produce an excellent Côtes du Roussillon, their ambitions are centred on the region's *vins de pays*. André Cazes would be happy to see a *vin de pays* at twice the price of an appellation wine. Hitherto they have planted good grape varieties in less good areas, but now they are going to start planting good varieties in the better sites. Two-thirds of their production is *vin de pays*, best exemplified in their red wine Le Canon du Maréchal, a Vin de Pays des Côtes Catalanes. The Marshal in question is Joffre, whose statue dominates the main square in Rivesaltes; André Cazes's grandparents bought Marshal Joffre's farm years ago. The wine is an interesting blend of Syrah, Merlot, Grenache Noir, a little Cabernet Sauvignon, some Cinsaut and some Carignan. Each gives something to the wine, and André Cazes is firmly against what he calls *monocépage* or varietal wines. It is a good glass of wine, very fruity and soft and easy to drink, more enjoyable than many an indifferent appellation wine.

Roussillon is covered by six *vins de pays*, which account for half the wine of the region. The two largest are Vin de Pays des Pyrénées-Orientales, which covers the whole department, and Vin de Pays Catalan for most of the southern part of the department, corresponding more or less to the appellation of Côtes du Roussillon. Vin de Pays des Côtes Catalanes is for the area north of Perpignan, around Rivesaltes and the beginning of the valley of the Agly, as far as Estagel. The much rarer Vin de Pays des Vals d'Agly covers the area around the villages of St-Paul-des-Fenouillèdes and Latour-de-France, while the equally obscure Vin de Pays des Coteaux des Fenouillèdes is centred on the village of Sournia in the north-west of the department. A new Vin de Pays de la Côte Vermeille was created in 1987 and covers the area around Banyuls and Collioure. Vin de Pays Catalan presents the most popular identity, while the Vignerons Catalans concentrate their efforts on Vin de Pays des Pyrénées-Orientales as they buy and blend wine from all over the department.

Cazes Frères are not the only producers to prefer the flexibility of *vins de pays* to the rigidity of the appellation regulations. Paul Chichet at Mas Chichet, south of Perpignan, who is a fifth-generation wine-maker and fourth-generation newspaperman, prefers to ignore the appellation regulations. He has just taken over responsibility for a property that his father inherited twenty years ago, at which time it was planted with Aramon and Carignan. Something had to be done, so his father pulled up the old vines and began replanting, so that the 32-hectare estate now consists of 14 hectares of Cabernet Sauvignon, 5 of Merlot, 4 of Grenache and 5 of Syrah, as well as experimental amounts of Chardonnay, Mourvèdre, Sauvignon and Chenin Blanc. M. Chichet now makes three wines, all Vin de Pays des Pyrénées-Orientales. There is a pink, made from Merlot, Syrah and Grenache by the *saigné* method of running off the juice after a few hours, giving quite a deep colour, which has a pronounced raspberry nose and an attractive fruity bite. The ordinary red *vin de pays* comes from Merlot, Syrah and Grenache, some of which is vinified in the classic way, and some by carbonic maceration. It is kept for ten months before bottling, and the result is a soft, fruity mouthful of wine, with an immediate impact of perfume and flavour. The *cuvée spéciale* consists entirely of Cabernet, 60 to 70 per cent Sauvignon and 30 to 40 per cent Franc, which is aged in wood for nine to twelve months. It is then given some bottle age before it is released for sale. The 1983 had a nose of blackcurrants and a fruity palate, with some of the stalkiness associated with Cabernet Franc. The 1981 had developed the character of mature cedarwood, with some slightly faded fruit.

Ultimately Paul Chichet would like to concentrate his efforts on Cabernet; he is searching for a constant product without great vintage differences and he has a much more thrusting, commercial view of life than many of his colleagues. His wine is made in a modern insulated warehouse, with steel vats and wooden barrels. He sees his chief problem not so much as one of making the wine, but as one of controlling the vines in the vineyard, for they are on the fertile alluvial plain south of Perpignan, where yields of 130 hectolitres per hectare are not uncommon. He tries to limit his production to 50 hl/ha by cutting off young bunches of grapes after the flowering, and no fertilizer has been added to the soil for twenty years.

As for white wine, he is interested in Chardonnay (especially as it is fashionable at the moment) and he would like to age it in wood; but as yet his production is still very much at an experimental stage. He has done some successful T-budding – grafting Merlot buds on to young Carignan – as a quick way of transforming the composition of his vineyards, but he is well aware that a decision on grape varieties will represent a commitment of at least twenty years. Cazes Frères and the Vignerons Catalans are also looking at white grape varieties, as it is generally accepted that white Côtes du Roussillon needs an injection of life. The Vignerons Catalans prefer Sauvignon to Chardonnay, as it does better in hot soil while Chardonnay prefers a higher and therefore cooler altitude. They find both difficult to vinify and yields are irregular, with Sauvignon averaging about 30 hl/ha while Chardonnay can reach 100 hl/ha. Chenin Blanc, surprisingly, they find too acid. André Cazes is also experimenting with Sauvignon and Chardonnay, which he has T-budded on to Macabeo and Grenache Noir as well as planting some. His ultimate aim is a white brand to complement Le Canon du Maréchal, which, since my visit, he has achieved, as a Vin de Pays des Côtes Catalanes and based on the Muscat grape variety.

The other most successful white *vin de pays* of the region has resulted from the poor sales of Muscat de Rivesaltes. An increasing number of producers are making a *vin de pays, cépage Muscat*, which when well vinified is a fresh, grapy wine that is not dissimilar to a Muscat d'Alsace. The Vignerons Catalans believe that a pure Muscat is too aggressive and astringent and they prefer to dilute Muscat d'Alexandrie with 15 per cent Macabeo and the same of Grenache Blanc. The co-operative in Rivesaltes is investing in stainless-steel vats and fermentation equipment for white wine, for, as the director said, so strict are the demands of hygiene that you need to make white wine in a dairy. They make two Muscat wines, both purely from Muscat d'Alexandrie, one of which is dry, with a pronounced spicy nose and flavour, while the second has 35 grams of residual sugar and is consequently sweeter and grapier. They also make a table wine from Macabeo but find that Grenache Blanc is not so satisfactory: its yields are too low and it ripens too early. Cazes Frères have been making Muscat as a table wine for about ten years. They do two pickings, so that the ripest grapes are used for Rivesaltes and the less ripe grapes (which would only reach about 11.5° to 12°) for table wine. This may be where the future lies for producers of Rivesaltes, since the gentle flavour and distinctive character of Muscat have a modern appeal.

Rivesaltes

Apart from table wine, Roussillon produces a considerable amount of *vin doux naturel*. There are Banyuls, Maury and, more important in area, Rivesaltes, which takes its name from a small town in the valley of the Agly to the North of Perpignan. The discovery of the process of making *vin doux naturel* is attributed to Arnaud de Villeneuve, who was a doctor of medicine at the University of Montpellier at the end of the thirteenth century. He added *eau de vie* to some fermenting grape juice with the result that the fermentation stopped; in 1299 he received a patent for his discovery from the king of Majorca, who also ruled Roussillon.

The wines of Rivesaltes have an old reputation. The earliest documentary evidence comes from 1394 when, as the Vatican archives record, Benedict XIII, the last of the Avignon popes, purchased through his *collecteur* in the diocese of Elne in Roussillon six charges of Vin Muscat de Claira. Claira is a village close to Rivesaltes. Roger Dion discusses this in his authoritative history of French wines, stating that evidently no wine of this type was made in the Rhône valley at that time and that hitherto wine of this kind came from Greece, Crete and best of all from Cyprus. During the fourteenth century, after Arnaud de Villeneuve's discovery, Grenache assumed importance as a grape for *vin de liqueur* or fortified wine. It seems that Spanish influence had a part to play here, for Grenache (or Garnacha) is Spanish in origin and Roussillon was then under Aragonese rule.

In a later century Voltaire sang the praises of Rivesaltes. He was the uncle of M. de la Houlière, governor of the fortress of Salses (which still produces Rivesaltes today), and wrote that 'he experienced great pleasure when he drank a cup of the Salses wine, although his frail human mechanism was unworthy of that liquor'. Arthur Young, travelling through France in 1787 and 1788, also enthused about Muscat de Rivesaltes. Rostand referred to it in Cyrano de Bergerac, while Grimaud de la Reynière, writing his *Journal des Gourmands et des Belles* in the early nineteenth century, considered it the best fortified wine of the kingdom.

All the nineteenth-century authorities rated it highly. For Jullien it was the best Muscat, not just of France, but of the universe, when it came from a good vintage and had aged for ten years. James Busby visited Rivesaltes in 1833 on a journey to France and Spain to collect vine cuttings to take back to Australia, and he wrote of how the grapes were left to shrivel on the vines. Guyot rated the Muscats of Rivesaltes better than those of Hérault, describing how the wines were made from dried grapes with no spirit added. Cavoleau also enthused about the Muscat of Rivesaltes, explaining that there were three grape varieties, Muscat Alexandrin, Rond Blanc and best of all St-Jacques, harvested in two pickings. The first grapes were left to dry until the others were picked.

Rendu gave the most detailed appraisal. Rivesaltes was the most important wine of Pyrénées-Orientales, covering 10,500 hectares, of which half were on slopes. The grape varieties included Carignan, Grenache, Mataro, Picpoule Noir and Clairette. Carignan was planted in three-quarters of the vineyards and blended with Mataro gave body and colour, while Grenache contributed sweetness and vivacity. What he called '*vin de commerce*' formed the principal income of Rivesaltes; Salses and Baixas were also mentioned as other important parts of the vineyard. The wines with a universal reputation were Muscat, Macabeo, Malvoisie, Grenache and Rancio. (Rancio describes a distinctive style of wine that has oxidized while ageing, as will be seen below in descriptions of visits in the area.) Muscat was dried on the vine and in the first year was more like a syrup than a wine, while the vinification for Macabeo and Malvoisie was slightly different as they were not dried. Rendu also mentioned the wines of Perpignan, including some excellent *rancios*.

Phylloxera had its usual catastrophic impact; the vineyard was subsequently reconstituted, but not over the whole of its former extent. Nevertheless fortified wines were popular enough in the pre-war years to make Rivesaltes one of the early appellations, dating back to 1936. Curiously, however, the appellation of Muscat de Rivesaltes was not created until 1972. At the same time a lesser appellation, Grand Roussillon, was created for wine that was not of the quality of Rivesaltes. In reality it is very rarely seen. The appellation of Rivesaltes covers a total of eighty-six villages; most of these are in Pyrénées-Orientales, and many of them are also within the appellations of the Côtes du Roussillon. Rivesaltes also includes a few villages in Aude, which are also part of the appellations of Fitou and Corbières. In this area an estate may concentrate on either fortified wine or table wine, but usually makes both.

Muscat de Rivesaltes is made from two grape varieties, Muscat d'Alexandrie and the more aromatic Muscat à Petits Grains. One of the best producers is the co-operative in the village of Lesquerde. Under the guidance of the leading oenologist of the region, Marc Dubernet, they are beginning to experiment with skin contact as part of the vinification process for the Muscat d'Alexandrie, in order to bring out more aroma. The grapes are still almost whole, just lightly crushed to release a little juice; skin contact lasts for as long as four days, before the fermentation really starts. Then the juice of both grape varieties is vinified separately, at a low temperature, and muted after ten days. The wine is bottled during the late winter, as early as possible, to keep the fragrance and freshness of the Muscat.

The principal grape varieties for Rivesaltes are Grenache Noir, Gris and Blanc, Macabeo and Malvoisie; in addition, 10 per cent of complementary grape varieties such as Carignan, Syrah and Cinsaut are permitted. Theoretically there are three types of wine in the appellation Rivesaltes: Rivesaltes Blanc or Doré, Rivesaltes Rouge and Rivesaltes Rancio, as well as Muscat de Rivesaltes. In practice the distinctions can be somewhat blurred.

Rivesaltes suffers from an identity problem. It covers a multitude of colours, tastes and flavours, so that the image of Rivesaltes and the market for it are in a very sorry state, as the director of the co-operative in Rivesaltes explained. The demand for *vin doux naturel* has declined dramatically in recent years, and the market for these wines (with the exception of Muscat de Beaumes-de-Venise) has only ever been domestic. In the 1930s everyone drank *vin doux naturel* and during the 1960s they enjoyed a golden age when they were popular, sought-after and expensive, costing the same number of francs in 1960 as now. Although that makes them much cheaper today, they are still more expensive than the average appellation table wine of the area. And consumer taste has evolved, turning against alcohol and sugar. Diet Coke is the absolute opposite of Rivesaltes! The modern consumer has discovered whisky, and these wines have come to be seen as the poor man's aperitif. Even the producers of Rivesaltes do not drink their own wine. When I was invited for an aperitif after a cellar visit, I was offered whisky or Martini! My hosts were surprised and pleased when I insisted on drinking their delicious twenty-year-old Rivesaltes. In fact the ageing process and the low yields would normally make Rivesaltes quite expensive, but it is often sold at an unrealistically low price, for otherwise it would not be sold at all.

There is an anomaly in the permitted yield of the appellation:

regulations state 40 hectolitres per hectare, but only 20 of the 40 hectolitres can actually be used for *vin doux naturel*. The remaining 20 hectolitres must be used for *vin de pays* or *vin de table* or for making base wine for the vermouth trade. The original idea behind this was to minimize a marked difference between different parts of the appellation. The vineyards around the town of Rivesaltes itself are in a very dry area (except the day I was there); they receive only about 400 mm of rain per year, about three-quarters of which would immediately be evaporated by the drying wind. The soil is very poor and any water drains away quickly so that it is impossible to obtain even 30 hl/ha. But the appellation includes vineyards further south in the region of the Aspres, where the land is much richer and it is easier to obtain 40 hl/ha. The aim was to give the appellation a uniformity to prevent one part of it from being disadvantaged. Sadly, the whole appellation now suffers from one big disadvantage: very few people are interested in buying Rivesaltes.

There are five or six hundred producers of the wine, including several co-operatives and *négociants* as well as individual estates. The quality and price variation is enormous and the market is very disorganized. In consequence, Rivesaltes can be sold for anything between 15 and 30 francs a bottle; in other words it may cost as little as a bottle of Minervois or as much as a bottle of Chablis. Worse still is its lack of reputation, and although a considerable amount of money has been spent on promotions, little has been achieved – Rivesaltes remains unknown. People prefer to drink whisky, or if they choose a wine-based aperitif it is more likely to be a vermouth or a Pineau de Charente, or even port, which is a very popular pre-meal drink in France. Rivesaltes suffers from what the director of the co-operative called 'a lack of locomotive'. There is no collective incentive to improve the situation, even though the quality of the wine itself has improved considerably over recent years. Ten years ago no one practised temperature control for fermentations, and if the fermentation stuck because it was too hot, this was not considered a problem as it had to be stopped anyway. Muscat de Rivesaltes was often a deep golden maderized colour with a caramelized taste, while today it can be honey-gold with a delicate flavour of the grape.

Fine Rivesaltes is aged for several years, a process which can only make the wine expensive. The traditional taste of Rivesaltes is the *goût du rancio*, of gentle oxidation. This may be achieved by keeping the wine in large oak casks for as long as six years. At the co-operative in Tuchan, where they also make Fitou and Corbières, their best Rivesaltes is first kept for a minimum of one year in vat, then for six months in large oak barrels, and finally outside in large glass demijohns, called *bonbonnes*, for nine months, so that the wine is subjected to all extremes of temperature. They are not airtight, nor are they completely filled, so that the oxidation is even more marked. With time the wine turns brown; it begins to smell of rich Christmas cake and to taste sweet and raisiny, with a lovely long, nutty tang. The Cazes brothers likewise subject their Rivesaltes Vieux to what they call a contrived oxidation. They have a cellar of old oak casks, which exude a warm smell of fruit-cake, walnuts and raisins; the wine itself tastes of nuts and prunes, with a dry finish. Surprisingly, given the slump in sales of Rivesaltes, André Cazes believes more strongly in the future of Rivesaltes than in that of Côtes du Roussillon, but I suspect his attitude is influenced by his interest in *vin de pays* and his disenchantment with the stifling attitude of the INAO.

Domaine Sarda-Malet is one of the old estates of the area. Their original cellars are now hidden in the urban sprawl of Perpignan, and far from easy to locate. With 50 hectares of vines, they make Côtes du Roussillon and *vin de pays* as well as Rivesaltes. The cellars are rustic and functional, with old vertical wooden presses and cement vats. M. Malet has 225-litre barrels of new oak for his Côtes du Roussillon, but he is convinced that wood is finished for *vin doux naturel*. You cannot put sweet wine in wood as the wood drinks the alcohol, and so he prefers to keep his wine in cement. Some of it is aged for as long as fifteen years, often depending upon sales. He is helped by his daughter and son-in-law who encouraged him to begin bottling his own wine a few years ago. M. Malet may be in his eighties, but his view of wine-making, encouraged by his children, is far from old-fashioned – only his ability to handle a motor car leaves much to be desired. He is one of the few producers to make a vintage Rivesaltes, a new idea in the appellation. These wines are sold young and, like vintage port, can be aged in bottle. They tend to have a deep colour when young with some sweet berry fruit, and are almost port-like with alcohol and tannin. For me, however, it is his Vieux Rivesaltes with its flavour of nuts and raisins that demonstrates the potential of the appellation.

Maury

The appellation of Maury forms a small enclave within the larger area of Rivesaltes and Côtes du Roussillon-Villages, and indeed, for table wine, Maury is one of the villages of the latter appellation. It stands in the valley of the Agly, and the appellation for *vin doux naturel* covers the surrounding vineyards where schist is the dominant soil. The production of Maury is dominated by the village co-operative, but there is one other sizeable estate, Mas Amiel, as well as two or three smaller producers.

Mas Amiel is a large property outside the village, with some 130 hectares planted mainly with Grenache Noir, the principal grape of the appellation. They have 90 per cent Grenache Noir (the appellation regulations dictate a minimum of 50 per cent) and they also have a little Macabeo and Muscat à Petits Grains. Other permitted grape varieties include Grenache Gris and Grenache Blanc; but it is Grenache Noir that gives Maury its flavour and character, for Maury, unlike Rivesaltes, is essentially a red *vin doux naturel*. Mas Amiel's distinctive method of vinification also contributes to the character and quality of the wine. They pride themselves on their '*parc de bonbonnes*', the large glass demijohns which have been abandoned by the other producers. All their wines spend twelve months, from June to June, outside in these demijohns, so that they are exposed to the full range of seasonal temperature changes. This is a region of hot summers and severe winters, for the Pyrenees are not far away.

The initial vinification is the same as for other *vins doux naturels* in that the grapes are hand-picked when they are overripe, a week later than for Côtes du Roussillon. They are destalked, all three varieties are fermented together, and after three days the mutage, the addition of the alcohol, takes place either on the juice alone or on the skins as well. If the juice alone is muted, the wine will be lighter and have relatively little tannin, but at Mas Amiel they prefer to add alcohol to the *marc* as well and then macerate it for three to four weeks before pressing, to give a stronger, richer, fuller-bodied wine.

Maury requires a minimum ageing of two years, but at Mas Amiel the youngest wine is kept for six years. Altogether they make three wines. The youngest, the six-year-old reserve, is fermented in cement vats and then spends the statutory year in glass demijohns, plus a further five years in 250-hectolitre vats of Austrian oak. They have seventeen of these enormous vats, which date back to 1920. They are topped up every so often; during six years the 'angels' share' in the form of evaporation amounts to some 20 per cent. The Cuvée Spéciale has ten years of oak ageing, and they have just introduced a fifteen-year-old wine, which I liked best of all.

The greatest change in colour comes during the period of ageing outdoors. The six-year-old reserve wine had turned a reddish tawny; it had quite a rich nose and tasted of sweet biscuits, with a clean, dry finish. The ten-year-old was drier, with more *rancio* on the nose and a raisiny bite, while the fifteen-year-old had a dry, nutty nose with hints of liquorice; on the palate it was very concentrated, quite sweet, with hints of violets and prunes – a delicious, original drink. At Mas Amiel they advocate drinking it either with chocolate at the end of the meal, or with *foie gras* at the beginning. I thought I would like it with walnuts. Certainly a wine like this deserves more than just a local reputation, and although its makers are promoting it energetically, I suspect they feel rather isolated.

Banyuls and Collioure

Banyuls is the last wine of France, for a few kilometres further south beyond Cerbère you cross the Spanish frontier into Catalonia. The road south of Argelès-sur-Mer, through the fishing villages of Collioure and Port-Vendres, hugs the coast and offers dramatic views at every turn. Here the foothills of the Pyrenees fall into the Mediterranean and the vineyards of Banyuls and Collioure rise on steep terraces. The winds can blow hard and the vines cling tenaciously to the hillsides. Banyuls is an attractive seaside resort and fishing-port.

The appellations of Banyuls and Collioure are coterminous and cover the vineyards of the four villages of Banyuls-sur-Mer, Collioure, Port-Vendres and Cerbère. The distinction is one of vinification: Banyuls is a *vin doux naturel*, while Collioure is an unfortified table wine. Banyuls was one of the first appellations to be created, as early as 1936, while Collioure came much later, in 1971. Until then, what is now Collioure was sometimes called Banyuls Sec; it seems that in the last century the two names were almost interchangeable, for both Banyuls and Collioure were praised as smooth, rich wines.

In the Middle Ages, when it was made by the Knights Templar who had settled in the area and adopted the methods of Arnaud de Villeneuve, Banyuls was enjoyed at the Aragonese court. But it was to remain something of a vinous backwater and received little more than a passing mention by the nineteenth-century authorities. Jullien cited Banyuls, Collioure and Port-Vendres in the second category of his classification of red wines, while Guyot described Banyuls as an exceptional wine and very sought-after. It was made only from Grenache, pressed immediately and muted with spirit. Cavoleau enthused about the good wines made from Grenache in Banyuls, Collioure and Port-Vendres, which at eight to ten years were velvety, rich but delicate and very agreeable. The best wines were very dark in colour and could be very sweet. Rendu, too, said of the wines of Collioure that they had a beautiful colour, body, a lot of richness and held the balance between fortified and dry wines; and that when they aged, they acquired finesse and a pronounced bouquet. They should not be bottled for ten years, by which time they should have taken on a *rancio* character.

In the twentieth century, Banyuls and Collioure have continued to be ignored outside their own region. The production of both wines is dominated by a group of five co-operatives, the Groupement Interproducteurs du Cru Banyuls, which was created in 1950 in an attempt to improve the market demand for Banyuls and to protect prices. Concentrated in Banyuls, Port-Vendres and Cerbère, they now account for 60 per cent of the production of Banyuls and 90 per cent of all Collioure.

The total appellation consists of 2,300 hectares, which could be increased but only with difficulty. The Spanish frontier limits the appellation to the south, in the north and west there are mountains, and to the east lies the Mediterranean. On the coast some vineyards have been lost to building land. But there are traces of overgrown terraces at 600 metres, whereas at the moment the vines only go up as far as 400 metres. The market for sweet Banyuls is static, but there is certainly interest in expanding the production of Collioure. The vineyards are interspersed with olive and almond trees, but little else apart from vines will survive on this rough terrain.

The vines grow on steep terraces where mechanization is difficult. The standard pruning is the *gobelet* system, so that the vines look like sturdy little bushes, without any supporting wires, and are able to resist the strong winds which can assault the exposed vineyards. The soil is infertile schist, and normally very little rain falls during the summer months. 1987 was a disastrous exception, when heavy rainstorms did considerable damage to the vineyards. Yields are low.

Thirty hectolitres and 40 hectolitres per hectare are allowed for Banyuls and Collioure respectively, but in reality these are never attained.

Alain Parcé of Domaine du Mas Blanc explained the elaborate vinification process of Banyuls to me. His father, Dr Alain Parcé, was one of the father-figures of the appellation and did much to re-establish the reputation of Banyuls in the post-war years. The family have been wine-growers since before the Revolution and they now have about 20 hectares of vines, split into numerous small parcels, making them one of the biggest independent growers. They vinify parcel by parcel, making several different *cuvées* of both Banyuls and Collioure. They generally make two-thirds Collioure to one-third Banyuls, but that proportion varies with each vintage.

The Banyuls appellation requires a minimum of 50 per cent Grenache Noir with 40 per cent Grenache Gris and Grenache Blanc and 10 per cent of other grape varieties such as Carignan, Cinsault, Syrah and Mourvèdre. The Domaine du Mas Blanc's Banyuls consists of 85 per cent Grenache Noir with a little Carignan and some Syrah and Mourvèdre; in some *cuvées* they also have some Counoise, which gives the wine a more spicy character. Carignan grows satisfactorily on the hillsides and M. Parcé described it as '*un cépage putain*' – a grape variety of doubtful virtue that will grow easily and very prolifically, but not on more difficult terrain. Mourvèdre is a late ripener and people are often too impatient with it. Before the phylloxera about two-thirds of the vineyards were planted with Mourvèdre, but in the subsequent replanting Grenache was preferred because of its higher alcoholic degree.

The terracing dictates that the grapes should be hand-picked, with the vintage beginning in early October when the grapes are overripe and turned almost to raisins by the drying wind. Picking is by plot of vines, rather than by grape variety. The grapes are destalked and the fermentation usually takes four or five days at 28°C, until it is stopped by the addition of alcohol when the wine has reached the required density, depending on whether the Banyuls is destined to be dry or slightly sweet. The juice is left on the *marc* for up to five weeks, which means a percentage of the alcohol is absorbed by the skins, but this method gives a traditional, long-lived Banyuls. If you simply mute the juice, the resulting wine is more like a pink wine than a serious red wine.

M. Parcé makes three different styles of Banyuls with three different ageing processes. The first is *rimage*, a vintage wine made only in the best years. *Rime* means 'grape' in Catalan, and so *rimage* translates literally as 'the age of the grapes'. The wine is aged in 5-hectolitre barrels in an insulated cellar for a year; the barrels are topped up regularly every week, so that there is no element of oxidation and the fruit flavour of the wine is retained. I was told it could age for fifty years and wondered whether this was France's answer to vintage port! Certainly, the 1986 Banyuls *rimage* that we tasted smelt not unlike good ruby port, with aromas of fruit-cake, chocolate and nuts.

Their second Banyuls is the same wine, but exposed to oxygen. It is aged in 40-hectolitre casks in a cellar that is subjected to severe temperature changes, reaching 28°C in summer and falling to 6°C in winter. The wines are topped up every six months and their evolution is closely followed; if they show signs of drying too much on the taste, they are transferred to cement vats for a while. They are bottled after six years. We tasted the 1967, which was a deep brown colour with a yellow rim, and had flavours of vanilla, orange, coffee, even a little chocolate, with a long, nutty finish. This is one of the very few wines you could drink with a chocolate pudding.

Finally they have a kind of solera system for ageing wine, begun by Dr Parcé back in 1929 and retaining an old family tradition. The solera is made up of three levels, or *sostres* as they are called in Catalan. Many of the original barrels are now in bad condition, so they have bottled some of the wine and amalgamated the rest, and are planning to start again with some new barrels. The wine will be bottled after six years. The sample we tasted was delicious, very concentrated, with a hint of oxidation and overtones of bitter chocolate, prunes and coffee.

The Groupement Interproducteurs du Cru Banyuls operates on a very much larger scale. I visited their principal cellars, the Cellier des Templiers in Banyuls. Here they ferment their wines in cement vats and age them in wood, depending on the desired style of wine. They have a forest of oak vats exuding a rich, raisiny aroma. The vats are neither filled to the brim nor topped up, a practice which their oenologist called 'controlled oxidation'. They also make some *rancio* wine which is never commercialized as such, but used in blends. Young wine is left in small barrels outdoors, exposed to climatic changes – in particular to the summer heat – for between two and four years. The deep red colour of the young wine changes to golden yellow. Before the Second World War a lot of *rancio* used to be produced, for small wine-makers would often leave their wine in barrels in the attic under the roof to obtain the *rancio* effect. Another co-operative in Banyuls, L'Étoile, ages wine outdoors in glass demijohns.

The Groupement Interproducteurs, or GICB as it is more conveniently called, is an enthusiastic exponent of Banyuls *grand cru*, a quality of wine which was incorporated in the appellation in 1962. It requires a higher minimum percentage of Grenache Noir, 75 per cent as opposed to 50 per cent for ordinary Banyuls, as well as a minimum of five days' skin contact during fermentation and a minimum of thirty months' ageing in wooden barrels of any size. M. Parcé considered it rather a meaningless distinction and explained that it had been instituted by the co-operatives in an attempt to encourage a greater selectivity with regard to grape varieties, as they wanted to promote Grenache Noir at the expense of Grenache Gris and Blanc. There is still a fair amount of Grenache Gris, but Grenache Blanc has virtually disappeared. A small amount of Muscat, both Muscat à Petits Grains and Muscat d'Alexandrie, is also grown in the area, but such vineyards have now been incorporated into the much broader appellation of Rivesaltes.

The GICB makes a broad spectrum of Banyuls of varying degrees of sweetness and age, with a variety of brand names. Banyuls Garance is kept only in cement to retain the fruit flavour of the wine, the cherry taste of young Grenache, which eventually develops into a raisiny flavour with prunes, reminiscent of young port. Banyuls Grand Cru Ancestral 1977 had more body and a drier flavour, originating from wood ageing, with overtones of vanilla and prunes. A 1979 was sweeter and more raisiny and was described as traditional Banyuls. Banyuls can even be pink in colour, but the better wines begin life as red wine, to age into tawny or deeper brown colours. Young Grenache will taste of cherries and other red fruit, while in the next stage of its development there are flavours of prunes and figs, which in turn age into aromas of dried fruits and raisins. A mature Grenache will finally have delicious overtones of coffee and vanilla. With flavours like these, there is no doubt that Banyuls deserves a revival in its reputation; it is one of the great undiscovered dessert wines of the world.

At its side is Collioure, which is far from being overshadowed by the older appellation. On the contrary, while the production of Banyuls is static, that of Collioure is growing, for there is always a

market for good red wine while a dessert wine, however fine, is often
neglected. M. Parcé makes two different *cuvées* of Collioure, named
after two small vineyards, Les Piloums and Les Cosporons Levants.
The first is made from 30 per cent each of Mourvèdre and Grenache
with 40 per cent Syrah, while the second unusually contains no
Grenache and consists of 40 per cent each of Syrah and Mourvèdre
with 20 per cent Counoise. He has not used Carignan in Collioure
since 1982. Vinification methods are traditional. Sometimes the
grapes are destalked, depending on their condition, and the stalks of
the Mourvèdre are always removed, as it has too many and the wine
would otherwise be too tannic. The fermentation is controlled at a
temperature of 25–28°C, with four or five weeks of skin contact. The
wine spends a year in wood, in 6-hectolitre barrels of old oak. Fining
is done with real egg-whites. It is a simple vinification designed to
make a long-lived wine. A comparison of Collioure with and without
Grenache offered an interesting tasting. Les Piloums was warm and
perfumed, with tannin and fruit reminiscent of a rich Châteauneuf-
du-Pape. In contrast Les Cosporons Levants was firmer, drier and
more tannic, without the fatness provided by the Grenache. It was a
more serious wine which will need longer bottle ageing.

The Collioure from the GICB is a lighter wine, aged in cement vats
rather than wood, except for the Mourvèdre which spends a few
months in wood; they consider that the Grenache does not benefit
from this treatment. As well as Grenache Noir and Mourvèdre, their
wine contains Carignan, Syrah and Cinsaut. At present Collioure is
very firmly a red wine, but steps are being taken to include pink in
the appellation. Collioure certainly has a future as a red wine of
quality, especially with the increased plantations of Mourvèdre,
which will enhance its ability to age and give it greater stature and
weight.

FITOU

Fitou is the oldest appellation for table wine in the Midi, created in
1948, although it was preceded by appellations for *vin doux naturel*
such as Rivesaltes and Banyuls. This may be indicative of an earlier
push towards quality that was not apparent elsewhere in the region
in the post-war period. Today, however, the differences are not so

great. As with every other appellation, much depends upon the individual producer.

The appellation of Fitou divides into two distinct areas: Fitou-Maritime, with vineyards on the coastal plains around the village of Fitou itself, and Fitou de Hautes-Corbières, with vineyards on the rugged hillsides of the Corbières range, where they are interspersed with those of Corbières itself. Nine villages make up the appellation: in Fitou-Maritime, Fitou, Leucate, La Palme, Caves de Treilles and Feuilla; inland, Cascatel, Villeneuve-les-Corbières, Paziols and Tuchan.

The origins of the vineyards of Fitou are Roman, for this was one of the many vineyards created by the Romans when they came to Narbonne; Roman amphorae have been found in the area. From then on Fitou seems to have fallen into oblivion. According to Hubrecht Duyker it was drunk at the court of Louis XIV, but otherwise was accorded little recognition. The nineteenth-century wine writers gave it scant mention. Jullien listed it amongst the wines of Narbonne, with Leucate, Treilles and Portet, and Rendu mentioned it as one of the most esteemed *crus* of Aude, along with La Palme, Sigean and Leucate.

It seems surprising that Fitou was singled out for appellation status before its neighbours, Côtes du Roussillon and Corbières. More recently, however, moves towards quality have taken place with an improvement in vinification methods following the introduction of carbonic maceration and the use of better grape varieties in the composition of the wine.

Unlike Corbières and Minervois, Fitou is firmly red, and there is no white or pink wine within the appellation. The principal grape varieties are Carignan, Grenache and Lladoner Pelut, which make up a maximum of 90 per cent of the wine, while Carignan cannot exceed 75 per cent of the total. The remaining 10 per cent can consist of Cinsaut, Syrah, Terret Noir, Mourvèdre and Macabeo. It is usually Syrah in the Hautes-Corbières and Mourvèdre in the Fitou-Maritime. Syrah prefers the drier atmosphere of the hills, where it ripens early and is usually picked at the beginning of the vintage towards the end of August. In contrast, Mourvèdre ripens later and needs the maritime atmosphere of the coastal vineyards, enjoying the early morning sea mists.

The maximum percentage of Carignan is decreasing gently but not significantly, and will probably stabilize at around 60 to 65 per cent.

It gives the wine structure and backbone. Thirty per cent is considered satisfactory for Lladoner Pelut or Grenache, which are interchangeable (although Grenache is the more common of the two), as both give a soft wine with body and alcohol.

There is a distinct difference of style between the two types of Fitou. Fitou-Maritime tends to be more supple, lighter, with less tannin, and is best drunk in relative youth. In contrast, the wine of the Hautes-Corbières has a firmer structure and will age longer. Both must in any case be kept for a minimum of nine months before bottling.

The production of Fitou is dominated by the co-operatives and there is only one individual producer of any significance, the Château de Nouvelles at Tuchan. Their 36 hectares are planted with 60 per cent Carignan, 30 per cent Grenache and 10 per cent Syrah. The cellars are delightfully traditional, with hundred-year-old oak casks. But they were the first in the appellation to vinify by carbonic maceration, beginning in 1974, with a small amount of Syrah. Their Fitou spends five years in cask before bottling, and when I visited the château in the spring of 1987 they were selling their 1980 vintage, which was long and elegant, with some good fruit. As well as Fitou they produce Rivesaltes and Muscat de Rivesaltes, and also Corbières. The property dates back to the Middle Ages and there are remains of a twelfth-century tower and ramparts.

Seven co-operatives account for 90 per cent of the appellation of Fitou; the largest is the Co-opérative des Producteurs de Mont Tauch at Tuchan in the Corbières. The mountain of Mont Tauch, at 900 metres the highest mountain of the Corbières, rises dramatically behind the village of Tuchan, which is situated on a plateau surrounded by mountains. This gives the area a particular microclimate with late springs and very hot summers. They produce a quarter of the appellation of Fitou, on average about 20,000 hectolitres, as well as Rivesaltes, Muscat de Rivesaltes, Corbières and the local Vin de Pays du Torgan. This is the new name for Vin de Pays des Coteaux Cathares. This region was very much at the heart of the Cathar heresy (see page 166), and it is scattered with some imposingly inaccessible castles such as the Château d'Aguilar. But marketing experts deemed that on the export market 'Cathares' was too reminiscent of a nasal complaint, and the name was duly suppressed.

The co-operative at Tuchan is well provided with modern equipment and has a forest of stainless-steel, self-emptying vats, linked by a maze of tubes and jokingly described as 'le petit Beaubourg de Tuchan', after the Pompidou Centre in Paris. All their better wine is vinified by carbonic maceration, and they are convinced that this brings out the quality of the Carignan. They have been doing this for ten years now. Unlike Château de Nouvelles their wines do not see any wood, as they do not consider that it adds anything to a wine that is already very tannic. Their wines therefore spend the statutory nine months and often longer in cement vats lined with epoxy resin.

They make several qualities of Fitou, dependent on various selection criteria based on soil and microclimate – what the French call *terroir*. Their best wine, Sélection des Terroirs, is vinified entirely by carbonic maceration; then there is a Sélection des Vignerons, from those growers who work well but whose vineyards do not have the appropriate *terroir*, which is sold under the label of Fitou d'Aguilar. Basic Fitou, destined for the supermarkets, is usually vinified in the classic manner.

Curiously, all the wines tasted as though they had spent some time in wood, especially the basic Fitou, which had a warm, fruity palate and a dry finish. Fitou d'Aguilar was much richer, both on nose and palate, quite earthy and warm, but with a similar dry finish. Liquorice and spice are supposed to be the characteristics of Fitou; this was certainly true of the Sélection des Terroirs, which had liquorice and almost herbal fruit on the palate, despite its rather dumb nose, while Château d'Aguilar proved to be the ideal accompaniment to lentils and sausage in the village restaurant.

Fitou has enjoyed considerable commercial success in recent years, but paradoxically this has now brought problems. It is certainly one of the better-known wines of the Midi, partly thanks to the efforts of the Vignerons du Val d'Orbieu. They extricated Fitou from the commercial doldrums of the early 1980s with the successful marketing of a Fitou under the name of Mme Claude Parmentier. Unfortunately the success has run away with them, so that there is insufficient wine to meet the demand. This success has gone to some producers' heads, too, resulting in an exorbitant increase in prices – 100 per cent in five months in 1987. Instead, the marketeers of the Val d'Orbieu will transfer Mme Parmentier and their attention to other wines, while Fitou d'Aguilar or Château de Nouvelles are still names to seek out for the warm flavour of the sun-soaked mountains.

CORBIÈRES

The vineyards of Corbières covers a large expanse of mountainous land to the south west of the city of Narbonne. In the north the appellation is limited by the valley of the Aude and in the east by the Mediterranean, while to the south the vineyards adjoin those of Roussillon. The area is dominated by the Montagne d'Alaric in the north and Mont Tauch in the south. The wine takes its name from this hilly region, called the Corbières, that extends to the foothills of the Pyrenees.

Corbières owes the introduction of viticulture to the Romans who settled in Narbonne in 125 BC. But development was interrupted by the invasions of the Visigoths and Saracens, and it was only in the high Middle Ages, with the foundation of abbeys at Lagrasse and Fontfroide, that viticulture took a firm hold on the landscape of the region. This was also the period of the building of the many Cathar castles on inaccessible hills – Aguilar, Tautavel, Queribus and others – to defend the heresy against Catholic conformity.

Corbières, along with most of the wines of the Midi, has lacked a distinctive identity. In the nineteenth century, Aude was described in general as an important wine-producing department. Cyrus Redding, writing in 1833, referred to the indifference to quality, noting that quantity was principally regarded here, and that the number of those who took a different view of things was small. Guyot gave the area of the vineyards in 1868 as 80,000 hectares, saying that viticulture provided the wealth of the department and Carignan was the most characteristic grape variety. In 1891 Corbières was described as having more stuffing than the wines of the Minervois and it was consequently used for blending with lighter wines. A distinction began to be made between the wines of the plain and the wines of the mountain, and in 1923 the area of Corbières was defined for the first time.

Corbières acquired sufficient identity after the Second World War to make it one of the early VDQS of France in 1951. But it did not become an appellation until 1985, when the area of the vineyards of Corbières was drastically reduced from 44,000 to 25,000 hectares. The former classification of Corbières Supérieures, which was an indication of higher alcoholic degree, was also suppressed. Within the area there is an enormous variety of microclimate and soil and many argue the case for further subdivision within the appellation – for a system of Corbières-Villages or of *crus*, to reflect these quite marked differences. Various *dossiers* have indeed been submitted to the INAO. In broad terms, Corbières could be divided into four *crus*. First would be the Montagne d'Alaric, with the villages of Lagrasse, Ribaute, Comigne and Camplong d'Aude. This area benefits from a particularly favourable microclimate and the geological survey has already been completed. Then there would be Hautes-Corbières, to the south around Durban and Castelmaure, and thirdly Corbières-Maritimes, including the coastal villages of Sigean, Portel and Bages. Finally would come the central part of the appellation, around the Bois de la Pinède, which for the moment is generally described as Corbières-Centrales. Some favour an even greater division, and most producers would like the concept of the Corbières *cru* to apply to both red and white wine, while the INAO is at present only interested in the red.

The soil varies, too. At Villeneuve there is schist, but clay and limestone also occur in proportions that vary from area to area. The climate is essentially Mediterranean, with mild winters and hot, dry summers. Such rain as there is usually falls in the spring and autumn. The region is also subject to the local winds – the Cers, the harsh, drying north wind, and the Marin, a gentler, humid wind which blows from the south east.

Like the other appellations of the Midi, the Corbières vineyards have undergone a gentle transformation through the introduction of improving grape varieties. The first tentative steps occurred in the 1960s, and the process gathered momentum in the 1970s. Carignan still remains the backbone of the vineyards, with as much as 70 per cent permitted, provided it is blended with 10 per cent Syrah. Only 60 per cent is allowed, however, if there is no Syrah and the Carignan is blended with just Grenache and Cinsaut. The coastal zones can plant Mourvèdre in preference to Syrah, and some people have both. Syrah is easier to cultivate, but near the coast the Mourvèdre gives good structure and flavour. Carignan, vinified by carbonic maceration and aged for twelve months, provides a good base for a wine. Eventually this method of vinification will become obligatory for Carignan. A minimum of 30 per cent Grenache gives weight and body, while Cinsaut, to a maximum of 20 per cent, makes for lightness and drinkability. As Carignan decreases, Grenache generally increases, and people plant Syrah or Mourvèdre depending on whether they are in the east or the west, with a Mediterranean climate or with some Atlantic influence.

The Corbières is an exciting region to visit, for there is an underlying optimism, a feeling that they are on the point of great achievements, with serious producers questioning established methods and working enthusiastically on improving their wine. Nothing is taken for granted any more. There is an open-mindedness and an infectious desire to experiment, and the creation of the appellation in 1985 has given the growers considerable impetus and motivation. As the director of one of the region's leading co-operatives at Castelmaure said, he is very proud to work in the Corbières as the vineyards are all new and there is greater open-mindedness than in vineyards with longer-established reputations. He was referring to Fitou, where there is a tendency to complacency, and he is firmly convinced that the Corbières are a vineyard of the future. I believe that he is right.

Vinification methods have improved almost beyond recognition. The development of carbonic maceration has had a profound effect on the quality of Corbières. The father of Marc Dubernet, today's leading oenologist of the Midi, was responsible for its introduction in the mid-1960s. The hard-skinned Carignan benefits particularly from this method, as the fruit and colour is extracted, but not the hard tannins. At first it was by no means universally accepted, as producers and co-operatives took time to equip their cellars; but now it is used to the extent that carbonic maceration will become obligatory for the vinification of Carignan.

The technique can be criticized for producing wines that do not last, but in fact the period of maceration in Languedoc is considerably longer than in the Beaujolais, which is the other region where it is widely practised. The results are quite different, especially as the Carignan is blended with the other grape varieties that have been vinified in the classic manner, giving the wine extra structure. Carbonic maceration necessitates hand-picking, and careful producers use small boxes, rather than large containers, to ensure that the grapes are not crushed and do not begin oxidizing before they reach the fermentation vat. Vinification temperatures are controlled as never before and there is greater selection within the crop, especially by the co-operatives, who now pay attention to soil and grape variety.

The point of carbonic maceration is to retain the perfume and fruit of the grapes. If the grapes are crushed, they oxidize and lose their perfume; if you protect them from oxygen with carbon dioxide, all the fruit is retained. If the grapes are kept intact, so that the fermentation actually begins inside each grape, the resulting alcohol helps to retain flavour when the grapes are actually pressed. With carbonic maceration, contrary to a classic fermentation, it is the pressed juice, not the free-run juice, that gives the wine quality. The free-run juice is less good because it has been in contact with the stalks of the grapes.

Corbières is not generally considered to be a wine for ageing. More adventurous growers, however, are experimenting successfully with oak barrels, sometimes making two wines, of which the better has spent a few months in oak. An excellent example is the Cave Co-opérative d'Embrès et de Castelmaure, a tiny percentage of whose wine is aged in 225-litre Bordelais barrels. Since 1978 they have set aside the wine made from grapes grown on the very best plots, which have been determined by geological analysis and aerial photographs. The vines themselves are at least ten years old and the vinification lasts as long as three weeks. The wine is matured for six months in wood, for which they have 170 barrels altogether, of which twenty-five are renewed each year. They make just 500 hectolitres, and the wine is sold as Cuvée des Pompadours. (The now ruined Château de Castelmaure was owned by a family called Pompadour, though they were not related to the more notorious Mme de Pompadour, mistress of Louis XV.)

There is an ever-growing number of serious producers of Corbières, both co-operatives and independent wine-makers. It would have been impossible to see them all, so what follows are my impressions of the people I did meet, who illustrate the current trends and prevailing optimism of Corbières.

Jacques Bergès has been president of the growers' association for fifteen years. He owns Domaine La Voulte-Gasparets in the village of Boutenac, where there have been vines since the 1700s, and he is the fifth generation of wine-growers there. Now his estate consists of 50 hectares, mainly of Corbières, though he also makes a little *vin de pays*. He has 60 per cent Carignan, 30 per cent Grenache and 10 per cent Cinsaut and Syrah. When he took over the property there was no Syrah at all, so he began planting some fifteen years ago; he may also try Mourvèdre, but not for the moment.

M. Bergès has a sound, objective view of his appellation, admitting the problems and himself illustrating some of the solutions. His cellar is neat and well run, and he has abandoned his old wooden casks in favour of cement vats. He also has a small ageing cellar of barrels that have already been used just once elsewhere, in which a little of his wine spends three or four months. His Cuvée Romain Paric, in memory of his great-grandfather, is made from eighty-year-old vines, 70 per cent Carignan and 30 per cent Grenache. He likes the wood to give the wine a hint of the taste of vanilla rather than add more tannin, as there is already enough from the Carignan. He admits that his first experiments with new wood in 1973 were not very successful, but the 1986 was concentrated and tough, with some attractive fruit to balance the tannin. We were also treated to a tasting of his 1984, which was a ripe, minty wine, drinking well in the spring of 1987, but with plenty of promise for the future. His 1977, not a great vintage, none the less illustrated the ability of Corbières to age.

Georges Bertrand at Domaine de Villemajou also worked on ageing Corbières. Sadly he has been killed in a car accident since my visit, but his family are continuing his work. He had created his estate over the last twenty years or so, starting from scratch, carefully selecting vineyards with the best aspect and soil (namely south-facing slopes on gravel and clay), so that there are now 63 hectares. At first he delivered his grapes to the local co-operative, but in 1969 he bought a cellar as he wanted to be able to make his wine himself, as well as grow grapes. All his wine is made by carbonic maceration and he said that at first he was criticized for this; but as the technique has developed and become more controlled, with a corresponding improvement in quality, it is now widely accepted. The period of maceration usually lasts about six to eleven days, depending on the temperature and the condition of the grapes. There are two schools of thought about carbonic maceration. Either you heat up the vat right at the beginning to about 33°C and then let it gradually cool down to 23°C; or you let nature take its course and allow the temperature to increase gently to about 33°C, maintain it at that temperature for a few days, and let it cool down to 22°C before you run off the juice. 22°C is the lowest feasible temperature, otherwise there is a risk of bacterial spoilage. M. Bertrand tried both methods and said he had not yet found 'the truth', but that he preferred the second method. If you heat the grapes at the beginning you get less tannin, but the grapes burst earlier and you can lose some aroma.

The barrels are kept in the cellar of the Château de Boutenac. He began in 1979 with twenty, then increased to fifty, then a hundred;

now there are 400 225-litre Bordeaux barrels that have been used once elsewhere. The wine spends between five and seven months in wood and the barrels are changed every year. His aim was to make a wine that is ready for immediate drinking as soon as it is bottled, not one that will need further ageing before consumption. We tasted a selection of M. Bertrand's wines, going back to 1978. On the whole they had developed well with time, and the younger wines had flavours reminiscent of what the French call collectively 'red fruit' – redcurrants, cherries, raspberries and so on. The 1978 had vegetal overtones, with a somewhat herbal finish, while the 1979 was rich and raisiny.

André Liguière at Château La Baronne is a doctor as well as a wine-grower and his wife Suzette also helps with the vines, so that both their names appear on their label. The château was built at the end of the nineteenth century for the Baronne de St-Vincent. Her son lived there alone for fifty years and after his death the château and vineyards were sold to Dr Liguière in 1955. He now has 45 hectares of vines altogether, 30 of Corbières and 15 of Vin de Pays de Hauterive en Pays d'Aude, where the valley of the Aude runs between the Corbières and the Minervois. We walked in his vineyards in the spring sunshine at the end of March and the vines were just beginning to bud. The vineyards, outside the village of Fontcouvert, lie on the slopes of the Montagne d'Alaric which dominates the skyline. Fontcouvert takes its name from an old spring which still exists and which watered a Roman villa. The village was on an old Roman road, and was later a halt for pilgrims on their way to Santiago de Compostela. Alaric was the famous Visigoth who sacked Rome; there is a local legend about a treasure that he is reputed to have lost in the area, but which has never been discovered.

The doctor's Corbières consists of 60 per cent Carignan, 25 per cent Grenache, 10 per cent Syrah and 5 per cent Mourvèdre. He first planted Syrah and Mourvèdre fifteen years ago. They are almost too far from the coast for Mourvèdre to grow successfully, but it was grown in the area before the phylloxera and a small drop gives the wine some character. *Gobelet* is the standard system of pruning for Corbières, with about 4,000 plants per hectare. All the grapes are hand-picked for carbonic maceration; Dr Liguière was one of the first to try out this technique in 1975, and in 1978 he took the step of installing vats for the purpose. He is also considering experimenting with wood, but at the moment has only six large casks which do not contribute much to the wine, so he would like to try out some new barrels.

Dr Liguière also makes white Corbières, which comes from Grenache Blanc and Bourboulenc, but he is prouder of what he calls *un vin vert* made from Grenache Gris, which is not allowed in the appellation. The grapes are picked before they are fully ripe and are fermented at a low temperature in stainless-steel vats to give a crisp, fragrant wine for the summer. White grapes used to be picked here when they were overripe to make a heavy, oxidizing *rancio* wine; you can still find Corbières *rancio*, but this is now dying out. The doctor's pink also contains a high proportion of Grenache Gris, as much as 70 per cent, which is blended with 20 per cent Cinsaut and 10 per cent Carignan to give an attractive, delicate raspberry flavour.

Claude Vialade at Château St-Auréol, outside the attractive village of Lagrasse, already has a full-time job running the export department of the Vignerons du Val d'Orbieu, but she and her husband still have the time to create what is to some extent an experimental vineyard under the guidance of the oenologist Marc Dubernet. For red wine they have planted Syrah and Grenache, and they also have some forty-year-old Carignan; they have paid particular attention to the *terroir* of each plot of vineyard. Since 1983 they have had 150 Bordelais barrels, already used for one wine, in which they keep their own wine for anything between eight and eighteen months, depending on the vintage. They are also planning to try out some new oak barrels. We drank the 1985 over lunch with that French national dish of steak and *pommes frites*. It was delicious. Nearly two-thirds of the wine is made from Grenache and Syrah; most of the Carignan that makes up the remaining 40 per cent is made by carbonic maceration, while the rest of the blend is vinified traditionally.

They are perhaps even more experimental with white wine. For this they have planted Malvoisie and Grenache Blanc, and as an even greater innovation have grafted Marsanne on to Macabeo which they dislike, as it oxidizes quickly. For the moment, however, the Marsanne is very much an experiment. At least the INAO has recognized that the existing grape varieties for Corbières Blanc do not give very exciting results and need to be enlivened with something more flavoursome; Marsanne may be the answer. Before the phylloxera there were many more white grape varieties in the region, but these have disappeared. Claude Vialade is in the lucky position of not depending upon her vineyard for her livelihood – she can afford to experiment and if necessary stand the expense of a mistake, though so far she has been very successful.

Yves Laboucarié at Domaine de Fontsainte is one of the leading growers of the village of Boutenac, and his family have been cultivating vines since 1604. Fontsainte takes its name from a spring which never ran dry, something of enormous value in this arid countryside. Asked about the future of the appellation, M. Laboucarié said, 'I am building it every day,' and indeed he is. The value of the appellation comes from the collective effort of all the conscientious growers in the area; as he says, you need lots of small bricks to build a big wall and everyone is contributing to that wall. You cannot make Corbières out of Chardonnay or Cabernet, so you must keep the basic grape varieties, namely Carignan and Grenache, and add other grapes to give aroma. Carignan does well with carbonic maceration, but that is not enough, so Syrah and Mourvèdre are also planted. He sees the *appellation contrôlée* for Corbières as the membership ticket into a club; it has certainly given the region an enormous boost.

M. Laboucarié is very aware of the geological and topographical differences between the various parts of the appellation. He is adamant that you cannot grow the same grape varieties all over, and that there are quite distinct characteristics in the different areas. For instance the wines of the Corbières-Maritimes tend to be light and aromatic, with finesse from the Mourvèdre, while those of the Corbières-Centrales, around Boutenac, are more substantial wines to be aged, as indeed his own is. He began his first experiments with oak ageing back in 1970, when the idea seemed quite revolutionary. He uses *demi-muids* of 600 litres, which is the traditional size of Languedoc, rather than Bordeaux barrels of 225 litres.

Corbières is still very much an adolescent appellation. There are people who remain untouched by these changes, the men who are approaching retirement and have no interest in the future; but those with a sense of direction are optimistic about its success. Even though the delimitation of the vineyards has drastically reduced the area of Corbières, the potential of the appellation is enormous. It could produce 1 million hectolitres, but for the moment not everyone has the right grape varieties in the required percentages. There is still a long way to go, but quality now comes first.

MINERVOIS

Minervois and Corbières seem to go hand in hand as twin appellations. They are separated by the valley of the Aude, with the vineyards of the Minervois on the foothills of the Massif Central facing those of the Corbières on the first slopes of the Pyrenees.

The Minervois takes its name from the isolated village of Minerve that perches in what seems an unassailable position on steep cliffs above the confluent of the Cesse and the Briant. If you approach the village from the east you pass the gorges of the Cesse, but in summer the river dries to the merest trickle. Suddenly there is a dramatic view of the village, which is Roman in origin and takes its name from Minerva, the goddess of wisdom. The surrounding countryside is wild and unforgiving, and in the spring rain it seemed harsh and sombre. Little grows but vines and olive trees on these arid, rocky hills that are the first foothills of the Montagne Noire.

The ramparts of Minerve were built in the twelfth century, and the village played its part in the Albigensian Crusade as one of the last strongholds of the Cathar heresy, which had a strong following in this part of France at the end of the twelfth century. The Cathars believed that all material things, including our own bodies, were the work of the devil; they therefore regarded wealth and possessions as evil, and were opposed to reproduction, marriage and family life. Pope Innocent III launched a crusade against them under the command of Simon de Montfort, father of the founder of the English parliament. Many Cathars died at Minerve after a successful siege by him in 1210.

The Roman legions who occupied Narbonne in the first century BC were responsible for introducing vines here. Cicero wrote of the vines of Minerve, that he called the Pagus Menerbensis, and Pliny the Younger preferred the wines of Minerve to those of Betoeres, i.e. Béziers. After the desolation caused by the Albigensian Crusade, Minervois faded from historical significance. It is said to have been drunk by various French kings – François I, Henri IV and Louis XVI – and in the fifteenth century Nicolas de la Jugie, Seigneur de la Livinière (which today is one of the principal villages of the appellation), sent wine to the papal court at Avignon for his uncle Clement VI.

The nineteenth-century writers accorded the wines of the Minervois no more than a passing mention, and the region suffered from phylloxera in the same way as did other wines of the Midi. The better-quality vineyards, planted on the arid slopes, fell into disuse and viticulture shifted towards the coastal plains to concentrate on an industrial production of '*le gros rouge*'. It is only in the last few years that the scales have begun to turn, with a shift in emphasis towards smaller production and better quality. Minervois was recognized as a VDQS in 1951 but it was not until 1985 that it became an appellation.

The appellation of Minervois covers a large and varied area. The town of Olonzac forms its administrative centre and it can be geographically and geologically divided into five different zones. Although these distinctions are acknowledged, as yet there is no move to obtain their recognition by the authorities of the INAO. Zone one is the easternmost part of the appellation, with vineyards on the pebbly plain around Ginestas; here the climate is influenced by maritime winds and rain. The second and largest zone is the area west of Olonzac, including the villages of La Livinière, Pépieux and Rieux-Minervois. This is the heart of the appellation, and the hottest, driest part. The third zone includes the vineyards between the villages of Caunes-Minervois and Azillanet, with vineyards on the south-facing foothills of the Montagne Noire. Again this is a very hot area. Fourthly there is what is called the Haut-Minervois, around the village of Minerve, where the vineyards are situated at an average altitude of 200 metres. The climate here is harsher and influenced by the mountains. Finally there is the westernmost part of the appellation, adjoining the vineyards of Cabardès, where the climate is more humid but still hot. Administratively, the appellation covers sixteen villages in the department of Hérault and forty-five in Aude.

Although white and pink wines are included in the appellation, most Minervois is firmly red. There is also an enclave of Muscat around the village of St-Jean-de-Minervois, of which more later. Twenty years ago the Minervois vineyards were planted with Carignan, Alicante Bouschet and Aramon, while today there is a strong presence of Grenache Noir as well as of Syrah and Mourvèdre, not to mention Cabernet Sauvignon and Merlot for *vin de pays*, and even some Pinot Noir. White Minervois consists mainly of Grenache Blanc, Bourboulenc and Macabeo, but there are some tentative plantings of Marsanne and Roussanne, and even of Chardonnay and Sauvignon.

The very first person to plant what were then, back in the

early 1960s, quite unorthodox grape varieties (namely Syrah and Mourvèdre) was Jacques Tallavignes at the Château de Paulignan. He is considered by many to have been the father of the appellation. Sadly he died a few years ago and his sons, while continuing their father's work, do not seem to have the same aptitude or talent.

The thinking wine-grower feels frustrated by the authoritarian practices of the INAO and resents the hold that the Bordelais maintain upon the planting of grape varieties like Cabernet Sauvignon and Merlot. They are grown in other parts of the world, so why not in the Midi too? The director of the co-operative at La Lavinière feels that the appellations of the Midi have been muzzled by the INAO. They want to be able to make a *vin de garde*, and Cabernet Sauvignon can only improve the quality of the appellation – but such is the power of the Bordelais.

The best way to convey an impression of the appellation of Minervois is to describe our visits to co-operatives and wine-growers with varying degrees of competence, enthusiasm and innovation. Several themes recur, such as the increasing use of oak barrels for maturing the wine, the development of the process of carbonic maceration and the changing composition of the vineyards. As will be seen, the producers do not always agree with each other and there is no one correct answer.

The co-operative of La Lavinière is generally considered to be one of the leading co-operatives of the appellation. It was instrumental in promoting the extensive use of the technique of carbonic maceration for the fermentation of the otherwise unyielding Carignan. It imposes very strict controls on its members at vintage time. They cannot bring more than 1,000 kilos of grapes with any one delivery, to ensure that the grapes intended for carbonic maceration are not already crushed on arrival at the cellar. The minimum alcoholic degree for Minervois is 11.5°, and a careful selection is made according to grape variety and vineyard (soil and aspect being the vital factors in the latter case). Most of their Minervois is vinified by carbonic maceration and their cellars are fully equipped for this purpose. Their fermentation vats have a 400-hectolitre capacity. They are each filled with carbon dioxide and about 30 tons of grapes. A little juice is inevitably released and is run off and heated; cultured yeasts are added to it and it is returned to the fermentation vat. The intact grapes are also heated so that a temperature of about 37°C is reached after a week. This heating fixes the aromas under the grape skins. The process is usually shorter for wines intended for early drinking as these require less tannin, whereas wines destined for some ageing will be kept for about twelve days in the fermentation vats. The juice is then run off, the grapes pressed and the juice cooled down to 20°C to avoid the development of any volatile aromas; the fermentation is then finished in the customary way. With carbonic maceration, unlike a classic vinification, the less free-run juice there is, the better the wine: its quality lies in the pressed juice. With a traditional vinification this should constitute as little as 20 per cent of the total, while in a vinification by carbonic maceration it should be as much as 60 or 70 per cent.

The co-operative at La Lavinière is also one of the producers best equipped for the oak ageing of Minervois. They have an attractive small cellar with Bordeaux barrels, bought second-hand from Château Chasse-Spleen at Moulis after the ageing of one or two wines, and they use them seven or eight times. The wine that is matured like this represents about a tenth of their total production of Minervois and it comes from vines planted on hillsides where the yield is lower than the statutory 50 hectolitres per hectare for Minervois. The 1985, tasted from the barrel in the spring of 1987, had some attractive flavours of vanilla and pepper and the wood had blended well into the wine, with balanced fruit. It was intended for bottling in June.

The vineyards of La Lavinière are still dominated by Carignan, which accounts for 80 per cent of the plantings. But only a maximum of 60 per cent is allowed in the appellation and there must be a minimum of 30 per cent Grenache, Syrah and Mourvèdre altogether, which is often exceeded. The remaining 10 per cent is made up by Cinsaut if necessary. At La Lavinière they favour Syrah rather than Mourvèdre. The locality suffers from drought, however, which Carignan can withstand, while Grenache, and Syrah even more so, need water. The soil here is a mixture of clay and limestone, rendered more porous by a fair quantity of gravel. The INAO allows the irrigation of Syrah, but only in May and June. The oldest Syrah vines at La Lavinière are now ten years old, which is still too young for the true quality of the grape to be established. They only have a little Cabernet Sauvignon and Merlot, as there is not sufficient suitable terrain for them. They are used for *vin de pays*, which is still the co-operative's largest product, either Vin de Pays de l'Hérault or a more local wine, Vin de Pays des Coteaux de Peyriac, which covers about a third of the appellation of Minervois in eighteen villages.

The more exciting wines generally come from individual estates. The Domaine de Ste-Eulalie, to the north of La Lavinière, is closely linked with the village co-operative: the manager here, Maurice Piccionini, is president of the co-operative. The estate actually belongs to Georges Blanc, who bought the abandoned property in 1979. Since then he has transformed this old estate, replanting the vineyards and equipping the cellars for carbonic maceration. The vineyards are south-facing, on stony clay-and-limestone soil. When I was there, the vines were turning russet in the autumn sunshine and there were views of the roofs of La Lavinière from the cellar door. Carignan has been reduced to 40 per cent, while Syrah reaches an unusually high 30 per cent and Grenache Noir 20 per cent. In addition there are 10 per cent white grapes (Bourboulenc and Macabeo) in this 25-hectare vineyard. Ideally M. Piccionini would like as little as 30 per cent Carignan in his vineyard, and plans to decrease his Carignan plantings in favour of Syrah in particular. Vinification methods are not dissimilar to those of the co-operative at La Lavinière, but the scale is smaller. The wine is vinified by carbonic maceration, and about a third of it is aged for six to twelve months in barrels from Châteaux Chasse-Spleen and Talbot. The white wine is vinified with twenty-four hours' skin contact after the grapes have been destalked, followed by a controlled fermentation at 14–16°C. The 1985 Minervois from Ste-Eulalie was a warm, peppery mouthful of wine with fruit and body, illustrating the potential quality of well-made Minervois.

The other leading estate of La Lavinière is the Château de Gourgazaud, which is owned by the amiable M. Piquet, the former managing director of the important *négociant* company of Chantovent. He is a friendly, unassuming man, who admitted that he much preferred growing grapes and making wine to running a company. He had always been fascinated by grapes, and when he bought the Château de Gourgazaud in 1974 he fulfilled a life-long ambition. Again, as at Ste-Eulalie, the vineyards were planted only with Aramon and Carignan. He now has only 30 per cent Carignan – he would like to get rid of it completely and described it rather rudely as a *cochonnerie* – with Syrah and Mourvèdre, not to mention Cabernet Sauvignon and Merlot, and unusually some Chardonnay and Sauvignon. He planted Syrah here in 1974; we take it for granted today, but it seemed revolutionary at the time. He feels that the future of Minervois lies with Syrah and to a lesser extent Mourvèdre; he does not like

Grenache as it oxidizes too easily. All his wine is made by carbonic maceration, and the very first experiment in the region with this process was carried out at Gourgazaud. Most of his Syrah and Cabernet Sauvignon is aged in oak barrels.

I have M. Piquet to thank for one of my most illuminating tastings, which demonstrated both his fascination with grape varieties and his healthy disrespect for the restrictions of the INAO. We began with a 1987 Sauvignon, which had been fermented in wood to see what happens. He has had Sauvignon in production for eight years but this was his first experiment with fermentation in oak. First the juice was given fifteen hours of skin contact and only the free-run juice was used. After fermentation the wine was racked and left in barrel on the fine lees. In order to retain some acidity, only about half of the wine will be allowed to do the malolactic fermentation. It will be bottled in the early spring and sold as Vin de Pays d'Oc, rather than as Vin de Pays de l'Aude, as the regulations are stricter. I liked the wine because the Sauvignon character was there, though with a fatness more reminiscent of the New World than of Sancerre. The oak was quite overpowering, but should tone down with time.

We went on to Chardonnay, which M. Piquet has been allowed by the INAO to plant as an experiment. He has just three rows, which gave him 30 litres of wine for his first vintage in 1987. The grapes were picked on 28 August, and with 12.5° of alcohol and 5 grams of acidity the wine has some crispness and weight, as well as a little buttery fruit that is a feature of the grape variety.

Then we tried some Minervois. M. Piquet admitted that his observance of the regulations governing grape varieties was not very orthodox, and that in practice there is no difference between the grape varieties for his *vin de pays* and for his Minervois. Both contain some Merlot, while he usually makes a varietal *vin de pays* from Cabernet Sauvignon. The 1986 had had four months in wood when I tasted it; it was perfumed with a peppery Syrah nose and had tannin, fruit and excellent structure. It will not be sold for another two years. Next we tried a 1979 – pure Syrah, made by carbonic maceration from five-year-old vines. It was quite surprising: rather elegant, with light, mature Syrah flavour and some herbal overtones. M. Piquet is very pleased with his Syrah, but he is expecting great things from his more recently planted Mourvèdre. People say it will not ripen here as La Lavinière is too far from the sea, but he wanted to take the risk, especially as he is very partial to Bandol, where Mourvèdre is at its best.

We finished with a 1985 Cabernet Sauvignon which had spent six months in wood and at the time of tasting had fifteen months' bottle age. It had some rich berry fruit, with tannin, acidity and a long finish. M. Piquet is adamant that he is not trying to imitate or rival a Château Latour. This is a relatively inexpensive wine for drinking tomorrow. He is also adamant that the use of oak must not be overdone and that his wines cannot stand up to new wood, so he ages them in Bordeaux barrels that have been used once before. Not only would new wood be too expensive, but also the wine would taste like an oak *tisane*! But good things can be done with early-ripening grape varieties like Cabernet Sauvignon, and he can compete with California and Australia.

M. Ormières at Château Fabas, near the village of Rieux-Minervois, is also conducting some serious experiments with oak-aged Minervois. His is a more traditional estate than Château de Gourgazaud. The château itself has its origins in a medieval fortified farm which belonged to the abbey of the nearby village of Caune. M. Ormières's family have owned it since 1938, and today attractive ranges of russet brick buildings surround a courtyard. There are 35 hectares of Minervois, and 18 of *vin de pays* (either des Coteaux de Peyriac or de l'Aude) which are gradually being transformed into appellation vineyards. It is all a question of grape variety. He began planting Syrah and Grenache twenty years ago, and Mourvèdre sixteen years ago. Grenache is the dominant grape variety at 31 per cent, with 24 per cent Carignan, 21 per cent Cinsaut, 12.5 per cent Syrah, 10 per cent Mourvèdre and a tiny 1.5 per cent Macabeo planted in 1987.

M. Ormières prefers to pick his grapes by mechanical harvester, which precludes a vinification by carbonic maceration. The fermentation usually lasts about twelve days to extract the maximum amount of tannin and colour, and the grape varieties are fermented separately then blended in December. The wine would then usually spend eighteen months in vat, but since 1985 M. Ormières has been experimenting with a little ageing in oak. Asked why, he replied that he likes wines that have been aged in wood – which seems as good a reason as any. He is working with a group of ten growers under the guidance of the oenologist of the Minervois growers' association. Their vineyards are in different parts of the appellation and they meet each month to taste and follow the evolution of their wines. He has tried three-, six- and nine-month ageing periods; so far six months seems to be the most satisfactory, but you need a wine with good body and sufficient tannin. Much depends upon the grape varieties, too. Carignan, for instance, is no good as it dries out in wood. Certainly the results augur well for the future.

There are numerous other independent growers making their mark on the appellation, such as the Château de Paraza, Guy Rancoule at Domaine de l'Herbe Sainte, Suzanne de Foncompret at Domaine de la Senche and Jacques Maris in La Lavinière – it would be impossible to mention them all. But I believe the most exciting producer of the appellation to be Daniel Domergue, whose cellars adjoin the Château de Paulignan. He sees himself as a twentieth-century Cathar, a voice crying in the wilderness against the restrictions of the INAO and the short-sighted attitudes of his fellow growers. 'We are a little anarchical here,' was one of the very first things he said to me. There is no family background of wine-making. He has a degree in German and his wife Hélène studied psychology, after which they ran a bookshop in Marseilles. Then, tired of the city rat-race and expecting their first child, they came to the Minervois and bought 5 hectares of vines that nobody wanted at Trausses. The vines were Carignan and Alicante Bouschet and were immediately pulled up. At the same time they studied viticulture and oenology, and planted 3.5 hectares with Syrah, Cinsaut, Grenache and Mourvèdre, and some Pinot Noir for Vin de Pays de l'Aude; not a single plant of Carignan. Minervois without Carignan was a revelation. The wines are quite different from any others I tasted, with richness and concentration and with flavours of prunes and liquorice, very powerful, very complex and needing several years of ageing.

M. Domergue's cellar is elementary, as financial restrictions have limited his investment in equipment. He ferments in an open-topped oak vat and does not have an *égrappoir* (destalking-machine). He does a *pigeage*, treading down the cap of grape skins with fishermen's waders twice a day for fifteen minutes. The juice spends eight days with the skins to extract colour and tannin, and he buys Bordeaux barrels (from Château Lagrange) in which his wine spends twelve to eighteen months. He is lucky in that his cellar is almost completely underground.

So far he only has red grapes, but he is thinking of Viognier and Roussanne. He says he owes a lot to Jacques Tallavignes, who gave him advice at the beginning.

Daniel Domergue is a fanatic and a maverick, with a cause that he pleads passionately. He is scathing of the restrictions and limitations imposed by the INAO, and considers the organization to be dominated by the Bordelais, Burgundians and Champenois who have imposed constraints upon the wines of the Midi after finally agreeing to let them into the club. He disagrees with the regulations about the number of vines that can be planted per hectare; the INAO imposes a minimum of at least 3,000 per hectare, which may work in Champagne but not here. In the eighteenth century there were a lot less, and planting in rows 2 metres wide with 2 metres between each plant would give a better distribution of foliage. He also believes that they would make better wine if they were allowed to irrigate in July, for rain in June is very important in this region and if there is none, the vines suffer excessively and cannot produce good grapes.

Daniel Domergue is a perfectionist aiming to make a great wine, and he is certainly well on the way to doing so. As he says, the Midi is full of 'good little wines', but with the climate and rainfall and small yields, you cannot be content with just a good wine; it can and must be great.

However, the last word on Minervois should go to M. Piccionini, who views the situation within the context of the appellation. He sees Minervois at a crossroads: 'If we take the right direction, we will succeed. If not, we shall be lost.' He fears the effect of the open market in 1992, when France will be open to wines from abroad, notably Spain, as never before. A large proportion of the members of the co-operatives, those who are reaching retiring age, will give up their vines; these vineyards will disappear and the area of the appellation will be reduced considerably, by as much as a third if not more. M. Piquet, too, feels that Minervois has plenty of future provided they can get rid of Carignan. The need to change the grape varieties is urgent; the climate is magnificent, but they are fifty years behind Australia and California. It will be a hard struggle, but the committed growers will win.

ST-JEAN-DE-MINERVOIS

The sleepy village of St-Jean-de-Minervois in the north east corner of the Minervois has its own appellation for a Muscat de St-Jean-de-Minervois. It is in the wildest, most arid part of the region, with its vineyards on the stony *garrigues*. I say arid, but on the afternoon in

March that I was there, heavy rain was the order of the day and we ran from car to cellar avoiding large puddles.

Our first visit was to Michel Sigé, who was at home as the rain was preventing him from pruning his vines. He explained that people began planting a little Muscat for their home consumption at the turn of the century and that it developed further during the 1930s, with the result that in 1950 Muscat de St-Jean-de-Minervois was given an appellation, with production regulations similar to the other *vins doux naturels* of southern France.

The grape variety is Muscat à Petits Grains, which has a very thin skin, making it fragile and susceptible to rot. Its yield is thus very irregular: in 1986 they only made 16 hectolitres per hectare because of damage from hail. Even in a good year the yield never exceeds 28 hl/ha. The grapes are picked by hand at the end of September, a full two weeks later than the Muscat of Lunel. The grapes are almost overripe, slightly dried, with a potential alcoholic degree of 14°. They are pressed immediately, and the fermentation is controlled at a temperature of 18–20°C and then stopped by the addition of alcohol when the right balance of sugar and natural alcohol is attained. No wood is used in its vinification, so that the flavour of Muscat is kept as fresh as possible. The wine develops more aromas with a little ageing, but would lose its character if kept too long. We tasted the 1985 vintage which, in the spring of 1987, was deliciously grapy and aromatic.

Altogether M. Sigé has 10 hectares of Muscat, and he works with his brother-in-law, M. Camman, who has 8 hectares. They also make some red Minervois, but consider Muscat de St-Jean-de-Minervois to be more rewarding. It has rarity value, whereas there is a glut of ordinary Minervois. The vineyards are concentrated around the village and their delimitation has been done. The total annual production is about 2,000 hectolitres, of which the village co-operative accounts for three-quarters, from 75 hectares of vines. We tasted their 1984 vintage, which was the colour of old gold, quite grapy on the nose, but tired on the finish. Marc Dubernet has recently taken over responsibility for their wine, however, so things can only improve under his control.

Muscat de St-Jean-de-Minervois is certainly one of the many unknown French wines of regional character that deserve a better reputation. A glass of Domaine Sigé or Domaine Barroubio, the other good independent producer, makes a delicious dessert wine on a summer's evening.

BLANQUETTE DE LIMOUX

Limoux is a cheerful, bustling town. At its centre there is an arcaded square which provides a focal point, while the Café du Commerce is the local meeting-place. Sit there long enough and you will see all Limoux. The square serves as the market-place, and on 1 May there are flower ladies with the traditional bunches of lily of the valley. The river Aude, crossed by the Pont Neuf which dates from the fourteenth century, flows through the town providing attractive riverside views. I stayed in the rather incongruously named Hôtel Moderne et Pigeon, which was not modern, nor did it have any pigeons – it was just an elegantly dilapidated town house that had once been one of two separate hotels.

Limoux lies south west of Carcassonne. The outskirts of the town proclaim its vinous interests, with loud signs advertising Blanquette de Limoux and offering cellar visits and tastings. The vineyards of Limoux cover quite an extensive area within a radius of some 20 kilometres of the town, between Carcassonne to the north and Quillan to the south, and bordering the Côtes de la Malepère to the west. In 1986 there were about 3,200 hectares of vines in production, planted mainly with Mauzac, but also with Chardonnay and Chenin Blanc. There is plenty of scope for extending the planted area, and there is a variety of different microclimates within the appellation, for it is a wild, undulating region. About five zones can broadly be defined. The area around Limoux produces the earliest-ripening grapes, while the villages of Pieusse, Pauligne and Malras have the most oceanic climate. Magrie, Tourreilles and Castelreng are the hottest localities, and in St-Hilaire and St-Polycarpe the vegetation is the most delayed; and in the Haute Vallée of the Aude, the highest part of the vineyards, with the coolest climate, the grapes ripen latest.

Limoux proudly claims to be the oldest sparkling wine in France, if not in the world, with an even longer history than champagne. The monks of the Benedictine abbey of St-Hilaire take credit for the discovery. The abbey still stands in a sleepy village, a Romanesque church with peaceful Gothic cloisters. The first records of viticulture in the region date back to the tenth century, and during the Middle Ages various privileges were granted to the inhabitants of Limoux regarding the sale of their wine. In 1388 the chronicler Froissart referred to the '*délectables beuveries de vin blanc Limouxin*'. Authorities have set the date of the discovery of sparkling wine as early as 1531, though the ultimate source for this date is unknown. Presumably the discovery was accidental, in that the monks found that their wine began to ferment again in the spring after the winter cold, and managed to contain the carbon dioxide. For several centuries Blanquette de Limoux was made by this *méthode rurale*, which you still find occasionally today.

Sixteenth-century archives refer to the white wines of Limoux. In 1544 Blanquette was sent to the Sieur d'Arques, and 1578 to the Prévôt-Général of the king. In 1584 the Duc de Joyeuse celebrated the capture of Brugairolles with Blanquette. By the eighteenth century its reputation had spread beyond the locality: in 1746 there was an order stipulating that thirty *pots* of Blanquette de Limoux should be sent to the students of the University of Paris, and in 1772 Paul-José Barthez, an eminent doctor of the University of Montpellier, recommended the use of Blanquette in the Paris hospitals.

In the nineteenth century it seems that Limoux was noted for its red as well as its white wines. Jullien said of the white wines that they had sweetness and elegance, enough alcohol and an attractive bouquet. A few years later Guyot compared the red wines with those of St-Georges d'Orques, saying that they were lighter, but could rival a good burgundy; they were made from Terret Noir, Picpoule, Carignan and Ribeyrenc. He mentioned Blanquette, but emphasized that the area was important for its red wines. Rendu cited Limoux as one of the esteemed *crus* of Languedoc and described Blanquette de Limoux as a white wine with a certain reputation; but he also said that the red wine from the hillsides was much better, though twice as expensive. He explained that Blanquette was bottled as soon as the tumultuous fermentation was finished, and that 10,000 hectolitres of red wine were produced as against 3,000 hectolitres of white. A few years later Mouillefert described Blanquette de Limoux as being very heady and having a good flavour.

Red wine is made at Limoux today, but only *vin de pays*, either de l'Aude, or de la Haute Vallée de l'Aude. Efforts are concentrated on Blanquette de Limoux, which became an appellation in 1938. In the first edition (1952) of his book on the wines of France, Alexis Lichine wrote of Blanquette de Limoux that the wines were small and an argument for insisting upon champagne. In the 1986 edition he is a little more complimentary, and things have changed so much in the last thirty years that today I would insist upon Blanquette de Limoux in preference to a cheap young champagne. There are moves afoot to modify the name of the appellation to Crémant de Limoux, in line with the names of the other principal sparkling wines of France.

Mauzac is the base of Blanquette de Limoux. It is called Blanquette (which means white in Occitan) in the region because of the white hairs on the underside of the leaves of the vine. Mauzac is typical of the appellation, and elsewhere it is only found in significant quantity in the vineyards of Gaillac. It can be distinguished by a characteristic taste of quince, a bitterness on the finish and some firm acidity which makes it suitable for a base wine for champenization. But pure Mauzac can produce a rather dull wine, and this has incited forward-thinking producers to experiment with Chardonnay and Chenin Blanc. The first plantings of these were made about twenty years ago, and from 1975 a maximum of 30 per cent Chardonnay and Chenin Blanc has been permitted in Blanquette de Limoux. Within this percentage the precise proportions can vary according to the producer's taste, so there may for example be 30 per cent of Chardonnay and no Chenin Blanc, or 15 per cent of each. In 1978 Clairette, of which 10 per cent had been allowed in the appellation, was removed as it was found to oxidize and age badly.

Chardonnay and Chenin Blanc, on the other hand, give good results and are growing in importance. Chardonnay is popular as it is one of the grape varieties of champagne and gives attractive aromas. It ripens early and is often picked at the end of August before it becomes overripe and loses its acidity. In contrast, Chenin Blanc ripens later and has a very good acidity level and an attractive bouquet when fully ripe. As yet, the area of vineyards planted with Chardonnay and Chenin Blanc is small – 264 hectares and 170 hectares respectively in 1984 – but they are both growing in importance. They undeniably improve the quality of Blanquette de Limoux, and all the best wines contain the maximum percentage of these two grapes.

The largest producer of Blanquette de Limoux is the Cave Coopérative de Limoux, which was founded in 1947 and now, with 630 members, is responsible for the production of three-quarters of the appellation. There are about six other large producers, some of whom make wine only from their own grapes and others who buy in grapes or juice, and altogether about twenty people who bottle Blanquette de Limoux. The installations of the co-operative are impressive for it has invested 75 million francs on new equipment, financed partly by loans, partly by government and EEC subsidies, and to a lesser extent by its own members. A cellar visit here rivals any champagne house. There are eight computer-programmed presses, and a forest of stainless-steel vats for temperature-controlled fermentations; most *remuage* is done on *giropalettes*, over a period of just five days. Cultured yeasts are used for both the first and second fermentations and the precise blending of the base wines before the second fermentation is done with the aid of the computer, which is credited with a better knowledge of the contents and character of each vat than any member of the cellar staff. They make three qualities of Blanquette de Limoux. Aimery is their basic wine, which spends one year on the lees of the second fermentation before *dégorgement* and includes 7.5 per cent each of Chardonnay and Chenin Blanc. Sieur d'Arques contains 15 per cent each of Chardonnay and Chenin Blanc and consequently is a more elegant, drier wine. Best of all is Prestige d'Aimery, with 20 per cent Chardonnay and 10 per cent Chenin Blanc, which can spend as long as six or seven years on the lees. I suspect that such a lengthy ageing period may have something to do with the fact that the co-operative's sales figures are not as impressive as their equipment. They admitted that they had overestimated the growth in sales, planting vineyards in anticipation of a market demand which failed to materialize. They say that sales are now improving and the situation is more stable. A minimum price – 14 francs per bottle at the beginning of 1987 – has been fixed by the Association Interprofessionnelle to prevent any excessive price reduction. At the moment the co-operative sells a surprisingly small percentage of its production to the export market, so obviously that is where its sales growth should lie.

Philippe Vergnes of Domaine de Martinolles near the village of St-Hilaire, one of the larger and newer estates, explained the details of the vinification process to me. In fact the principle is identical to that of champagne. You are allowed to produce a basic yield, which can be modified annually, of 6,500 kilos of grapes per hectare, giving you 50 hectolitres per hectare. As with champagne, the grapes must be hand-picked; they are put in 25–30-kilo containers and pressed immediately to avoid oxidation. They press 3,000 kilos at a time, which takes one and a half hours. The pressing is divided into three parts, each part being kept separately: the first 45 per cent of the juice is the *cuvée*; the next 45 per cent is the *taille* and the final 10 per cent the *rebêche*. Each grape variety is fermented separately using cultured yeast, and the fermentation is controlled at 17–18°C and lasts for two to three weeks. The wines are fined and undergo cold-treatment for tartrates, but no malolactic fermentation. They are then blended, ready for the second fermentation. The *cuvée*, especially of Chardonnay and Chenin Blanc, is kept for the better wines, while the basic wines are made from the *taille* of the Mauzac. Under the appellation regulations the wine must be aged for a minimum of nine months, but in practice it is often kept for longer. M. Vergnes uses mechanical *giropalettes* for the *remuage* of his basic *brut* and *demi-sec*, but for his very best wines he prefers manual *remuage*. He finds that sediment does not settle as well with mechanical *remuage*. After *dégorgement* some *liqueur d'expédition*, a mixture of wine and sugar, is added and the wines are aged for a few months before sale.

They use the brand name Berceau, as St-Hilaire is seen as the cradle of Blanquette de Limoux. In addition to the *brut* and *demi-sec*, there are two better wines: Le Flascon, which comes in a special bottle, and La Régente.

Domaine de Martinolles is a family property bought by Philippe Vergnes's grandfather just after the war. At that time it produced common table wine, and continued to do so until Philippe and his brothers took over the running of the estate in 1973. Then there was just 1 hectare of Mauzac, while today they have 40 hectares of Mauzac, 15 of Chardonnay and 5 of Chenin Blanc, as well as 20 hectares of Alicante, Carignan, and Cinsaut for Vin de Pays de l'Aude. They deliver these grapes to the co-operative of St-Hilaire, but they do make some *vin de pays* of their own, *cépage* Chardonnay. Our tasting showed a well-made wine, with some light varietal character, which they would eventually like to be able to age in wood. Certainly the future looks rosy for them, as they are making and selling their wine successfully and have plans for expansion.

Another producer with an excellent reputation is Jean-Pierre Robert at Domaine de Froin. Unfortunately he was not at home when we called, but we were welcomed by his daughters and his father, who explained his range of wines. The most individual is a wine labelled 'Au Temps de Pépé'. Pépé is an affectionate term for grandfather in French, and Pépé himself explained how this was the traditional method of Limoux. They use the ripest grapes, which are picked at the end of the vintage when they have a potential alcohol of 12°, rather than 9° or 10°. The fermentation is stopped by chilling the juice, and the wine is bottled and kept for a few months before being allowed to ferment again; it then undergoes ageing on the lees and *dégorgement* in the normal way. It was a delicious glass of wine, elegant and creamy.

Carte Ivoire, made purely from Mauzac and aged for eighteen months, is their basic wine; then there is Carte Noire, again pure Mauzac, but aged for three years; finally Dame Robert, a vintage wine, contains some Chenin and Chardonnay. In fact there are few vintage differences, though a non-vintage wine may occasionally be a mix of years. They also produce a *vin de pays* from Chardonnay, and more unusually a Cabernet Blanc de Noirs – in other words a pale pink wine from Cabernet grapes that are pressed immediately so that the juice absorbs very little colour from the skins. The most traditional still wine of the area is Limoux Nature, made from Mauzac. The example I tasted, from another producer, Guinot, was unexciting, with some dusty fruit and crisp acidity. As with the still wine of champagne, you can appreciate why sparkling wine is preferred in Limoux. To give the last word to Pépé: 'Blanquette should be yellow like gold and sweet like honey.'

CÔTES DE LA MALEPÈRE

If France divides broadly into three large viticultural regions, the Côtes de la Malepère are where two of them meet, for they lie on the frontier between Languedoc and Aquitaine. What the French call '*le partage des eaux*' between the Atlantic and the Mediterranean is at Castelnaudary, some 30 kilometres to the west.

The vineyards of the Côtes de la Malepère are a melting-pot of grape varieties. Those of the Midi mingle with those of Bordeaux, giving the wines an originality which is relatively recent in creation. The Massif de la Malepère is a range of hills just south west of the city of Carcassonne, with its medieval citadel, and north west of Limoux. The vineyards are on south-facing slopes around the villages of Routier, Alaigne and Malviès. Viticulture was virtually the only form of agriculture here, but in the early 1960s the wines produced in the region were fit for little other than blending with heady brews from North Africa. With the independence of Algeria in 1963, that market was lost. The Carignan and Aramon with which the region was planted gave neither yield nor alcohol, and certainly not quality. Something needed to be done to save the region's agricultural economy, with the result that various responsible organizations, notably the Chambre de l'Agriculture de l'Aude, decided to create an experimental vineyard to establish which were the most suitable grape varieties to plant in the region.

It had already been recognized that although the Côtes de la Malepère, positioned in the department of Aude, belong geographically to the Midi, climatically the area has more affinity with the south west. There are fewer hours of sunshine than on the coastal plain, and there is not the same lack of summer rain, so that vines here do not have to withstand periods of drought. The natural vegetation of the area illustrates the climatic mix: one finds the holmoaks and Alep pines of the Mediterranean, the *chêne pubescent* of the sub-Mediterranean, the common or pedunculate oak of the Atlantic and finally the beech of the mountains.

A research station was set up in 1965, at Domaine de Cazes in the village of Alaigne, to study the behaviour of several grape varieties in relation to the various microclimates and also to the soil of the region. The feasibility of introducing Bordeaux grape varieties was soon realized, and the present *encépagement* of Côtes de la Malepère consists of three principal varieties: Merlot, Cot and Cinsaut. A maximum of 60 per cent of each of these is allowed. The secondary varieties, of which a maximum of 30 per cent each is allowed, are Cabernet Franc, Cabernet Sauvignon, Grenache Noir and Syrah. The range and permitted percentages allow plenty of room for manoeuvre, but whereas it is possible to make Côtes de la Malepère without any Midi grape varieties, it would be very difficult not to include some Bordelais varieties. The first Bordelais varieties were planted in commercial vineyards about 1970 and the region first became a VDQS in 1976; but then bureaucracy decided that it should have been a *vin de pays* first, and it did not finally and conclusively become a VDQS until 1983.

The area is dominated by co-operatives. They were partly responsible for setting up the research station and they are now linked in one of the large producers' associations of the Midi, UCCOAR, which stands for Union des Caves Co-opératives de l'Ouest Audois et du Razès. (The Razès is a small area within the Côtes de la Malepère.) The UCCOAR may have originated in the area, but it has extended its activities far beyond, concentrating primarily on *vins de pays*. Nevertheless it is responsible for 90 per cent of the production of the Côtes de la Malepère and originated from a need to promote the area and to plan and control the investment necessary to finance the development of the vineyards. The co-operatives of the Côtes de la Malepère may have saved the region's viticulture, but I suspect that the few private properties feel somewhat swamped by their presence today.

I saw two independent producers. First of all I went to the sleepy village of Routier to the Château de Routier, where Michèle Lézaret runs the family estate. Her grandfather bought the château in 1960, and after studies in literature and law she took over the property in 1984 and turned her energies to agriculture. She had a functional cellar at the entrance to the village, and the russet leaves of her vines stretched across the valley in the autumn sunshine. Her 50 hectares of vines are planted principally with Merlot, Cabernet Franc, Cabernet Sauvignon, Grenache and Cot, as well as some Cinsaut, although she is not in favour of it, seeing it as a kind of Aramon. She makes pink as well as red wine, but white wine does not yet feature in the appellation. Her pink was fresh with fragrant raspberry fruit, while the red had some attractive flavours, but lacked the depth that will eventually come with older vines.

Château de Malviès, an elegant Bourbon Restoration house built under Charles X, is the principal building in another tiny village, Malviès, which cannot even boast a café to its name. It is owned by Mme Gourdou, whose husband is a surgeon in Toulouse; although she takes an active interest in her family property, the wine is made by her cellar manager. She has 45 hectares of vines, 20 of VDQS and 25 of *vin de pays*. The latter wine is Vin de Pays des Côtes de Prouille, but the name is rarely found on a label. Mme Gourdou's Côtes de la Malepère is made from 60 per cent Merlot and 20 per cent each of Cabernet Franc and Cabernet Sauvignon. Hers was the first wine of the area that I tasted, and after ten days in the vineyards of the Midi, the contrast was marked. The influence of Bordeaux was immediately apparent, for after the warm wines of the south, this Château de Malviès had the tannic structure of Cabernet and Merlot. Her wine spends a year in vat, followed by six months in barrels if it is a special *cuvée*, and then by six months in bottle before it is ready for sale. She also makes some pink, by the *saigné* method of running off the juice, from Cinsaut and Cabernet. Some Chardonnay has also been planted, but is not yet in production.

The research station continues to function under the direction of Camille Vilotte, who explained his more recent projects. He has 21 hectares of experimental vineyards planted with eighty-five different grape varieties, including varieties from elsewhere in France and new varieties that are crossings of established ones. For this he works under the guidance of the stations of the INRA (Institut National de la Recherche Agronomique) in Bordeaux and Montpellier. He is looking for grape varieties that both ripen early and give aromatic flavours, such as the Portan, a crossing of Grenache Noir and Portugais Bleu designed especially for *vin de primeur* – it is very fruity, but has absolutely no ageing potential. There is also the Chenonçon, a crossing of Grenache Noir and Jurançon Noir, which is being developed for *vins de pays*. It is light and fruity, easy to drink, without much tannin. Similarly there is the Arioloba, a crossing of Sauvignon Blanc and Arrufiat, named after its inventor who was Basque. It combines the aroma of the Sauvignon with the resistance to rot of the Arufiat. The Chasan, a cross of Chardonnay and Listan, is also planted to see how it grows in the area. These varieties were developed by the research station in Montpellier.

Côtes de la Malepère is a small VDQS with only about 200 hectares of vines and an average annual production of 10,000 hectolitres. But the potential of the area is much greater, for as the co-operative members change the composition of their vineyards to obtain the right combination of grape varieties, which can hardly be done overnight, so will the area gradually increase. For the moment the production of Côtes de la Malepère is a small drop compared to the region's production of *vin de pays* and (to a lesser extent) *vin de table*. They aspire to the status of an appellation, for as M. Vilotte said, it is that or nothing.

The Côtes de la Malepère are one of the forgotten vineyards of France, and I am ashamed to admit that I nearly missed them out of this book. We had driven from Carcassonne to Limoux and had passed close to them without realizing their existence. It was only a mention on the hotel wine list that sent us searching for the Château de Malviès. They deserve better recognition, for the combination of the warmth of the Mediterranean and the structure of the south west is unique.

CABARDÈS

Cabardès is separated from the Côtes de la Malepère by the city of Carcassonne and the plain, across which run the Canal du Midi and the Autoroute des Deux Mers that both link the Atlantic and the Mediterranean. In the east Cabardès adjoins the vineyards of the

Minervois, but it has more in common with the Côtes de la Malepère. Here, too, Midi and Bordeaux grape varieties meet. The regulations of the VDQS permit a similar diversity with Cabernet Sauvignon, Cot, Merlot, Grenache and Syrah. Cinsaut has been virtually eliminated from the area while a maximum of only 30 per cent Carignan is permitted, and although Fer Servadou is included in the regulations, it is not planted. The best wines of Cabardès are in practice made from Cabernet Sauvignon, Merlot and Grenache, and sometimes from Syrah.

As in the Côtes de la Malepère, the climate is part Mediterranean and part Atlantic, a fact which allows for the diversity of grape varieties. But it generally tends to be warmer and drier than in the Côtes de la Malepère and more like the Minervois, the vineyards being on the better-exposed slopes of the foothills of the Montagne Noire. Even so, Bordeaux grape varieties perform better here than in the Minervois. It is a very windy region, for the Marin and the Cers can both blow hard, though the Montagne Noire, the last outpost of the Massif Central, protects the area from the winds of the north. The soil is varied, too, so that Bordelais grape varieties can flourish on richer, deeper soils while those of the Midi are planted on thinner, poorer ones. Syrah does not perform so well here, as it is susceptible to rot if the weather is too wet.

Like so many of the wine regions of France, Cabardès fell into oblivion after the phylloxera crisis. 'Le gros rouge' was its prime production until people began to plant Cabernet and Merlot at the end of the 1960s, a move which saved the area from terminal decline. Cabardès, or the Côtes du Cabardès et de l'Orbiel to give the region its full name, was recognized as a VDQS in 1973 for red and pink wine; the same status has not yet been accorded to white wine, although there are some tentative plantings of Chardonnay. Altogether fourteen villages are covered, of which the most important are Aragon and Montolieu near the town of Conques-sur-Orbiel.

Co-operatives are much less important for Cabardès than for Côtes de la Malepère, as the co-operatives of the district concentrate their activities on *vin de table*, plus some Vin de Pays de l'Aude or the local Vin de Pays des Coteaux de la Cité de Carcassonne. The production of Cabardès is mainly in the hands of private producers, and there is a better feeling of cohesion than in the Côtes de la Malepère.

Mme Françoise de Lorgeril at Château Pennautier runs a total of 96 hectares, with a wide range of grape varieties including Cabernet Franc and Cot, as well as those in the appellation. She still has quite a high proportion of Carignan, which is slowly being reduced year by year, and has planted some Chardonnay, which is not yet in production. Château Pennautier is a handsome edifice mainly of 1620, though two wings were added later in rather austere grey stone. We talked in Mme de Lorgeril's elegant drawing-room and she explained that the château has never left her family, although the name has changed with the female succession. Their archives date back to 1700 and show that an ancestor, Pierre-Louis Rech de Pennautier, sent wine from his property to the French armies during the War of the Spanish Succession. In contrast, the cellar is modern and functional. Each grape variety is usually fermented separately, and blended in the following spring for relatively early bottling. The wine has a grassy, herbal flavour, not unlike a warmer version of a Chinon or Bourgueil.

The other leading producer is the Comte de Cibeins at the Château de Rayssac outside Conques-sur-Orbiel. He also owns the Château de Cabriac in the Corbières. His parents bought the run-down Château de Rayssac in 1962 and since then they have replanted the vineyards. In his 25 hectares he has a substantial amount of Cabernet Sauvignon and Grenache, some Merlot and Syrah, and a little Mourvèdre. He is the only producer to have planted Mourvèdre, which is allowed, but is considered to be at its limit here and difficult to ripen. M. de Cibeins, however, feels that it gives his wine an interesting structure and quality. It is planted on the edge of the *garrigues* in a vineyard that faces due south. He has also planted some Chardonnay to make a *vin de pays*, in the hope of eventually obtaining a white appellation.

Vinification methods are classic, with a little carbonic maceration for Syrah, Carignan and Mourvèdre. He vinifies in cement vats and has a few old wooden vats for storage. He usually blends his wines in the spring and begins bottling soon afterwards. He gave me my first taste of Cabardès, which was an interesting comparison with his Corbières. The Corbières was warm, full and southern, while the Cabardès had a different structure, with more tannin and flavours of pepper and blackcurrants. The wines can be drunk young but should have some ageing potential; as yet, however, there is little experience of this in the area. Like Côtes de la Malepère, they too would like the elevated status of an appellation; as a mere VDQS they suffer from the French snobbery about appellations, and, like Côtes de la Malepère again, they deserve better.

COTEAUX DU LANGUEDOC AND CLAIRETTE DU LANGUEDOC

Coteaux du Languedoc is a large appellation that stretches from Narbonne to Nîmes, covering many of the vineyards of Hérault and a small part of those of Aude. As well as the basic appellation there are fourteen *crus*: (travelling roughly west to east) Quatourze, La Clape, St-Chinian, Faugères, Picpoul de Pinet, Cabrières, St-Saturnin, Montpeyroux, St-Georges d'Orques, Pic St-Loup, Méjanelle, St-Drézery, St-Christol and Coteaux de Vérargues. In other words it is rather like Bordeaux, with a basic appellation covering the whole area and specific villages of particular quality singled out for special mention. The Coteaux du Languedoc was first recognized as a VDQS in 1961, whereas some of the *crus*, such as Quatourze, were given that status as early as 1951. The VDQS covered all three colours, and in particular the vineyards between Pézenas and Lodève and around the village of Langlade. In 1982 two of the *crus*, Faugères and St-Chinian, were recognized as appellations in their own right and in 1985 the all-encompassing appellation was created; initially it only covered red and pink wine, but it now includes white. There is another distinct white appellation, namely Clairette du Languedoc.

One of the most distinctive wines of the basic appellation of Coteaux du Languedoc comes from the Prieuré de St-Jean-de-Bébian just outside Pézenas. It is a ruined twelfth-century priory that is now owned by one of the most individual wine-growers of the Midi, Alain Roux. He has been there for ten years now, and although his father was a *négociant*, he had no particular training in wine-making and says that he is self-taught. He has 32 hectares on the slopes around the property, and is insistent that his vineyards have soil identical to those of Châteauneuf-du-Pape. They certainly have the large stones of the southern Rhône – though here they have come from the Massif Central – with virtually no earth. Nothing apart from vines will grow in such soil and the yields are tiny, an average of 30 hectolitres per hectare. M. Roux has planted all thirteen grape varieties of Châteauneuf-du-Pape; Grenache is the most important, but there are also sizeable percentages of Mourvèdre and Syrah, as well as Muscardin, Terret Noir, Vaccarèse, Counoise, Cinsaut, Clairette, Bourboulenc, Picpoul, Picardan and Roussanne. They are all fermented together, including the white grapes; he considers that this gives the wine better harmony. The grapes are picked when they are almost overripe and the fermentation lasts fifteen to twenty days. M. Roux feels very strongly that varietal wines are an oenological error and that a blend of several grape varieties gives a wine greater subtlety. When I suggested that there were several grape varieties in his vineyard that were not permitted in the Coteaux du Languedoc, he said, with cheerful disregard of the regulations, that it was of no importance. Who can tell, if the wine tastes good? And that it certainly does, with a flavour and concentration of fruit that is unique amongst the Coteaux du Languedoc.

Langlade, in the eastern part of Hérault, almost adjoining the Costières de Nîmes, is an important village for Coteaux du Langue-doc. It had a reputation for its wine back in the seventeenth century. Perhaps its most historic moment was in 1703 during the struggles with the Camisards, the Calvinists who rebelled against Louis XIV after the Revocation of the Edict of Nantes. The Maréchal de Montrevel was sent a consignment of wine from Langlade by the wife of the Lieutenant of Languedoc, Mme de Baville. It was intercepted by the Camisard leader, Jean Cavalier, with disastrous results: he was unprepared for the next battle and lost the fight.

The nineteenth-century authorities gave Langlade a passing mention, but otherwise its reputation has declined and its vineyards have fallen into disuse. There are diplomas for gold medals dating from the Paris fair of 1900, and at the beginning of the century Langlade was considered part of the Côtes du Rhône. The vineyards virtually disappeared with the First World War.

So often in the Midi it is a newcomer to viticulture who has made the most impact. In the village of Langlade that person is Henri Arnal, who was a manufacturer of steel girders until he sold his business in 1975 and became a wine-maker, fulfilling a long-standing ambition. As he said, 'I am lucky enough to live out my passion.' The Midi is in a pioneering period and he is determined to play his part. It takes time to change vineyards and men, but he firmly believes in his cause. He certainly has courage and determination and he sees the situation more clearly than most of his fellow wine-growers.

He believes they must make the most of their originality and not produce false Bordeaux, but real Coteaux du Languedoc. He has wines without Carignan or Cinsaut; if you do not have these varieties, you can dispense with Grenache as well and can make a pure Syrah or a pure Mourvèdre. Mourvèdre used to grow here before the phylloxera, when it was called the Espar and also the Plante de St-

Gilles from the nearby town of the Costières de Nîmes. However, it disappeared from the region as it proved too difficult to graft. M. Arnal would like Langlade to be a *cru* of Coteaux du Languedoc, but it will take time. There is great potential in the *garrigues* of the village of Langlade, but they need to be cleared of scrub. The other growers in the village are not interested or sufficiently motivated, so for the moment he is something of a voice crying in the wilderness.

M. Arnal began replanting his vineyards in 1976 and now has 20 hectares, 10 of Coteaux du Languedoc and 10 of Vin de Pays de la Vaunage – mainly for white wine, with a little red from Merlot and Cabernet Sauvignon. His Coteaux du Languedoc vineyards are planted with one-third each of Grenache, Syrah and Mourvèdre, providing an amazing example of a Midi wine without the ubiquitous Carignan. From these he makes several different wines, experimenting with the blend. We tasted one wine made from 40 per cent each of Syrah and Grenache and 20 per cent Mourvèdre. Any more Mourvèdre would completely overwhelm the rest, as he found with the 1985 which was one-third of each. Grenache gives a good base, but it ages badly. A pure Mourvèdre was perfumed and fruity, with some tannin, but without the meaty, animal character of Bandol. His wine is not destined for a long life and it should have immediate appeal. To use his own musical metaphor, his red wine is Rossini and not Wagner. Whichever composer it took after, it tasted delicious with a *ragoût d'olives* from his own olive trees.

Chenin Blanc has been planted experimentally, and a pure Chenin from vines that had only been in production for two years was rounded and fruity, again without the sharp acidity you sometimes find in the Loire valley. M. Arnal also makes a blend of one-third Chenin to two-thirds Grenache Blanc, for on its own Grenache Blanc is too aggressive. He has also planted a little Chardonnay; the 1985, made from three-year-old vines, had the makings of an interesting wine but was still rather reticent.

Great care is taken with vinification methods. Fermentation temperatures are meticulously controlled and nitrogen is used to avoid any oxidation. There are no wooden barrels, only metal vats, and the use of sulphur dioxide is kept to a minimum. Grape varieties are fermented separately and then blended as desired.

Wine for M. Arnal is his hobby, or, more poetically, what the French call his *violon d'Ingres*; but it is more than just a hobby, it is a passion. He has a challenge and seems a contented man, living with his two dogs Giscard and Anne-Aymone, who were born the day Giscard d'Estaing was elected President, and making wine of which he could be proud. As yet, however, he is too modest: he does not want to establish a reputation for himself until his wine is better. He is going in the right direction, and it is people like him who will give a direction to the Coteaux du Languedoc.

The vineyards of Clairette du Languedoc total 1,200 hectares in ten villages between Pézenas and Clermont l'Hérault, namely Adissan (which once had a particular reputation for its Clairette), Aspiran, Le Bosc, Cabrières, Ceyrac, Fontès, Nizas, Paulan, Pérat and St-André-de-Sagonis. Most Clairette du Languedoc is produced by the village co-operatives and is of indifferent quality. There are, however, two good independent producers.

Clairette du Languedoc was the earliest appellation of the area, created in 1948. The sole grape variety is Clairette, but the regulations failed to define the method of vinification. Consequently there were enormous variations, so that the wine could be young and dry, old and maderized, sweet, and even a *vin doux naturel*; as a result, production fell. It was the Jany family at Domaine Condamine-Bertrand to the north of Pézenas who did much to restore the reputation of Clairette du Languedoc. The estate is now run by Bertrand Jany, an enthusiastic young man who talked about his grandfather's efforts for the appellation, and of his great aunt who had been the secretary of the growers' association. Bertrand Jany took over the family property in 1980, and at that time he was the largest producer of white wine in the area, apart from the co-operatives, and the only one to make Clairette du Languedoc.

Clairette, with its small, thick-skinned grapes, is a difficult variety to grow. It is relatively resistant to disease, but can suffer from *coulure* and needs correct pruning in the *gobelet* system. M. Jany told us of an old wine-grower's belief that if you prune your vines at the old moon, this will prevent *coulure* the next year. All his Clairette vines are very old, planted by his grandfather or even his great-grandfather, but he will gradually renew them. If Clairette is too ripe, it makes very alcoholic wine; and it can ripen very quickly, gaining as much as half a degree in a day if the weather is very hot. It used to be picked at 13° or 14°, but it makes much better wine at 12°.

Compared to other white grape varieties in the area, Clairette ripens late and is not picked until the middle of September. Vinification must be carried out with meticulous care as Clairette has a tendency to oxidize. The grapes are picked in the morning when they are cool and the pressed juice, of which only the first pressing is used, is left to cool for twelve hours at 6°C so that it will fall clear. Yeast and bentonite are added, and the fermentation is controlled at 16–17°C and lasts about three weeks. There is no malolactic fermentation, in order to retain the acidity, and the wine is fined, cold-treated and bottled in November.

It is a wine to drink when it is young and fresh, for it does not age well. We sat in the elegant salon of the château beneath a fine painted ceiling and tasted the 1986 vintage; it had a distinctive flavour, with hints of almonds and some leafy fruit. For M. Jany, aniseed is one of the characteristics of Clairette. It is quite a full mouthful and certainly the most individual white wine of the Midi, with some original regional flavour.

Another young grower has followed M. Jany's example with Clairette – Jean-Louis Randon at Domaine St-André, just outside Pézenas. He has some fifty-year-old vines, which only give an average yield of about 18 hectolitres per hectare. His wine is fermented slowly at 18°C and the result is a full, rather nutty, biscuity-flavoured wine.

No wine-grower can make a living from Clairette du Languedoc alone, and M. Jany's other wines also deserve a mention. He has other white grapes which make a *vin de pays* or a white Coteaux du Languedoc. Ugni Blanc and Carignan Blanc are disappearing and he is concentrating on Grenache Blanc, plus some experimental Roussanne, Chenin Blanc and the new variety called Chasan, which is a cross between Chardonnay and Listan. It is possible that Chenin Blanc may eventually be included in the appellation of Coteaux du Languedoc, as it is generally recognized that the traditional white grape varieties of the Midi need a boost of flavour. His first vintage of Chenin Blanc was 1986; the wine we tasted had a dry, honeyed character and was fuller and less acid than its counterpart from the Loire.

Red Coteaux du Languedoc also forms a substantial part of his production. For this he has a high 30 per cent of Syrah, the same of Grenache and 10 per cent of Mourvèdre, which was planted only five years ago; the balance is made up of Carignan and Cinsaut. No Carignan has been planted on the estate for twenty years and now hardly any is left. Cinsaut can be useful to reduce the alcohol level in a blend – you add Cinsaut instead of water to dilute the wine! It also makes good pink wine when blended with Grenache.

As well as the southern grape varieties M. Jany has some Merlot and Cabernet Sauvignon, and (unusually) some Petit Verdot which is not really allowed. He would also like to plant some Pinot Noir, but that is not permitted either. The Bordelais grape varieties can be made into Vin de Pays de l'Hérault, Côtes de Ceressou or Côtes de Thongue. The Petit Verdot is vinified with the Cabernet Sauvignon and he would like to age it in small barrels. In contrast, the Merlot makes an attractive wine for early drinking. The Coteaux de Languedoc is aged in large barrels during the cooler months, between October and May, but as they are old ones that belonged to his great-grandfather, he is tending to use them less, for wood is only interesting if it is in good condition. All this promises well for the future.

Quatourze

Quatourze is the westernmost *cru* of the Coteaux du Languedoc. The vineyards are within the parish of Narbonne and many are sadly being eaten up by suburban development. There is only one grower of any note, Yvon Ortola at Château de Notre-Dame-de-Quatourze, with 32 hectares of vines. The co-operative accounts for a good quarter of the production and there are a couple of other producers of some size, but many of the vineyards are being abandoned as the land is so much more valuable for building. M. Ortola, who is president of the growers' association, fights a battle every five years when the *plan d'occupation du sol* is revised, to ensure that the area of Quatourze continues to be registered as an agricultural zone. For the moment there are some 200 hectares in production, but the total could be doubled.

Narbonne itself is the northern limit of the area, while to the south it is bounded by the Étang de Bages, to the west by the motorway, and to the east by the plain of Narbonne. The vineyards are on a plateau that rises only some 17 metres above sea-level. There are two theories as to the origin of the name Quatourze, both based on the fact that *quatourze* means 'fourteen' in Occitan. The area is known for its lack of rainfall, so that the wine made here is strong and alcoholic, often reaching a natural 14°; alternatively, in the Middle

Ages when taxes were based on a percentage (usually a tenth), the king only took a fourteenth in this arid and infertile land.

M. Ortola is a fourth-generation Algerian, who bought this abandoned property in 1974. In Algeria he grew clementines and wheat as well as grapes. He feels at home here for there are figs and almonds as well as vines; he has adapted happily to life on mainland France, but obviously it has not been easy. His first vintage in 1975 made just 720 hectolitres of wine.

When Quatourze became a VDQS in 1951, Carignan was the sole grape variety. Now the composition conforms to that of the other wines of the Coteaux du Languedoc, so that M. Ortola's vineyards are planted with 40 per cent Carignan, 10 per cent Mourvèdre and Syrah, 20 per cent Grenache and 25 per cent Cinsaut. The remaining 5 per cent are Macabeo for white wine, but it is really too hot an area for successful white. But there is more rain than in Algeria and they are allowed to irrigate between 15 June and 15 July, which can give good results, with a yield of about 60 hectolitres per hectare. The soil is poor and pebbly but clay-based, so that it tends to retain the water, and ditches have had to be dug for drainage.

M. Ortola's cellars are functional, with cement vats, but well equipped for controlling the fermentation temperatures. The white and pink fermentations are kept at 17°, while the red is fermented in the classic manner, usually for about ten days at 29°C. Syrah is picked first, then Grenache and finally Carignan, and each is fermented separately and blended after the malolactic fermentation is finished. This is not a wine to age – 'We leave that to the Bordelais.' Certainly the red wine had a warm, peppery flavour, making an agreeably chewy mouthful of wine. The pink, made half from Grenache and half from Cinsaut, was fresh with a tang of raspberry. The white was the least successful of the three; at present it is made purely from Macabeo, but M. Ortola is considering Rolle or Marsanne as possible additions to improve the rather dull, peppery flavour of the Macabeo.

M. Ortola is an enthusiast and described himself as '*un amoureux du vin*', who could not imagine life without it. He certainly needs all his enthusiasm, for one suspects that life is pretty tough when you are trying to maintain an appellation against the odds. There are no young people left except M. Ortola's own son, and everyone thought he was mad to buy land in Quatourze when his fellow-growers were being tempted by the lure of building contracts. Yet you can see why M. Ortola felt at home here, for it is a beautiful spot. Hundred-year-old olive trees line the driveway, and from the cellar door you look over the vineyards; there is a lovely distant view of the unfinished cathedral of Narbonne. The sun shines most days, but the wind is 'diabolical'. Indeed, the day we were there the Mistral was blowing hard. Somehow the vines seem to survive.

La Clape

The hill of La Clape, the rocky mountain to the north of Narbonne, was once an island. It became part of the mainland in the Middle Ages, when the River Aude silted up. Until that time Narbonne was an important port and a prosperous city; the unfinished cathedral of St-Just demonstrates both its former aspirations and the dramatic effect of the loss of its sea trade. La Clape is a wild, rocky outcrop that contrasts sharply with the surrounding plain and the gaudy seaside resort of Narbonne-Plage. The road round the mountain is spectacular: the scenery changes sharply from mountain to sea, with the blue water contrasting vividly with the rough, scrub-covered hillsides.

La Clape is one of the better-known vineyards of the Coteaux du Languedoc. At home it benefits from the tourist trade of the Mediterranean, and in English-speaking countries its name has unfortunate associations which make it memorable to those who have never drunk it.

The most individual grower of the appellation is Jean Ségura at Domaine La Rivière-Haute. He was proud to tell us that he had flown with the RAF during the war. He came originally from North Africa and his father-in-law bought the estate in 1955. He was serious and friendly, and had firm views on how his wine should be made. There are 1,000 hectares of vines on and surrounding the mountain of La Clape, of which 950 hectares are planted with red grapes. M. Ségura has 13 of the 50 hectares of white grapes – Bourboulenc, Grenache Blanc and Terret Blanc – and unlike most producers of La Clape, he concentrates on white wine.

M. Ségura described himself as 'an ecologist of wine', with very definite views of how wine should be made. He adds no sulphur at the vintage – it's filthy stuff – and he does not clean his juice before fermentation, for otherwise the wine is too light and important elements are removed. He uses neither pesticides nor fertilizers in the vineyard, for he prefers to leave such things to nature; and with the drying sea winds, there is no problem with rot. His belief in the balance of nature goes to the extent of encouraging swallows to nest in his cellar, which is more like a large barn and has cement vats. The birds return to the same nests each year, and pieces of cardboard are fixed to the rafters at strategic points to prevent any problem with droppings! Spiders' webs are left undisturbed, for the spiders eat the flies, and there is a resident toad who answers to the name of Auguste.

M. Ségura is proud of his wine, and rightly so, for it is very good – an old-fashioned wine in the very best sense of the word. His white La Clape, on which his reputation rests, is made from 40 per cent Bourboulenc, 12 per cent Grenache Blanc and 48 per cent Terret Blanc. He believes in 'the marriage of grape varieties'. The wine has quite a deep golden colour, with a rather closed nose, but on the palate the 1986 vintage was rich, fat and rounded, and almost sweet on the finish. It was full and long, with flavours of nuts and honey. It is not aged in wood, only in vat, and bottled as required.

He also makes a red wine, that he described as *un vin de conversation*. It comes from a blend of Carignan, Syrah, Mourvèdre, Cinsaut and Grenache, and is fruity and perfumed, with a dry finish, but without the stature of the white wine.

Even within a very small area there are quite considerable variations of climate and soil, and a difference of altitude of 250 metres between the highest and lowest vineyards of La Clape. Those nearest to Narbonne itself tend to face north, while those further east face the sea and benefit from the sea breezes. The soil ranges from sand near the sea and where the river has silted up to clay from the erosion of the mountain. This is one of the sunniest parts of France, enjoying 3,000 hours of sunshine annually and rivalled only by Hyères in Provence. Even Corsica, the most southerly part of France, only registers 2,500 hours. M. Ségura's vineyards lie at only 16 metres above sea-level, while those of Château La Rouquette-sur-Mer, in the heart of the mountain, are much higher.

Château La Rouquette-sur-Mer is, as its name implies, on the seaward side of the mountain. The present château is less than a hundred years old, but there is a much older building lying lost in the *garrigues*. This was abandoned after the phylloxera, when people noticed that the vines survived in the sandier soil nearer the sea and the vineyards shifted towards the coast. Today the reverse is taking place. The estate now belongs to Jacques Boscary, who took over the family property about twenty years ago and replanted the vineyards. The vines had already been destroyed during the war, but when his grandfather was restoring the property in 1945, he followed the bad advice of the Ministry of Agriculture to replant with hybrids. So M. Boscary had to start again, which he did with Grenache in particular, on the advice of M. Dufays from Château Nalys in Châteauneuf-du-Pape, who even gave him his first Grenache vines. He cleared the *garrigues* of scrub and turned the flatter land over to *vin de pays*.

M. Boscary makes both red and white wine, as well as a little pink. For white he has Bourboulenc and Clairette; when pushed, he admitted to 'a little experiment' with Marsanne, but was reticent about conclusions. For the present, Bourboulenc is very much the dominant grape variety in his white wine, which is delicious – quite different from that of M. Ségura, but similar in that it avoids the sterile squeaky-cleanliness of many supposedly well-vinified wines of the Midi, for which so much attention is paid to fermentation temperatures and acidity levels that the wine is devoid of any regional characteristics. M. Boscary's wine, which is followed by Marc Dubernet, has a delicate fragrance with a fresh, slightly nutty flavour and a gentle 'dustiness'. M. Boscary himself said the bouquet was the smell of vine flowers in the vineyard, but sadly my walks in the vineyards during the flowering have been so infrequent that I am unable to confirm that opinion.

The grapes at La Rouquette-sur-Mer are all hand-picked. Spaniards from the same village in southern Spain have been coming here for the last twenty-seven years and the same man has always led the team, so it is a friendly, colourful occasion, unspoilt by mechanical harvesters. The red wine is made of Syrah, Cinsaut, Grenache and Carignan. The Carignan is vinified by carbonic maceration, while the rest undergo a traditional vinification, each variety separately, before blending. The cellar is functional and well run. Some of the red wine is aged for a few months in new Bordelais barrels, which are only used twice. M. Boscary's great ambition is to build an underground cellar beneath the mountain of La Clape itself, but for the moment that is no more than a dream.

Both red wines had an attractive fruity pepperiness, but the oak-aged wine had a more solid structure, with more tannin. M. Boscary plans to increase the percentage of Syrah at the expense of Carignan, while still maintaining the latter as a base of 40 per cent. He would also like to plant some Mourvèdre.

The ideal composition of the vineyard is one of the moot points of the area. M. Braqueslanges at Château Moujan, which is the first property you reach as you approach La Clape from Narbonne, is convinced that Carignan ripens well here, contrary to its performance in Hérault where it does not ripen properly. It is a mistake to group the vineyards around Narbonne with those around Montpellier, as conditions are quite different. But they are in the minority here and so will be obliged, like the rest of the Coteaux du Languedoc, to reduce Carignan to 40 per cent by 1990. Here it gives body and tannin, but not around Montpellier. When I asked if he had Carignan, the reply was 'Certainly, fortunately.' For him Mourvèdre is the subject of much questioning: because his vineyards are on the north side of the mountain, away from the sea, he is not sure whether it will ripen properly. No one has Mourvèdre of sufficient age for the results to be assessed, while Grenache is unsatisfactory because its sensitivity to *coulure* leads to low and erratic yields. In 1986 it gave just 18 hectolitres per hectare. M. Braqueslanges was one of the first to plant Syrah here some fifteen years ago, and is happy with it, but you must not have too much. As for Cinsaut, it's like water – juice with neither colour nor alcohol.

In addition to these Midi grape varieties there is also some Merlot; but 'the Bordelais don't want us to compete with them', so this is used for a Vin de Pays des Coteaux de Narbonne. Some white vines have also been planted, Malvoisie and Bourboulenc, as well as Grenache Blanc, but for the moment they too are destined for *vin de pays* as they are too young for the appellation wine.

Château Moujan is a very old estate with 74 hectares of vines. M. Braqueslanges' wife's great-grandfather was the engineer responsible for levelling plains in the area around Narbonne, so that the vineyards could be flooded as a preventative measure against the phylloxera louse. The life-cycle of the louse includes forty days below ground, so if the vineyards are flooded for that period, the louse will die. With vineyards at only 80 centimetres above sea-level, they quite often flood naturally anyway. This was also done in the Camargue and around Agde in Hérault.

The cellars at Château Moujan did not seem a model of hygiene, with large old barrels and cement vats, and more unusually some 200-year-old stone fermentation vats. The wine, however was remarkably good. The best wine is made by carbonic maceration from the oldest vines on the steepest slopes. It was peppery and perfumed, quite full-bodied, but not a wine to age. M. Braqueslanges also considers his pink to be a speciality, with its fresh taste of raspberries.

Domaine de la Pech Céleyran is separated from the main mountain of La Clape as the estate stands on an isolated hill of its own. (*Pech* means 'hill' in the local patois.) It is owned by the St-Exupéry family, who have cousins at Château Tiregand in Pécharmant. The property also has associations with Toulouse-Lautrec. In 1850 the estate was divided between two sisters. The elder, Adèle Tapie de Céleyran, the mother of Toulouse-Lautrec, took what was then considered to be the better half, with vineyards on the plain, while the younger took this half with vineyards on the hill opposite, where today the better wine is made. In the Toulouse-Lautrec museum in Albi there are water-colours painted at Château Céleyran.

The Domaine de la Pech Céleyran has belonged to the St-Exupéry family for three generations. The estate consists of 80 hectares of vines, half in the appellation of La Clape and half producing Vin de Pays des Côtes de Pérignan. The appellation vineyards are planted mainly with Grenache, plus some Mourvèdre, Syrah and Carignan, while for *vin de pays* they have Merlot, Cabernet Sauvignon and Malbec, as well as the more traditional Cinsaut and Alicante Bouschet. They also make two white *vins de pays* from Macabeo and Chardonnay. Malbec has been grown here for twenty-three years, while Cabernet Sauvignon was planted in 1970 and Merlot in 1975. The Chardonnay, grafted on to Alicante Bouschet, only came into production in 1987.

The striking feature of the cellars is thirty-seven 300-hectolitre barrels. They were built in 1850 with the cellar, and are an impressive sight. The red La Clape spends two years in them after a traditional vinification lasting ten to fifteen days, with each grape variety fermented separately and blended in the following January. In fact I preferred the *vin de pays*, which had not stayed so long in wood. It contains a high proportion of Merlot and has an attractive smoky character, which comes apparently from the soil, as it repeated in their other wines. In contrast the La Clape, made mainly from Grenache and Syrah, was firmer and drier, with a slightly herbal flavour, but none the less a good taste on which to leave the area.

St-Chinian

St-Chinian and Faugères are the two most important *crus* of the Coteaux du Languedoc, for they were both appellations in their own right, St-Chinian since 1982, before they were brought under the umbrella appellation of Coteaux du Languedoc in 1985. St-Chinian is a large area, covering twenty villages with 2,500 hectares of delimited vineyards, stretching from the Minervois in the west to Faugères in the east. The village of St-Chinian is the largest of the appellation, more the size of a small country town, while others are mere hamlets. It has a Maison du Vin in the Grand Rue where you can buy and taste wines from all the producers of the appellation.

The very earliest records of vines in St-Chinian go back to the ninth century, when a monk named Aniane (who was to become St Aniane, thus giving his name to St Chinian) planted vines in 826. During the Middle Ages viticulture was a subject of dispute between lay landlords and the Church, which tried to maintain a monopoly over the sale of wine. The town of St-Chinian was destroyed during the Wars of Religion in the sixteenth century. In 1590 it was recorded that the Duc de Montmorency ordered the villages of St-Chinian, Berlou and Pierrerue to provide him each week with eighteen sheep and three *charges* of wine.

Viticulture has evidently played a vital part in the economy of the region throughout its history. Little else will grow on the rugged foothills of the Cévennes, which form the greater part of the appellation. The area is divided geologically by the River Vernazobre, with quite different soils to the north and to the south, giving two completely different wines. The north western half of the area is based on schist, and includes St-Chinian and the villages of Roquebrun, Berlou, and Murviel, while the soil in the southern part of the appellation is a mixture of limestone and clay. Consequently there are two very different styles of St-Chinian. The wine produced from schist is light, eminently fruity and destined for early drinking, while that from the clay and limestone is more solid and substantial, and benefits from some ageing.

St-Chinian boasts the leading co-operative of the Midi. Ask any reputable producer in the region who else he rates in Languedoc, and the co-operative of Berlou is bound to feature in his list. The Cave de Berlou was founded in 1965, which makes it almost the youngest co-operative in the Midi. That of nearby Roquebrun came one year later. The motive for this late development was the search for quality. The wines of Berlou had formerly been destined for '*vin de médecin*' to boost the weaker wines of the plains, but the situation had become no longer acceptable. Something had to be done, and the mayor of Berlou, Georges Dardé (who is also the president of the co-operative), proved to be the leading force in the creation of this exceptional institution that sets an example to the others of the region.

Another wine-grower of St-Chinian described Georges Dardé as an enlightened dictator, for although he has had no education, he has intelligence and flair, he knows what he wants for his co-operative, and he makes sure he gets it. He enjoys the whole-hearted support of his members. Under the guidance of Marc Dubernet this co-operative produces some of the most attractive wines of the Midi. It is equipped for vinification by carbonic maceration and it is on this technique that its reputation is based. Its wines include Berlou Prestige and another brand name, Schisteil, from a fusion of schist and *soleil*, the two principal elements that contribute to the wine.

Since 1978 increasing amounts of Grenache, Syrah and Mourvèdre are being planted in the area. The appellation regulations dictate a maximum of 50 per cent Carignan and there is talk of reducing that still further. For the moment Grenache must represent a minimum of 10 per cent, a proportion which will be increased to 20 per cent in 1990. At the same time Syrah and/or Mourvèdre will increase from 5 to 10 per cent. There is a feeling that Carignan should not be decreased much more as it gives the wine acidity and backbone, without which the wine would be too soft. Cinsaut is the variety to eliminate as it is too light and too soft, with excessive yields. Unfortunately some misguided people have been replacing Carignan with Cinsaut, under the illusion that Cinsaut was preferable, which it is not. The original plantings of Grenache were done without any thought of clonal selection, but today only the correct clones can be planted. Syrah is now quite accepted in the appellation, whereas Mourvèdre is only just beginning to be planted. There are just 5 hectares in the village, and these are not yet in production.

The village of Berlou was called Berloup in the Middle Ages and its name is thought to have come from the Latin *ver luporum*, meaning 'spring of wolves'. Maybe there were once wolves in the nearby Forêt des Albières. At the end of the nineteenth century the Hérault directory recorded that the village of Berlou produced excellent wine that rivalled that of Roussillon.

The co-operative makes two styles of red wine, one by carbonic maceration and the other by a classic vinification, as well as white and pink wine. The vintage is not until the end of September at Berlou for the vineyards, planted on terraced hillsides, are at an altitude of 200 metres and the nights are cool, so that the grapes ripen slowly.

The wind is another peculiarity of the microclimate: the Cers can blow hard and there can be storms during the summer, but otherwise there is very little summer rain. Nor does the soil retain water. A storm at the equinox in September can double the size of the vintage without necessarily spoiling the quality by overdiluting the wine; a local saying holds that 'the crop goes away during the summer and comes back at vintage time'. The best grapes are vinified by carbonic maceration, the selection being computer-controlled and stream-lined. The grapes are heated to 30°C and the fermentation usually lasts for twelve or fourteen days. This wine ages better than that of a traditional vinification which lasts only six days, as there is more tannin from the longer maceration.

Unlike many of the co-operatives of the Midi, that of Berlou faces a positive future. There is no doubt that it is on the road to success and will do much for the reputation of its appellation. Georges Dardé and his director Bernard Goût make an excellent team and they are good publicists of their wine. Lunch in the village café provided an opportunity to taste the range and there was no doubt that Berlou Prestige was the perfect accompaniment to a magnificent jugged hare. The enlightened dictator was in an expansive mood as he had just become a grandfather.

Although the co-operatives of St-Chinian account for 60 per cent of the production of the appellation, there are several important independent producers. François Guy at Château Coujan near Murviel-les-Béziers is one of the largest, with 100 hectares of vines. You drive out of the village along a dirt track lined with vines and ending at an elegantly decaying château. The vineyards are full of fossilized coral, which looks rather like pieces of honeycomb. You find it when you dig deep into the soil, and it provides excellent drainage.

Asked about grape varieties, M. Guy replied, 'I have them all.' He makes St-Chinian, Vin de Pays des Coteaux de Murviel and even some basic *vin de table*. His St-Chinian is made from 30 per cent Cinsaut, 30 per cent Grenache and 40 per cent Mourvèdre. He does not like Carignan as it is too coarse, and although he has had Syrah for twenty-five years, he says that it does not satisfy him; on the other hand he is delighted with Mourvèdre. His *vin de pays* comes from 75 per cent Merlot and 25 per cent Cabernet Sauvignon, and everything else that is left goes into the *vin de table*.

M. Guy is hospitable, and a tasting of his wines in his cellar – with two rows of enormous old barrels forming a gallery – demonstrated the extent of his enthusiasm and love of experimentation. We began with a *vin de pays*, a Sauvignon, with a smoky tang of gooseberries. The juice is given three hours' skin contact and then fermented, beginning at 12°C and rising to 20°C. He is not so keen on pink though he does make a little, mainly from Cinsaut as it does not have much colour anyway. And now, 'We move on to serious things, that is to say, red wine.' First we tried a 1986 St-Chinian, for which the three grape varieties are fermented separately and then blended; this he described as a happy marriage, after which the wine spends ten or eleven months in large barrels. On the nose it has lots of red berry fruit, with peppery tannin on the palate.

We then tried the 1982 St-Chinian, which was the first vintage with any significant quantity of Mourvèdre. People said it would not ripen properly here, but M. Guy has proved them wrong. The nose had the meaty, animal character of Mourvèdre, what the French call *viandé*, with some lovely rich fruit, slightly reminiscent of liquorice. It was supple and rounded, with a good balance of tannin and acidity and a lovely long finish. He had tried carbonic maceration, but is not very happy with it and prefers traditional vinification; in any case, this enables most of his grapes to be picked by machine.

M. Guy was one of the very first people to plant Cabernet Sauvignon and Merlot back in 1966, when the INAO authorized them. His first vinification in 1968 consisted of just 50 hectolitres, for which his broker was prepared to pay him a little more than for his Aramon, but less than for the wine made from *teinturier* varieties like Alicante Bouschet. Such was the standard view of the innovatory grape varieties. As he could only sell the wine in bulk at a ridiculous price, he began to bottle it. We compared two vintages, 1985 and 1975. The 1985 was rich and powerful with a slightly bitter finish, while the 1975 was much more elegant, with flavours of mint – indicative of what the 1985 could become with age. There are no very marked vintage differences in this part of France. Cabernet and Merlot are early-ripening varieties here, so they have a short vegetation cycle and are usually picked before the equinoctial storms.

M. Guy's enthusiasm is endless. This year he has picked Viognier for the first time and made four demijohns of wine 'just for fun'. Viognier is not officially allowed in St-Chinian, but in the Rhône valley it gives interesting wine, and more adventurous growers consider it another possibility to enliven the generally dull white wines of the Midi. As in the Rhône valley, however, it is quite difficult to grow. M. Guy views the appellation with the eyes of someone who is not an outsider, but who has seen the outside world. He was trained in law before the war with thoughts of a career in the civil service, but he was the only son amongst five children, and so took over the family property. He has travelled to other continents and enthused about California, comparing it with Languedoc. 'California is here,' he said, gesticulating at eye level, 'while Languedoc is down here,' the hand now at knee level, making a motion of waves, 'with a few islands. I am an island!'

M. Guy also has a wicked sense of humour. He realized that our practical experience of wine-making was limited, and inquired whether we had ever put our noses right into the fumes of a fermenting vat of wine. We admitted we had not, so there we were, kneeling on the cellar floor to sniff the vapours from a vat beneath our feet. It is an experience I shall never forget, or wish to repeat, with a sensation of sharp needles of carbon dioxide attacking the back of the nostrils. We were also given the dubious treat of trying some untreated olives. The oval-shaped green Les Lucques may be the best olives of the Midi, but until they have been treated they taste unpleasantly astringent.

Although St-Chinian is mainly a red wine, some good pink is also made here, notably at Domaine Guiraud-Boyer. Patricia Guiraud is one of the many examples of an outsider coming to the area with a fresh, open-minded attitude. She is slowly persuading her husband to replace their Aramon and Carignan, from which their red is still made. The pink, a *vin d'une nuit*, which comes from Syrah, Cinsaut and Grenache, was a delicious mouthful of fresh raspberry fruit and a fitting taste on which to leave St-Chinian.

Faugères

The appellation of Faugères, created in 1982, three years before that of Coteaux du Languedoc, covers seven villages that lie between the valley of the river Orb and the plain of Béziers, in the foothills of the mountains of the Espinouse, an outpost of the Massif Central. This is some of the most beautiful countryside of the Midi vineyards. The land is hilly, and narrow lanes wind from hamlet to hamlet. Little will grow apart from vines on this poor soil of schist, and although there are some olive and chestnut trees and a few animals grazing, vines remain the sole agricultural activity of any importance.

The soil of the vineyards of Faugères is the same schist as in the adjoining vineyards of St-Chinian. The grape varieties are the same too, though Faugères has been slower to introduce the *cépages améliorateurs*. The first Grenache was planted just after the war by Gilbert Alquier and his estate also has a high proportion of both Syrah and Mourvèdre, but others have been slow to follow his example. At present the appellation regulations require a minimum of only 5 per cent of Mourvèdre and Syrah together and 10 per cent of Grenache, which for the 1990 vintage must be increased to 10 and 20 per cent respectively. Fifty per cent is the maximum percentage for both Cinsaut and Carignan.

Grape varieties and vinification methods vary with the individual. There are wines made purely by carbonic maceration and wines made only by traditional methods; wines with a high proportion of Syrah or Mourvèdre and wines with hardly any at all. Some cellars have the traditional old oak casks, and in others they have been abandoned.

The co-operatives, of which there are three (at Antignac, Laurens and in the village of Faugères itself), dominate the production, but in addition there are some twenty private growers who bottle their wine. The co-operative at Faugères was created in 1960 (making it one of the most recent in the area) to help the many small producers who were unable to equip their own cellars. Its original aim was to concentrate on making Faugères, but inevitably it was too difficult to exclude the *vin de table*, and Faugères only accounts for half of its production. Even so, it makes 15,000 hectolitres out of the total average annual production of 60,000 hectolitres of Faugères. The area of the appellation at present stands at 1,200 hectares, with an average yield of 50 hectolitres per hectare. The area has potential for expansion as hillsides are cleared of scrub and people plant the right grape varieties for the appellation. But there is still too much Carignan and Aramon and not everyone has Syrah yet, which is obligatory for Faugères. The story is the same as elsewhere: the old members of the co-operative are not interested in change, and there are not many young people who are sufficiently motivated. Sadly the quality of the wine is unexciting, but the taste of Faugères should not be judged by that of its co-operative.

Bernard Vidal at La Liguière is certainly not lacking in energy, for while his father had the estate of Château de la Liguière, he created his own estate. He has now taken over his father's vineyards and has 60 hectares of Faugères altogether, planted with 20 per cent Carignan, 30 per cent Grenache, 30 per cent Cinsaut and the rest Syrah and Mourvèdre. There is more Syrah than Mourvèdre, and the Mourvèdre is only just coming into production. M. Vidal is an enthusiastic exponent of carbonic maceration and all his red wine is made that way. He was the first to vinify Faugères by this method back in 1967, guided by the man who introduced the technique to the Midi, the father of the oenologist Marc Dubernet. His wine is not at all typical of Faugères, for although it is well made, it has the distinctive taste of carbonic maceration which tends to camouflage any regional characteristics. A blend with a traditional vinification would give a more typical taste.

M. Saur at Château de Haut-Fabrègues near Cabrerolles is a more traditional producer, although his family have been there for only twenty years. The château itself goes back to the sixteenth century, when it was part of the estate of the lords of Grézan until it was sold at the Revolution. Cabrerolles takes its name from the herds of goats that used to abound in the area. This was a region predominantly of stock-rearing until about a hundred years ago when people began to plant more vines. On M. Saur's 50 hectares of vines, which are untypical in being in one large parcel around the château, he has 20 per cent Carignan, 20 per cent Cinsaut and 25 per cent Grenache, the balance being made up of Syrah, which he first planted in 1979, and Mourvèdre. He is particularly keen on increasing the Mourvèdre as it is good for ageing, and he finds that it performs well in the acid soil of Faugères. It ripens at the same time as Carignan, but the results are much better.

White wine was included in the VDQS in 1948, but hardly any is made today. However, M. Saur has carried out an experimental planting of Marsanne and Roussanne; he also has Macabeo, Terret Blanc, Grenache and white Carignan, as well as a table grape called Servant, which ripens late and gives a high level of acidity. His small production of pink wine is made by the *saigné* method from Grenache and Cinsaut.

For his red wine, he uses carbonic maceration for Carignan. All the other grape varieties are vinified separately in the traditional way, with a short fermentation which only lasts three or four days, while the carbonic maceration takes ten days. The wine is blended and then aged for three to six months in hundred-year-old 70-hectolitre barrels. Syrah and Mourvèdre have increased the ageing potential of Faugères; M. Saur's wine is certainly not a wine to drink young, but one that will benefit from a four or five years' bottle age. He makes two *cuvées* – a selected wine with a higher proportion of Mourvèdre, Syrah and Grenache, and an ordinary generic wine. In the spring of 1987 his basic 1986 was a solid mouthful of tannin and fruit, while the 1985 selection was more elegant, with a lovely long finish. For M. Saur the character of Faugères comes from the dry schist soil, which gives the wine a distinctive flavour, a slightly smoky taste that he calls gunflint or *pierre à fusil*.

Another traditional grower of Faugères is Gilbert Alquier in the village of Faugères. His cellars are behind an ivy-covered facade on the outskirts of the village. The date 1874 on the house marks the beginning of the estate. His father planted the first Grenache vines here just after the war and he has some photographs that show how difficult it was. It seemed as though there was no soil at all in the vineyards, just large stones; they had to add soil to help the roots of the young vines. In the hallway where we tasted, there is a photograph of his grandparents at the 1920 vintage.

He has 25 hectares of vines, planted with 25 per cent Syrah (which he has had since 1964), 25 per cent Mourvèdre (which was planted in 1970), 25 per cent Grenache and the same of Carignan. As well as red wine he makes a little pink, but his reputation rests firmly upon his red. His is a classic vinification, with an eight- to twelve-day fermentation controlled at a temperature of 25°C. The grapes are not destalked and each variety is fermented separately and blended afterwards. The 1986 vintage, tasted in October 1987, had a deep colour with a very attractive perfumed fruitiness, reminiscent of 'red fruit', coming from the Syrah, and some subtle tannins. The 1985 had begun to develop a taste of maturity, being softer and more rounded. In 1983 M. Alquier began to make a Cuvée Prestige from a small proportion of his better grapes; this is aged for ten to twelve months in new 225-litre barrels of Tronçais oak. We tasted the 1985, and although the flavour of the wood was still very apparent on nose and palate, so that it needed more age to mellow, it was just one of the many examples of a talented and thinking grower trying to make the best wine within his means.

Picpoul de Pinet

Picpoul de Pinet is a rather surprising oasis of white wine in a sea of predominantly red Coteaux du Languedoc. Picpoul is the grape variety, and it is grown in a small area centred on the village of Pinet near Pézenas. Picpoul is virtually unique to this area, but no one quite knows why it is grown here and nowhere else of any significance. It has been like that for generations, they said.

The largest producer of the wine is the Cave Co-opérative de Pinet, which was founded in 1923. At that time it was simply a co-operative of producers of white *vin ordinaire*, for Picpoul de Pinet had no reputation to vaunt. The wines were made without care and sold as base wines for vermouth, notably to Martini. That outlet has long since gone. Picpoul de Pinet became a VDQS in 1947 and an appellation under the umbrella of Coteaux du Languedoc in 1985. The delimitation of the vineyards had already been carried out in the five villages of the appellation, namely Pomerols, Mèze, Castelnau-de-Guers, Montagnac and Pinet itself. For the moment there are some 200 hectares in production (out of a possible total of 2,500), and the area is gradually increasing with the encouragement of the co-operative. The regulations of production did not change with the creation of the appellation; the only difference was psychological – for the status of *appellation contrôlée* brought a greater incentive for quality. This is certainly apparent in the co-operative of Pinet, for when I visited them, new vinification equipment, with stainless-steel vats, was being installed.

A comparative tasting demonstrated the improvements effected by their changed production methods. I had always thought of Picpoul as a rather dull, flabby grape variety and wondered why it should have been singled out when it seemed no more interesting than the other white grapes of the Midi, such as Bourboulenc, Macabeo, Terret Blanc and so on. When it is carefully vinified, however, it can be encouraged to produce a rather delicate smoky flavour; it certainly proved very quaffable with a large plate of seafood at a restaurant in the colourful fishing harbour of nearby Sète.

Apart from the co-operative at Pinet, the producers of significance include the co-operative at Pomerols and a couple of independent growers, namely Claude and Ludovic Gaujal at Domaine de Gaujal and the Bézard-Falgas family of Domaine Genson. As well as Picpoul, both these growers as well as the co-operative members have red and other white grapes for the local Vin de Pays des Côtes de Thau (the vineyards are not far from the large Étang de Thau). The terrain is fairly flat, and they are too close to the sea to come within the appellation of Coteaux du Languedoc for red wine. There are also some experimental plantings of Chardonnay and Sauvignon, but for the moment the grape variety of Pinet is very firmly Picpoul with its fragrant, nutty flavour.

Cabrières

Cabrières is one of the villages of the Coteaux du Languedoc, situated in the hilly countryside towards the foothills of the Massif Central, near the town of Clermont l'Hérault. The name means goat, coming originally from the Latin *caper*. Between the two world wars there were as many as 3,000 goats and sheep in the village, and a human population of only 300. Today the goats have gone, for the last goatherd died in 1984 and the village now concentrates on wine.

The vineyards of Cabrières, situated only in that village, are close to those of Faugères. Virtually the sole producer is the village co-operative, along with one insignificant private estate. Cabrières has a historic reputation for its pink wine, going back as far as 1357 with a reference in the archives of Montpellier to the *vin vermeil* of Cabrières. Forty years ago the co-operative made only pink wine; now red is more important, and there is also a little Clairette du Languedoc.

Today the basic pink of Cabrières is based on Cinsaut, while the better-quality pink, called L'Estabel, includes some Grenache as well as some Syrah, which was first planted in the village about ten years ago. The *saigné* method is used, the juice being run off after a few hours on the skins. On the whole, however, the red wine is better. The Cuvée Fulgand Cabanon, named after the village priest who is said to have introduced the wine of Cabrières to Louis XIV, consists of 50 per cent Syrah with some Grenache and Carignan and is a solid, rounded mouthful of wine. The co-operative began working with carbonic maceration in 1986, mainly for Carignan, but much of their wine is still vinified in the traditional manner. Generally the wines are better than adequate, but fail to excite.

St-Saturnin

St-Saturnin is another village of the Coteaux du Languedoc, with vineyards adjoining those of Montpeyroux. The countryside is wild and rugged, especially from the viewpoint at the Rocher des Vierges behind the village. Little grows here apart from vines, and St-Saturnin itself shows few signs of life apart from a mobile grocer's van and the village co-operative. The village is Roman is origin, and used to be called St-Saturnin-de-Lucian after a Roman notable called Lucianus who settled here. Later the bishop of nearby Lodève used it as a summer residence. Today viticulture is virtually the sole activity apart from a few olive and almond trees. Of the 180-odd members of the co-operative, a third make a living from their vineyards.

The Cave Co-opérative de St-Saturnin is one of the most dynamic of the Midi in terms of attitude and export achievement. In 1983 it opened an impressively equipped bottling hall, financed partly by EEC subsidies but mainly by its own members. The entire production of St-Saturnin rests in the hands of the co-operative; there is only one producer in the village outside the co-operative, and he does not have the right grape varieties for the appellation. The members of the co-operative have committed their vineyards to it for fifty years, giving it long-term control of the appellation. Its hold seems quite authoritarian: a young man who inherits his father's vines is obliged to deliver his grapes to the co-operative, whether he likes it or not, until the year 2001, if his father was a founder member of the co-operative in 1951.

Nevertheless the co-operative has been responsible for encouraging the gradual planting of *cépages améliorateurs*, though so far, of the 780 hectares controlled by the co-operative, only 340 hectares produce St-Saturnin. That figure is slowly increasing, but people are slow to change. The mentality of the elderly members is conservative in the extreme. We were given an example of a man who has 10 hectares of vines, of which 2 are planted with Grenache and the rest with Cinsaut and Carignan. If he would but plant just half a hectare of Syrah, he could make St-Saturnin, rather than ordinary *vin de table*, but he will not. The basic grape variety is still very much Carignan, although there are 85 hectares of Grenache, 50 of Syrah (of which the first vines were planted about twelve years ago), and just 7 hectares of Mourvèdre, which are much more recent and which they are hoping to increase in the next few years.

As for white wine, they have planted a little Chenin Blanc on an experimental basis, for use in their Vin de Pays du Mont de Baudile; there is also a little Ugni Blanc and Terret Blanc, as well as Chasselas, for Clermont l'Hérault was also a region of table grapes. But the principal production of St-Saturnin is red wine, including a very light red, a *vin d'une nuit*. This was first made accidentally when the cellar manager emptied a vat by mistake, but as it tasted good they have continued to make it. They are not equipped for carbonic maceration, but do have some sophisticated rotating vats to extract the maximum aroma during fermentation.

The vineyards of St-Saturnin extend into the villages of Jonquières and St-Guiraud and the soil is a mixture of clay and limestone, very pebbly with good drainage. As well as St-Saturnin the co-operative also makes some Coteaux du Languedoc; St-Saturnin can also be declassified into Coteaux du Languedoc, though in fact St-Saturnin is the better-known name and therefore tends to sell better. Château de Jonquières is sold as a single-estate Coteaux du Languedoc, while Château d'Arboras is an individually vinified St-Saturnin. Several different wines, as well as the *vin d'une nuit*, are based on selections of grapes and vineyards, but unfortunately those we tasted lacked substance and the flavours failed to attain the anticipated quality.

Montpeyroux

The co-operative at nearby Montpeyroux, to the north of Clermont l'Hérault, seemed in some ways more successful. Montpeyroux is the last wine village before the Massif Central, and the most northern vineyard of the Midi. The skyline is dominated by the mountains, with Mont St-Baudile (which gives its name to the local *vin de pays*) rising to 847 metres. There are 700 hectares of vines in the village of Montpeyroux, most of which could produce appellation wine, but they are not planted with the correct grape varieties. There are two private growers and a cooperative with 254 members, of whom forty live from their vines alone. Some of them have vineyards in other villages and therefore also deliver grapes to other co-operatives.

The co-operative was created in 1950, but just produced *vin ordinaire* until Montpeyroux was made a VDQS in 1958. It is now part of the appellation of Coteaux du Languedoc. Virtually all the wine of Montpeyroux is red; there is a little drop of pink, but no white at all. Ten years ago the vineyards were planted almost entirely with Carignan, but they are now gradually being transformed. The first Syrah was planted in 1982 and there are also Grenache and Cinsaut, while Carignan is slowly being reduced. But it does give good results where the yields are low, and here in this poor, stony soil they rarely reach more than 40 hectolitres per hectare. The vines suffer from drought in the summer months and they never irrigate.

They would like to increase the proportion of Grenache, but the yields are often very tiny, as little as 13 hl/ha, as it is so susceptible to *coulure*. At the moment the *encépagement* for Montpeyroux is 50 per cent Carignan, 15 per cent Syrah, 20 per cent Cinsaut and 15 per cent Grenache. They could plant Mourvèdre, too, but many of their members are reluctant and slow to change. However, in the last few years they have considerably increased the area of vines that can make appellation wine. The total production of the co-operative is an average of 38,000 hectolitres; in 1982 only 6,000 hectolitres would have been appellation wine, but that figure had increased to 18,000 hectolitres with the 1987 vintage.

The director of the co-operative described their wine as a very traditional product. It is all made by the classic methods of vinification with no carbonic maceration, for the consumers of Montpeyroux, who are mainly the local population, seem fairly conservative in their tastes. The co-operative is well equipped and able to control its fermentations efficiently. Each grape variety is fermented separately and blended after the malolactic fermentation. The wine is cold-stabilized and then kept in cement vats for about eighteen months. The Vin de Pays du Mont Baudile differs only in the selection of grapes, the method of production being identical.

The co-operative of Montpeyroux produces several different *cuvées*, based on a selection of grapes and vineyards. I best liked the basic Montpeyroux, which was rounded and rugged with some soft fruit. The Sélection Terroir is made from vines (mainly Grenache and Cinsaut) that are at least ten years old, from better sites, and is aged in bottle rather than vat. It was solid and peppery, with rather a hard finish. Le Souverain, which they consider to be their best wine, had the rather alcoholic vegetal fruit character of Grenache.

They have just opened a new tasting- and sales room. Most of these co-operatives sell a lot of wine by *vente directe* and some, like Montpeyroux, are well equipped to do so, with a smart shop. The Cuvée Inaugurale to mark this opening is a blend of the best wines available for the occasion, a solid, traditional wine – a bit tannic and rugged, like the scenery.

St-Georges-d'Orques

The village of St-Georges-d'Orques lies close to the western suburbs of Montpellier on the flat coastal plain. At first glance the terrain does not appear as propitious for the production of good wine as that of the villages in hilly countryside like Cabrières and Montpeyroux. But it seems that St-Georges-d'Orques is an oasis of quality in the plains and its wines have long enjoyed a reputation. In the seventeenth century they were exported as far afield as Russia, Switzerland and the Netherlands as well as to England. There is a record of a purchase of St-Georges-d'Orques by the Earl of Bristol in 1715. In the early nineteenth century the English who were 'interned' in Montpellier during the Napoleonic Wars acquired a taste for it, and according to Morton Shand in *A Book of French Wines*, decanter labels bearing the name St-Georges referred not to the better-known village of Nuits in Côte d'Or, but to St-Georges-d'Orques. Thomas Jefferson discovered the wines of St-Georges-d'Orques when he was ambassador of the newly independent United States in Paris.

The village was mentioned by the nineteenth-century authorities. Jullien listed it with Vérargues, St-Drézery and St-Christol, writing in 1816 that the wines had an agreeable taste with body and alcohol, and after five years' ageing made distinguished bottles that could compare with those from Burgundy. Rendu wrote that there were 500 hectares of vines, of which Terret Noir and Prian formed the base, with Œillade and Clairette, while Carignan, Mourastel and even Aramon had been introduced and the wines were distinguished by their honest taste. They were heady wines that developed after three years into something better than average. Mostly they were drunk in Paris. Vizetelly, at the end of the century, said that St-Georges was the only wine of real character in Hérault.

Today St-Georges-d'Orques is one of the *crus* of the Coteaux du Languedoc. The wine is made by the village co-operative, which accounts for two-thirds of the appellation, and by a handful of individual producers. It is a standard co-operative, founded in 1948, and built to the usual drab design of French wine co-operatives. Inside there are cement vats and also a few oak barrels, for it is one of the more forward-looking co-operatives of the Midi and four or five years ago began ageing its better wines in 225-litre barrels, as well as in 30-hectolitre casks. It makes a variety of different wines. The Cuvée Tradition comes from Carignan, Grenache and Cinsaut vinified in the traditional way, as is the Cuvée Prestige which includes some Syrah. The Cuvée Macération, as the name implies, is produced purely by carbonic maceration, while the Cuvée Millénaire was a special wine made to celebrate the thousandth anniversary of the founding of the city of Montpellier. Syrah and more especially Mourvèdre are recent introductions and there are also Cabernet Sauvignon and Merlot for Vin de Pays de l'Hérault. The appellation wine still forms only a relatively small part of their production – 15,000 hectolitres out of a total of 55,000 – while the rest is *vin de pays*, *vin de table* or destined for the distillery.

Pic St-Loup

The appellation of Pic St-Loup takes its name from the mountain that dominates the skyline some 20 kilometres north of Montpellier. The story goes that in the early Middle Ages a man called Loup from the village of St-Martin-des-Landes at the foot of the mountain fell in love, but he had two rivals. The three men decided to go on the Crusades to prove their valour, but when they returned a few years later, the object of their love had disappeared. Disillusioned, they each took the vows of a hermit and Loup settled on the nearby mountain.

Today the vineyards cover thirteen villages to the north of Montpellier, with a potential area of 5,000 hectares. In fact only about 600 hectares are planted with the correct grape varieties. Some of the wine is sold as Vin de Pays du Val de Montferrand, and a very large proportion is no better than *vin de table*. The Vin de Pays du Val de Montferrand covers quite a large part of Hérault, from the outskirts of Montpellier as far north as the town of Ganges. The Château de Montferrand is at the foot of the Pic St-Loup outside the village of St-Mathieu-de-Tréviers.

The Co-opérative de St-Mathieu-de-Tréviers is one of the larger producers of Pic St-Loup and it is working hard to improve the quality of its wine. There are strict criteria for assessing the grapes, relating to grape variety, alcoholic degree, the situation of the vineyard, the condition of the grapes and whether or not they are machine- or hand-picked. Hand-picking is of course essential for carbonic maceration, and they have built a new reception area with a rolling carpet for the grapes destined for this type of vinification. They also do classic vinifications and even thermo-vinifications (when the juice is heated) for *vin de table*.

There is still too much Carignan in the village, but over the last seven years they have planted 25 hectares of Syrah, Mourvèdre,

Cabernet Sauvignon, Merlot and Grenache, of which the Bordelais varieties are used for *vin de pays*. Twenty-five hectares may seem a very small area, but they have to fight the conservative attitudes of many of their members, and it was only in 1980 that they took the decision to improve their installations and amend the grape varieties. The VDQS of Pic St-Loup also allowed for white wine and there is a little Ugni Blanc, as well as some young experimental plantings of Sauvignon, Chardonnay, Grenache Blanc and Marsanne. Rolle and Chenin Blanc are other possibilities that are being considered in view of the need to enliven the white wine of the region.

Their basic Pic St-Loup is made from one-third Grenache and Carignan, vinified by carbonic maceration, one-third Syrah and one-third Grenache, Carignan and Cinsaut vinified in the classic manner; it was a solid, slightly sweet, chewy mouthful of wine. They have two estates which are vinified separately, Domaine St-Aunès and Domaine Ste-Lucie, while their best-seller is what they call a *vin de café*, a red wine that you can drink without food. The juice has only spent thirty-six hours on the skins and the result is a light, fruity wine that is perfectly innocuous and has no distinguishing characteristics.

Méjanelle

Méjanelle is almost indistinguishable from the south eastern suburbs of Montpellier, with vineyards in Mauguio, St-Aunès and Montpellier itself. At times we seemed horribly lost in the vicinity of the airport of Fréjorgues in our search for the Château de Flaugergues, which is one of the leading estates of the *cru* of Méjanelle. Here, unlike in the rest of the Coteaux du Languedoc, co-operatives are unimportant and Coteaux de la Méjanelle is made by several independent growers.

In the Middle Ages the bishops of Montpellier had vineyards here and the wines were said to be strong and full-bodied, with plenty of spirit and substance. In 1596 Thomas Platters described his peregrinations around Montpellier and the tasting he had at the Château de Grammont. At that time the wine of Méjanelle was called *vin de grès* – a reference to the soil of the vineyards, with its large stones called *galets* or *grès*. In 1626 a certain Abraham Goelnitz wrote that the wines of the Coteaux de la Méjanelle were the most alcoholic wines of the whole of France. I would not say that this holds true today, but the wines of Henri de Colbert at the Château de Flaugergues have a certain charm. So does the man himself. He is a direct descendant of Louis XIV's great minister, who did so much for the economy of France. He compared wine-making to the birth of a child.

M. de Colbert is an enthusiast, and it is men like him who can do much for the wines of the Midi. He clearly loves his wine and what he is doing. First there was a Roman villa on the site, then the monks of Grammont cultivated vines here from the eleventh century until 1690, when one of M. de Colbert's ancestors on his mother's side, Étienne de Flaugergues, bought the estate. The rather austere château that you can visit today dates back to the seventeenth century. The façade is Italianate but simple, and the interior contains a magnificent staircase of 1710, hung with Brussels tapestries depicting the life of Moses, and a wonderful old kitchen with a huge fireplace and copper pans.

The vineyards are planted round the property, 50 hectares in all. The soil, such as it is, consists of large stones or *galets* similar to those in the vineyards of Châteauneuf-du-Pape. M. de Colbert is intent on undoing the bad work of the last century and is aiming to suppress Carignan completely. His vineyards are planted mainly with Syrah, Grenache and Mourvèdre, as well as with some Cinsaut, Cabernet Sauvignon and Merlot. Each grape variety is vinified separately, by the traditional method rather than by carbonic maceration, and he makes two qualities of Méjanelle, as well as a Vin de Pays de l'Hérault, wines with warm southern fruit and flavours.

St-Drézery

St-Drézery, like neighbouring St-Christol, received a passing mention from Jullien and Guyot. Today the village co-operative dominates the appellation, which is the smallest *cru* of the Coteaux du Languedoc. There are also a couple of independent producers, such as Louis Spitaleri at Domaine du Mas de Carrat. M. Spitaleri is a stocky farmer who arrived here from Tunisia in 1962. As he says, he landed here and he stayed. First of all he reared pigs; but he also planted his first vines in 1968 and gradually the vines took over, so that his vats are now housed in the old pigsty! Various improvised gadgets give his cellars an air of Heath Robinson, but they seem to work.

He now has 33 hectares of vines; Grenache is the main grape variety, but there is a little of everything – some Syrah, Cinsaut, Carignan and Mourvèdre, as well as Merlot for *vin de pays*. He planted Syrah in 1979 and his first Mourvèdre came into production in 1987 – he is pulling up Carignan to plant more Mourvèdre. He has had Merlot since 1975 and is more than pleased with it. His son, taking advantage of the benefits offered to young wine-growers, is also planting vines and is following the INAO's advice for white wine, with Grenache Blanc, Marsanne and Roussanne coming into production. Father's vinification methods are usually traditional, though he tried carbonic maceration for the first time in 1986. He is well equipped to control his vinification temperatures and also makes a pink wine by pressing the grapes, which he considers gives a better balance to the wine than by running off the juice as in the *saigné* method. The wine is rough and ready with some good honest fruit; it might benefit from a little bottle age, but M. Spitaleri has no resources for ageing his wine – for that you need space and money.

St-Christol

St-Christol is a village to the east of Montpellier, not far from the departmental boundary with Gard. The particular stony soil of the area, a formation that the French curiously call *poudingue*, gives the wines of St-Christol their character. As always, Carignan is the dominant grape variety; but there is quite a high percentage of Grenache, as well as some Syrah and Mourvèdre, and also some Merlot and Cabernet Sauvignon for *vin de pays*. A considerable effort has been made to improve the grape varieties, and Mourvèdre and Syrah perform well on the slopes around the village.

The village co-operative dominates the appellation, but of its total production of 55,000 hectolitres only 6,000 are sold as St-Christol. They also make some Vin de Pays de la Bénovie and as much as 15,000 hectolitres goes to the distillery. Vinification methods are the standard ones of the average co-operative. There are several different wines, some with fanciful names. Péché de Bacchus contains 90 per cent Grenache and Noces de Cana is based on Carignan, while their most attractive wine, labelled simply St-Christol, included Mourvèdre and Syrah as well as Grenache, and had a smoky, peppery flavour with some perfumed fruit.

Coteaux de Vérargues and Muscat de Lunel

The Coteaux de Vérargues are the most easterly *cru* of the Coteaux du Languedoc. The vineyards cover nine parishes, including the village of Vérargues, as well as the town of Lunel, while the appellation of Muscat de Lunel is found in the three parishes of Lunel-Viel, Vérargues and Saturargues. Producers of Muscat de Lunel make Coteaux du Languedoc as well, and one such is Jean-Philippe Servière at the Château du Grès-St-Paul.

M. Servière took over the family estate some ten years ago. His family have had vineyards there since 1840, and at the beginning of this century his great-grandfather built an Italian-style château. He was a successful *négociant*, but his son, M. Servière's father, was not interested in the estate and it had been abandoned to tranquil decay. Bourgeois families did not tend their own vines, but employed someone to do it for them. M. Servière, however, with his degree in political science and doctorate in law, decided he had had enough of the Parisian rat-race. The rest of his family thought he was mad and they were certainly not prepared to make any financial contribution to the estate. As he said, suggesting to a Parisian that he should invest in Languedoc has about as much appeal as suggesting to a Laplander that he should invest in reindeer!

M. Servière is a courageous and determined man and he is making a success of what is a challenging and at times difficult venture. His red wine is made from Syrah, Grenache, Cinsaut and Carignan and he also has some Cabernet Sauvignon and Merlot that he planted eight years ago. He admits to putting a little in his Coteaux du Languedoc, even though one is not allowed to. He feels they give the wine a better structure and compensate for the Carignan, which he cannot afford to and does not want to pull up immediately; he wants to replant the vineyards gradually so as not to have too high a proportion of young vines. He is also planning to plant some Mourvèdre. His grapes are picked by machine, and the traditional fermentation takes four or five days and produces a warm, fruity wine with peppery flavours for fairly early drinking.

M. Servière prefers his red wine to his Muscat de Lunel. I enjoyed both. He is one of three independent producers of Muscat de Lunel. This appellation is dominated by the co-operative of Lunel which, although it vinifies its wine relatively efficiently, is inexpert in marketing it. Having accumulated four years' stock in its cellars, it does a great disservice to the reputation of the appellation by selling wine that is tired and oxidizing.

Lunel is an attractive little country town. It proudly proclaims itself 'La Cité du Muscat'. Laurence Sterne, writing in 1760, described Muscat de Lunel as the best Muscat wine of the whole of France;

some was sent to Napoleon by his sister, Pauline Borghese, when he was in exile on the island of St Helena. Jean-Jacques Rousseau also enjoyed the Muscat de Lunel at the Auberge du Pont du Vidourle towards 1750.

Muscat de Lunel was given an appellation in 1943 and is made entirely from Muscat à Petits Grains, grown on poor stony soil. The average yield is small, 25 hectolitres per hectare. Altogether there are 270 hectares in the appellation, giving an average production of 8,000 hectolitres, of which the co-operative is responsible for 95 per cent. M. Servière has 5 hectares of Muscat and is eventually planning to plant another 16. The wine is made with meticulous care, so that the fruit of the grape is retained and the taste is not too syrupy. The grapes are hand-picked and pressed, without any skin contact. The fermentation takes place at 17°C and between 5 and 10 per cent alcohol by volume is added when the sugar content has dropped to 125 grams per litre. A minimum level of natural alcohol is added to retain the maximum amount of fruit. The use of the alcohol is carefully controlled: its purchase has to be declared, and officialdom demands that some grape juice is added to it as soon as it arrives in the cellars, so that it cannot be used for any other purpose. The wine is not aged, but bottled in the spring. It is usually blended with some wine of the previous year, so that there is no marked difference in taste from one year to the next.

The vinification of Muscat for *vin doux naturel* is an object of some experimentation. M. Servière explained that growers in other appellations using Muscat were trying to harvest at night (so that cool grapes were picked) and were putting the grapes in a cool chamber, to give them five hours of skin contact. Vinification temperatures are also a matter for discussion, for if the fermentation is too cold, say 10°C, the wine tastes more like apple juice. M. Servière would like to give up using any sulphur, but that is easier said than done and he would like the wine to have a lower sugar level, so that it is lighter and finer.

Muscat de Lunel is not an easy wine to sell. Muscat de Beaumes-de-Venise is much better known, and there is competition from other Muscats from outside France. But M. Servière is optimistic for the future, for although the consumer needs educating, the wine does have great appeal. You can drink it like Sauternes – not just as a dessert wine but as an aperitif, or with *foie gras*, or even with blue cheese.

MUSCAT DE FRONTIGNAN

Frontignan, the home of the best-known of the three *vins doux naturels* of Hérault, is an unprepossessing town. It lies on the Étang d'Ingril and the skyline is dominated by a petrol refinery. The main road from Montpellier, which skirts the edge of the town, is lined with gaudy notices advertising Muscat in bottle or in cubitainer, luring the unsuspecting tourist with promises of tasting. What they fail to say is that most of this is imported Muscat, coming not at all from the vineyards of Frontignan, but from much further afield – Greece, particularly the island of Samos. It looks rather like a fairground, and quite belies the real quality of Muscat de Frontignan.

Frontignan boasts a long-standing reputation. Pliny the Younger described the Muscat wine of Frontignan in his letters and called it '*viae apianae*', the paths of bees. Arnaud de Villeneuve, the doctor who discovered the effects of adding alcohol to fermenting grape juice, wrote in the early fourteenth century that on the advice of the king of Aragon (who was lord of Frontignan) he had been drinking two glasses of Muscat de Frontignan every day for several weeks and already felt ten years younger. He proposed to continue treating himself with this wonderful wine until he was only twenty years old.

In later centuries Muscat de Frontignan travelled to Paris, where in 1704 the *limonadiers* of the capital included it amongst the wines they were allowed to sell *en gros*. It was drunk in England in the seventeenth and eighteenth centuries, and was labelled Frontiniac. John Locke, the English political philosopher, sang its praises in 1676. Voltaire, too, ordered wine from Frontignan, writing to his supplier in 1774 with the words: 'Keep me alive, by sending me a small quarter of the best wine of Frontignan.'

But perhaps its most famous customer was Thomas Jefferson, who visited Frontignan in 1787 while he was the American ambassador in Paris. His correspondence with a Dr Lambert, who was mayor of Frontignan and a producer of Muscat, has been preserved in various archives in the United States. In 1790 he asked for wine to be sent across the Atlantic: 'Although I am far away from you at the moment, Sir, I would still like to receive your excellent wines. Please therefore have the kindness to send ten dozen bottles for our President, General George Washington, and five dozen for me, of both white and red, but more of the latter.' Evidently Frontignan produced red as well as white wine at that time; certainly, a century or so later Rendu mentioned both red and white Muscat and compared the red with the 'Vin de Constance' (a reference to Constantia from South Africa).

Of the nineteenth-century authorities, Jullien was the most appreciative of the quality of Muscat de Frontignan. After the Muscat of Rivesaltes he rated it as the best in the kingdom, writing that it was distinguished by its sweetness, with a lot of body and a very pronounced taste of fruit and a very smooth perfume. It benefited from ageing, would keep a long time and could withstand a journey by land or by sea. It certainly sounds a rather more robust wine than that of today.

So what of Muscat de Frontignan towards the end of the twentieth century? I drank and enjoyed that of Yves Pastourel at Château de la Peyrade. This light golden wine had delicious overtones of apricots on nose and palate, and was gently sweet without being cloying.

Unlike Muscat de Rivesaltes, Muscat de Frontignan is made purely from Muscat Blanc à Petits Grains, otherwise itself confusingly known as Muscat de Frontignan in France, or as Muscat Frontignan in California or even White Frontignan or Frontignac in Australia. It performs well in the chalky soil around Frontignan. The vineyards are on the eastern side of the Étang de Thau which, combined with proximity to the sea, ensures a suitably warm microclimate. The area of the appellation has been delimited to 2,100 hectares, but only about 850 are in production. Three-quarters of those are cultivated by members of the co-operative which was created in 1909. In addition there are half a dozen private producers, among whom Yves Pastourel at Château de la Peyrade is the largest, and has an excellent reputation.

The Pastourel family came to Frontignan in 1977. They were already wine-growers at Pézenas, but were attracted by the reputation and challenge of Frontignan. They bought the Château de la Peyrade and now have 25 hectares of vineyards planted just with Muscat à Petits Grains. The château was built during the 1830s and is an elegant but rather sombre building, standing back from a busy roundabout on the edge of the industrial complex of Sète. You do not come here for the view, for the vineyards are like an oasis in the midst of tarmac and concrete. Yves Pastourel is a charming, enthusiastic man, with an intelligent and inquiring view of his appellation. He works with his two sons on the estate. As he said, they had the luck to come here with 'brand new eyes'.

In the last ten years they have acted as a motive force for improving the quality of Muscat de Frontignan, which had sadly declined and fallen into disrepute. It used to be a syrupy, heavy, oxidized wine; so they worked with new vinification methods, avoiding any oxidation, controlling their fermentation temperatures and making a lighter wine with more perfume and refinement. Not everyone followed their example, for some people are immovable. A fermenting vat must be carefully followed to determine the right moment to add the alcohol. Often they spend the night in the cellar, checking the density of the must every hour or so. If you mute the wine too soon, you have too much sugar, and if you wait too long, you will have too much alcohol. The finished wine must have a minimum of $15°$ alcohol, including between 5 and 10 per cent by volume of added alcohol. The wine stays in vat all the winter and the new wine is not bottled until after Easter. Even then it is blended with some wine from the previous year, so that there is not too marked a difference between any two wines; for the taste of Muscat can change quite significantly in the course of a year, as the wine matures.

Yields for Muscat de Frontignan, or simply Frontignan, as the Pastourels would prefer the appellation to be called, are low at 30 hectolitres per hectare. They would also like to experiment with giving the juice some skin contact before fermentation, but to do this you need very healthy grapes, without a trace of rot. They are also trying to make a dry white wine, picking the grapes at a potential of $12°$ alcohol and giving the juice ten to twelve hours of skin contact. 1987 saw their first experiment, and no one else has yet followed their lead. They would also like to do the mutage with a lower sugar content in the juice – 110 grams as in Beaumes-de-Venise, rather than 125 grams as the appellation regulations dictate – and add less alcohol, just to see what the resulting wine would be like. But here they run the risk of upsetting the authorities of the INAO, for they would be disturbing a regulation that has been fixed since Frontignan was given its appellation in 1936.

Muscat de Frontignan enjoys a good reputation in France, where it sells well, but perhaps not well enough. Abroad it is less well known and although it is available in England, we have tended to follow the fashion for Muscat de Beaumes-de-Venise, which is our loss, as Muscat de Frontignan is a suitable rival. This is an appellation that needs and deserves to be revitalized and shaken out of its dormancy.

MUSCAT DE MIREVAL

Muscat de Mireval is somewhat overshadowed by its larger neighbour, Frontignan. Mireval is a sleepy, unprepossessing little town, a few kilometres east of Frontignan, where we looked in vain for a café. Nor has it attracted much attention in the past. François I is said to have drunk it, and Rabelais also praised it in *Pantagruel*: '*Puis vint à Montpellier ou il trouva fort bon vin de Mirevaulx et joyeuse compagnie.*' The nineteenth-century authorities are remarkably silent about it.

The vineyards of the appellation are confined to the parish of Mireval and the adjoining village of Vic-la-Gordiole. Yields are small, a basic 28 hectolitres per hectare. The production of Muscat de Mireval is dominated by the co-operative, appropriately called La Cave Rabelais. You can try their wines in a smart roadside tasting-room with a shop.

There are also a couple of independent growers, Domaine de la Capelle and Mas des Pigeonniers. We visited the former, where they have 30 hectares of vines altogether, of which 17 are planted with Muscat à Petits Grains, while the rest produces red *vin de table* or *vin de pays*. There are hopes that the red wine of Mireval may eventually be included in the appellation of Coteaux du Languedoc.

There seems very little difference between the Muscats of Mireval and Frontignan; the grapes are picked with a minimum of 15° potential alcohol and alcohol is added when the sugar content has dropped to 125 grams per litre. The cellars at Domaine de la Capelle were unsophisticated, with basic cement vats and no real means of controlling the temperature, so that the wine ferments at 25–30°C. The resulting wine was quite a rich golden colour, derived from the deep-coloured skins of ripe Muscat. I detected apricots on the nose, and on the palate it was rich, quite sweet and not too cloying, but slightly spoilt by a faint alcoholic burn on the finish. Considering the basic equipment, however, it was remarkably good – a wine to be drunk young, and certainly much fresher and fruitier than the wine we tasted at the co-operative, where apparently they leave their Muscat to age for twelve months before bottling, as they prefer a more mature style of wine. The demand for Muscat de Mireval seems purely local, and for the moment is likely to remain so.

VIN DE PAYS OF THE MIDI

The most exciting *vins de pays* are made in areas where there are no competing appellations or VDQS. The regulations, although strict, allow scope for experimentation in a way that is not possible with the appellations, which must follow the '*usages locaux loyaux et constants*' of the region. Grape varieties that are not part of a region's tradition can be grown under the broader umbrella of the *vin de pays*. But in areas where there are also appellations, the *vins de pays* are usually very much the second string of the wine-maker's repertoire; consequently, although he may indeed use them for experimental Cabernet Sauvignon or Chardonnay, he is just as likely to use them for the Carignan or even Aramon that he has not yet pulled up. Also the wine from young vines, not yet in full production, will become *vin de pays*, as will any vats of wine that are not up to scratch. They inevitably provide an outlet for the second choice.

Nevertheless there are parts of the Midi, notably on the coastal plains, where there are no appellations. It is there that talented and inspired wine-makers are producing exciting wines under the designation of *vin de pays*. On paper the wines may have a lower status than wines with an appellation, but in the glass the differences are very much less clearly defined. There are so-called *vins de pays* that rival some of the best appellations in quality, and there are some appellation wines that are no better than many a *vin de pays*. What really matters is who made the wine and whose signature is on the label.

The most famous example of a *vin de pays* that has acquired a reputation and a price to compete not only with neighbouring appellations but also with appellations from the more classic parts of France is Mas de Daumas Gassac, which according to the label is a simple Vin de Pays de l'Hérault. The wine, however, is far from simple. It has been described as the Lafite of Languedoc and it represents an exciting example of just what can be done in the Midi with ability and talent, as well as money. Not to put too mercenary a note on it, money is essential if you are to change a vineyard in the dramatic way that Aimé Guibert has done. Luck and imagination have helped, too.

Aimé Guibert and his wife Véronique bought Mas de Daumas Gassac, which lies between the small towns of Aniane and Gignac, about 30 kilometres north west of Montpellier in the heart of Hérault, in 1970. They wanted a house in the country, not a vineyard. M. Guibert is a lawyer and his family come from Millau in Aveyron, where they have a tanning business. Véronique Guibert is equally removed from wine, for she is an ethnologist, specializing in Celtic traditions.

Quite by chance they discovered that they were sitting on a viticultural gold-mine. Henri Enjalbert, who was not only the leading geologist at Bordeaux University but also an enthusiastic archaeologist and a great friend of the Guiberts, came to Mas de Daumas Gassac because there are Iron Age remains in the area. While he was there, he noticed the soil of the property, a half-million-year-old red glacial powder. He told Aimé Guibert that with such soil he could make great wine. The challenge was taken up. This glacial powder is rare: being so fine, it is highly susceptible to wind erosion and has usually been blown into rivers or disappeared into the sea. How it came to form such a hill at Mas de Daumas Gassac is open to speculation. Possibly a tornado was responsible, since the lack of round stones indicates that the soil was created by wind rather than by water. It is deep, poor and without humus.

There were already vines at Mas de Daumas Gassac, since this was an area of polyculture, but none that had any pretensions to quality. M. Guibert planted his first vines in 1974; he now has 12 hectares in production and is aiming eventually for about 20, planted for red wine with 80 per cent Cabernet Sauvignon and approximately 3 per cent each of Merlot, Cabernet Franc, Syrah, Pinot Noir, Tannat and Cot. As for white wine, the grape varieties are mainly Viognier, Chardonnay and Petit Manseng, with some Muscat à Petits Grains, and also Nelerschol, a biblical grape associated with Moses. This may seem far-fetched, but Numbers chapter 13, verse 23 reads: 'And they came unto the brook of Eshcol and cut down from thence a branch with one cluster of grapes, and they bare it between two upon a staff; and they brought of the pomegranates, and of the figs.' The grapes must have been enormous to require two men to carry them. Aimé Guibert has ten vines, cuttings from a vineyard on the borders of Jordan and southern Syria, that were given to him by an Israeli student who was studying oenology at Montpellier. These ten plants yield as much as 100 kilos of fruit, with each vine limited to just two *grappes*, each averaging 5 kilos but sometimes attaining 10 kilos, like the grapes found by the followers of Moses. Not all these grape varieties are in full production yet and the 1986 white was mainly

Viognier, with some Chardonnay and a drop of Muscat. Asked why he chose such a mixture, M. Guibert simply said, 'You can't explain a crazy man! If something is too simple, it is not interesting – the more disorder, the more fun!'

At Mas de Daumas Gassac you have left the broad coastal plain behind you; the vineyards are at an altitude of 200 to 300 metres, but with a microclimate more appropriate to land at 500 to 600 metres. The aspect is north westerly, so that the vineyards are not exposed to the suffocating heat of the south, and being in the shadow of other hills causes the vines to flower here three weeks later than usual for the area. Similarly, the vintage is three to four weeks later than on the plains.

They practise organic viticulture at the property, something that they are able to do without too much difficulty as they are on the edge of the *garrigues* and isolated from other vineyards. For 1 hectare of vines they have 3 or 4 hectares of scrub with its smells of thyme, laurel and lavender contributing to the wine. The vines are treated with the traditional Bordeaux mixture of copper sulphate, and the only fertilizers are natural compost and manure.

Professor Émile Peynaud, the eminent Bordeaux professor of oenology who in his retirement has become consultant to numerous estates all over Europe, has played his part in this wine. He made the first two vintages in 1978 and 1979, but now, M. Guibert having gained experience, simply acts as a consultant. The hand-picked grapes are checked for rot, destalked and loaded into stainless-steel fermentation vats by gravity. The different grape varieties are fermented separately for about three weeks, to allow complex flavours to develop, and then blended before the malolactic fermentation. Two-thirds of the pressed wine is used and blended with the free-run juice after the malolactic fermentation is complete.

There was once a flour mill at Mas de Daumas Gassac and the cellars have been built over the old mill's water reservoir, so there is a constantly cool temperature; also, water is available from the springs for cooling the fermentation vats by running cold water over them (a technique called *ruissellement*), although in fact they have never had to resort to this expedient. The fermentation temperature is kept at 30°C in the centre of the tank and at 20°C on the outside. For *remontage* they follow Peynaud's principle, pumping over the juice with oxygen for the first three days and without oxygen for the rest of the fermentation period.

The wine is aged in second-hand barrels from Château Margaux; these will be used for ten years. The tannin of new wood is not needed for there is already enough natural tannin in the wine. The length of ageing depends upon the wine's development; the 1978 vintage, for example, was aged for three years before it was released for sale.

It was with the sale of the first vintage that luck played its part. There were 20,000 bottles to be sold and M. Guibert had no customers, no reputation and no salesmen. So he persuaded five fellow Aveyronnais, owners of Parisian brasseries, to take a small quantity of his wine. As he says, it was an instant miracle. The wine critic of *Le Figaro* was given it to taste in reply to the question, 'What's new?' Likewise Gault-Millau, who described it as the Lafite of Languedoc. For Peynaud this wine was the proof that Enjalbert was right. In 1987, six years after its release, the 1978 had flavours of cedarwood and tobacco, and a combination of elegance and richness; 1985 had a blackberry concentration of depth and power.

The first vintage of the white wine is also remarkable, with tastes reminiscent of peaches and apricots. The grapes were pressed after four days of skin contact, then given a long, cool fermentation which lasted at least six weeks. The wine was then left on its lees for three weeks and spent three weeks in wood before being bottled at the end of March.

A little pink is also made, from Pinot Noir, Syrah, Cabernet Franc and a little Cabernet Sauvignon. The fermentation takes about six weeks at 16°C, and some natural carbon dioxide is retained to make what M. Guibert called a *vin de soif* – a wine to quench your thirst – with flavours reminiscent of rose-water and strawberries.

The future of Mas de Daumas Gassac will be exciting to observe. In the short space of nine years Aimé Guibert has established an enviable reputation for his wine. He is lucky in having money at his disposal, but he was also fortunate in having the unusual soil of his vineyards, which in his view makes his wine quite out of the ordinary for the Midi. He would tell you that his wine is not a Languedoc wine, it is Mas de Daumas Gassac. The fact remains that his vineyards are firmly in Languedoc, and he cannot fail to provide an inspiration for other ambitious wine-makers and reputation-seekers in the region. Mas de Daumas Gassac demonstrates just what can happen in the Midi, given money, luck and talent.

The Vin de Pays des Côtes de Thongue covers the valley of the

Thongue to the west of Pézenas and includes about fifteen villages. They are outside the Coteaux du Languedoc. We went to see Louis-Marie Tesserenc of Domaine de l'Arjolle in the village of Pouzolles. He is a youngish, solid, bearded man, with a certain *joie de vivre*. His welcoming words were, 'Come into the cellar, we'll have a drink and I will tell you my life story.' Well, he did not quite tell us the whole story, but he told us a good deal about his wine while we drank some delicious dry Muscat – a table wine, not a *vin doux naturel*.

He works in a GAEC (Groupement Agricole d'Exploitation en Commun) with his brother, and they have 70 hectares of Vin de Pays des Côtes de Thongue which are planted with all kinds of grape varieties which are unorthodox for the Midi. There is Cabernet Sauvignon, Merlot, Cabernet Franc, Sauvignon Blanc, Chardonnay, Muscat and even a little Viognier. When they took over the property in 1974 they pulled up the Carignan, Aramon and Cinsaut that had made vulgar *vin de table*. M. Tesserenc sees himself as a pioneer, for 'that is what is interesting. You have to learn everything from scratch and sometimes you make mistakes, but if you had inherited a Bordeaux château, you could only go down – here you can go up.' He is not interested in appellations, for with *vins de pays* you have complete freedom. You can play *la carte des cépages* and *la carte de vin nouveau*, which can be released much earlier than an appellation wine. We tasted the 1987 *primeur* in October. Louis-Marie Tesserenc has, as he said, a lot of ideas in his head, but not much in his wallet. Again money plays a crucial part in projects of renovation and replanting, and he has invested a lot in the vineyard; now he is going to turn his attention to the cellar.

He still has his father's large old barrels, in which some of his red wine is aged. There are various different blends, most of them based on Merlot and Cabernet Sauvignon. He is well equipped to control his fermentation temperatures. The juice of his Sauvignon and Muscat is given a few hours of skin contact. His Chardonnay and Viognier are not in production yet. Ultimately he would like to make wine to age; that demands an underground ageing cellar, but he is lucky as he will be able to use the cellar at the Château de Moujan, which is a rented estate and provides their other label. There is no doubt that the Tesserenc family is quite the exception in the Côtes de Thongue, for most people are still firmly traditional in their adherence to Carignan in quantity.

When you visit a producer of *vin de pays* you never know quite what to expect, for there are none of the constraints of an appellation to lay down guidelines for a wine. François Henry, at Domaine St-Martin-de-la-Garrigue outside the village of Montagnac, could make Picpoul de Pinet if he wished, but it is of no interest to him. He prefers Chardonnay to Picpoul, and in addition has a variety of red grape varieties, both from Bordeaux and the Midi. The property is Roman in origin for St Martin was a name that was commonly used when a Roman site was converted to Christianity. There is a tiny chapel that was built in the ninth century and archives refer to the priory of St-Martin-de-la-Garrigue in 847. In the Middle Ages there was a fortified *bastide*, and in the eighteenth century two wings were added to the central façade.

We went on a tour of the vineyards, which are on the hills around the château. This proved somewhat hazardous as it was the first day of the shooting season and I had visions of being mistaken for a pheasant by a short-sighted huntsman. When M. Henry's father bought the property in 1975, the vineyards were planted with 40 per cent Carignan, 40 per cent Aramon and a few plants of Grenache; the remaining 20 per cent were red and white hybrid varieties that were 'worse than deplorable'. Over the last twelve years they have been transformed. Although there is still a little Carignan left for financial reasons, all the Aramon and certainly all the hybrids have been pulled up and 20 of the 35 hectares have been replanted. The vineyards are surrounded by *garrigues* and the soil is a mixture, which allows for a variety of different grapes. Since 1986 these vineyards have been classified within the Vin de Pays des Coteaux de Bessilles, and although the name may be unknown, it still has a better *image de marque* than Vin de Pays de l'Hérault.

M. Henry makes three styles of red wine. The first is what he calls his Cuvée Tradition, for which the grape varieties are indeed traditional – a blend of Carignan, Grenache and Cinsaut, vinified in the classic way, without any wood ageing. This is a wine for early drinking. In the mid-1970s, when he was replanting the vineyards, the French market was orientated towards the taste of Bordeaux. Consequently he planted Merlot and Cabernet Sauvignon, and his Cuvée Réserve is made from 40 per cent each of Merlot and Cabernet Sauvignon and 20 per cent Grenache and Cinsaut. Pure Cabernet and Merlot are too Bordelais, so he has '*méridonialisé*' the wine with Grenache. After a long *cuvaison* it is aged in large oak barrels for two years. Finally there is the Cuvée Bronzinelle, which is my favourite of the three. The better grape varieties of the Midi, Syrah and Mourvèdre, came later and only went into production in 1985. At the moment it is made from equal parts of Grenache, Syrah and Mourvèdre, but the eventual aim is to increase the Mourvèdre to 50 per cent. It is a spicy, peppery wine that has spent a year in large barrels of Hungarian oak, some of which are a hundred years old. They require an enormous amount of maintenance and the tartrates are removed regularly. M. Henry is against carbonic maceration because everyone uses it. He is also against what he calls technological wine; as he says, everyone is so solicited by technology that everyone could make the same wine – you just pay a cheque for the equipment and follow the recipe.

As for white wine, he has Terret Blanc, which does well on the limestone soil; when well vinified, it has an attractive smoky character. He plans to try some skin contact for it. But it is his Chardonnay that excites him most. When asked why he had planted Chardonnay rather than any other variety, he answered quite simply: 'I adore white Burgundy.' His Chardonnay is still very much at an experimental stage. In the first year, 1984, he fermented it in wood, for which he had just one barrel; but it was not very satisfactory, probably because the vines were still too young. He is aiming for the '*méthode ancienne*' of Burgundy. In 1985 he fermented half the crop in stainless steel and then blended it with the rest in barrels for the malolactic fermentation. It became too woody too quickly, so in 1986 he fermented it all in stainless steel and then transferred it into wood for three months, as opposed to six months in 1985. As for 1987, he told me with glee, 'I have treated myself to two new barrels' (the others are five years old), so that he now has fifteen altogether.

It is all very well for an estate to make wine that flouts the preconceived ideas of the region, but the wine also has to be sold. This is where an organization like Delta Domaines comes into play. It is basically a marketing company, run by a bright young man called Dominique Rivière and based on six go-ahead estates around the Bassin de Thau, between Cap d'Agde and Sète. This may be the heart of the coastal plain of Hérault, but the group is intent on realizing the potential of the region for good, sound, everyday drinking wine. The leading estate, the flagship of the group, is Domaine du Bosc at Vias. It is owned by Pierre Bésinet, a chemical engineer by training; when he took over the estate from his father in 1978, he had not only expertise but also the outsider's vital gift of imagination. His father had already planted some Cabernet Sauvignon and Syrah, which was very original at the time, but he still had hybrids that had been producing wine for an aperitif company in Sète.

The 50-hectare estate now includes an enormous variety of different grapes: Syrah, Merlot, Cabernet Sauvignon, Grenache Gris and Cinsaut; and for white wine, Marsanne, Sauvignon, Muscat d'Alexandrie, Grenache Blanc, Viognier and a little Ugni Blanc. Their philosophy is to make wines of pure grape varieties, thus establishing an identity other than mere *vin de pays*. The volcanic soil at Domaine du Bosc is particularly suitable for white wine.

The other properties in the group are Domaine de la Grange Rouge, Domaine de la Fadèze, Domaine de la Gardie, Domaine St-Victor and Domaine des Pourthié – all situated between Vias and Marseillan on the west side of the Étang de Thau. At Domaine de la Fadèze they are achieving exciting things with Terret Blanc. This grape used to have a bad reputation: it was alcoholic but neutral, and was used by vermouth-makers, in particular Noilly Prat. The vermouth market has declined and something had to be done with the wine. At reasonable yields (not the 200 hectolitres per hectare for vermouth), picked early, with some acidity remaining, and vinified properly with a cool fermentation, it can make a deliciously fragrant glass of wine. The grape enjoys the maritime influence of the lagoon. Domaine St-Victor has the same soil as La Fadèze, with similar wines, while Domaine de la Grange Rouge has worked on Chasan with some success. They also have Chasan at Domaine des Pourthié at Agde, where the reds are good, too, while La Gardie shares the volcanic soil of its neighbour, Domaine du Bosc, and makes good Grenache Blanc.

Other estates would like to join Delta Domaines. You need money and the right attitude. If you have money, you can achieve something in three years. You can buy equipment and begin to change your vineyards. But attitude is important, too. The people who are achieving things are the young people who return to a family property, or who buy land after doing something else. They come fresh to wine. You cannot expect a man of fifty to change his ideas after twenty or thirty years of *bêtises*. All six estates share the same oenologist, the Peynaud of the Midi, Marc Dubernet. Improvements over the last ten years have been enormous. Dominique Rivière described a 1977

Merlot from Domaine de la Grange Rouge, saying that in 1978 it was considered wonderful, but today would not be rated at all.

I began my circuit of *vins de pays* with something that is small and beautiful and I will finish with an absolute contrast – the largest vineyard-owners of France, Les Salins du Midi, who are responsible for most of the Vin de Pays des Sables du Golfe de Lion. As the name implies, their principal activity is not wine but salt. They were started in 1856, seven years before phylloxera was found in the Midi, and by 1875 it was noticed that the vineyards that they owned on the coastal sand dunes, to provide wine for their salt workers, remained unaffected by phylloxera. The phylloxera louse cannot survive in very sandy soil. By 1900 they had 700 hectares of vines and by 1987 1,700 hectares. These included three estates around the Camargue; Domaine de Villeroy, near Sète; Domaine de Jarras and Domaine du Bosquet outside Aigues Mortes; the Abbaye de St-Hilaire in the Coteaux Varois; and Château La Gordonne in the Côtes de Provence. In all, they own 37,000 hectares of land, mainly of salt flats on the coast, which makes them the largest landowners in France after the state and the Church. More surprising is the fact that they are the largest producers of Cabernet Sauvignon in France.

For the last forty years they have been at the forefront of new measures, both in vineyard and cellar, to improve the quality of the wines of the Midi. Until the Second World War their vineyards, like everyone else's, were directed towards quantity. Quality was a secondary consideration, but when the emphasis changed after the war, they had a golden opportunity to adapt their vineyards accordingly. Their coastal vineyards had been heavily mined so that they had to start again from scratch. At that moment they acquired a far-sighted young director, Pierre-Louis Jullien, fresh from oenology studies in Montpellier. It was he who instigated the first plantings of Cabernet Sauvignon in the Midi; he finally retired in 1986, having devoted his entire career to the Salins du Midi.

They did not bottle any wine themselves until 1958, when the brand name Listel was created. It comes from the name of an island, the Ile de Stel (which is one of the sandbanks of the Rhône delta and lies south-west of Aigues Mortes), where they have vineyards, and where vines have been grown since the fifteenth century. In Occitan the name Ile de Stel means simply 'island of sand'.

Each of the three Midi estates has its speciality. Domaine de Villeroy, with its vast area of vineyards on the sandbar that separates the Bassin de Thau from the Mediterranean, concentrates on white wines, including a lightly sparkling Brut de Listel and a slightly alcoholic grape juice called Pétillant de Raisin. You can see the vineyards from the viewpoint above Sète: a flat expanse of vines with the lagoon on one side, and the sea on the other stretching to the horizon. Here they grow Chardonnay, Sauvignon Blanc, Clairette and Ugni Blanc for Listel Brut, and Chenin Blanc, Riesling and Muscat d'Alexandrie for the Pétillant de Raisin. Plantings of Chardonnay are being increased. All these wines are either sold as Vin de Pays des Sables du Golfe de Lion, or as Vin de Pays d'Oc. Their technical expertise for the vinification of white wine is impressive and they use the latest methods. Their use of sulphur dioxide is minimal, well within the limits for organic wine. They make their own yeast cultures and cool fermentations are meticulously controlled by computer.

Domaine de Jarras near Aigues-Mortes concentrates on *gris* and pink wines made from the traditional grapes of the Midi, Carignan, Cinsaut and Grenache. When these varieties are grown on sand, the skins do not turn fully red, but remain *gris*, an almost bluish colour. The regulations for the *vin de pays* allow them to produce a Gris de Gris, which is unique, for elsewhere where the wine is *gris* (such as in the Côtes de Toul), the grapes themselves are red, not *gris*. The vinification is given the same meticulous care as for the white wine. The light pink colour comes from no more than about twenty minutes of skin contact. Listel Gris de Gris is their flagship and accounts for half of their total wine production. The other peculiarity of Sables du Golfe de Lion is that it is the only wine outside the Loire valley to allow for bottling *sur lie*. This practice is usually restricted to Muscadet, where the wine is bottled off the fine lees of the fermentation, so that the wine retains a hint of carbon dioxide and thereby some additional freshness.

The cellars of Domaine de Jarras are impressive and they still house the original oak barrels. These enormous barrels of Russian oak were built with the cellars in 1883 and are still used to age the basic red Listel for a period of nine months. In contrast, outside stands a forest of enormous stainless-steel tanks, and those who have a good head for heights and can climb to the top are rewarded with views of the Camargue and its flamingos in the evening sunset. At night during vintage time you can see mechanical harvesters at work, huge beasts prowling through the vineyards; they prefer to pick during the night so as to have cooler grapes. The prototypes of the now commonplace Brand harvester machines were developed here.

The third estate, Domaine du Bosquet, which is also close to Aigues-Mortes, concentrates on red wine. The vineyards here are planted with Cabernet Sauvignon, Cabernet Franc, Merlot, Syrah and Carignan. Methods at Domaine du Bosquet are less refined and they say they still have a lot to learn about red wine-making. Natural factors are much more important in red wine, for they reckon that red wines are made 60 per cent by the soil or *terroir* and 40 per cent by the man, while for white wine the percentages are reversed. They use two methods for red wine vinification: the traditional method, with regular *remontages* to extract colour and tannin, and thermal vinification, which entails heating the must and which they were one of the first to develop during the 1950s. Heat destroys rot and, more important, it acts as a colour solvent; so that at a high temperature, say 70°C, you get colour but not tannin. They use it for Carignan and also for Cabernet Franc, but not for Cabernet Sauvignon, as it does change the aroma of the grape. On the other hand they do not use carbonic maceration as they find it gives a wine which is wonderfully fruity for a few months, but then suddenly fades. They want to age all their red wines before sale.

The Vin de Pays des Sables du Golfe de Lion is the only *vin de pays* with a geological delimitation, for the vineyard area is defined by the presence of sand. The local growers' association would like to become an appellation. Les Salins du Midi, however, who are responsible for 80 per cent of the wine, prefer the flexibility that is offered by the *vin de pays*. They could have had an appellation for Listel back in 1972, but it would have imposed unwelcome restrictions, especially on grape varieties. *Appellation contrôlée* is still of no interest to them for, in common with some smaller producers of *vins de pays*, they have their own objectives that have little to do with the limitations of an appellation.

COSTIÈRES DE NÎMES AND CLAIRETTE DE BELLEGARDE

The Costières de Nîmes are where the Rhône meets Languedoc. It is quite a large appellation, covering a plateau to the south of Nîmes and limited by the Rhône in the east and the Camargue in the south.

The motorway, 'La Languedocienne', is on the northern edge and to the west there are the vineyards of the Coteaux du Languedoc. The wines from the eastern part of the appellation resemble their neighbours in the Côtes du Rhône, while the wines of the west have more similarity to those of Languedoc.

The viticultural origins of the Costières de Nîmes are firmly Roman. Nearby Nîmes, with its magnificent arena and the Maison Carrée, was an important Roman city. But the viticultural history of the region has been unspectacular. In the seventeenth century wines from Bellegarde, Vauvert and St-Gilles were sent to Paris, and in the nineteenth century the same wines were sent from Sète and Aigues-Mortes to northern Europe. Guyot wrote favourably of the Vins des Costières, mentioning in particular those made from Mourvèdre, which was also called the Plante de St-Gilles. Mourvèdre disappeared from the area with the phylloxera crisis.

The area was recognized as a VDQS in 1951 with the names Costières du Gard and was elevated to appellation status in 1986 and then to avoid any potential confusion with Vins de Pays du Gard the name was changed with the 1989 vintage to Costières de Nîmes. The area of the appellation has been carefully delimited so that it covers altogether about 25,000 hectares in twenty-four villages, although only about 12,000 hectares are planted, and of those only 3,500 hectares actually produce the appellation wine. As in the rest of the Midi, there is still a considerable amount of replanting necessary to obtain the desired grape varieties. Vin de Pays des Coteaux Flaviens, which is named after the Roman imperial dynasty, covers the same area and gives some identity to experimental plantings of Merlot and Cabernet Sauvignon, as well as to the excess production of Carignan.

The vineyard area is strictly limited to a particular type of soil, the grès, an especially stony soil of gravel and large pebbles brought down from the Alps by the Rhône. It tends to be of a distinctive orange–red colour, with a subsoil containing a high proportion of clay; this retains moisture and prevents the vines from suffering too much from lack of rain during the summer. The proximity of the sea also has a tempering effect, bringing a certain degree of humidity. At the same time the large stones in the vineyard absorb daytime heat and radiate it back on to the vines at night, ensuring that the grapes are fully ripe.

The grape varieties of the Costières de Nîmes are, as elsewhere in the Midi, in a state of transition. The composition of the vineyards has changed since 1970, when Carignan was the principal variety, followed by Aramon and various hybrids. There was no Syrah or Mourvèdre and hardly any Grenache. Today Carignan is still the main variety, with a maximum of 50 per cent which will be decreased to 40 per cent, and there is a growing amount of Grenache, which will have to account for a minimum of 25 per cent by 1990, as well as some Syrah and a little Mourvèdre. Inevitably this transition is a slow process; as the director of one co-operative said, 'A vineyard is not a plantation of lettuces.' It cannot change overnight, and fifteen years ago they were receiving subsidies to plant Carignan whereas now they are pulling it up.

Costières de Nîmes is predominantly a red wine, although a small amount of pink is made as well as a drop of white. In addition to white Costières de Nîmes there is a separate appellation called Clairette de Bellegarde covering a small area within the Costières de Nîmes. The grape varieties for white Costières de Nîmes are Grenache Blanc, Macabeo and Ugni Blanc, with an occasional drop of Marsanne and Roussanne, while Clairette de Bellegarde is made purely from Clairette, like Clairette du Languedoc.

Unlike most of the appellations of the Midi, Costières de Nîmes is not dominated by the co-operatives; they only account for 30 per cent of the production, while independent producers are far more important and are making considerable efforts to improve the quality of their wine. I spent four days in the appellation, with the very competent secretary of the growers' association, Alexis Guyot, as my guide. I was left with an impression of an appellation that was bursting with energy and no longer half asleep like parts of the Coteaux du Languedoc, but full of motivation to improve its wines. Appellation status has certainly lent impetus to the drive for quality, and considerable efforts have been made and continue to be made, with some exciting results.

Our first visit was to the Co-opérative de St-Gilles. This is the town that serves as gateway to the Camargue, that vast area of marshland at the estuary of the Rhône which forms such a wonderful nature reserve, with wild ponies and flocks of flamingos. The co-operative is one of the largest in the area, but even so only a small percentage of its production is Costières de Nîmes; it also makes Vin de Pays des Coteaux Flaviens and Vin de Pays du Gard, as well as a large quantity of *vin de table*, of which a hefty dollop goes to the distillery.

They appreciate the problems caused by such a large output of *vin de table*, but it is a difficult and lengthy process to convert a vineyard from high yield to quality. The soil is rich and has been over-fertilized for years, and the vines must be adapted accordingly, with different clones, pruning and density of planting. They stopped adding nitrogen to the soil fifteen years ago, but there has been no reduction in the vigour of the vines for the soil is deep and has accumulated reserves of nitrogen. Above all they have to combat the conservative attitude of their older members, for a grower who has been used to *'faire pisser la vigne'* for the last fifty years is not going to give up the habit of a lifetime overnight. They are making considerable efforts, however, with a programme of replanting 165 hectares over the next five years. They have already replanted about 25 to 30 hectares each year since 1970, using Grenache and Syrah and more recently Mourvèdre. They have also tried T-budding, but it is very expensive and a specialized skill, and the technique is not yet perfected. Syrah is proving particularly successful in the Costières de Nîmes as it is a relatively early ripener and can be picked before the equinoctial rains in September, while Mourvèdre ripens later and is therefore more delicate. It also needs ageing which represents an investment. As for white wine, they would like to plant more Grenache Blanc at the expense of Ugni Blanc, which they described as the Carignan of white wine.

Vinification methods are improving, too, and they make a careful selection of their grapes, imposing a certain discipline on their members. In common with so many co-operatives of the Midi they were not equipped for efficient temperature controls until 1982. They have experimented with carbonic maceration, but it would necessitate an investment of some 600,000–800,000 francs, which they cannot yet afford. But they are trying some oak ageing of their best wine, from Grenache and Syrah, in small Bordelais barrels which have already been used for one wine. The best *cuvée* of their 1986 vintage had an attractive chewy fruitiness.

The Château de Campuget is a historic estate that is now owned by M. Dalle. He is partly of Flemish origin, which accounts for the northern resonance in his name. His father bought the estate in 1941. In the twelfth century, however, it belonged to Guillaume de Nogaret who destroyed the power of the Knights Templar. The present château was built in the sixteenth century and partly rebuilt under Napoleon III. It had remained in the hands of the Maigre family from the time of Nogaret until 1917. The estate consists of 95 hectares in which the grape varieties have changed considerably in the last ten years, as well as the methods of cultivation. They now have 5,500 vines per hectare instead of 3,300. This gives lower yields of better wine. There are already some Grenache Blanc and Clairette, but Marsanne and Roussanne have also been planted; in 1986 5 hectares of Chardonnay were added. Chardonnay is the centre of a great debate as to whether or not it gives more aroma and flavour. Grenache Blanc is certainly improved by the addition of 20 per cent of Marsanne and Roussanne, which provide extra flavours and fruit. A red wine made from 60 per cent Grenache and 40 per cent Syrah really showed the potential of the Costières de Nîmes, with a smoky, rather meaty nose, and on the palate tannin, structure, lots of fruit and some ageing potential. Merlot, planted for *vin de pays*, is doing well here and there is also a little Cabernet Sauvignon.

Quite one of the best Costières de Nîmes that I tasted came from the Château de Rozier, the family property of Louis de Belair, who inherited it from an old aunt. He has had no wine training at all, and worked on the stock exchange in Lyons till he came to the Costières de Nîmes in 1977 with the objective view of an outsider. We talked in his reception room, with its large fireplace. An Alsatian was asleep in front of the fire and the cat, who was definitely top dog, settled herself on the dog, who hardly stirred, and went to sleep too. As well as vines there are peach trees and wheat on the estate.

The Côtes du Rhône are only 7 kilometres away and there is no natural break between the two appellations, only a departmental boundary; so M. de Belair is looking to make a wine similar to a good Côtes du Rhône, and he is succeeding. He feels that they are penalized by the image of the former Costières du Gard, but it is producers like him who will succeed in changing that image. He makes two red wines; his better *cuvée* has a high proportion of Grenache, with some Syrah and a little Cinsaut and Carignan. It had a warm, rich nose, with flavours of prunes, some tannin and some long, rich, chewy fruit. The basic wine, made from 30 per cent each of Grenache and Cinsaut with 40 per cent Carignan, was also good; it lacked the depth of the other, but had some warm fruit. For reasons of finance, however, he cannot afford to make too much of the better wine.

For someone who has had no formal training in oenology, M. de Belair's methods are meticulous. He takes great care that the grapes are fully ripe and ferments each grape variety in stainless-steel vats; the maceration lasts eleven to thirteen days with two *remontages* a day. The blending is done at the end of April for bottling in May and September. He makes no pink wine as he does not want to spoil the quality of his red.

Bellegarde is the centre of the small white appellation of Clairette de Bellegarde. There are just three producers, with a total combined production of about 3,000 hectolitres – the Co-opérative de Belle-garde, Domaine de l'Amarine and Domaine de St-Louis-la-Perdrix. All three have a much larger production of Costières de Nîmes. The unprepossessing village of Bellegarde has had a reputation for its white wine for many years, and it was given an appellation in 1949 for a white wine made purely from Clairette. The wine is really little more than a local curiosity with a historic reputation, and the appellation was never developed. Clairette is a difficult grape to vinify well as it oxidizes quickly, but when vinified properly it makes a distinctive but rather old-fashioned wine – dry and nutty, with a certain amount of character and weight.

Domaine de l'Amarine at Bellegarde is the property of Nicolas Godebski. His father was Polish, but the estate has been in his mother's family since the twelfth century. She was a Mlle de Bernice, from an old regional family; the Hôtel de Bernice is one of the finer town houses in Nîmes. M. Godebski has 37 hectares of vines, but only 4 are planted with Clairette. Grenache is the most important red grape and there are also Syrah, Cinsaut, Carignan and Mour-vèdre, as well as Grenache Blanc for white Costières de Nîmes, and a little experimental Marsanne and Chardonnay.

M. Godebski is one of the growers who have retained their large old oak barrels and he has no cement vats, only steel ones. Eventually he plans to refurbish his cellar with stainless-steel vats. He vinifies his white wine in wood and then transfers it into vats; red wine is subjected to the reverse procedure and is given about fifteen months' wood ageing before bottling, which is rare in the Costières de Nîmes. We tasted his 1984, made from 70 per cent Grenache and 30 per cent Syrah. Grenache needs to be balanced by a more substantial grape which does not age so quickly and the 1986 vintage will have some Mourvèdre. As for the 1984, it was a warm, peppery mouthful of wine.

Some pink wine is also made, from Grenache and Cinsaut, and also a sparkling pink by the champagne method, which restored our spirits when we were forced to have a picnic lunch on the forecourt of the Ford garage in Nîmes when my car had broken down!

The Domaine de St-Louis-la-Perdrix is run by Mme Lamour and her daughters. Her husband Philippe Lamour was a great friend of Baron Le Roy who laid the foundations for the *appellation contrôlée* in Châteauneuf-du-Pape; he in turn set up the framework for the system of VDQS, and was one of the great personalities of the original Costières du Gard. He is now an old man and takes a back seat in the affairs of the appellation and of the estate. He was the first, however, to see the potential of the wines of the plateau back in the 1950s, and the credit for the initial creation of Costières du Gard is his.

The estate was once a hunting-lodge belonging to the Duchesse d'Uzès, hence the partridge. It has belonged to the Lamour family since 1942; they have 60 hectares of vines altogether, including only 3 of Clairette. Their red wine is made from Grenache and Carignan, 40 per cent of each, with Syrah or Cinsaut for pink. The white Costières de Nîmes comes mainly from Grenache Blanc with 20 per cent Clairette. There is a special *cuvée* called Marianne, after one of the daughters, with a higher percentage of Syrah; it also contains a drop of Cabernet Sauvignon which provides more structure and substance. Although some Cabernet is grown elsewhere in the area for *vin de pays*, it is unusual to find any infiltrating the appellation wine. Other growers said that Cabernet was the worst thing possible as it does not like the soil of the Costières de Nîmes. The Lamours no longer have their large old barrels, which were burnt for firewood ten years ago. Theirs is a neat, functional cellar of cement vats, with classic methods of vinification, all carefully controlled. Their wine certainly does justice to the reputation of the estate and its owner, and demonstrates the untapped potential of the Costières de Nîmes.

6

Wines of Provence

There is a moment as you drive south from Lyons, somewhere around Orange, when the atmosphere subtly changes and you know that you have reached the warm south and arrived in Provence. True, a motorway sign, bearing the symbols of a blazing sun and a parasol pine, tells you 'Vous êtes en Provence'. But it is more than that. The sun is stronger, the light is brighter and there are the warm scents of lavender, thyme and pine trees. Just before Aix-en-Provence the Mont Ste-Victoire looms into view, conjuring up the bold colours of Cézanne's paintings. If you have ever holidayed on the Côte d'Azur, sat at a café in St-Tropez, eaten bouillabaisse in Marseilles and sipped the local wine, the chances are that you drank a pink Côtes de Provence from a funny amphora-shaped bottle. But the wines of Provence are so much more than pretty pink wines for holidays and picnics; there are serious reds and whites offering a myriad tastes and flavours.

The largest and best-known appellation of the area is Côtes de Provence, but it can be red and white as well as pink. Around the town of Aix-en-Provence are the vineyards of the Coteaux d'Aix-en-Provence, with a sub-region, the Coteaux des Baux-en-Provence, with vineyards on the foothills of the Alpilles. Between these two larger areas comes the Coteaux Varois, a recent addition to the hierachy of VDQS, and then within these larger areas are four smaller, more prestigious appellations. Cassis has a reputation for white wine, while Bandol is known above all for substantial red wines based on the Mourvèdre grape. Palette is a tiny appellation outside Aix-en-Provence, with just one estate of consequence, Château Simone, and hidden in the suburbs of Nice are the vineyards of Bellet. Finally we have a new appellation, the Côtes du Lubéron, with vineyards around the town of Apt on the foothills of the

Montagne du Lubéron, and the lesser-known VDQS of the Coteaux de Pierrevert, which is enjoying something of a revival.

CASSIS

The first time I headed down the motorway towards the sun, my destination was Cassis. In summer sunshine, Cassis is a cheerful, bustling port, for holiday yachts rather than fishing-boats. Frédéric Mistral said of it, 'He who has seen Paris, but has not seen Cassis, has seen nothing.' In the holiday season it is full of sailing enthusiasts, but I preferred it in the autumn wind of late October. The port is lined with cheerful restaurants offering *bouillabaisse* and *fruits de mer*. The remains of an old castle dominate the hill overlooking the port. Outside the town are the dramatic cliffs of Cap Canaille, at 416 metres the highest cliffs in France. They offer a striking view of the turquoise Mediterranean and the town of Cassis.

The Greeks of Phocaea brought vines to Cassis about the same time that they came to Marseilles, around 600 BC. The Romans continued to plant vines here, usually on coastal land. During the Middle Ages the vineyards gradually shifted to more suitable sites inland. The first reference to a precise vineyard in Cassis dates from 1199. There are subsequent occasional mentions in the local archives, and in 1530 it was recorded that the Albizzi family, who came from Florence, planted vines to the north of the town. The principal activity of Cassis was always maritime, but by the nineteenth century agriculture had also become important. Vines, olive trees and fruit trees were planted together on the hillsides outside the town, and wheat was grown.

Today the reputation of Cassis rests on its white wine. In earlier centuries, however, it was known for its Muscat wine and also for fine red wines. René of Anjou did much to establish the reputation of the wines of Provence, Cassis included, in the fifteenth century. He is said to have brought the Muscat grape to Provence from Italy. In 1672 the governor of Burgundy asked for two small barrels of white Cassis wine to be sent to him for the visit of Louis XIV. In the nineteenth century Rendu described Cassis as the best white wine of Provence, and classed the red wine in the first rank of fine wines of the department. The white wine was both sweet and alcoholic and very strong, and enjoyed by those who like very strong wine. A

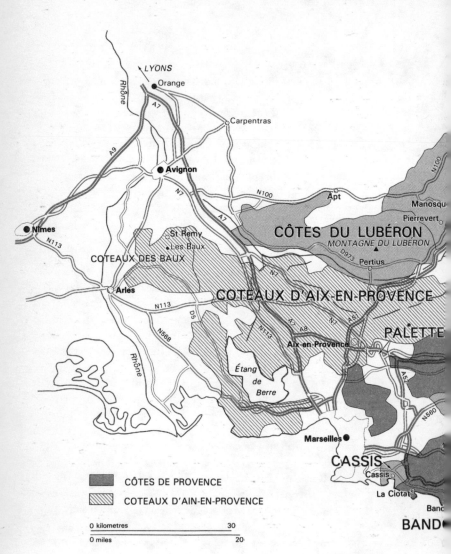

LYONS

Rhône

Orange

A7

Carpentras

A9

N7

Avignon

N100

Apt

Manosqu

Pierrevert

Nîmes

N113

St Remy

Les Baux

CÔTES DU LUBÉRON

MONTAGNE DU LUBÉRON

COTEAUX DES BAUX

A7

D973

Pertius

Arles

N113

D5

COTEAUX D'AIX-EN-PROVENCE

N7

N569

N113

A7

A8

N7

A51

PALETTE

Aix-en-Provence

Étang

de

Berre

A51

Rhône

N560

Marseilles

CASSIS

Cassis

La Ciotat

Banc

BAND

CÔTES DE PROVENCE

COTEAUX D'AIN-EN-PROVENCE

0 kilometres   30

0 miles   20

Mediterranean Sea

Provence

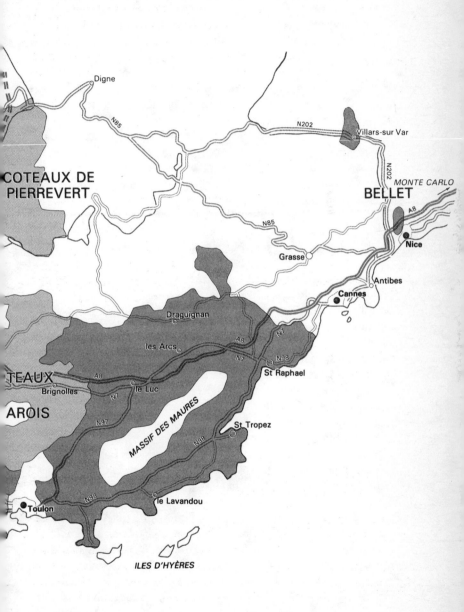

COTEAUX DE
PIERREVERT

Digne

N85

N202   N202   Villars-sur Var

MONTE CARLO

BELLET

N85   A8

Grasse   Nice

Antibes

Cannes

TEAUX
Brignolles

AROIS

A8

Draguignan

les Arcs   A8   N7

N7   N98

le Luc   St Raphael

N97

MASSIF DES MAURES

St Tropez

N98

N98   le Lavandou

Toulon

ILES D'HYÈRES

Muscat wine was also made, from two-thirds Muscat and one-third Mourvèdre, that was not without merit.

The vineyards of Cassis were completely destroyed by the phylloxera; they were reconstituted soon afterwards, but not to their former extent. In the mid-nineteenth century there were 498 hectares of vines in Cassis, an area which has fallen today to 170 hectares occupied by just twelve producers. The vineyards are limited to the parish of Cassis itself. Sadly the land is more valuable for building holiday villas, and there is a strong temptation to sell to building contractors as the town sprawls into the hinterland.

Cassis prides itself on being one of the three earliest appellations in France in 1936, along with Arbois in the Jura and Châteauneuf-du-Pape. The appellation allows for red, pink and white wine, for the Muscat wines disappeared with the advent of the phylloxera. But not everyone makes red wine, and the reputation of Cassis today is for a dry, rather substantial white wine. The permitted grape varieties for the white wine are Ugni Blanc, Clairette, Marsanne, Doucillon (which is the local name for Bourboulenc) and – rather unexpectedly – Sauvignon. Red and pink can come from Grenache, Cinsaut, Carignan and Mourvèdre.

Ugni Blanc is the basis of Cassis as of all southern French white wines. It gives a dry white of little character, but produces good yields with unfailing reliability, and so is useful *'pour faire la quantité'*. Clairette Blanche has declined in popularity as it suffers badly from *coulure*, although it is a very old grape variety of the Midi and gives a certain character to Cassis. Marsanne, which has been grown in Cassis for as long as people can remember, complements the Ugni Blanc and Clairette, giving the fragrance and fruit that the others can lack. It is increasing in importance while Doucillon is declining. Sauvignon Blanc has always been grown here, and the majority of producers have a little drop of it as it adds character and bouquet to their wine; but it too has the disadvantage of susceptibility to *coulure*.

The Mistral can blow hard in Cassis, so virtually all the vines are pruned in the *gobelet* system, without wires which might damage them. Wooden posts provide support, and sometimes the weaker young vines suffer. But the advantage of the Mistral – and this applies throughout Provence – is its deterrence of rot. The drying winds keep the vines healthy. Admittedly, at Cassis there are also some cooling sea breezes. Drought and rain can both be a problem. Most rain falls in the spring. In 1986 there was no rain from Easter until the end of

August, but then the clouds burst and half the average annual rainfall fell in the space of just two hours, causing considerable damage.

The soil is poor and pebbly, a mixture of clay and limestone. Yields are low: 40 hl/ha are allowed, but often only 30 hl/ha is reached. Most of the vineyards are on terraces, notably on the slopes of Cap Canaille. The terraces prevent the erosion that would be caused by the heavy rains. There have been few new plantings of vines, the single exception being by François Sack at Domaine Clos Ste-Magdeleine, just outside Cassis. There are the most wonderful views of the Mediterranean from his courtyard. He has built new terraces on the slopes of Cap Canaille, clearing scrub with the help of a bulldozer; the site is superb.

François Sack now has 12 hectares of vines from which he makes white wine and a little pink, but no red. His white is made from equal parts of Ugni Blanc, Clairette and Marsanne, with about 5 per cent of Sauvignon. Sauvignon ripens before the other varieties, but the yields are tiny – only 25 hl/ha in 1987, for example, and in 1986 a mere 5 hl/ha. He believes that a little drop of Sauvignon gives an extra something to his wine, but he is not sure that he will keep it. For him Clairette and Marsanne provide finesse, and Ugni Blanc quantity. His pink wine comes from Cinsaut and Grenache, with a little Mourvèdre. Vinification methods are standard and his 1986 white Cassis was dry and nutty, full with a dry finish – an old-fashioned style of wine.

Jean-Pierre Santini at Domaine du Paternel has 14 hectares of vines, mainly for white wine. Forty per cent of Ugni Blanc gives him volume, the same amount of Marsanne provides alcohol – the minimum alcohol content for Cassis is 11° – and 10 per cent Clairette contributes acidity, as does a small amount of Bourboulenc. He also has a drop of Sauvignon, but it does not perform well with *gobelet* pruning, and the *guyot* system is forbidden in the appellation. His small amounts of red and pink are made from Grenache, Mourvèdre, Cinsaut and Carignan. In contrast to the situation in the Languedoc, Carignan accounts for only a small proportion of the vines at Cassis. Grenache tends to be the most important grape variety, despite its susceptibility to *coulure*. Mourvèdre used to be more widely planted before the phylloxera crisis but is now gaining in popularity again, and Cinsaut is considered a useful complement, without adding a great deal of character to the wine.

M. Santini's red wine comes half from Mourvèdre and half from

Grenache; the other grapes are used for pink. His methods are standard and efficient and his white wine was more lively than others we tasted. We also sampled the 1987 *bourrut*, which is not fully vinified but retains a little unfermented sugar. It looked like grapefruit juice, had a smoky flavour and proved deliciously quaffable. We were told it should be drunk with smoked chestnuts.

The puzzle of Cassis is how such a white wine has acquired its reputation, for these solid, rather dry, nutty white wines are certainly not to the modern taste. They lacked the zingy fruit enjoyed by the fashionable palate. But they did go remarkably well with the local seafood, and most are drunk in Provence, washing down a plate of *fruits de mer* in warm sunshine down at the harbour.

BANDOL

Paul Bunan, one of the leading growers of Bandol, described the appellation as '*un grand méconnu*', a great unknown. He is right. Although Bandol can be pink or white, the best wine of the appellation is undoubtedly red and it deserves a much greater reputation than it enjoys. For me, Bandol was one of the great discoveries of this book, a wine of stature and depth and an illustration of the complexity of the Mourvèdre grape.

The wine takes its name from the port from which the produce of the surrounding vineyards has been shipped for the last 200 years. The harbour itself was built surprisingly late in the history of the town, not until the mid-eighteenth century. Greeks from Phocaea on the west coast of Asia Minor brought viticulture to this part of France when they founded their colony on the site of present-day Marseilles around 600 BC. When the Romans arrived here in 125 BC, they found viticulture sufficiently well established for them to send wines back to Italy. Roman amphorae have been found on the seabed between the Ile de Bendor and the coast, indicating the existence of a lively export trade.

The archives illustrate the importance of viticulture in the Middle Ages, showing that in 1023 a certain Étienne gave vineyards at La Cadière to the monks of the nearby abbey of St Victor. Numerous documents from the fourteenth century to the sixteenth relate to the sale and circulation of grapes, to vines and harvests. Until the harbour at Bandol was built, barrels of wine were thrown into the sea to be taken on board by ships anchored off the coast. A local nobleman, M. de Boyer Bandol, wrote at the beginning of the seventeenth century that these wines kept well and even improved during long journeys. He should have known for he exported them in large quantities to the Iles Françaises, as the French West Indies were called at the time. Louis XV favoured Bandol and was said to drink wine only from the Rouve district, which is within the village of Le Beausset and part of the present-day vineyards of Bandol.

The project of building a deep-water harbour at Bandol was first discussed in 1754. This was to make a considerable difference to the reputation of the wine. During the Napoleonic Wars, when all shipping was escorted by convoys from Toulon, the town of Bandol obtained the privilege of marking barrels of its wine with the letter B in order to distinguish them from other wines of the region. In the first half of the nineteenth century, Bandol was sent not only to Italy, northern Europe and America, but as far as India and Brazil. It was deemed to improve with a long sea voyage and could withstand the heat. During the last years of the Second Empire the town of Bandol was a flourishing port with a thriving cooperage trade. Rendu, writing at the time, described Bandol as a wine that was rich in colour, body and alcohol, coming from Beausset, La Cadière, Castellet and St-Cyr. The vines were grown on limestone slopes and Mourvèdre was almost the only grape variety. At first the wines were hard and coarse, but they improved with age and could withstand a sea voyage.

This prosperous scene vanished with the arrival of the phylloxera louse, which virtually destroyed the vineyards of Bandol between 1870 and 1872. Few had the heart to replant their vineyards and those that did chose hybrid varieties, or possibly Grenache, Carignan and Cinsaut. Bandol had to wait until the end of the middle of the twentieth century for its renaissance. It was one of the earlier appellations, dating from 1941. Even then Mourvèdre needed only to account for a minimum of 10 per cent in the red wine, but since 1986, thanks to the efforts of Lucien Peyraud and others, 50 per cent is the absolute minimum and the better wines contain much more.

Lucien Peyraud is the grand old man of the appellation of Bandol. He arrived here in 1940, the year before Bandol became an appellation, when he married Mlle Lucie Tempier of Domaine Tempier. He came from the industrial town of St-Étienne in the department of Loire and went to agricultural college in Aix-en-Provence. As he says,

'I liked this place so much that I stayed.' When he arrived at Domaine Tempier, most of the vineyards were planted with Carignan for making indifferent *vin ordinaire*. It was only in 1951 that Mourvèdre began to acquire any significance or importance.

First we were taken to see the vineyards. This necessitated a very bumpy ride in a Citroën 2CV up a dirt track to the viewpoint at Le Beausset-le-Vieux. There is an old chapel that has been restored by the villagers. The views across the valley to the Mont de Ste-Baume are magnificent. The vineyards of Bandol seem to form an amphitheatre of terraces, and indeed Bandol has been called 'the appellation of 10,000 terraces'. Some of them were actually built by the Phocaeans, but many were abandoned as the vineyards returned to scrub and woodland after the phylloxera. They are essential, however, in preventing erosion on the steepest hillsides. Mixed with the vines there are olive trees, but otherwise little else can be cultivated here.

The soil is very poor. Basically it is a mixture of clay and limestone, but the proportions of each, and the gravel content, vary considerably within the area of the appellation. The region is also known to geologists for the Renversement du Beausset, a formation in which geological layers have somersaulted, so that the older rocks lie above the later ones.

The appellation of Bandol covers the parishes of Bandol itself, Sanary, La Cadière, Le Castellet and parts of Le Beausset, St-Cyr-sur-Mer, Ollioules and Évenos. The area under vines now totals some 940 hectares, a considerable increase from the 100 hectares of 1941. More vineyards could be planted, but alas, in areas by the coast the land is more valuable for building holiday villas. Today Bandol is an attractive port, full of pleasure-boats and fishing-boats. Cafés and restaurants line the harbour. Le Castellet and La Cadière are both old hilltop towns, but while the former has preserved its medieval charm, the latter has allowed some encroachment by the twentieth century.

The Mistral can blow hard here, even on an otherwise fine day. The drying wind provides a wonderful treatment for rot. As Paul Bunan said, 'The Mistral is our best friend; it is he who treats the vines.' In fact the climate as a whole is very favourable to viticulture, for there are long hours of sunshine. Sea breezes temper the heat of the day, while at night cooler air from the mountains also helps to offset the daytime temperatures. Normally there is little rain, rarely more than 60 centimetres per year; but the south east wind can bring rain, and the elegant Éric Boisseaux of Château Vannières informed us that when this happens the wine-growers say (rather less elegantly) that it is *les vaches qui pissent*, such is the torrent of water that falls out of the sky – as it did when we were there.

Indisputably it is the Mourvèdre grape that gives red Bandol its character. Mourvèdre shows its true quality and potential, unmatched anywhere else, in the vineyards of Bandol. Mourvèdre is of Spanish origin; in other parts of the world it is called Mataro, so that Mataro in Valencia and Murviedro in Catalonia both claim to be its home. Nevertheless it has been grown in southern France for over four centuries.

The Mourvèdre likes to see the sea, for it enjoys the sea breezes; but it also demands hot Provençal sunshine and likes clay soil. As Paul Bunan put it, 'It likes its head in the sun and its roots in the damp, in cool soil.' Its bud-break comes late and it is thus also a late ripener. The vintage in Bandol takes place in late September and Mourvèdre is the last grape variety to be picked, often not until well into October. In the drying conditions of the Mistral, its tough, thick-skinned berries rarely suffer from rot. But it can be a difficult vine to graft on to American rootstock, which explains its disappearance from the vineyards of Bandol for so long. It is only in the last ten or twenty years that it has returned, but it now occupies a growing proportion of the appellation's vineyards.

Pink Bandol comes from the same three grape varieties as red Bandol, but tends to contain more Grenache and Cinsaut. White Bandol, which only accounts for 10 per cent of the total production of the appellation, is based on Clairette Pointu (the same Clairette as Clairette de Bellegarde) and Ugni Blanc. Some growers have Bourboulenc, and others, more successfully, Sauvignon. Some, such as Domaine Tempier, make no white wine at all.

Domaine Tempier, which today is run by Lucien Peyraud and his son sons, François and Jean-Marie, consists of 27 hectares distributed between three vineyards: Le Plan du Castellet, around the cellars; La Tourtine, which consists of 8 hectares; and Le Mijoua, near the chapel at Le Beausset, which at 250 metres is the highest in altitude. The vinification is all centralized at Le Plan du Castellet. Mme Peyraud's great-grandmother built the cellars in 1880, but they have since been modernized. Everything works by gravity, so that they avoid pumping the wine unnecessarily. They used to ferment their red wine in large wooden barrels, but that dried up the wine; so they were replaced first with cement vats and later, when the cellars were enlarged in 1968, with stainless-steel tanks.

At Domaine Tempier they make their wine as naturally as possible. They assert that they are craftsmen in wine, and not aiming for a commercial product; they say that some wine-growers have oenologists who put in more chemicals than are necessary, thereby deforming the character of the wine. In the vineyard they use no chemical fertilizers and no weedkillers, and they respect the composition of the soil; if you spoil it with chemicals, you get unbalanced grapes. In the cellar, sulphur dioxide is kept to a minimum.

Their red wine is fermented in stainless-steel or cement vats for seven days at a temperature of 25°C. All the grapes are fermented together, for they consider that the 'best marriage' takes place in the vat at the beginning. The appellation regulations require a minimum of eighteen months' ageing, which ideally should be in wood. At Domaine Tempier they use large oak barrels. The wood is too old to contribute anything to the wine but there is already enough tannin so it just allows a gentle oxidation, which is not possible with cement or stainless steel. The ageing period is often longer, always at least two years, and the more Mourvèdre you have, the longer the time you need. The best vintages, such as 1985, 1982 and 1975, stayed in wood for three years.

They experiment with different *cuvées* from the three estates, so that the precise proportions of grape varieties can vary from one estate to another, and from one vintage to another. They have a very small amount of Syrah, but do not find that it performs well in Bandol. It ripens too early and is better suited to the cooler conditions of the northern Rhône. 'Mourvèdre is the king and you have to kneel before it.' Grown without wires, pruned in the *gobelet* style, it gives low yields, never more than 40 hectolitres per hectare and often less.

About a third of the appellation is pink for the whole of Provence is dominated by pink wine, notably Côtes de Provence of indifferent quality. Normally it is a wine for the seaside and the summer, but at Domaine Tempier they aim for a pink for connoisseurs, not simply a thirst-quencher. Good pink wine is difficult to make. The blend is 35 per cent each of Cinsaut and Grenache, plus 30 per cent of Mourvèdre from young vines, i.e. less than ten years old. Half is made from pressed grapes and half from free-run juice; in contrast to their red wine, they ferment it (at 25°C for ten days) in wood. It is then bottled early to provide a fresh, fragrantly fruity wine to drink within the year. Good though their pink may be, the reputation of Domaine Tempier and of Bandol rests firmly on red wines, with their delicious, complex flavours of Mourvèdre – flavours that develop with bottle age.

The *grande dame* of the appellation of Bandol is the Comtesse Arlette de Portalis, who shares with Lucien Peyraud some of the credit for re-establishing Mourvèdre in the vineyards of Bandol. She is now a rather frail old lady, with an air of eccentricity, who hardly stirs from her bedroom; she received us there with the words, 'What can I tell you, my dears?' She reminisced about the old days, saying that Mourvèdre was the only grape variety before the phylloxera, but that the Provençaux were lazy and preferred to plant the easier Aramon and Carignan. But even as a *vin de table* Bandol had a good reputation.

Another very old estate is Domaine de la Laidière, which has been owned by the Estienne family for several generations. Jules and his son Freddy now have 25 hectares of vines on south east-facing terraces near Le Beausset. The estate has grown since 1941 when Jules's father had just 6 hectares of vines and a press for olive-oil. When all the olive trees were killed in the bad frost of 1956, they turned to wine. They make all three colours of Bandol, including some of the best white of the appellation. The blend for the white wine is 60 per cent Clairette and 40 per cent Ugni Blanc. Great care is taken to avoid any oxidation during the vinification, and the fermentation is carefully controlled at 20°C. In the autumn of 1987 the 1986 had a fresh, fruity nose and a dry, nutty flavour.

Their vines range in age from one year old to sixty; the output of vines that are less than ten years old goes into the pink wine, for which the blend is usually 40 per cent each of Carignan and Mourvèdre with 20 per cent Grenache. It is a wine for early drinking, with a tang of raspberries.

The cellars have been equipped with stainless-steel vats and the fermentation temperatures are controlled by running cold water over the outside of the vats. The red wine is fermented at 30°C for eleven days, with a daily *remontage*. They used not to destalk the grapes, but now they do, preferring the tannin from the grapes to that from the stalks. In this way some of the former astringency is removed and the wine also needs less ageing and is ready to drink after five years.

The blending is done after the malolactic fermentation has finished, and the red wine usually consists of 50 per cent Mourvèdre with 25 per cent each of Cinsaut and Grenache. M. Estienne does not believe in pure Mourvèdre, maintaining that without the complement of the other varieties it is too tough, tannic and overpowering. His 1982, a particularly good vintage, was a real mouthful of wine, still very young and concentrated, with meaty overtones. In contrast the 1985, which had just been bottled, was lighter, rather spicy, with flavours of red fruit.

There have been many newcomers to the appellation of Bandol over the last ten or twenty years. Some arrived here more by accident than intention, such as the Comte de St-Victor at Domaine de Pibarnon. He says that in 1973 he hardly knew of the existence of Bandol; when he took the train to Nice he was vaguely aware of a loudspeaker calling, '*Bandol deux minutes d'arrêt*,' but no more. But he was looking for a wine estate to buy and he did stop in Bandol; he had a lousy meal, but the wine was wonderful. 'Beware of what you drink in restaurants; that's what led me here!'

After some searching he bought Domaine de Pibarnon, which at 300 metres is the highest estate of the appellation. You approach it along a narrow road from outside La Cadière and on a fine day you can see La Ciotat and the coastline. The estate was run-down, with 5 hectares of vines and some pigs. So from working with patents, with a degree in political science, M. de St-Victor turned wine-grower.

He is full of ideas and enthusiasm, for he has come to wine-making with no preconceptions. He is convinced of the qualities of the Mourvèdre and has increased the percentage in his vineyard from 50 to 80 per cent. This is complemented with 10 per cent each of Cinsaut and Grenache, whereas previously it was 40 per cent Cinsaut and 10 per cent Grenache. The vineyard has been extended to 25 hectares. He has a small, neat, traditional cellar, equipped with stainless-steel fermentation vats and wooden casks. His grapes are not destalked and all three grape varieties are fermented together; he considers this to be better than blending afterwards, for it is like cooking a stew when you just put everything in together! The wine is aged for between eighteen months and two years in large casks and then demands some bottle age before it is ready to drink. He is also experimenting with some pure Mourvèdre in new 228-litre barrels. With this, vanilla and fruit were the dominant flavours, while the same wine in large casks was tougher and more concentrated. His 1979, which was a lighter vintage, was elegant, with meaty overtones and flavours of mushrooms. 'This is the style of wine that led me here,' and one could see his point.

The independence of Algeria brought an influx of newcomers into the area. The Bunan family, who own Moulin des Costes and Mas de la Rouvière, had vineyards in Algeria. They bought their first estate in Bandol in 1962 and the second seven years later. They also rent Domaine du Belouvé, which makes them one of the largest producers of the appellation. The only other estate of comparable size is Château Romassan which is part of Domaines Ott, whose activities are discussed on page 267. All the Bunans' wine is made at Moulin des Costes near La Cadière d'Azur, and in practice there is no difference between the three estates. Theirs is one of the most modern cellars of the appellation. Their white Bandol consists of Ugni Blanc and Clairette, with 5 per cent each of Sauvignon and Bourboulenc to give some extra fruit and character. They are trying three or four hours' skin contact for the white wine, and are achieving successful results with Sauvignon. They have also made a pure Sauvignon as a Vin de Pays de Mont Caume, which is the *vin de pays* that covers the appellation of Bandol.

Their pink wine consists mainly of Grenache, with 25 per cent Mourvèdre and 15 per cent Cinsaut. The juice is given some skin contact before the grapes are pressed. Methods are modern: the juice is centrifuged and fermented in stainless-steel vats for ten or twelve days, with the temperature carefully controlled around 15°C.

The Bunans' red wines tend towards the lighter style of Bandol; but they are none the worse for that, for it makes them more accessible, with more immediate fruit. Mourvèdre usually represents about 65 to 75 per cent of the blend and it is not destalked, whereas Cinsaut and Grenache are. The fermentation takes about twelve to fifteen days at about 23°C, which is low for red wine, and the length of ageing varies. The lighter 1983 spent eighteen months in wood, compared with two years for the tougher 1982. They too are experimenting with ageing Bandol in new small barrels – the 1982 tasted very oaky. They also have some Cabernet Sauvignon for Vin de Pays de Mont Caume; they planted these about ten years ago as they wanted to make *vin de pays* of a completely different style, rather than an indifferent lesser Bandol. Often the same grape varieties are used for the *vin de pays* as for the appellation; when this happens, either grapes from young vines are used, or alternatively the less successful vats of Bandol are declassified into *vin de pays*.

At Domaine de Terrebrune, you not only receive a warm welcome from Georges and Claire Delille, but also from their dogs, Snoopy and Sultan. This is the most easterly estate of the appellation, outside Ollioules. As its name implies, the soil is indeed brown. The Delilles bought the estate in 1961. There were some vines from the 1900s, but the land was mostly used for market gardening – artichokes and flowers – so they started from scratch. They built south-facing terraces, left the land fallow for several years, and gradually planted 20 hectares of vines. 1975 was the first year they made wine, and until then they simply sold their grapes.

Like Domaine Tempier they practise organic viticulture, treating their vines only with copper sulphate on the rare occasions that some treatment is necessary. The Grenache is trained on wires, as otherwise it tends to flop on to the ground, causing the grapes to rot. The Mourvèdre is grown in the *gobelet* system with 4,500 plants to the hectare; they also have a little Syrah, but it is not very satisfactory. They make no white wine, and the pink (made mainly from Cinsaut, with 25 per cent Mourvèdre and 30 per cent Grenache) spends six months in large casks. It is dry and fragrant.

Half of the grapes for the red wine are destalked, and the juice is fermented in stainless steel and then aged for two years in wood. The barrels are topped up every fifteen days. They are particularly enthusiastic about their 1982 and I liked it, too. Its nose reminded me of smoky bacon and it had flavours of raspberries and cherries, with very good structure and balance; it was lighter than some Bandol, but a delicious glass of wine.

Château de Vannières is one of the most attractive properties of the appellation. It is owned by the Boisseaux family, who also have vineyards on the Côte de Beaune, though Éric Boisseaux prefers to spend his time in Bandol. The estate has its origins in the sixteenth century with André de Lombard, Seigneur du Castellet. The present château was built by a Scotsman about 1850 and then belonged to the family of the French minister Bénazet, whose heirs sold the estate to Éric Boisseaux's grandfather in 1957. The original sixteenth-century vaulted cellar is now used as a tasting- and sales-room, and there are delightful gardens and a 300-year-old pine tree in the courtyard of the château. You enter the cellars via a magnificent sixteenth-century staircase.

The vineyards have been replanted, and there are now 30 hectares producing all three colours of Bandol. White is made from Ugni Blanc, which will probably be pulled up. Pink comes from one-third each of Grenache, Cinsaut and Tibouren, which are pressed and fermented at a cool temperature.

The red wine consists of 50 per cent Mourvèdre, 20 per cent each of Grenache and Cinsaut and as much as 10 per cent Syrah. The grapes are not destalked or crushed, but put into the fermentation vats intact, all four varieties mixed up together. After a traditional fermentation, controlled at 25–27°C, the wine is aged in large casks for eighteen months. Château Vannières is one of the lighter wines of Bandol and with its gentle, meaty nose and hint of blackcurrants, the 1983 went well with barbecued lamb flavoured with thyme. In 1986 it still needed another year or so of bottle ageing.

There are other private estates worthy of note in Bandol and I have enjoyed wine from Domaine de la Bastide Blanche, with its excellent white wine, Domaine de Cagueloup and Domaine de Frégate. There is also the reliable co-operative La Roque, with its cellars near La Cadière d'Azur.

There is a general optimistic feeling about the future of Bandol. Serious growers are concentrating on making a wine of quality and character, displaying the unique qualities of the Mourvèdre, which is undoubtedly at its best on the sun-soaked terraces of Bandol.

PALETTE

Few people who leave Aix-en-Provence by motorway in the direction of Marseilles notice a small vineyard up on the hillside outside the town; they have flashed past it in an instant, ignoring the sixteenth-century building of Château Simone. The appellation is Palette, one of the very smallest in France, with just 25 hectares.

Château Simone accounts for 80 per cent of Palette – all the white and pink wine, and most of the red. The colour breakdown within the estate is 50 per cent red, 30 per cent pink and 20 per cent white. There is just one other producer of red Palette, Château de la Crémade, but the quality there bears no relation to that at Château Simone. For lovers of Provence wine, Château Simone *is* Palette.

The name Palette comes from a hamlet outside Aix-en-Provence and the appellation lies within the adjoining village of Meyreuil. In the sixteenth century the estate belonged to Les Grands Carmes d'Aix, the Carmelites. It was they who planted the first vines and built the magnificent cellars that are still used today. A subsequent owner of the property was a Mlle Simone and for over two centuries, since the reign of Louis XVI, Château Simone has been in the hands of the Rougier family. René Rougier is the seventh generation.

He talked of his father's and grandfather's contributions to the reputation of Château Simone. His grandfather lived to the age of 103 and had known Cézanne and also Winston Churchill, who painted the Mont Ste-Victoire from a vantage point by the humpback bridge, the Pont des Trois Sautets, near the entrance to the property. Churchill sent him a telegram on his hundredth birthday. René Rougier's father was one of the pioneers in Provence for selling wine in bottle: he first bottled Château Simone back in 1921, following the example of Châteauneuf-du-Pape and demonstrating the ageing potential of his wine.

Palette was one of the early post-war appellations, recognized in 1948. M. Chappaz, vice-president of the INAO, who was responsible for the creation of the early appellations, notably that of Bandol, appreciated the geological distinctiveness of Palette and Château Simone. At that time the surrounding appellation of Coteaux d'Aix-en-Provence was not even dreamt of, and Château Simone was a small estate in a sea of *vin ordinaire*. But it is at the centre of a geological formation called the Cercle de Palette, and the soil consists of limestone debris called the Calcaire de Langesse.

The Rougier family would have liked the appellation of Palette to cover just their own vineyards, following the example of Château Grillet in the Rhône valley. However, the Cercle de Palette extends over a larger area of about 300 hectares. For geological reasons, neighbouring land had to be included, but most of it is forest which is very unlikely ever to be cut down. The forest contributes to the microclimate of the vineyards, which are surrounded by pines. The river Arc crosses the appellation, providing an element of humidity, and the vines face north, so that the sun's rays are more gentle. They are protected from strong winds by an amphitheatre of hills which also concentrates the heat in the vineyard even though it is north-facing. Consequently the grapes ripen perfectly, though not usually until the beginning of October. The vines are cultivated in the traditional way, with no chemical fertilizers or weedkillers.

Phylloxera destroyed the vineyard in 1875, but the Rougier family replanted their land with the traditional grape varieties of Provence. Some of the oldest vines go back to 1890. There is a high percentage of Mourvèdre, Grenache and Cinsaut, as well as several other red grapes: Syrah, which has always been grown here, a little Carignan, red Picpoul, Muscat Rouge and two unknown Provençal grapes, Manosquen and Castet. The white wine is made from Ugni Blanc, Grenache Blanc, white Picpoul and various types of Muscat. Fifteen hectares are in production at Château Simone, with another 5 hectares planned. Yields are small, never more than 40 hectolitres per hectare, giving an annual production of 60–80,000 bottles. The different grape varieties are mixed up in the vineyard, and thus all fermented together. Any precise blending would be anathema.

Methods here are traditional. 'This is the house where the most respected word is tradition. That is what gives our wines strength. We try to adapt the techniques of modern science, while respecting the practices of the old days that made the reputation of Château Simone.' It works! Château Simone is not only one of the very best wines of Provence, but ranks amongst the great wines of France.

The white wine is fermented in large oak barrels and fermentation temperatures are left to nature, for there is no danger of the must overheating in these cool underground cellars. The fermentation usually takes a couple of weeks. A light dose of sulphur dioxide prevents a malolactic fermentation and then the wine is aged in 600-litre barrels for one or two years, during which time there are regular rackings and *ouillages*, or toppings-up. They have two qualities of white wine, determined by the period of wood ageing. The 1986, aged for one year in wood, had a gentle, leafy nose and a slightly nutty flavour; the 1983, with two years in wood, was a much fuller, more complex wine, rich in flavour, almost honeyed, with hints of acacia and lime. M. Rougier reckons it will take seven years to reach its plateau, and will last for a further ten years.

The pink wine is also made to last. This is not a wine to quaff in youthful freshness like most Provençal pinks. On the contrary, it has body and weight after two years' ageing in large oak barrels.

Although M. Rougier studied at Montpellier and Beaune, he says that Château Simone's methods of vinification have not changed since his grandfather's day. The red wine is fermented in cement vats for about twelve to fifteen days, and the temperature reaches at least 30°C, which gives good colour, extract and aroma. The grapes are partially destalked, but there is no *pigeage* and only one *remontage*, at the end of the fermentation. The red wines are fined with real egg-whites and are aged first in large barrels and then in smaller ones. A few of the barrels are new replacements, but most have been carefully looked after and are quite old. The malolactic fermentation usually takes place in the spring: 'We are not in a hurry here.' These are wines to age in bottle, and they still have wine from the earliest bottlings in 1921. The label is delightfully old-fashioned; it was designed soon after the First World War and they have never seen the need to change it.

We tasted the 1983, which had not yet begun to age in colour. There was an excellent balance of fruit and tannin, with lots of both, and flavours of prunes, plus a hint of animal and a slight earthiness, all leaving a long finish. M. Rougier reckons the 1983 has very good potential; amongst other great vintages he rates 1975, 1971, 1969, 1964 and 1947. These are wines to drink with red meat, ideally wild boar and other game from the woods of Palette.

BELLET

The vineyards of the tiny appellation of Bellet nestle amongst the suburbs of Nice and there are many amongst the city's 400,000 inhabitants who fail to realize that there are vineyards within the city boundaries. You can ask for a bottle of Bellet in one of the open-air fish restaurants of the old town, and your request will be treated with sceptical disbelief as to the existence of Bellet.

If you leave behind the elegance of the Promenade des Anglais and the bustle of the city, and drive up into the hills to the outlying village of St-Romain-de-Bellet, you come to vineyards that are often overlooked by suburban villas. In the nineteenth century Alpes-Maritimes, which only became part of France in 1860, was an important viticultural department, with many vineyards which have long since disappeared. Vines gave way to carnations, which are now the main crop.

The earliest historical reference I could find to the wines of Bellet was a letter from a certain Marshal de Catinat, writing to the governor of Nice on 26 August 1696 and saying, 'You ask me for news of the wine from Bellet that you sent to me. I can assure you that it was found to be admirable and better than the wines of France that we have here, although they were well chosen.'

Two centuries later Guyot was rather less enthusiastic, saying that if the vineyards were well kept they would give delicious wine and that Bellet was good if it was well made, but often it was not. He mentioned Braquet as being a very fine and rich grape, accounting for a fifth of the vineyards, while Fuella, the present day Folle Noire, accounted for three-fifths and the rest was Roussanne, Négret, Pignerol and Clairette.

The appellation of Bellet was created in 1941 and 600 hectares were delimited, but only 55 hectares are currently planted. This figure is very unlikely to increase, as any available land is greedily snapped up by building contractors. The appellation of Bellet had a rather chequered early career, for the quality – or rather lack of quality – of the wine was such that it was nearly demoted in 1943. But Philippe Bagnis's grandfather, at Château de Crémat, one of the principal producers of Bellet, asked for two years' grace and managed to negotiate a stay of execution. The appellation really only began to emerge from the doldrums in the early 1960s. Today there are five bottlers of Bellet, among whom the most important are the Bagnis family at the Château de Crémat and the de Charnacé family at the Château de Bellet. Without these two families, the appellation of Bellet would have disappeared.

The Château de Bellet is a charming building of a soft russet colour, and dates from the fifteenth century. One of its owners, Pierre Roissard, was created Baron de Bellet by the Duke of Savoy in 1777 and the property is still owned by his heirs. I was given a warm welcome by Ghislain de Charnacé and a less enthusiastic one by the Belgian sheep-dog Attila, who was firmly told, 'Attila, you do not eat the guests.' First we went to the vineyards. At an altitude of 300 metres, on terraced slopes facing the Alps on the east bank of the Var, they are much cooler than many of the vineyards of Provence. The vintage here does not begin until the end of September. There are always gentle cooling breezes from the sea and from the mountains, but no strong winds – just the tail end of the Mistral. In winter there are frosts and sometimes snow. They like rain in the spring and in June after the flowering, so that the vines have enough water to be able to withstand the summer drought.

Bellet can be red, white or pink. The principal grape variety for the white wine is the Rolle, a variety rarely found outside Bellet, and never outside Provence. Since 1955, thanks to the efforts of the Bagnis family, Chardonnay has also been permitted. The grape varieties for red and pink Bellet demonstrate the area's links with Italy, for the two most important ones are the Braquet, which is the Brachetto of Piedmont, and the Folle Noire, which is no relation of the Folle Blanche and for which a synonym is Fuella. Grenache and Cinsaut are also grown; other grape varieties feature in the appellation decree, but are not found in the vineyards.

 Ghislain de Charnacé is an enthusiastic exponent of the qualities of Braquet. He explained how the variety had almost disappeared from the area because of its fragility; it gives only a small amount of fruit, but wine of great finesse. In contrast the Folle Noire provides colour and tannin, and the Grenache alcohol. He is working on restoring Braquet to the vineyards of Bellet. There were a few remaining vines from which to take cuttings, but Braquet also demands the right pruning, a type of *guyot*, and compatible rootstock (from the *vitis rupestris* or *vitis berlandieri* family). Even then yields are low, an average of 25 to 30 hectolitres per hectare. But for M. de Charnacé, Braquet gives red Bellet its true character. Philippe Bagnis at the Château de Crémat disagrees. He thinks that Braquet should be used for pink wine, while Folle Noire makes fuller, longer-lasting red wine. M. de Charnacé, however, does not make a red wine to age and his 1983, tasted in September 1986, was light, perfumed, peppery and quite individual. In contrast the red of M. Bagnis was a more solid, substantial mouthful.

 Both age their red wine in large oak barrels. At the Château de Bellet the grapes are crushed but not destalked, and the fermentation takes place in vats for about ten days at 30°C with two *remontages* every day, after which the wine is aged for twelve months in wood. In contrast, at the Château de Crémat, where the red wine is made from 60 per cent Folle Noire with equal parts of Grenache and Braquet, the fermentation takes place in wood and the wine is aged first in large barrels and then in small ones, also for a total of twelve months.

 It was undeniably the white wine of Bellet that excited me the most and that which I tasted at the Château de Bellet certainly has a greater ageing potential than their red wine. M. de Charnacé believes that the stony chalk soil is much better suited to white wine than red. We compared his 1985 and 1980 vintages. The younger had an attractive nutty flavour that developed well in the glass, with a long finish. The taste had none of the heaviness that can spoil the white wines of Cassis, which is the only other white Provençal wine of any reputation. The

1980, which is only considered to be an average vintage, had developed a rich, leafy flavour with nutty overtones, so that comparison with a white Burgundy from the Côte d'Or would not have been completely out of place.

The Château de Crémat was built in the middle of the last century. Philippe Bagnis told the story of how, as a boy, his grandfather used to be brought out to St-Romain-de-Bellet for Sunday outings and would look at the château and say, 'When I am grown up that is the house I will buy.' Years later, in 1957, he achieved his ambition. A Roman road, the Via Augusta, ran through St-Romain-de-Bellet, where there was a look-out tower and a provisions point; the cellars of the château incorporate two Roman galleries.

The Bagnis family were successful Provence *négociants* before they became wine-growers at Bellet, and are responsible for the well-known Côtes de Provence brand L'Estandon. They now own 13 hectares of vineyards, rent 7 hectares, and buy the grapes of the very small growers of the appellation who do not have the means or inclination to vinify their own wine. The wine from their own vineyards is vinified separately. Their cellars have been modernized recently and are now streamlined with stainless-steel vinification vats, equipped with efficient temperature controls, for white and pink wine. There are new 225-litre barrels and some larger twenty-five-year-old casks.

The pink wine of Château de Crémat is dominated by Braquet, with 20 per cent each of Folle Noire and Cinsaut; this combination makes quite a full-flavoured wine, with hints of raspberry. The white wine contains 10 per cent of Chardonnay, which gives more nerve to the flatter Rolle.

For me the vocation of Bellet must undoubtedly be its white wine. The Rolle, with a little Chardonnay, benefits from the cooler climate of this part of Provence to give a white wine that is individual and distinctive. I enjoyed the elegant red wine of Château de Bellet, for there was an attractive aromatic quality that compensated for the lack of body in the Braquet. In contrast, the red wines with a higher proportion of Folle Noire seemed coarser. But my enthusiasm lies firmly with the whites of Bellet.

CÔTES DE PROVENCE

Contrary to the implications of its name, Côtes de Provence covers a relatively small part of Provence. The former Provincia Romana, from which came the name of Provence, covered five modern departments – Vaucluse, Alpes-de-Haute-Provence, Bouches-du-Rhône, Var and Alpes-Maritimes – while the appellation of Côtes de Provence is centred on Var, with some vineyards in Bouches-du-Rhône and Alpes-Maritimes. Vines have been grown here since the Greeks colonized Marseilles in the sixth century BC, and the Romans did more to establish viticulture here. Julius Caesar founded the town of Fréjus (formerly Forum Julii) and wrote about the region's wines, which found their way to Rome, in his commentaries.

In the early thirteenth century the marriage of Eleanor of Provence to the English King Henry III brought the wines of Provence to England. René of Anjou, the last Count of Provence, appreciated his country's wines. Born in Angers, titular king of Naples, Sicily and Jerusalem, responsible for ceding Provence to Louis XI of France in 1480, he was a man of letters who is also credited with the introduction of the Muscat grape to Provence as well as with the invention of the method of making *vin clairet*, a deeper-coloured pink wine.

In the seventeenth century, that inexhaustible letter-writer Madame de Sévigné often stayed at Entrecasteaux near Draguignan and referred to the wines of the region. It was not until the nineteenth century that wine became the most important product of Provence, for until then it was overshadowed by cereals, olives, fruit and vegetables. The vines grew on terraced hillsides, mixed with olive and fruit trees, and wheat was cultivated in the valleys.

None of the nineteenth-century authorities wrote of the wines of Provence with any great enthusiasm. Jullien tells us that 92,900 hectares produced 1,687,000 hectolitres in 1816, of which 889,000 were drunk locally. The most sought-after were the Muscat wines and the *vins cuits* or cooked wines. He says that the variety of grapes grown was enormous, but the mixture gave no specific taste to the wine and took away all its qualities without giving it anything. No mention was made of any pink wine, only red and white, *vins cuits* and Muscats. For Rendu the wines of Provence were mostly in the class of common wines for local consumption, and there was a lack of good grapes and careful vinification. Cavoleau wrote that the wines of Provence had little reputation and were only sought after in

France when there was a small harvest in other vineyards. He thought they could be good, with good grapes and climate, but that there was a lack of attention to the production process.

Phylloxera wrought havoc in the vineyards of Provence in the 1870s, and with the subsequent replanting the small-yielding Mourvèdre was abandoned in favour of the more prolific Carignan. But the early years of this century saw the arrival of pioneers of improving grape varieties from outside the region. Marcel Ott came from Alsace and bought Château de Selle near the village of Taradeau in 1912; in the spirit of experimentation he planted the vineyards with all the main grape varieties of France, including Gewurztraminer, Riesling, Cabernet Sauvignon, Sémillon, Sauvignon and so on. Others were to build upon his work. In the 1930s there were the first tentative efforts towards a recognition of a standard of quality, with the formation of an association dedicated to obtaining an appellation.

This ambition was not achieved until 1977, although a VDQS was granted for Côtes de Provence in 1951. The issue was confused by the union of a group of *crus classés*, formally recognized by the INAO in 1955, comprising some twenty-three estates. One of the founders of this group was the distinguished Count Henri de Laval, who today is still the proprietor of Château Ste-Rosaline, one of the more traditional estates of the appellation. These estates were considered at the time to be the best, but in practice they were those who regularly bottled their own wines rather than selling in bulk to the local *négociants*. Although the classification still exists as the only system of *crus classés* outside Bordeaux, it is meaningless and has no connection with reality. The fortunes of these twenty-odd properties have fluctuated; some have disappeared altogether and only a handful merit any distinction today. There are other, newer estates that would merit inclusion, but the INAO – firmly backed by the Bordelais – has forbidden the extension of the classification. Here, for the record, is the list of estates recognized in 1955: Domaine de Mauvanne, Coteaux des Ferrages, Domaine de la Source Ste-Marguerite, Castel Roubine, Domaine de l'Aumérade, Domaine de la Clapière, Clos du Relars, Domaine de Rimauresq, Château Ste-Rosaline, Château de Selle, Clos Mireille, Château St-Martin, Domaine de la Croix, Domaine de St-Maur, Clos Cibonne, Domaine du Galoupet, Domaine de Bregançon, Château Minuty, Domaine de la Grande Loube, Domaine du Noyer and Domaine du Jas d'Esclans. Those that are worthy of note today include the two Ott properties, Clos

Mireille and Château de Selle, Château Ste-Rosaline, Château Minuty and a handful of the others.

The area of Côtes de Provence was delimited to 18,000 hectares in 1951, and was not significantly altered with the introduction of the appellation in 1977. The vineyards cover a wide area. The greater part of the appellation is in the department of Var, including the coastal region south of the Massif des Maures and a large area to the north of the mountains. On the west side it is limited by the recent VDQS of the Coteaux Varois. The city of Toulon interrupts the coastal vineyards so that these are mainly in the west, around the appellation of Bandol and towards Cassis in the department of Bouches-du-Rhône. Finally there is just one parish of the appellation, Villars-sur-Var, in the department of Alpes-Maritimes. The average annual production of 750,000 hectolitres of Côtes de Provence breaks down into 60 per cent pink wine, 35 per cent red and 5 per cent white.

Pink wine accounted for the early popularity of Côtes de Provence, and now for its lack of success. When the Côte d'Azur became a popular holiday resort and tourists flocked to Provence, they wanted light, refreshing wines to quench their thirst in the warm sunshine. Pink Côtes de Provence was the ideal drink, a pretty, frivolous wine for holidays and picnics. With few exceptions this is not a region of white wine, but the grapes that make red wine could easily make pink to meet the holidaymakers' requirements. Outside the tourist season, however the demand for pink Côtes de Provence was non-existent. For the majority of Frenchmen, the first requirement of a wine is that it should be red. Consequently, in the past few years, perhaps prompted by the granting of appellation status, there has been a gentle drift towards red wine among more serious growers.

The large area of the appellation covers a considerable variety of terrain and microclimate, and consequently produces a diversity of wines. The soil changes, too, for clay and limestone are the dominant constituents inland, while shale with quartz is more common in the coastal vineyards. In either case the soil is poor, stony and lacking in humus, the type of soil that vines love and in which little else can grow.

The climate is Mediterranean, with hot dry summers, cool winters and little rainfall. What rain there is usually falls at the end of the autumn and in the spring. The summer months are usually free of rain and vines can suffer from drought. In some instances, where the water table is high, the vines' roots are able to tap underground sources of water. Provence is the region of the Mistral and the wind can blow hard, sometimes damaging the younger, more fragile vines, but generally it does more good than harm, preventing the humidity that causes the development of rot and disease. For those who practise organic viticulture, and there are several in the appellation, life is made easier by the drying effect of the Mistral.

Such a variety of soil and microclimatic conditions inevitably encourages a diversity of grape varieties. The small amount of white Côtes de Provence comes mainly from Ugni Blanc, with some Clairette, Sémillon or Rolle. The more serious producers concentrate on Sémillon and Rolle to enliven the ubiquitous Ugni Blanc. Clos Mireille, one of the Ott estates, is known for its delicious white wine made from equal amounts of Sémillon and Ugni Blanc. The best white wine at Domaine de la Bernarde includes 40 per cent of Sémillon blended with the wine from seventy-year-old Ugni Blanc vines. In contrast, at Château Ste-Rosaline there is no Ugni Blanc at all and the white wine is made from 30 per cent Sémillon and 10 per cent Clairette, with the greater part of the blend coming from Rolle.

Black grapes account for 95 per cent of the vineyards, with a considerable choice available to any producer of Côtes de Provence. Changes were implemented with the elevation of the area to an appellation. The high-yielding Carignan was the principal grape variety for both red and pink Côtes de Provence, but the results were dull and uninspiring. A gradual change has therefore been programmed. Whereas Carignan accounted for 70 per cent of red and pink Côtes de Provence in 1978, the proportion has now been decreased to 40 per cent. It is being replaced by Grenache, which gives warm, full-bodied wines. Cinsaut is popular for pink wines and the soft-skinned Tibouren also contributes to successful pinks. Mourvèdre performs better at Bandol than in the Côtes de Provence; a local saying insists that it should see the sea to ripen well, and inland it does indeed sometimes fail to ripen fully.

The two grape varieties which have attracted the most interest are Syrah and Cabernet Sauvignon. They can both enhance the sometimes bland wines of the Côtes de Provence, but must not exceed more than 30 per cent of a blend. Indeed, the appellation regulations are littered with limitations on maximum and minimum percentages. They determine what is planted in a vineyard, but who is to say that a wine does or does not contain a certain percentage of a particular grape variety, provided that it tastes 'typical' of the appellation? Cabernet Sauvignon is enthusiastically viewed for its potential to enliven the more solid grape varieties of the south. However, serious producers are adamant that it should not be allowed to overwhelm the true flavour of the appellation; they do not want to produce a Provençal claret. Even so, it is undeniable that a small amount of Cabernet Sauvignon provides aroma and backbone in a wine without changing the essential character of a Côtes de Provence. Syrah, which is more commonly associated with the northern Rhône, has been slowly encroaching upon the vineyards of the south, and certainly contributes flavour and fruit, again without detracting from the true character of the appellation. The object is to improve, but not to transform.

Vinification methods have improved enormously during the ten years of the appellation. Well-equipped cellars ferment their white and pink wines at a cool temperature of around 18°C. Pinks are generally made by the *saigné* method, with the juice spending anything from four to twenty-four hours on the skins depending on the wine-maker's particular aims and preferences, and also on the condition of the grapes and the amount of colour they are likely to give the juice. After the desired time the juice is run off and fermentation takes place in the normal way. The residue of juice and skins is often topped up with more red grapes for a classic red fermentation. In contrast, a pink wine is sometimes made simply by pressing the grapes, for enough colour for a pale pink will be absorbed during this short contact with the skins.

There is more scope for variety with red wine vinification. Carbonic maceration is practised by some wine-makers and its main exponent in the Côtes de Provence is Guy Meulnart at Domaine de la Bernarde. Château Minuty also practises a variation of carbonic maceration, crushing the soft-skinned grapes and putting the tougher-skinned grapes whole into the fermentation vats. Some producers ferment each grape variety separately and make a careful blend of precise proportions, while others vinify all the different grape varieties together. Sometimes the grapes are destalked, sometimes not; sometimes the pressed wine is used in the blend, or in the regional *vin de pays*, or not at all – in which case it probably ends up at the distillery. Perhaps the greatest variation comes in the ageing of the vine before bottling. New 225-litre barrels represent a fashionable trend in some of the world's wine areas and Côtes de Provence is no exception.

While some estates use new barrels of this size, others use no wood at all, while most common of all are the large oak casks, called *foudres*, that contain 70 hectolitres or more of wine. A traditional estate will give the red and maybe even the pink wine at least one year's ageing in these large barrels, which are traditionally made of Slavonic oak.

The producers of Côtes de Provence therefore have enormous scope. The following paragraphs describe some of the better producers and relate who does what. The co-operatives account for two-thirds of the appellation; some are efficient and dynamic and others quite the opposite. Many of the co-operatives have changed from selling their wine in bulk to local *négociants* to bottling and marketing their wine themselves, often without thoroughly exploring the commercial implications. The unfortunate result is that a large amount of pink Côtes de Provence remains unsold each year, and there are serious problems of over-stocking of a wine that does not improve but deteriorates with age. Unions of co-operatives have been formed to relieve some of the pressures, most notably the Union des Maures et de l'Esterel and Univar, the Union des Vins du Var.

The most energetic co-operative of the appellation, however, is undoubtedly the Maîtres Vignerons du Presqu'île de St-Tropez. Legally they have co-operative status, but in practice they are not a traditional co-operative, but a group of twelve properties on the peninsula beyond St-Tropez who each vinify their own wine, but since 1974 have shared bottling and commercial facilities. The wine from one of the larger estates, Château de Pamplonne, is kept separately, while the wine from the others is blended together into two different qualities of Côtes de Provence, Cuvée du Cep d'Or and the better Carte Noire. Their best pink wine comes only from Grenache, and their best red from Grenache with some Syrah and Mourvèdre. They are keenly aware of the problems of selling pink wine, which only enjoys a seasonal demand as a *vin de café*. For them the future lies with better red wines and they are working hard to associate Côtes de Provence with red as well as pink wine. Cuvée Chasseur, with its attractive series of labels depicting game birds, is one idea of theirs.

The best-known name of the Côtes de Provence is Domaines Ott. Altogether the family owns three estates in Provence: Clos Mireille and Château de Selle, which are both in the appellation of Côtes de Provence, and Château Romassan in Bandol. Their offices are at

Antibes. Marcel Ott bought the dilapidated estate of Château de Selle near Taradeau in 1912. It is a beautiful old château, with a soft pink stone façade and terraced vineyards. On the winding road to the property you pass the remains of a Saracen tower and a Christian chapel on the same hilltop. The estate was used by the counts of Provence for hunting wild boar, and the existing château was built in the eighteenth century.

While Marcel Ott worked on his vineyards, establishing grape varieties like Cabernet Sauvignon and Sémillon, his son concentrated on the commercial aspects of the business and created the distinctive Ott bottle, the design of which is based on the Provençal *jarres*, the large earthenware pots which today you often find filled with geraniums. This nearly became accepted as the Provence bottle; instead there is now a plethora of different shapes, including a standard *négociant* and a standard producers' bottle, as well as several special shapes for individual growers, while more serious producers favour the tall, shouldered claret bottle for their red wine.

The Ott estates practise organic viticulture and each has a flock of sheep to provide the vines with natural manure. Many of the vines are trained on wires, contrary to the usual practice in Provence. The Ott reputation rests upon their pink wine from the Château de Selle, called Coeur du Grain, which travels the world to forty-odd countries. It certainly is one of the better Côtes de Provence pinks, and also one of the most expensive. Great care is taken with its vinification, with the Grenache being pressed immediately while the other grapes are fermented as for a *vin d'une nuit*. The usual blend is one-third each of Grenache, Cabernet Sauvignon and Cinsaut.

The red wine at Château de Selle is serious, too, made from 50 per cent Cabernet Sauvignon and equal parts of Grenache and Cinsaut. It is given eighteen months' ageing in large casks and is usually at its best after about another five years' bottle age. A 1981 drunk in 1988 was a deliciously rounded, harmonious glass of wine, while a 1957, which was an exceptional vintage, was a wonderful glass of wine with flavours reminiscent of both Burgundy and Bordeaux, with hints of cedarwood and vegetal overtones.

At Clos Mireille you can walk down to the Mediterranean from the vineyards, and this proximity to the sea means that the grapes are ripened by reflected heat and light from the water. The soil here is quite different from Château de Selle, being based on mica-schist and quartz. Here they concentrate on white wine, made from equal parts of Sauvignon and Ugni Blanc. Methods are traditional and Henri Ott, who runs the estate, sees no reason to change. He makes a white wine that will age; after fermentation in wood it spends two or three months in 600-litre barrels, and a little carbon dioxide from the fermentation is retained at bottling. The 1984, tasted in 1986, was developing rich, leafy flavours almost reminiscent of Chardonnay, but there were hints of Sémillon honey on the finish, and the faintest prickle of carbon dioxide. With a good balance of firm acidity they expect the wine to last for several years. It is a white Côtes de Provence that is quite out of the ordinary, with more in common with a wine from Bellet than with other white wines of the appellation.

Guy Meulnart at Domaine de la Bernarde reckoned Domaines Ott to be the leaders for white and pink Côtes de Provence, but he considered his red wine to be better. The Meulnart family bought Domaine de la Bernarde in 1974. Guy Meulnart's father had worked in industry, running a company that manufactured reels for fishing-rods, but wine was his passion and with the purchase of Domaine de la Bernarde he fulfilled a lifelong ambition. Guy Meulnart himself trained first as an architect and then as a mechanical engineer before coming to the estate in 1983.

He is an enthusiastic exponent of carbonic maceration; all their red wine is made like this, and not just for youthful drinking, but also with some ageing in mind. After fermentation it is kept in vat for several months, given a year's bottle age before sale, and not usually sold until it is two or three years old.

They make three red wines. The lowest quality is a *vin de pays*, from vineyards at the bottom of a hill that are not classified as Côtes de Provence; they are planted mainly with Carignan and sold as Domaine de Boudéry. Domaine de la Bernarde is made from equal parts of Cabernet Sauvignon, Syrah and Grenache, while Clos de la Bernarde comes mainly from Syrah and Cabernet Sauvignon. Their style is very distinctive, with perfume, fruit and flavour; peppery, chewy and quite soft, but with enough tannin to make a very enjoyable glass of wine. The Clos de la Bernarde has more tannin than Domaine de la Bernarde, and thus more substance and weight. A half-bottle of 1980 Clos de la Bernarde tasted in 1986 provided a warm, mellow mouthful of flavour, with hints of herbs and black-currants, admirably demonstrating the ageing potential. They are very distinctive wines, to be either loved or hated, with no half-measures.

The white wines from Domaine de la Bernarde are also good.

Sémillon, Clairette and Ugni Blanc are the main grape varieties, giving some full-flavoured, nutty wines. The two pinks (made principally from Grenache, Cinsaut and Tibouren) taste of fresh raspberries, with some attractive fruit and acidity. Later we sat under a fig tree at a nearby restaurant and washed down a *terrine de lapin* and some freshly grilled *cèpes* with pink Clos de la Bernarde. In the warm Provençal sunshine, all seemed right with the world.

Perhaps the most traditional estate of the appellation is Château Ste-Rosaline, which is owned by Baron Henri de Rasque de Laval, whose father was one of the pioneers of the appellation of Côtes de Provence. The property was formerly an abbey dating back to the twelfth century, and has beautiful cloisters of that period. Four religious orders have been here: Templars, Cistercians, Carthusians and Observantines, until the Revolution. M. de Laval's family have owned the estate since 1878 and were also owners of another good Côtes de Provence property, Château de Rasque. As for St Rosaline, she was a prioress here at the beginning of the fourteenth century and was canonized by Pope John XXII.

M. de Laval began working here in 1942, continuing his father's work in the cellar and vineyard. Although modern improvements have been accepted, there is still an aura of tradition, with an imposing cellar of old oak casks in which the pink wine spends a year and the red even longer. Carignan and Ugni Blanc have been uprooted, so the white wine is made from Rolle, Sémillon and Clairette, the pink from Mourvèdre, Cinsaut, Tibouren and Grenache in equal parts, and the red from Mourvèdre, Cabernet Sauvignon and Syrah, with a traditional fermentation of twenty days. The object is to make a wine that will age, and the taste is warm, rich and southern.

Another old estate is Château Minuty, which goes back to the eighteenth century. The present château was built under Napoleon III, with the addition a few years later of a tiny chapel in the grounds to commemorate a son killed in the Franco-Prussian war. A mass is said there every year for the grape-pickers. Since 1936 the estate has belonged to the Farnets, an old St-Tropez family, and today is run by M. Mattron, a lawyer by profession, who married Mlle Farnet. The estate has been completely reorganized over the last fifty years and they now have 45 hectares of vines, planted with Grenache, Cinsaut, Carignan, Mourvèdre, Cabernet Sauvignon and Syrah for red wines, and Tibouren for pink. White wine is made from Ugni Blanc, Clairette (which is known locally as Olivette de St-Tropez, as

the berries look like tiny olives), Rolle and Sémillon. They also
have a little Chardonnay, which is not very successful, and some
Sauvignon, which gives better results, but neither is allowed in the
appellation. Cabernet Sauvignon and Sémillon were here before the
phylloxera, so once they had been re-established by the Ott family
there was no problem in including them in the appellation.

The red wine here is made mainly by carbonic maceration. The
soft-skinned grapes are crushed and put into the vat first, with the
tougher grapes on top, uncrushed. The temperature is raised to 32°C
to extract the maximum amount of colour. With this method the
free-run juice is more tannic as it comes into contact with the stalks,
while the pressed juice is more perfumed and aromatic. The wine
then spends eight to twelve months in *foudres*; they have a magnificent
cellar, a real show-piece of old barrels. As for the taste, it is peppery
and perfumed – a youthful, fruity wine.

There are numerous other estates that merit a mention, such as
Commanderie de la Peyrassol, Château de Barbeyrolles and Château
St-André de Figière, but these are just the few that I was able to visit
of those which are characteristic of the injection of new energy into
the appellation of Côtes de Provence. Although most producers
continue to make a sizeable amount of pink wine, providing the
holiday-makers with a refreshing drink of varying quality, the far-
sighted amongst them are seeking to develop the potential of red
Côtes de Provence. The area of the Côtes de Provence is large, so that
there are numerous differences in soil and microclimate; some people
would like to see an amended appellation with a Côtes de Provence-
Villages, differentiating for example between the vineyards of the
coast around St-Tropez and those further inland near Cuers, along
the lines of Côtes du Rhône-Villages. There is a feeling that parcels
of vineyards that produce wines of a distinctive character and quality
are at present drowned in a sea of mediocrity and deserve some
distinction.

In the meantime an association has been formed, the Association
des Crus de la Côte d'Azur, which covers the vineyards of Provence
from Cassis to Bellet, but not as yet those of the Coteaux d'Aix-en-
Provence. Its members include the more dynamic producers of these
appellations and their objective is to create a marketing image for
the whole region and to promote and sell the wines of Provence.
Membership, which totals about forty estates, implies a certain
quality level.

Gérard Magrin, the director of the Comité Interprofessionnel des Côtes de Provence, whose shop-front is a brand new Maison du Vin at Les Arcs in the heart of the appellation, feels that the problem with Côtes de Provence lies in the lack of understanding of pink wines. People do not realize that pink wines are more difficult to make than either red or white wine, and the producers themselves have no pride in their pink wines. Pink Côtes de Provence is desperately in need of a quality image, so it is not surprising that many of the more serious growers have turned to red wine, where the potential is enormous. It may well be that the future of Côtes de Provence lies with red wine rather than pink. The reds can aspire to some stature, while the pinks, even at their best, will rarely be seen as more than attractive summer seaside wines.

COTEAUX D'AIX-EN-PROVENCE

The attractive town of Aix-en-Provence lies on the south east edge of the appellation to which it gives its name. Once these vineyards were called the Coteaux du Roy René, after the last count of Provence to hold his court at Aix. Although King René ceded Provence to the French king Louis XI on his death in 1480, Aix has remained the capital of the area. The tree-lined Cours Mirabelle, with its fine fountain, has elegant town houses and lively cafés. Aix-en-Provence hosts an annual arts festival and you can visit Cézanne's studio.

Vines have grown on these hillsides around Aix for centuries. Even so, in the early nineteenth century Jullien wrote that there was no vineyard that merited the attention of gourmets. Later writers ignored the area completely. By 1956 the vineyards of the Coteaux d'Aix-en-Provence were sufficiently distinguished from the surrounding mass of *vin ordinaire* to be recognized as a VDQS. There was disappointment in 1977 when they were not given an appellation to match the nearby Côtes de Provence. But I cannot help suspecting that this has proved a blessing in disguise, for the supposed slight to the Coteaux d'Aix-en-Provence provoked a considerable effort to improve the quality of the wines, with the result that Coteaux d'Aix-en-Provence became an appellation in 1985 and now compares very favourably with Côtes de Provence. It has one distinct advantage over Côtes de Provence: the larger part of the production is red, so it is not tainted by association with pink wine.

The appellation of Coteaux d'Aix-en-Provence covers forty-nine villages, two in the department of Var and the majority in Bouches-du-Rhône. Nominally, the appellation extends all round the Étang de Berre to the outskirts of Marseilles. In practice industry has taken over here, and the vineyards are concentrated on the foothills of the Mont Ste-Victoire. They spread as far as Rians in the east and to Les Baux in the west. The vineyards set in the dramatic lunar landscape of the Alpilles are entitled to a subdivision of the appellation, Coteaux des Baux or simply Les Baux. In theory it is not a separate appellation, but in practice the words Coteaux d'Aix-en-Provence are often omitted from the label.

A large mixture of grape varieties is allowed in the appellation, more than for Côtes de Provence. As one grower said, '*C'est toute une salade!*' For white wine you are allowed Bourboulenc, Clairette, Grenache Blanc, Sauvignon, Sémillon and Ugni Blanc, while for red and pink there are Cabernet Sauvignon, Carignan, Cinsaut, Counoise, Grenache, Mourvèdre and Syrah. Permitted percentages vary, so at the moment 70 per cent is the maximum for any white grape; but that figure will be reduced to 40 per cent for Ugni Blanc and 30 per cent for Sauvignon and Sémillon. Much more Carignan is allowed in Coteaux d'Aix-en-Provence than in Côtes de Provence. At present it can represent up to 60 per cent, like all the other red grape varieties, but it is being progressively reduced to 30 per cent by 1995. Forty per cent will become the maximum percentage for any other red grape variety in 1991.

However, there are those who do not conform to the regulations at all. Chardonnay is grown too, ostensibly for Vin de Pays des Bouches-du-Rhône, and there is one determined grower at Domaine de Trévallon who persists in making his wine from Syrah and Cabernet Sauvignon alone.

The most spectacular estate of the appellation is Château Vigne-laure, on the stony plateau outside the village of Rians, on the eastern edge of the appellation. The owner, Georges Brunet, bought a dilapidated château and run-down vineyard in 1964. He had already restored Château La Lagune in the Médoc to its former glory, and here in the beautiful, arid hills outside Aix-en-Provence he took up a new challenge. When Dr Guyot wrote his survey of the vineyards of France in 1865, he said you could make a great wine in this region by mixing Syrah and Cabernet Sauvignon. He considered that Syrah gave structure to the Cabernet Sauvignon, for this was the period of

'Lafite *hermitagé*', when the wines of the northern Rhône were not infrequently sent to Bordeaux to boost less substantial clarets. Cabernet Sauvignon was grown here in the nineteenth century and Guyot wrote that the wines made from it had a velvet flavour, while wines from Syrah were rich and full of flavour, like those of Hermitage.

Georges Brunet was guided by Dr Guyot's advice just over a century later, but he also included a more traditional grape variety of the region, Grenache; the 55 hectares of vineyards at Vignelaure are thus planted with 60 per cent Cabernet Sauvignon, 30 per cent Syrah and 10 per cent Grenache. Viticultural and wine-making methods here are meticulously neat and thorough. The first you see of Vignelaure is neat rows of vines, planted on south-facing slopes, with hardly a leaf out of place. The soil here is clay and limestone mixed with sand, which gives excellent drainage. But the water table is 7 or 8 metres below the surface, which the vine roots can easily reach.

It is hard to believe that these impeccable cellars are actually used for wine-making. Georges Brunet believes in the kinship of the artist and the wine-maker, and his cellar walls are decorated with the works of contemporary French artists. Most appealing was a photograph by Cartier-Bresson of an old man contemplating a nearly empty bottle of wine. You could almost hear him saying, 'Ah, that was a good bottle!' Each grape variety is fermented separately, as in Bordeaux. The blending is done in February or March after the malolactic fermentation, and then the wine spends a further eighteen months in wood or maybe longer, depending on the characteristics of the vintage. M. Brunet prefers the oak from the Allier to that of the Limousin or the Vosges as it is finer-grained and gives a more elegant flavour to his wine. His barrels are made in Cognac, by steaming, not charring.

It would be difficult to deny the quality of the results. The 1983, sampled in September 1986, had the predominant taste of youthful Cabernet Sauvignon, with a flavour of blackcurrants and an underlying richness. The 1981 was elegant and balanced, very stylish, with some delicious fruit, while the 1975 – which M. Brunet described as 'a fake great vintage', especially in Bordeaux – was drinking beautifully: elegant and complex, with length and nuances of flavour. A second wine, in the Bordelais fashion, is called Le Page and comes from younger vines and is given less wood ageing. The artistic association with wine has been extended into the literary domain, and instead of artists to design labels, there are authors to write back labels. Anthony Burgess has written: '*Quand je bois le vin de Vignelaure, j'entends des violons lointains.*' *Laure* in Provençal means a sacred spring, so Vignelaure is literally the vine of the sacred spring.

You have to go to the other side of the appellation to find a grower who has followed Dr Guyot's advice single-mindedly. Éloi Durrbach at Domaine de Trévallon, on the foothills of the Alpilles in the Coteaux des Baux, has Cabernet Sauvignon and Syrah in his vineyards, but no Grenache. This is a new wine estate and Éloi Durrbach is an excellent example of the outsider coming to an area with an energetic approach and no preconceived ideas. He inherited a family property, a tumbledown old farm that belonged to his mother. He had studied mathematics and architecture, but not oenology; he was tired of life in the capital, so came here and planted his first vines in 1974.

He now has 16 hectares, 60 per cent Cabernet Sauvignon and 40 per cent Syrah. The INAO would like him to plant some Grenache, too, but for the moment he chooses not to oblige. He is the only grower to take this independent stand. He is also planting white vineyards of Chardonnay and Roussanne, and Viognier also tempts him. The soil is very poor and chalky, often with large solid chunks of chalk as well as traces of iron. The hills of the Alpilles provide a peculiarly local microclimate, for they are only 30 kilometres long by 5 wide. The vines are planted on their slopes in a north–south orientation, to withstand the Mistral better. It is hot here so that the grapes ripen well, and with very ripe grapes it is almost impossible to make pink wine. M. Durrbach practises organic viticulture and insists on the importance of working the land. He treats his vines with nothing but the traditional Bordeaux mixture of copper sulphate.

His cellar was built in stages. At first the stainless-steel fermentation vats were outside, then a roof was put over them. The two grape varieties are fermented separately at a high temperature to obtain the maximum extraction of colour and tannin, which takes ten to twenty days, much longer than with any other producer of Coteaux des Baux. The wine goes into wood immediately the fermentation is finished. M. Durrbach did experiment with new wood, but found that it destroyed the regional character of his wine. He prefers old casks, old beer barrels which have been renovated. The wine usually spends about eighteen months in wood and his 1985 was bottled in May 1987.

We were treated to a comprehensive tasting of the wines of Domaine de Trévallon. The 1985 was rich and concentrated, with blackberries on the nose, while the 1984 also had blackberries, with some vanilla. The 1983, with a yield of only 20 hectolitres per hectare, was rich and concentrated, and had the peppery nose of the Syrah and the blackcurrants of Cabernet Sauvignon, with tannin and length. The 1982 had hints of tobacco on the nose and made a very attractive glass of wine in September 1986, and we subsequently finished the bottle over a picnic in the shadow of the Alpilles. The 1981 was the least attractive, with hints of rubber, while 1978, the first serious vintage, was almost Burgundian, with vegetal overtones and some Cabernet cedarwood.

One of the oldest estates of the Coteaux des Baux is Mas de la Dame. It is now run by M. Chatin, whose Burgundian father-in-law, Robert Faye, did much for the region in the post-war years. The estate has been in the family since 1921; he was the first in the area to replace his hybrid vines with noble varieties and began bottling his own wine in 1949. He dreamt of a large, all-embracing appellation for the wines of Provence, that would have included several smaller appellations such as the Coteaux des Baux as separate entities. This was not to be, for the Coteaux d'Aix-en-Provence wanted to retain the Coteaux des Baux. But there is much more homogeneity within the Coteaux des Baux than within the Coteaux d'Aix-en-Provence; all the estates are grouped around the Alpilles and the attractive hilltop town of Les Baux, while those of the Coteaux d'Aix-en-Provence are much more spread-out. The microclimate of the Alpilles is hot and dry, and as there is less rain than in the Coteaux d'Aix-en-Provence, the vines can suffer from drought. The only difference within the sub-appellation is that the grapes grown on the southern foothills of the Alpilles ripen a few days earlier than those on the northern side. They would still like to see a separate appellation for the Coteaux des Baux – 'We dream about it a little' – but for the moment they will have to remain Coteaux d'Aix-en-Provence, Les Baux.

The origins of Mas de la Dame are fifteenth-century and there have always been vineyards and olive trees here, as well as fruit trees, apricots and almonds. They still have the old olive presses, and in 1889 Van Gogh chose the house as a subject. Grenache is the dominant grape variety, but they are planting some more Cabernet Sauvignon. There are Syrah, Cinsaut and Carignan, too, as well as some new plantings of Clairette and Sémillon. They make two qualities of red wine, one for early drinking and one, with more Syrah and Cabernet Sauvignon, for ageing. Both are aged in large barrels.

The most isolated estate of the Coteaux d'Aix-en-Provence is Château Calissanne, a large estate near the Étang de Berre. Some of the vineyards lie at a mere 15 metres above sea-level. The microclimate here is hotter than in the rest of the appellation and the vintage is often two weeks earlier. They have 120 hectares of vines and there are also olive trees and *garrigues*, rocky scrub with thyme, lavender, and rosemary where they hunt rabbits and partridges. Rows of cypresses act as windbreaks to protect the vines from the Mistral. The origins of the estate are Roman, and behind the hills facing the château are the remains of a Roman oppidum.

We sat in the old-fashioned kitchen of the château, with its large open fireplace, talking and tasting with Denis Langue, the manager of the estate. He is new to Provence, having come from Burgundy, but he is excited by the opportunities that are offered in Provence. Here you are not a prisoner of tradition and outsiders can bring their new ideas. The owners of the estate allow him freedom to experiment, something that he could never do in Burgundy.

They make two wines of each colour, with a variety of different grapes. Their best white wine is a blend of Sauvignon and Sémillon which they are considering ageing in wood. In contrast, the basic white is made from Ugni Blanc and Clairette. The Rosé Tradition is a blend of Grenache, Cinsaut, Carignan and a little Mourvèdre, while the Rosé Prestige is pure Syrah, which is fresher and more lively. For the basic red, a blend of Cinsaut, Grenache, Carignan and a little Cabernet Sauvignon gives a peppery wine with herbal overtones. The bouquet was the smell of the surrounding scrub, with the scent of wild herbs. The Cuvée Prestige, on the other hand, has Mourvèdre and Syrah as well as Grenache and Cabernet, and is a more chewy, substantial wine that has been aged for several months in wood. Each grape variety is fermented separately, so the exact proportions inevitably vary from year to year. They are planting more Mourvèdre, as it ripens well in these coastal vineyards.

Denis Langue is optimistic for the future, and is convinced that the area has yet more to offer, for the notion of *terroir* is more developed, and that, combined with the technical improvements of recent years, will achieve great things for the appellation. His optimism is shared by Jean-Stanislas de Taisne at Château de Fonscolombe.

Fonscolombe is in the heart of the appellation, not far from the town of Aix. The heaviest concentration of vineyards is here, around the villages of Meyragues and Le Puy-Ste-Réparade near the northern limit of the appellation, marked by the River Durance. Fonscolombe is an old estate owned by the Marquis de Saporta. Yannic, as his friends call Jean-Stanislas de Taisne, came to wine by marriage. Trained as a mechanical engineer, with no experience of wine at all, he agreed to help his father-in-law out for a couple of years back in 1978. In 1988 he is still there.

Again, outside experience has made its impact. He has a broader view of the potential of the region, appreciating the enormous variation that is possible from the same grape varieties. He also saw the desirability of changing the style of the wine. It used to be kept in wood for several years and made to age, the inspiration being nearby Châteauneuf-du-Pape; Yannic's objective, however is a soft, fruity, aromatic wine to sell and drink young.

Yannic encouraged his father-in-law to plant more white grapes, notably Sauvignon, but also Ugni Blanc, Grenache Blanc and Clairette. Sauvignon is the first to ripen, as early as the middle of September, while Ugni Blanc is often not ripe until the middle of October. Their best white wine is made from equal amounts of each of the four grape varieties, and in the taste there is a hint of gooseberries from the Sauvignon. They also have some Chardonnay, supposedly for the *vin de pays*, but sometimes a drop finds its way into the appellation wine. Grenache Blanc is not found that often in the appellation, for although it gives good yields, it is quite difficult to cultivate.

Grenache is the basis of their red wine, and there are also Carignan, Cinsaut, a generous dollop of Cabernet Sauvignon and an increasing amount of Syrah; the better pink is made from Grenache, Cabernet Sauvignon and Cinsaut. They are less enthusiastic about a combination of Syrah and Cabernet Sauvignon, finding that the two grape varieties do not blend so well, but sometimes they make what they call 'a sandwich vat', with a layer of Syrah grapes between two layers of Cabernet Sauvignon. Their vinification method for red wine is a variation of carbonic maceration: they put whole grapes into the vat, but add no carbon dioxide. Some grapes are crushed by the weight of the grapes above them; the free-run juice is run off, the remaining grapes are pressed, and the two musts are blended. As yet there is no wood ageing of the red wine.

When the present Marquis de Saporta took over the estate around 1960, his vineyards were planted with Aramon and other hybrids. In the last twenty-five years he has gradually replanted, in three successive waves. First came Grenache, Cinsaut and Syrah in the mid-1960s, then Cabernet Sauvignon in the early 1970s, and last of all Sauvignon and Chardonnay around 1980. Some Carignan has been retained as it performs well here.

The Château de Fonscolombe is one of the largest producers of white wine in the appellation. It is the Domaine du Château Bas, however, that has established a reputation for its white wine in preference to its red or pink. The estate is near the village of Vernègues in the northern part of the appellation. There are substantial remains of a Roman temple behind the cellar buildings; the château itself, which is twelfth century in origin, has acquired piecemeal additions over the centuries. They also have the remains of the old Roman olive-press in the cellars. The estate is now owned by a German industrialist who has invested a considerable amount of money in modern cellar equipment, with stainless-steel vats, efficient means of temperature control and centrifuges.

Although the white wine has Ugni Blanc as the main grape variety, this is balanced by a hefty dollop of Sauvignon which dominates the palate and nose, with gooseberry fruit and fresh acidity. There is also a small drop of Grenache Blanc in the blend. Each grape variety is vinified separately, with the fermentation temperature kept around 18°C; the malolactic fermentation is prevented, and the wine is blended for bottling in early spring.

Red and pink wines are made from Cabernet Sauvignon, Grenache and Syrah, with a small amount of Carignan. The red wine is aged in large casks for six to twelve months and they are experimenting with small barrels for Cabernet and Grenache, but only for a three-month period. A prestige wine, Cuvée du Temple, is made from two-thirds Cabernet Sauvignon and one-third Syrah, following the good Dr Guyot's recipe. It had the rich, peppery flavour of Syrah blackcurrant-gums, which toned down the more austere, tannic flavours of the Cabernet Sauvignon. Their red wine is usually made from one-third each of Cabernet Sauvignon, Syrah and Grenache; the Cinsaut is kept for the pink wine, which is made by the *saigné* method, with three hours' contact with the skins to give a pale and pretty shade of pink. The Carignan is used for the Vin de Pays des Bouches-du-Rhône, which is sold under the name of Domaine de St-Césaire.

Coteaux d'Aix-en-Provence has undergone an enormous transformation in the last twenty years or so. It would seem that its original failure to be elevated to an appellation alongside the neighbouring Côtes de Provence gave the more dynamic growers the necessary incentive to improve the quality of their wines. The influx of newcomers – men like Georges Brunet, Éloi Durrbach and Yannic de Taisne – has achieved great things for the appellation. The Coteaux d'Aix-en-Provence are more dedicated to red wine than their neighbours; they are closer to the villages of the Côtes du Rhône, and the Coteaux des Baux are closer to Avignon than to Aix-en-Provence itself. All this contributes to current optimism for the future of the appellation.

COTEAUX VAROIS

The vineyards of the Coteaux Varois lie between those of the Coteaux d'Aix-en-Provence and those of the Côtes de Provence. They thus form a zone of transition between the two appellations. The sleepy town of Brignoles is at their centre, surrounded by twenty-seven villages. This northern part of the department has a slightly cooler climate; the vineyards are on a rocky plateau, still not too far from the sea. The Coteaux Varois were one of the very first *vins de pays*, created at the early stages of the classification back in 1973. In 1984 they were promoted to a VDQS for red and pink wine, but not white.

In some respects the Coteaux Varois remain a sleepy backwater. Of the potential 2,400 hectares of vines, only about half are planted. The production of the area is dominated by co-operatives who continue to produce unexciting Vin de Pays du Var, and even less inspiring *vin de table*, from grape varieties like Carignan and Aramon. But the improved status of VDQS has given the more energetic growers an element of motivation. A growers' association was created along with the VDQS in order to promote the wine with the limited funds available. Individual members are working hard to improve their wines, and there are a number of serious estates to consider.

The most exciting estate is the Domaine de St-Jean-de-Villecroze on the edge of the appellation near the village of Tourtour, which claims to be the highest village of France and calls itself '*le village dans le ciel*'. The night we were there it was the village in the clouds. The Domaine de St-Jean-de-Villecroze is owned by an American from New Jersey, Alan Hirsh, and his French wife Denise, who bought this abandoned property in 1974. Their energy was one of the contributory factors in the success of the application for VDQS. They had to plant a vineyard from scratch and now have 34 hectares of vines – Cabernet Sauvignon, Cinsaut, Syrah and Grenache. The principal grape varieties of the Coteaux Varois are in fact Carignan, Cinsaut, Grenache, Mourvèdre and Syrah, while Cabernet Sauvignon and Tibouren are permitted as secondary varieties. The maximum allowed for any one of the principal varieties is 70 per cent, with 30 per cent for the secondary varieties. Since 60 per cent of the Hirsh's vineyards are planted with Cabernet Sauvignon, they also make some excellent varietal wine from both Syrah and Cabernet Sauvignon. They have to market this as Vin de Pays du Var, but it is far superior to any ordinary *vin de pays*, and indeed they sell it for a higher price than their Coteaux Varois.

No expense has been spared in equipping the cellars at Domaine St-Jean-de-Villecroze. Advice was sought from California on the construction of the winery, and a cellar was cut into the hillside and equipped with stainless-steel vats with glycol blankets to control the fermentation temperatures. After a traditional vinification most of the red wine spends some months in wood. Each year they hire a Californian oenologist to mastermind the wine-making. Their Coteaux Varois is a blend of equal amounts of Syrah and Cabernet Sauvignon with a little Grenache, vinified separately and blended a year later. The wine we tasted had the dominant peppery character-istics of Syrah. The pink wine is made from Cinsaut.

At Domaine du Loou we were treated to a comprehensive tasting by Dominique de Placido. He is an Italian who has taken over his father-in-law's estate, and when he arrived here there were a few vines, but also sheep, wheat and almond trees. Now there are 47 hectares of Grenache, Cabernet Sauvignon, Syrah, Carignan and a little Mourvèdre, from which he makes a variety of different wines, both Coteaux Varois and *vin de pays*. *Loou* is the old Provençal word for '*labourer*' or to work the land: in this context, it means a place where land is cultivated. The origins of the estate are Gallo-Roman, and M. de Placido found the remains of tombs from that period when he was replanting the vineyards.

His cellars are functional, with cement vats and some wooden barrels of varying sizes. At the vintage he decides which grapes will be destined for what wine. Cabernet Sauvignon is usually vinified on its own and the others are all fermented together. We tasted a 1983 Coteaux Varois from Grenache and Syrah which was soft and peppery, while another 1983 from Cabernet Sauvignon as well as Grenache and Syrah, which had spent some time in wood, was a more solid mouthful. There was also a *vin de pays* from Cabernet Sauvignon, with hints of blackcurrant, and a more traditional *vin de pays* from Grenache and Carignan. The 1985 Coteaux Varois from Syrah and Grenache had been aged in small barrels and had an attractive peppery fruitiness.

The largest estate in the Coteaux Varois, the Domaine de l'Abbaye de St-Hilaire at Ollières, is owned by Les Salins du Midi. They too have a high proportion of Cabernet Sauvignon for *vin de pays*, but are also planting more Syrah and Grenache. The 1985, which is not aged in wood, was rounded and ripe, with flavours of blackcurrant. Domaine des Chaberts, owned by a Mrs Pitt-Rivers, and Domaine de Deffends also have good reputations.

As Emmanuel Gaujal, one of the leading oenologists of Provence, with a consultant laboratory at Brignoles and relations making wine in the Coteaux du Languedoc, said: 'The Coteaux Varois need not be ashamed of their pink wines.' As for red, the slightly cooler climatic conditions are often more favourable than in the Côtes de Provence. There is no doubt that it is the private estates that are leading the way in the Coteaux Varois, although the co-operatives are doing their best to follow. People with means have invested in the area and shaken up the intransigent older growers; the potential is considerable.

COTEAUX DE PIERREVERT

The vineyards of Pierrevert are a natural continuation of the Côtes du Lubéron, and form a sleepy backwater away from the mainstream of Provençal viticulture. The hilltop village of Pierrevert is at the centre of the vineyards and Manosque – with one claim to fame, as the birthplace of the writer Jean Giono – is the only town of any size. Coteaux de Pierrevert was made a VDQS in 1959, and the overall area was defined to cover forty-two villages in the southern part of the department of the Alpes-de-Haute-Provence. Many of these villages do not in fact have vineyards, most of which are concentrated around Pierrevert. But the precise delimitation was not done for nearly another thirty years, and the INAO inspectors were completing their work during my visit to the area in 1986. Back in 1959 the co-operative at Pierrevert was the only producer; it has been in existence since 1925, at which time the region had a reputation for sparkling wine. What they called Clairet de Pierrevert won medals in the 1930s, but the 1980s version, a *méthode champenoise*, would not win prizes today. The co-operative now has ninety-two members with about 200 hectares of vines around the village. As well as Coteaux de Pierrevert, they make Vin de Pays des Alpes-de-Haute-Provence. Further north in the department are some of the highest vineyards of France, near the town of Digne.

The first independent producer came to Pierrevert in 1963, a M. Charles Pons-Mure, who also runs an estate in Lirac. But there is no cellar on his estate at Domaine La Blasque, so his wine is made at Domaine de Régusse by another newcomer to the area, Claude Dieudonné. He started from scratch in 1972, clearing scrub and planting vines. He has had no oenological training, but he had always wanted to be a wine-maker and has learnt in the vineyard.

Altogether M. Dieudonné has nineteen different grape varieties, as the VDQS regulations allow for a real hotchpotch of flavours. For white wine there are Ugni Blanc, Marsanne, Clairette, Picpoul and Grenache Blanc, while for red and pink the varieties include Grenache, Syrah, Carignan, Cinsaut, Mourvèdre and Aubun. These are grapes of the south, but M. Dieudonné believes that they are not suitable for the cooler conditions of the Coteaux de Pierrevert, as they often fail to ripen properly; he has also planted Chardonnay, Aligoté, Pinot Noir, Cabernet Sauvignon, Merlot and Gamay. These are vinified as varietal wines and labelled as Vin de Pays des Alpes-de-Haute-Provence, while to confuse the issue further, some of his vineyards are within the adjoining appellation of Côtes du Lubéron. Louis Latour in Aloxe-Corton have offered advice on Chardonnay and Pinot Noir, and also provide used Burgundian barrels.

The quality of M. Dieudonné's wines varied quite considerably. Best of all I liked a 1983 red Coteaux de Pierrevert made from Grenache, Cabernet Sauvignon and Merlot, which had some per-fumed, peppery fruit. A 1982 pure Cabernet Sauvignon was quite dry with some good sound fruit, while the 1985 Pinot Noir had some potential. Potential is probably the key word in describing Coteaux de Pierrevert. The wines will never be great but they will improve, and can provide some enjoyable drinking; M. Dieudonné has courage and deserves to succeed.

CÔTES DU LUBÉRON

The Côtes du Lubéron are where the vineyards of the Rhône valley meet those of Provence. They are separated from the appellation of Coteaux d'Aix-en-Provence by the broad River Durance and the vineyards stand on the slopes of the Montagne du Lubéron, an attractive area of small villages and hilly countryside. The plains are devoted to market gardening. Vines have been commonplace here since Roman times, but have had little historical significance. The Côtes du Lubéron were given their appellation with the 1987 vintage, when the area was restricted to include only hillside vineyards; those on the plains were declassified to Vin de Pays de Vaucluse.

Co-operatives were founded during the twentieth century, and seventeen are now grouped together to sell their wines under the 'Cellier de Marrenon' label. They are responsible for 90 per cent of the appellation, as well as for a considerable amount of Côtes du Ventoux and Vin de Pays de Vaucluse. It was they who introduced Côtes du Lubéron to the popular wine market and put the area on the map. Their installations are well equipped with modern technology and their wine is accordingly reliable.

However, it was two private estates, the oldest properties of the area, that really contributed to the reputation of Côtes du Lubéron: Château Isolette and Château de Mille. Unfortunately neither of them was receptive to visitors during the vintage. I am told their wines are made in the traditional way, with classic fermentations and ageing in oak. My own appreciation of Côtes du Lubéron comes from visits to two newcomers to the appellation, who in themselves provide an interesting contrast.

My first impression of the Côtes du Lubéron came from Jean-Pierre Margan of Château La Canorgue near Bonnieux. He took over his father-in-law's neglected estate in 1976 and completely refurbished the cellar and replanted the vineyards. They are old cellars that go back to the fifteenth century; they are vaulted in soft stone and an old chapel has been incorporated into them. You reach them through the vegetable gardens, walking past fat tomatoes and shiny aubergines. The dog came too, whose name is Cabernet, 'Because I am not allowed to plant any!' After further conversation, however, it transpired that M. Margan did have some Cabernet Sauvignon, although officially it is not allowed within the appellation.

M. Margan has 20 hectares of vines and his colour breakdown is 80 per cent red, 15 per cent pink and 5 per cent white. His red wine is made from Syrah, Grenache, Cinsaut, Mourvèdre and what he called 'sundries', mainly Merlot and Cabernet Sauvignon. He adores Merlot as it is less obvious in the wine and marries well with Syrah. His pink wine is made from the same grape varieties as the red, except that Mourvèdre is excluded. Although the Côtes du Lubéron cannot be considered a coastal vineyard, M. Margan finds that Mourvèdre ripens well here provided you eliminate half the crop after the flowering. White wine is made with Clairette, Ugni Blanc and other varieties, mainly Sauvignon. Again Sauvignon is not allowed by the INAO, so officially it should be used for Vin de Pays de Vaucluse; but there is a feeling that the INAO is too restrictive towards new ideas. There is the same attitude towards plantings of Chardonnay.

Although the Côtes du Lubéron are geographically close to the Côtes du Rhône, their wines are lighter in alcohol, fruitier and more aromatic. M. Margan was adamant that they should not be compared with their neighbours. All his grapes are picked by hand for he believes that mechanical harvesters damage the grapes too much. If he had to have one, he would change jobs. He makes one wine of each colour, usually putting the different grape varieties together at the fermentation. His is an empirical approach: he never does the same each year, as every vintage has its own particular characteristics, which he tries to enhance. In a cooler year the fermentation is longer, taking ten or twelve days as opposed to six to eight days in a hotter year. His red spends six to nine months in wood, which is usual amongst the private growers of the appellation. We tasted the 1985 red which had spent ten months in wood. It was full and substantial with flavours of liquorice and vanilla, as well as some tannin; and a 1979, a particularly good vintage, had aged well, with some warm, mature fruit.

M. Margan had followed his grandfather and father by studying oenology at Montpellier, and his first vintage was only in 1978. Wine-making is not only his job, but his love. He exudes enthusiasm combined with common sense and is quietly ambitious to do his best.

He admits to being pleased with his white wine – well, 99 per cent pleased, for you are never 100 per cent satisfied. I liked it, too.

My visit to Château Val Joanis near Pertuis was just as exciting, but in a different way. This was quite a different scale of operations: a large estate with 120 hectares of vines, in which an enormous amount of money has been invested by the Chancel family. They came to wine from olive-oil, and when they bought the estate in 1978 there were just 5 hectares of vines adjoining the sixteenth-century château. The first thing they did was to bring in the bulldozers and clear scrub from where there had been vines before the phylloxera, for they found the remains of crumbling terraces. The bulldozers achieved more gentle slopes, and 70 hectares were planted immediately with Syrah, Grenache, Cinsaut, Chardonnay, Sauvignon and Ugni Blanc. Other grape varieties have since been added: Mourvèdre, Gamay, Cabernet Sauvignon, Merlot and Bourboulenc; they have even T-budded some Chardonnay on to Ugni Blanc.

We went on a bumpy tour of the vineyards in an old jeep used by the Americans in the war. Running through the estate is a dirt track that was once the old coach road between Aix and Avignon, and a tumbledown cottage was once a coaching inn. White grapes are planted in the valley and red grapes on the slopes. All are trained on wires and dressed for mechanical harvesting. Val Joanis also employ people to sort the grapes and remove any rotten ones, so they have not put their trust in machines alone. Before planting they had to lay pipes for drainage channels, as the soil is a mixture of clay and limestone, with *galets* or large stones in parts of the vineyard, as in Châteauneuf-du-Pape.

The cellars show the same attention to detail, with efficient, functional installations. Everything is in stainless steel. The different grape varieties are fermented separately and then blended in the spring. Only the best grapes are used for the appellation and the rest are Vin de Pays de Vaucluse. They have tried some carbonic maceration, but prefer traditional vinifications for their red wine. Temperatures are very precisely controlled, at 25–28°C for red wine and much cooler for white and pink. They are experimenting with ageing their red wine in barrel, and are also considering different bottling times.

The quality of the wine reflects the attention that is given to the vinification. The white wine, made from two parts Ugni Blanc to one part Chardonnay, has a nutty hint of Chardonnay. A Vin de Pays de

Vaucluse using some young Sauvignon was crisp and fresh. The pink is made mainly from Cinsaut and Grenache, with a little Gamay, while the red comes from Syrah and Grenache with a little Mourvèdre. Officially, Cabernet Sauvignon and Merlot may only go into the *vin de pays*. The 1985 red Val Joanis was a solid, peppery mouthful of fruit and flavour.

The Chancel family have invested over 60 million francs in the Château de Val Joanis since 1978. They could have bought a classed-growth property in Bordeaux for the same price and make wine that they would be able to sell at a much higher price than Côtes du Lubéron. But Bordeaux or Burgundy were too safe; an estate in the Côtes du Lubéron offered an adventure and the opportunity to create a reputation. This enterprising spirit has made a major contribution to the rising star of the appellation.

7

Wines of Corsica

I fell in love with Corsica at first sight. Maybe it was something to do with leaving London on a grey, sleety February morning and arriving in Ajaccio to find spring sunshine, a blue sky and flowering almond and mimosa trees. It was irresistible and I was enchanted. The Greeks were right when they called Corsica Kallisté, which means the very beautiful. Later the name became Kersiké, for the rocky mountains, and finally Korsia, for the forests, which was to change to Corsica in Latin, or Corse in French.

The Greeks arrived here from Asia Minor in 565 BC and founded the town of Alalia on the site of present-day Aléria, on the east coast of the island. They probably brought vines with them, and in the museum at Aléria there are certainly Greek artefacts depicting vintage scenes. After the Greeks came the Romans, and in 35 BC Virgil wrote of the wine of the Balagne, the area around Calvi, describing the ruby-coloured wine that was so agreeable to the palate.

The next important influence on viticulture came from Pisa, which had control of the island from 1077 until ousted by the Genoese in 1284. During the period of 'Pax Pisana', viticulture prospered. The Genoese, too, encouraged viticulture, along with the other crops of Corsica – olives, sweet chestnuts and figs. In 1572 every landowner was obliged to plant ten fruit trees and four vines, or else risk a fine. Many Corsicans were nomads at heart, taking their sheep to summer pastures in the mountains and only returning to their homes for the winter. Such a migratory life was not conducive to the cultivation of the vines. But the Genoese persisted, and wheat, olive-oil and wine were sent to Genoa. Evidence of the Genoese hold on the island remains today, for scattered along the coastline are the ruins of Genoese look-out towers. Other nations had designs upon Corsica: the Saracens, the Aragonese and the French, who finally gained control of the island in May 1769, three months before the birth of Napoleon Bonaparte in Ajaccio.

By the end of the eighteenth century there were 9,800 hectares of vines on Corsica, rising to 11,304 hectares in the census of 1814. (The total comprised 1,468 hectares in Ajaccio, 6,462 in Bastia, 2,059 in Corte, 933 in Sartène and 382 in Calvi.) It was an island of polyculture, for as well as an enormous population of sheep, there were olive and chestnut trees, and small fields of wheat. The vines were planted on the hillsides in terraces. Boswell praised the wines of Corsica, while the French writers enthused over the favourable climatic conditions for viticulture, but were less complimentary about the wines themselves. Rendu, writing in 1856, said that Corsica enjoyed a magnificent climate which could enable her to become one of the richest producers of dry wines and fortified wines, but the grape varieties were badly chosen and there were insufficient cellars. The wines were manipulated without intelligence and they were strong but vulgar.

Dr Guyot wrote that vines grew beautifully in Corsica at Cap Corse, at Bastia, Vescovato, Cervione, Corte and Ajaccio, where he observed that the vines were vigorous and only asked to bear fruit, and gave excellent results with the right grape varieties. It was the same at Calvi and Sartène. In 1874 an official report cited viticulture as the principal resource of three-quarters of the population. That was to change dramatically when the phylloxera arrived on the island later the same year. By 1914 the area under vines had fallen to 6,000 hectares.

The First World War had a disastrous demographic effect on Corsica. More than 40,000 men were killed, more than from any other department of France, out of a total population of 230,000. Many more preferred to remain 'on the continent', as the Corsicans call mainland France, or to emigrate further afield. The war left Corsica with a severe problem of rural depopulation, which was not really solved until the enormous influx of *pieds-noirs* in the early 1960s. Over 17,000 people from North Africa settled here, bringing with them, for better or for worse, their own viticultural experience.

The arrival of the *pieds-noirs* galvanized the economy of the island, but its indigenous viticulture suffered badly at the hands of the newcomers. Many of them had grown grapes in Algeria and Morocco in conditions which gave generous quantities of *vin ordinaire* with minimal production costs. They expected to find the same conditions

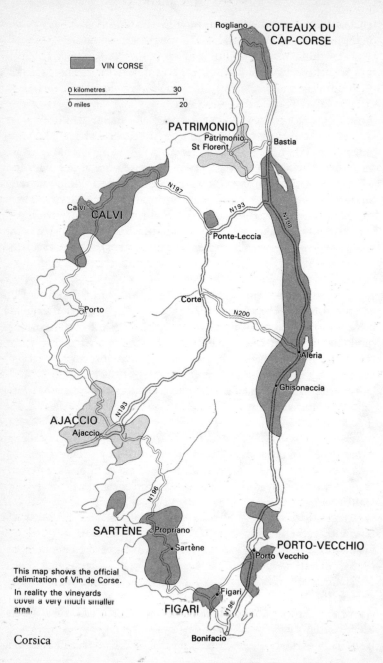

VIN CORSE

0 kilometres 30
0 miles 20

COTEAUX DU
CAP-CORSE

Rogliano

PATRIMONIO

Patrimonio
St Florent

Bastia

N197

N193

Calvi

CALVI

N198

Ponte-Leccia

Corte

N200

Porto

Aleria

Ghisonaccia

N193

AJACCIO

Ajaccio

N196

SARTÈNE

Propriano

Sartène

PORTO-VECCHIO

Porto Vecchio

This map shows the official
delimitation of Vin de Corse.

In reality the vineyards
cover a very much smaller
area.

FIGARI

Figari

N198

Corsica

Bonifacio

290

in Corsica. Vast expanses of the *maquis*, the scrub that covers much of the interior of the island, were *démaquisé* or cleared without consideration of the suitability of the terrain. It was often impossible to assess this beforehand and there was no attempt to control the plantings. The eastern coastal plain was the prime target of the new arrivals. They planted the grape varieties which they had grown in North Africa – Grenache, Cinsaut, Carignan and Alicante Bouschet. Quantity, not quality, was their objective. The extension of the vineyards on the eastern side of the island was such that, whereas in 1958 there had only been 9,000 hectares, by 1973 there were 32,000. But yields were much lower than in Algeria. Even the favourable financial terms given by the French government could not make viticulture pay as well as it had there. There were various 'wine scandals'. On an island which should have no problem in obtaining sufficiently ripe grapes, nearly 8,000 tonnes of sugar were used for chaptalization in 1971. The immigrants had completely disrupted the island's traditional viticulture.

The failure of many of these new vineyards has been recognized and many have been pulled up; by 1987 the area of vines in Corsica had fallen to 10,000 hectares. Where once there were subsidies for planting vineyards, there are now *primes d'arrachage* for grubbing them up. Some are being allowed to revert to *maquis* and others have been converted to follow a new fashion, kiwi fruit. The future of Corsican viticulture lies mainly with the traditional grape varieties that form the mainstay of the appellations of Corsica. The island's first appellation was Patrimonio in the north, which achieved that status in 1968; it was followed by Coteaux d'Ajaccio in 1971, the name of which was changed to Ajaccio in 1984. These remain separate from the all-embracing Vin de Corse that was created in 1976 with the *crus* of Sartène, Figari, Porto-Vecchio, Coteaux du Cap Corse and Calvi. There is some Vin de Corse produced in the centre of the island near Ponte Leccia and on the east coast south of Bastia, but otherwise most of the vineyards outside the *crus* and the appellations of Ajaccio and Patrimonio are covered by the Vin de Pays de l'Ile de Beauté.

Native grape varieties provide a substantial proportion of the appellation wines. There is Sciacarello, which in the Corsican language, that is closer to Italian than to French, means 'the grape which bursts under the teeth', for it does have a hard skin and plenty of juice. It is at its best on the granite soils of Ajaccio and Sartène.

Occasionally you find a pure Sciacarello, but it is usually blended with Nielluccio or with Grenache (which is sometimes called Alicante de Corse), or maybe with Syrah or, less frequently, Carignan and Cinsaut.

Nielluccio, in contrast, is a tougher, more substantial and tannic grape. In Patrimonio you can find pure Nielluccio, and at present it must represent a minimum of 60 per cent of the appellation. Elsewhere it is blended with other grape varieties.

The most important white grape variety is Vermentino, which confusingly is also known as Malvoisie de Corse, although it bears no relationship to any other Malvoisie. It is found in neighbouring Sardinia and is a close relation of the Rolle of Bellet in Provence. You can also find it in Spain and Portugal.

There are other island grape varieties: Carcagiolu, Barbirossu, Montaccio, Pagadebit, Bianco Gentile and so on. These are of much less importance than either Nielluccio and Sciacarello. Corsica is well behind the rest of France in the field of viticultural research, but efforts are being made to catch up and a research station was established in 1981 under the auspices of the CIVAM. (The French love acronyms and this one stands for the Centre d'Information et de Vulgarisation pour l'Agriculture et le Milieu Rural.) It is tiny, with a minute vineyard of just thirty vines of each of eighteen different Corsican varieties, and with vinification equipment on an equally small scale. Some work has been done on clonal selection and they now have three clones of Vermentino in an experimental vineyard on Cap Corse. Some selection has been made for Sciacarello, but Nielluccio is proving more problematic as it is very susceptible to viruses. The research station also carries out maturity tests in the vineyard just before the vintage in an attempt to persuade the growers to think in terms of acidity rather than of potential alcohol.

There is a third strand to Corsican viticulture, which causes the purist growers of Ajaccio and Sartène a certain amount of unease. This is the more recent introduction of grape varieties such as Cabernet Sauvignon, Merlot, Chardonnay and Chenin Blanc. The traditional appellations are anxious that these mainland varieties should not infiltrate the appellations of the island. At the moment they can only be included in the Vin de Pays de l'Ile de Beauté, and are planted on the eastern plain south of Bastia.

AJACCIO

My first visit to Corsica began in Ajaccio. This is the city of Napoleon, who was born in August 1769 in the old quarter, in a substantial town house which is now a simple museum. The main square, the Place des Palmiers, has a statue of the French Emperor emulating his Roman predecessors, with toga and laurel wreath. The vineyards of the appellation are on the hillsides overlooking the Gulf of Ajaccio. The climate is mild and at the end of February you could feel the hesitant warmth of the spring sunshine. Two weeks earlier, however, there had been 70 centimetres of snow on the hills. Mountains dominate the skyline. Corsica's highest peak, Monte Cinto, rises to 3,000 metres and is snowcapped even in the height of summer.

The individuality of the wines of Ajaccio derives from the combination of the Sciacarello grape and granite soil. Sciacarello must represent 40 per cent of any red wine, and probably 95 per cent of all Sciacarello is grown on the 213 hectares of the appellation. A typical blend may be 60 per cent Sciacarello with Grenache and maybe some Cinsaut or Carignan. Sciacarello gives a wine bouquet, while Cinsaut will provide weight and Carignan body. Grenache has the disadvantage of easy oxidation.

First I went to Domaine de Peraldi, in the hills just outside Ajaccio. It is owned by an elderly aristocratic gentleman, Count Louis de Poix. He told me that a de Poix shot the arrow that killed William Rufus in the New Forest. Peraldi was the name of his mother's family, who have owned the estate for 400 years. He himself had a career in industry in Paris, and came to wine in retirement. His estate may be old, but his cellar is modern, well equipped for cool fermentations and for treating his Carignan grapes to carbonic maceration. He has some small oak barrels for ageing his red wine. I liked his pink wine, for which the juice spends eight hours on the skins; consequently it is quite deep in colour, with the full-flavoured fruit of raspberries. The raspberry, almost young Burgundy, flavour also came out in a red wine which was unusual in being a pure Sciacarello, made initially as an experiment. The count's Vermentino, for white wine, is just coming into production. We finished our visit with a glass of champagne, looking at wonderful views of the Gulf of Ajaccio in the sunset.

A complete contrast was my first visit the next morning, to Martin Santini in the little village of Appietto. He has an old cellar carved out of the rock underneath his house. The large barrels made of chestnut were constructed in the cellar. M. Santini is a wizened old man of seventy-three, who cultivates his 5 hectares with his son. He said his wine, both red and pink, was aged in barrels for five years. I was told that it was very good, and made according to the original Corsican tradition. Sadly there was none available to taste. Instead I was amused by M. Santini's view of the growers who are members of the co-operative. He thought they had an easy life: 'They look after their vines from January to July, spend August and most of September by the sea, come home in time to pick their grapes and then go hunting every day during November and December!'

François-Noël Mercurey at Domaine de Paviglia is the historian of the appellation. From his cellar door you can see almond trees and mimosa blossom. The mimosa seemed so fragile and ethereal, but I was told that it grows like a weed. The cellars at Domaine de Paviglia were built in 1820 and M. Mercurey has plans for a small wine museum, with old barrels and tools. He has found a *mâche-bouchon*, which was used at the beginning of the century to soften corks. The donkey was the usual form of transport in Corsica and M. Mercurey's collection includes a *barulazza*, a 65–litre flat-sided barrel which could be carried from a donkey's saddle.

His 1982 red wine was tough and tannic in February 1986. As well as Sciacarello it contained small amounts of Carignan, Grenache and Cinsaut. The grapes are not destalked, which enhances the tannin. The 1978 vintage of the same wine had lasted well, with some perfume and fruit, while the 1974 had faded, developing a smell reminiscent of stables. M. Mercurey was insistent that Corsican wines will age, and he is worried that the island's developing tourist trade will burden Corsica with a false image based on summer holiday wines.

SARTÈNE

From Ajaccio we took the winding road to Sartène. It is 30 kilometres as the crow flies but 50 by road. Sartène is one of the old towns of the island, perched on the side of a hill, with narrow streets leading to a central square. It seemed a rather sombre place in the early evening light, with its grey stone houses. Sartène is famous for its religious festival at Easter, which is described so vividly in Dorothy Carrington's evocative book *The Granite Island*.

Sartène is one of the island's firmly traditional appellations and covers a wide area to the north and south of the town. Vines are really the only practicable crop on the poor soil, but many vineyards have disappeared since the waning of the first flush of enthusiasm of the *pieds noirs*. Old people are retiring and a few young people are replanting, but only with Corsican grape varieties. Sciacarello and Nielluccio must account for a minimum of 50 per cent in the appellation wine, while Carignan is restricted to 10 per cent. There are Grenache, Cinsaut and Barbarossa too, as well as Vermentino and Ugni Blanc for white wine.

The most dynamic grower of the appellation is Félix Andréanni of Domaine Fiumiccioli, just north of the town. His estate is named after the nearby river. He has planted 30 hectares, with Corsican vines only, during the last ten years. He was a mathematics teacher, but took over his parents' vineyard. He is convinced of the quality of the indigenous Corsican grapes, and as well as Nielluccio and Sciacarello he has some of the more obscure varieties. He considers that the wines of Corsica have been spoilt by the introduction of Grenache, Cinsaut and Carignan. Grenache was here before, but the *pieds-noirs* increased it; and Cinsaut and Carignan have changed the flavour. His red wine comprises equal parts of Sciacarello, Nielluccio and Grenache. They are destalked and the fermentation lasts four to seven days at 28°C, with a *remontage* twice a day. Then the wine is aged in stainless-steel vats for two years. M. Andréanni would like to have some small barrels, but it is a question of space and practicability. He racks his wine but does not fine it, and he expects his red wine to last for five or six years after bottling. He does not believe in introducing Merlot or Cabernet Sauvignon, for they would change the character of Corsican wines. There are plans to replant the vineyards, taking advantage of subsidies to pull up unsuitable vines and replace them with local varieties.

The soil of Sartène is flint-based, almost sandy, with very good drainage. The vines like it and the yields can be high. People making *vin de table* can obtain as much as 200 hectolitres per hectare, but for the *cru* of Sartène the basic limit is 45 hl/ha. M. Andréanni's wines are good and include some fragrant, nutty white wine, a pale orange pink wine, and a full-flavoured red with some distinctive fruit and tannin.

FIGARI

From the vineyards of Sartène I headed south towards Figari. The roads are slow in Corsica, but that allowed time to admire the views of the rocky coastline. At the end of February the sky was blue and you could see Sardinia in the distance. Figari is in the southern corner of the island, near the historic town of Bonifacio. This is an area that has particularly suffered from the influx of immigrants from North Africa. The co-operative of Figari was founded in 1962 to accommodate the new arrivals, and it now functions at only one-third capacity for the remaining ten members, who have 200 hectares of vines between them. A lot of vineyards are being declassified here in order to obtain subsidies for the vines to be pulled up.

More successful was the nearby Cave Poquet at Poggiale. Roger Poquet was a wine-grower in Algeria and he works with Marco de Peretti at Domaine de Tanella. They cleared extensive areas of *maquis* and now cultivate 100 hectares of vines, which accounts for a third of the total appellation of Figari. At the height of the planting there were 1,400 hectares here in the mid-1960s, but three-quarters of the vines have now been grubbed up. Labour proved to be too expensive and mistakes were made – often it was impossible to tell, before you cleared the *maquis*, if the land would be suitable. Large expanses were not. Although Corsica is hot, it is not as hot as Algeria. In Corsica the vintage takes place at the end of September, while in Algeria they begin picking grapes in the middle of August.

They make white wine mainly from Ugni Blanc, with some Vermentino, while pink wine comes from Cinsaut, Grenache and Sciacarello and the red mainly from Grenache, with some Carignan, Sciacarello and Nielluccio. It reminded me of a cheerful, peppery Côtes du Rhône, but did not really taste of Corsica.

PORTO-VECCHIO

Porto-Vecchio has also experienced the influx of *pieds-noirs*. Once there were numerous tiny vineyards in the area around the port; people had wheat and olive trees, too, and led a nomadic life with their animals, shifting between the coast and the mountains. Then the immigrants arrived and pulled up the *maquis*. But the soil is poor and granitic, and the large yields of North Africa could never be achieved here. Today there is one estate at Porto-Vecchio, Domaine de Torraccia, owned by Christian Imbert. He came here in 1966 after a varied career in other parts of the world. His neighbours treated him as the '*fou du coin*', for there was nothing but a spring at Torraccia when he arrived. He cleared the *maquis* and planted 40 hectares of vines, mainly of Corsican grape varieties, as well as 25 hectares of olive trees.

His cellars are new and functional, designed to operate by gravity. We were accompanied by two puppies, César and Cléopatre, who were learning to negotiate flights of stairs, with much squeaking and squealing. Christian Imbert's basic red wine comes from Nielluccio, Sciacarello, Grenache and a little Syrah, for sometimes the Corsican grape varieties can lack colour, which the Syrah supplements. He has also experimented with pure Nielluccio vinified by carbonic maceration. His best red, however, is a blend of 80 per cent Nielluccio and 20 per cent Sciacarello called Oriu, which is aged in vats for at least one, if not two years before bottling. It has the warm, fruity, perfumed flavour of Corsica. His white wine, mainly from Vermentino with some Ugni Blanc and Clairette, is fragrant and fresh. The pink comes from 50 per cent Nielluccio with 10 per cent Sciacarello and 20 per cent each of Grenache and Cinsaut. Some of the Nielluccio is pressed immediately, as its character can be rather overwhelming if it is all *saigné*. The flavour is fresh and fruity, with a good acidity balance.

Christian Imbert is president of an organization called Uva Corse, which was formed by the leading independent producers with the object of promoting their wines. They are all people who make and bottle their own appellation wine from their own grapes, and share a similar philosophy. The members use the special bottle of Uva Corse, with the embossed motif of the Moor's head with two Tritons and a crown. Legend has it that Corsica is guarded by male mermaids, while the Moor's head is the island's emblem. There are all sorts of tales associated with the Moor's head, going back to the struggles between the Christians and the Saracens in the Middle Ages; similar stories occur in Sardinia and Aragon. The members of Uva Corse are working hard to promote their wines, and are achieving some success.

Christian Imbert is certainly one of the more dynamic wine-makers of the island. He set out to create a reputation and he is succeeding. He is optimistic about the future of Corsican wines, explaining that when he arrived twenty years ago, there was very little drinkable wine. Now, after all the upheaval of uprooting vineyards, they can see the light at the end of the tunnel. The problem with Corsicans is that they have no idea how to sell their wines, for they are not salesmen, but shepherds and warriors. Someone else described them as good-for-nothings, at least those who have stayed on the island. It was always the more dynamic people who emigrated, even if only as far as mainland France. But there is no doubt that the quality of Corsican wine has improved enormously over the last few years, for on the first occasion that wines were submitted to analysis and tasting for the appellation, many were refused their *labelle*. Things are much better now.

VIN DE PAYS DE L'ILE DE BEAUTÉ

North of Porto-Vecchio the coastline opens out into the vast Plaine Orientale. This is where most of the island's *vin de pays* is produced, mainly by co-operatives. The co-operative of Aléria, which is where the Greeks settled so many centuries ago, is part of the Union des Vignerons de l'Ile de Beauté. There is an archaeological museum at Aléria, but little else to recommend the town. The co-operative makes simple Vin de Corse, with a maximum yield of 50 hectolitres per hectare, as well as Vin de Pays de l'ile de Beauté for which they can produce 80 hl/ha. Their appellation wine, under the brand name of Réserve du Président, comes from 50 per cent Nielluccio with some Grenache, Cinsaut, Carignan and Syrah. Merlot and Cabernet Sauvignon are grown for the *vin de pays* and they would like to include 10 per cent in the appellation. This is what is feared by the more traditional producers of Sartène and Ajaccio, but at Aléria these traditionalists are criticized for their refusal to progress.

The vineyards of Aléria are most suitable for red wine, so the co-operative has encouraged the planting of Merlot and Cabernet Sauvignon, and retained Nielluccio, Grenache and Syrah while eliminating Carignan and Cinsaut. Vermentino has been kept, too, but no Ugni Blanc; they also have a little Chardonnay. The cellars of the co-operative of Aléria are well run. From the top of the tall outdoor vats you can see flat expanses of vines stretching to the sea. They are well equipped to control their fermentations in either concrete or stainless-steel vats. White and pink wines ferment at 15–20°C and there is no malolactic fermentation, otherwise the wines would be too flat. The better red wine is aged in small barrels for a few months.

The co-operative of Casinca, near Bastia, is part of the same group and has a similar attitude towards the continental grape varieties. Both co-operatives aspire to their own appellations, of Aléria and Casinca. It is the Co-opérative de la Marena, however, which has the most dynamic attitude towards viticulture on the coastal plain. They are part of the Union des Vignerons Associés du Levant, commonly known as UVAL, which is responsible for 2,300 hectares in all. They have taken the decision to concentrate on varietal wines and to leave the traditional flavours of Corsica to the small wine-growers. Their objective is 'high-tech table wine' for the export market, and they want their members to earn money. Certainly, they had an appreciation of the economic facts of life that was rare on the island.

They explained that Corsica has an exceptional climate, equivalent on the coastal plain to the Californian climatic zone 3, which includes the top of the Napa valley. There is no risk of frost and summer temperatures are not excessively hot; there are 2,500 hours of sunshine annually, and 500 millimetres of rain is the same as in Bordeaux. The rain falls in the autumn and in the winter months of January and February. The mountains of central Corsica reduce the amount of sunshine by an hour per day and create a good contrast between day and night temperatures. They have found that Carignan ripens badly in Corsica, not until the middle of October, while Chardonnay is ready to be picked at the end of August.

They have developed a range of varietal wines, consisting of an unusual Blanc de Syrah (vinified as a *vin gris*, which is not really allowed), Cabernet Sauvignon, Nielluccio, Chardonnay and Chenin Blanc. The Nielluccio is in fact an appellation wine, but that is irrelevant to the co-operative's aims. Their marketing policy concentrates upon the grape variety, and considerable efforts have been made with the presentation. The label depicts a carving of a vintage scene from the Norman church of St-Michel de Murato. They have worked hard to develop their vineyards; considerable areas of Carignan and Alicante have been T-budded with Chardonnay, with some success, and they also have plans for Pinot Noir and Merlot. Their cellars are probably the most modern on the island, with sophisticated equipment for cooling the fermenting juice and the finished wine. They use cultured yeast, centrifuge the must, and control everything very closely. There is no complacency in their approach; one feels that they are constantly seeking to improve their wines, and the results are impressive.

COTEAUX DE CAP CORSE

The coastal plain ends at Bastia, which is the old capital of Corsica. For the brief two-year period that Corsica belonged to England, during the Napoleonic Wars, the Viceroy, Sir Gilbert Elliot, held his court there. There is a colourful port, with fishing- and pleasure-boats, overlooked by gently decaying houses. From Bastia I drove north to Macinaggio, almost at the top of Cap Corse. The road is narrow and winding, with more than its fair share of potholes. Before the phylloxera there were 1,800 hectares of vines on Cap Corse and you can still see the remains of crumbling terraces. Today the vineyards have almost disappeared, leaving less than 20 hectares shared between four producers of the appellation of Coteaux de Cap Corse. The villages of Morsiglia, Rogliano and Santa Severa are all that remain of a vineyard that once covered the whole of Cap Corse. The best and largest grower is Jean-Noël Luigi at Clos Nicrosi, who has 10.5 hectares of white grapes – 7 of Vermentino, plus 3.5 of Muscat that are not in the appellation. He is also planting some Nielluccio and a little Grenache, but his reputation rests upon his white wine, which is quite the best in the island.

The wind was blowing hard outside and carrying spray from the sea, so we sat by the log fire and talked and tasted. It is Toussaint Luigi who owns the estate, but his nephew Jean-Noël now does all the work. They explained that the Muscat à Petits Grains is typical of Cap Corse and that it is picked when the potential alcohol is 14°, usually in mid-September; it is then left in the vineyard to dry for a week in the sunshine, so that the berries dehydrate and the potential alcohol rises to 18°. It is then vinified like a *vin doux naturel*: the grapes are pressed and the fermentation is stopped, leaving 100 grams of sugar per litre and the alcohol level is raised to 17°. Yields are tiny, only 20 hectolitres per hectare. For the moment their Muscat, or Muscatellu in Corsican, does not have an appellation. Nevertheless it deserves one, with its lovely rich, honeyed, Muscat nose and flavour; it needs a year's ageing for the alcohol to marry properly with the wine.

It is the dry white wine that makes the appellation Coteaux de Cap

Corse. Here the Vermentino gives an average yield of 30 hl/ha. The juice is never given any skin contact and it is fermented at 17–18°C, with no malolactic fermentation; they do not need to add acidity, and the wine is bottled in April. It should age for about three years. It had a perfumed flavour that I did not find in any other Vermentino on the island, and in the spring of 1986 the 1985 was a light golden colour with a full, nutty nose. In the mouth it reminded me a little of Viognier, having a perfumed flavour and an almost oily texture. In comparison the 1982 had a richer, more leafy, buttery flavour and was delicious with some local fish.

The soil of Cap Corse is schist, which suits the Vermentino. Unusually for traditional Corsican vineyards, the vines here are trained on wires, for the wind can be so strong that they need the extra support. The microclimate of Cap Corse subjects it to the south west Libeccio in the summer, and the Sirocco blows from the east. A strong wind at the flowering can easily destroy two-thirds of the crop. However, they have less rain than the rest of the island – except the day that I was there.

PATRIMONIO

In the afternoon, as I drove down the other side of the Cap Corse towards Patrimonio, the clouds cleared. The road was narrow with overhanging cliffs, and there were breathtaking views of rocky bays and coves. In 50 kilometres I met no more than five cars. The village of Patrimonio is set at the base of Cap Corse, but first I headed for the estate of Dominique Gentile, just outside the lively town of St-Florent.

Patrimonio is the oldest appellation of Corsica, but dates only from 1968. But the reputation of its wine goes back to the Middle Ages: the monks of the abbey of Farinolle cultivated vines and sent wine to the papal court in Rome. Today there is a feeling that the potential of the appellation is not fully realized. This is the area for Nielluccio above all, for it flourishes on the clay and limestone soil which occurs nowhere else in Corsica. The vineyards are terraced on the steep slopes of Mont St-Angelo, which dominates the skyline of Patrimonio.

Thirty years ago there were vines everywhere around Patrimonio and St-Florent – 600 hectares cultivated by some 250 growers, mostly people with other crops as well, who sent their grapes to the local co-operative. The appellation covers seven villages, for as well as Patrimonio and St-Florent there are Oletta, Farinole and Casta to the south and Poggio d'Oletta to the north, where there are the most vines. Then in August 1960 disaster struck in the form of a severe hailstorm which wiped out the crop for that year and destroyed many of the vineyards. Older people with only a few vines were reluctant to replant, and others left the area and abandoned their vines. Today there are 350 hectares, with only about twenty wine-growers who make a living from their wine. Of these there are three whose wines excel. Quality is unreliable amongst the others, and the co-operative of Patrimonio has fallen into financial difficulties and gone into liquidation.

Dominique Gentile is a friendly, enthusiastic man and gave me a warm welcome. He was delighted to have the opportunity to talk about Patrimonio. Its individuality comes from the Nielluccio grape, which dominates the blend for the red wine. It is the Sangiovese of Italy and was brought to the island by the Pisans and Genoese. Purists, such as Dominique Gentile, would like the wine to be made from Nielluccio alone. At the moment up to 40 per cent Grenache is allowed, and by 1990 the required amount of Nielluccio will be increased to 90 per cent. He gives his red grapes, which are destalked first, a six-day maceration to extract colour and tannin, with a *remontage* at least twice a day. The fermentation temperature is maintained at 30°C. Afterwards the wine spends seven or eight months in cement vats and is bottled in the spring. Ideally he would keep his wine for longer before bottling, but the great problem in Corsica is the effect of summer temperatures. However, he has plans for an underground cellar for storage.

A dry white wine is made from Vermentino, with a carefully controlled fermentation. There is no malolactic fermentation, so that sufficient acidity is retained in the wine. The pink, also from Nielluccio, is made by the *saigné* method with about twenty-four hours' skin contact, depending on the conditions of the vintage.

Although M. Gentile's father had been a wine-grower, his vines had been pulled up; so his son started from scratch, clearing 13 hectares of *maquis*. People thought he was mad to plant vines back in the early 1970s. But he is realistic about the future of Patrimonio: 'It declined because of the men, but the soil, the climate and the grape varieties are still there.' It is interest and motivation that are lacking.

Fortunately there are others who share M. Gentile's enthusiasm. From St-Florent we headed for the tiny village of Oletta on the hills below the Col de Teghime. On a fine day you have views of both the Gulf of St-Florent and of the east coast of the island. When we were there, there was swirling cloud and the Sirocco was blowing hard. But it brought no rain, and there had been none all summer. We drove past the old cathedral of St-Florent and up into the hills through bleak wasteland, the result of a forest fire a week earlier. There was ash in the air and an atmosphere of desolation, not unlike a First World War battle scene. The vines, however, seem to resist the ravages of fire more than the drier scrub.

Yves Leccia has 20 hectares of vines scattered around the village in ten small parcels. He makes all three colours of Patrimonio and has a small near-cellar under his house, equipped with stainless-steel vats. His white wine from Vermentino is fermented at 19°C for about ten days and bottled in the spring. It tastes fruity and rounded, with the slightly bitter, nutty finish that is typical of Vermentino. The pink, which is a blend of Grenache and Nielluccio, is given the same careful fermentation when the juice has been run off after twenty-four hours of skin contact; it has a gentle raspberry flavour. The red consists of 80 per cent Nielluccio with 20 per cent Grenache, which are destalked and fermented on the skins for three to five days and then aged in stainless-steel vats for a year. It is a rounded mouthful of wine, warm, perfumed and peppery with some tannin. The experimental station of the island, the CIVAM, is experimenting with ageing Nielluccio in wood, but M. Leccia is rather hesitant about this, as it is not obvious that wood ageing will make better wine. His Muscat is similar to that of Dominique Gentile in method and flavour; sweet, honeyed and grapy. He sees the strength of the appellation as lying in the Corsican grape varieties, for they contribute individuality; now it is up to the people to contribute quality.

The village of Patrimonio stretches across the hillside, and the road from the Col de Teghime is lined with signs advertising *vente directe* and tastings of Patrimonio. The sixteenth-century church stands in splendid isolation. Outside the village we found another young enthusiast, Antoine Arena, at Clos de Morta Maio. He and Messieurs Gentile and Leccia seemed like three musketeers, fighting for their appellation. He has 7 hectares of vines planted with Nielluccio, Vermentino, Muscat and a little Grenache (which is not very popular as it suffers badly from *coulure*).

His small, rather chaotic cellar houses old barrels and new stainless-steel vats, and produces some delicious wine. The Vermentino had an attractive perfume with a slightly bitter finish. He keeps his Muscat in large oak barrels for six or seven months and then it should have twelve months in bottle. Cap Corse and Patrimonio are the only areas where the tradition for Muscat has been retained; originally it was made for family consumption on high days and holidays, as a special treat, rather like Vin Santo in Tuscany. As for his red wine, the fermentation starts in stainless-steel vats and is then finished off in wood. When we tasted the 1986 in September 1987, it had just been bottled and was a bit dumb, but it promised well. In the tasting-room there was a sign saying, '*Un repas sans vin est comme une soirée sans amis*'.

CALVI

From the lively port of St-Florent, with its harbourside restaurants where you can dine off fish that were still in the sea just a few hours earlier, I headed towards Calvi. The road goes through some of the wildest terrain of the island, an arid, uninhabited area called the Désert des Agriates. With little vegetation for nourishment, there were not even any sheep. Calvi is the centre of the district of the Balagne, that stretches from L'Ile Rousse nearly as far south as Porto. Three river valleys from the core of the appellation of Calvi: that of the Regino, near L'Ile Rousse, and the valleys of Calenzana and Galeria. Calvi itself is a seaside resort. In February it looks desolate in the rain, with the cafés closed for renovation, but in September it is more cheerful and bustling, with its port and the picturesque old town dominated by the Genoese citadel. Local pride asserts the claim of Calvi to be the birthplace of Christopher Columbus, for the town was Genoese in 1441.

My introduction to the wine of Calvi came from Paul Suzzoni at Domaine Colombu, or in French Colombe, just outside the town. His 25-hectare estate is planted with Nielluccio, Sciacarello, Grenache and Cinsaut, as well as some Barbarossa and Syrah. He does not make any white wine. He began planting his vines in 1970; his father had land for sheep, cows and wheat, but he saw no future in these. There is a healthy market for wine, however, provided by the summer tourist trade. Although he went to agricultural college, he has had no formal viticultural training, learning by experience. As a man of the land he is insistent on the importance of vine-husbandry; he uses no insecticides or chemical fertilizers and prunes his vines very severely, trying to do everything as naturally as possible. 'You have to follow nature, and help it,' but he is against any chemical products in his wine. Nor is there anything special in his vinification methods. 'The wine makes itself. If you have worked well in the vineyard for eleven months, it is the grapes that make the wine.' I liked his wines, for they had an attractive perfumed flavour, with the warm, peppery taste of the island.

More established is Fabien Paolini at Clos Landry. You approach his estate along a bumpy road hedged by mimosa, which was in brilliant flower in February, providing a bright splash of colour on a grey afternoon. He has 24 hectares of vines – Nielluccio, Sciacarello, Grenache and a little Cinsaut and Syrah – from which he makes two bottles of pink to every one of red. He is not interested in white wine. I preferred his red to his pink, which lacked fruit, although it seemed efficiently vinified. The red wine had been kept in old barrels for a few months, which allowed gentle oxidation rather than any wood ageing. It was quite tough, with some perfumed fruit, and promised well.

My last taste of Calvi came from a young grower in the hills outside Calvi near Muro. Michel Raoust happily guided me out to Clos Reginu along narrow roads with wonderful views of the distant coastline. We arrived at his estate, 25 hectares of vines apparently in the middle of nowhere. The vineyard had been planted by his father-in-law and Michel Raoust had taken it over after a varied career of numerous jobs, the last one with the French equivalent of the Water Board! I liked his wine enormously. His red is mainly from Grenache, Nielluccio and Sciacarello, with some Syrah and Carignan; it was tannic and astringent, with plenty of balancing perfumed fruit. He would like some Mourvèdre, but you are only allowed to plant Nielluccio, Sciacarello or Vermentino here. In 1984 he began experimenting with oak ageing, envisaging that his red wine would ultimately spend one year in vat, followed by a year in wood and a year in bottle before being ready for drinking. His first vintage was only in 1981.

And there my tour of the island ended. I headed back to the airport at Bastia, over the hills that run down the centre of the island. Corsica suffers from its insularity. No one produces bottles, corks or capsules on the island, so that all these have to be brought from mainland France. The tourists provide a ready sale for the wines in the summer, but they are a limited market. Although the island is part of France, it is often neglected or simply ignored in the line-up of French wines. Yet there are wines of great character and individuality to be found. The indigenous grape varieties with their distinctive flavours, which were nearly drowned in the tide of vulgar grapes from North Africa, now represent the future of Corsican viticulture.

8

The Upper Reaches of the Loire, and the Lyonnais

CÔTES DU FOREZ

The little-known Côtes du Forez is a small oasis of vines in the centre of France, in the department of Loire. It is easy to forget that this majestic river of fine châteaux begins its course as a tiny trickle near Le Puy in Haute-Loire. It flows through the department of Loire, past the vineyards of the Côtes du Forez and the Côte Roannaise. Downstream near Nevers it is joined by the Allier, whose roughly parallel course has taken it past the vineyards of St-Pourçain and the Côtes d'Auvergne. It is these rivers and a spectacular chain of volcanoes, the *puys* of the Massif Central, that link the four islands of vineyards. The Côte Roannaise and Côtes du Forez are not very far from the Beaujolais, and there are similarities in grape variety and vinification methods; St-Pourçain and the Côtes d'Auvergne, on the other hand, have a more localized character.

Côtes du Forez covers a fairly static area of some 200 hectares planted almost entirely with Gamay Noir à Jus Blanc. Virtually the entire production is vinified by the Cave Co-opérative des Vignerons Foréziens at Trélins, outside the town of Boën-sur-Lignon. This co-operative is working well for its wine. It was created in 1962, six years after Côtes du Forez was recognized as a VDQS, and now has 220 members. Only one grower lives from his vines alone, for this is very much a region of polyculture with orchards, vegetables and dairy farming. Three of the members choose not to bring all their grapes to the co-operative and vinify a little themselves, but the quantity is insignificant.

I spent a morning with the director of Les Vignerons Foréziens, Alain Coudurier, who is young, enthusiastic and energetic. He has broader horizons than many a co-operative director buried in the

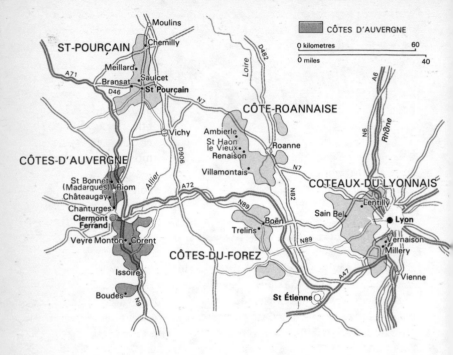

The Upper Reaches of the Loire Valley

heart of France. He comes from Chambéry in Savoie and has spent time in Australia, working in the Barossa valley.

M. Coudurier explained that the history of the vineyards of the Côtes du Forez goes back to the Romans. In 980 mention was made of the vineyard of L'Annet at Boen, and the Benedictine monks of the abbey of Cluny and the counts of Forez developed the vineyards during the Middle Ages. Between 1173 and 1376 the region was governed by the counts of Forez from the château of Montbrison, and it did not revert to the French crown until the reign of François I. In 1606 Anne d'Urfé, a member of another important local family and the sister of Honoré d'Urfé, wrote that Boen was a small town in a wood where there were good vineyards, especially in a place called Courbine that produced good wine, even at the end of the autumn.

The vineyards of the Côtes du Forez were at their greatest extent with 5,043 hectares of vines in 1885; at that time they supplied the people of the mountains of the Massif Central, where no vines could grow. In 1956 Côtes du Forez became a VDQS for vineyards in the villages of Boen-sur-Lignon, Trélins, Marcoux, Marcilly and Pralong, covering the hillsides on the edge of the plain of Forez. These are the foothills of the Massif Central, and the vineyards are some of the highest in France at an altitude of between 400 and 550 metres. In the distance you can see the snow-covered caps of the old volcanoes. In 1976 the area was extended to include several more villages, making a total of twenty-two, but in practice the most important are Boen and Marcilly.

The soil is mainly granite and clay with some volcanic extrusions and sand. Climatically the region is one of transition between the hard continental climate of the north and softer, warmer climate of the Mediterranean.

Monsieur Pâtard, the vice-president and a founder member of the co-operative, talked of the measures involved in obtaining the VDQS. It was necessary to establish the former reputation of the vineyards by tracing diplomas from before the First World War. Clearing out his attic, what should he find but the diploma awarding his grandfather a silver medal at the Concours de Montbrison in 1899. Perhaps more interesting was a medal the grandfather had won as a nurseryman, grafting vines in the struggle against phylloxera, at a Concours de Greffage de Vignes Françaises sur Vignes Américaines (a competition for the grafting of French vines on to American rootstock), and his Diplôme de Greffeur of 1893.

Les Vignerons Foréziens are better equipped than many a co-operative, with a new vinification plant that has ten shining stainless-steel vats, blanketed for efficient temperature control. The grape variety is Gamay and the method is that of the Beaujolais. Whole bunches are picked, so there are no mechanical harvesters here, and the fermentation vats are filled by gravity. No extra carbon dioxide is added, a system that they call semi-carbonic. The fermentation of the red wine is maintained at 25°C, and the length of the fermentation varies according to the particular *cuvée* for which the wine is destined. A *primeur* will have four or five days and a prestige *cuvée* seven or eight days. The free-run juice is blended with the pressed juice and all the wines are bottled in the spring after the malolactic fermentation, fining and filtering, apart from the *primeur* which is released on 1 December.

Some pink wine is made, for which the grapes are either pressed immediately or left with the skins for about twenty-four hours. For that the fermentation is maintained at 18°C. More unexpected was their pink *méthode champenoise* wine, which is not included in the VDQS and goes under the poetic name of Moussette d'Astrée. Moussette is a more picturesque name for *mousseux* and Astrée another name for the region, recalling one of the early novels of the seventeenth century, *Le Romain d'Astrée* by Honoré d'Urfé.

For the moment no white wine is made, for the Côtes du Forez have never been a region of white wine. However, some Chardonnay has been planted as an experiment by three growers in different parts of the area, but the vines are not yet in production.

The co-operative has had the commercial shrewdness to develop a range of different *cuvées* appropriate to its customers, such as Le Train Bleu for the restaurant in the Gare de Lyon; another is La Cuvée de l'Écrivain, produced for the annual book fair in nearby St-Étienne and named each year after a contemporary French writer. In 1985 it was René Fallet, who wrote (perhaps inappropriately) *Le Beaujolais nouveau est arrivé* and in 1986 Robert Sabatier, the author of *Les Allumettes suédoises*. A prestige *cuvée* is made from the oldest vines with the smallest yields, 30 hectolitres per hectare as opposed to the more usual 60. The wines are good and they have an attractive Gamay character that would not be out of place in a line-up of Beaujolais, while the prestige *cuvée* could happily compete with a Morgon or a Fleurie.

CÔTE ROANNAISE

The rather dreary town of Roanne gives its name to the second wine of the Loire valley (that is, as you travel downstream from the river's source). Another reason for visiting Roanne might be the highly acclaimed starred restaurant of the Frères Troisgros – fortunately for my bank balance it was closed the evening I was in Roanne!

Benedictine monks from the nearby abbey of Ambierlé can take much of the credit for planting vines here in the Middle Ages, and the town of Roanne became an important port on the Loire, which provided a link with Paris via Orléans. The declaration of the local wine brotherhood notes with pride that on what is said to be the earliest wine list found in France, dating from the reign of Louis XIII, mention is made of the wines of Pommard and of Villerest, a village in the Côte Roannaise. Certainly during the eighteenth century wine was sent by river and canal to Paris, and there are records of wine being loaded at Roanne, notably on 16 May 1755 when Sieur Xavier-François de la Marette from the village of St-Haon-le-Châtel sent ninety-eight barrels of both old and new wine by river to the Quai de la Tonnelle in Paris.

At the beginning of the twentieth century the area produced 700–800,000 hectolitres of wine annually and the village of Lentigny had fifteen wine-growers. Today there is only one and the total area of the Côte Roannaise has shrunk to around 100 hectares, with an average annual production of 5,000 hectolitres. The Côte Roannaise became a VDQS in 1955, which gave the region some much-needed encouragement to work towards quality and to abandon hybrid vines and common table wine. The area now covers twenty-four villages, of which the most important are Ambierlé, St-Haon-le-Vieux, St-Haon-le-Châtel, Villemontais, Lentigny and Villerest; the vineyards stand on the slopes of the Monts de la Madeleine, part of the foothills of the Massif Central, and face south east at an altitude of 370 metres. The climate is gentle and frost is rare, although hail can be a problem.

The soil is predominantly granite, so that Gamay flourishes, while Pinot Noir is less suitable. Many of the vineyards are very steep and some are even terraced. Most are planted in wide rows with about 5,000 vines per hectare, and are pruned in the *guyot* system with five or six eyes; an alternative system consists of narrow rows with 10,000 vines per hectare on a square grid and 1 metre apart. Yields vary so that one grower may only average 35 hectolitres per hectare, while others reach 50 or even 60 hl/ha.

The vineyards of the Beaujolais are not so far away, about 70 kilometres as the crow flies, so it is no surprise that Gamay Noir à Jus Blanc is the dominant grape variety; but here it is a different clone, called the Gamay Romain. A little Pinot Noir is also grown; this used to be much more important, but Gamay has the overwhelming advantage from the growers' point of view that it gives much higher yields. Consequently only one person retains Pinot Noir in any quantity in his vineyards.

White wine does not feature in the VDQS. Some was made at the beginning of the century but had disappeared by the time the VDQS was created; it is only recently that there have been one or two tentative plantings of Chardonnay, which can be sold as Vin de Pays d'Urfé. Certainly the wine-growers of the Côte Roannaise would like it included in the VDQS, just as they would like to be promoted to an appellation.

Pierre Geaume, the president of the growers' association, is fairly representative of the area and is the only wine-grower in the village of Lentigny. His house, with its cellars and dovecot, is built round a pleasant courtyard adorned by pots of geraniums. He used to have a large herd of cows, but milk quotas have encouraged him to turn to vines and he now has 3 hectares, including 50 ares of Chardonnay. For him the character of Côte Roannaise comes from the Gamay grape vinified the same way as in the Beaujolais. There is little formal training in wine-making in the area – for that, 'We went to our neighbours in the Beaujolais.' The grapes are not destalked but are fermented in whole bunches for about five days, and the wine is usually bottled in the early spring. M. Geaume is not equipped to cool his fermentation vats, but there is usually little problem. The temperature remains below about 28°C as his vats are quite small. He is replacing his old cement vats with stainless-steel ones. The cement is virtually indestructible: 'If only bank safes were as solid.' He is removing his father's old wooden barrels, too.

In contrast to Pierre Geaume, Paul-Louis Lapandéry at St-Haon-le-Vieux has continued the old tradition of Pinot Noir and aims to make a wine to age. He is rather isolated in his enthusiasm for Pinot Noir and scorns his colleagues' allegiance to the methods of the Beaujolais. He is dismissive of the resulting young wine, that only became characteristic of the Côte Roannaise as more people began to bottle their own wines ten or fifteen years ago.

His methods, too, are traditional, for the grapes are destalked and fermented in old oak vats at a temperature of about 30°C for eight or ten days. He has some elementary cooling equipment and still uses an old vertical wooden press. His wine is aged in 15-hectolitre oak barrels for eighteen months, so that his 1985 vintage was not bottled until the spring of 1987. The wine is racked a couple of times but it is fined with real egg-white, one and a half eggs per barrel. M. Lapandéry considers his 1985 to be one of the best wines he has ever made, along with the 1971, the 1957 and the 1947, the last bottle of which he drank in 1972 when it was thirty-five years old. The 1985 was delicious – quite a solid mouthful of fruit with some acidity and not much tannin. It went very well with Mme Lapandéry's home-cured ham and home-made sausages.

CÔTES D'AUVERGNE

It was quite a surprise to be told that a hundred years ago the department of Puy-de-Dôme was the third most important viticultural department of France, for today you have difficulty in distinguishing the few remaining vineyards from the sprawling suburbs of Clermont-Ferrand. In 1890 there were 60,000 hectares of vines and entire hillsides were covered with terraced vineyards. Today they are reduced to 2,100 hectares, of which 500 produce the VDQS Côtes d'Auvergne, with its five *crus* of Corent, Madargues, Boudes, Châteaugay and Chanturgues.

The first records of viticulture go back to the Gallo-Roman period. Coins have been found near the village of Corent depicting bunches of grapes. In the fifth century Sidonius Apollinaris, bishop of the Auvergne, described the Limagne, the fertile foothills of the Massif Central around Clermont-Ferrand, saying that there was wheat on the plain, vines on the slopes and pasture on the tops of the mountains, and that the wines of the hills were comparable to those of Palermo or Chios. Viticulture was evidently an important part of the region's economy and continued to be so throughout the Middle Ages. From the twelfth century the river port of Ris sent wines to Paris. Letters from Charles VI in 1416 refer to wines of Ris being sold in Paris, and in 1454 there is mention of a merchant from Orléans bringing a large load of wine from Ris.

A notable change took place in the eighteenth century, a change in grape variety from Pinot Noir to Gamay, which has never been reversed. Gamay has an advantage over Pinot Noir in that it produces more wine. It was after this transformation that Jullien described the wines of the Auvergne as rather indifferent, that they were in general for early drinking and would not travel except during the first year and deteriorated if they were exposed to the summer heat. He said they were low in alcohol and rarely kept for more than two years and were very suitable for blending, going well with other wines.

When the wines of the Auvergne were at their peak, they profited from the devastation caused by the phylloxera in other parts of France. The phylloxera did not reach the vineyards of the Auvergne until 1890, but when it came the effect of the attack was such that by the end of the century the vineyard area of Puy-de-Dôme had fallen to around 26,000 hectares, a drop of 50 per cent in less than ten years, and the decline continued. The harvest of 1910 is remembered for its devastating attacks of mildew. Many wine-growers were killed in the First World War, and by 1919 there were only 15,000 hectares of vines in the region. The rural exodus of farmers lured by the Michelin factories of Clermont-Ferrand continued the decline and viticulture lost its appeal.

Today many of the vineyards of the Côtes d'Auvergne are fighting the encroaching urban sprawl of Clermont-Ferrand. Viticulture has been reduced to negligible importance and one cannot help feeling that the remaining wine-growers of the Côtes d'Auvergne are fighting something of a rearguard action. They are proud of their product, its tradition and its history, even though the wines of the Auvergne have lost their reputation in Paris and enjoy little more than local interest. One has to admire the courage and tenacity of the men and women who are striving to maintain the precarious existence of their vineyards against considerable odds.

The vineyards of the Côtes d'Auvergne are amongst the most isolated in France. The INAO classes them with those of the Loire valley, to which they are connected by the River Allier. There are no other vineyards nearer than those of St-Pourçain to the north of Vichy. The Côtes d'Auvergne are very scattered, forming small oases of vines over the hillsides north and south of Clermont-Ferrand. Altogether fifty-four villages are included in the VDQS area, which was delimited in 1977. Of these the most important in terms of quantity are those closest to Clermont-Ferrand, such as Aubières, Pérignat-les-Sarlièves and Veyre-Monton, which is the home of the rather depressing regional co-operative. The five *crus* owe their status more to historic reputation than to a currently flourishing vineyard.

Corent is a small, sleepy village on a steep hill near Clermont-Ferrand. You approach it by a narrow, tortuous road and it quietly ignores its proximity to the Michelin tyre capital with a firmly rural, gently dilapidated atmosphere. Odd signs hanging from houses advertise Rosé de Corent. I stopped to taste the wine made by Paul Champroux. His daughter showed me their cellar, which contained some old wooden barrels, made by her grandfather who was a cooper, and a couple of cement vats. They have 8 hectares of Gamay as well as some wheat and asparagus. Corent is the only pink wine among the *crus* of the Côtes d'Auvergne, probably because the grapes never ripened sufficiently to make red wine, as the vineyards are on north west-facing slopes. The soil is volcanic, based on red lava. The colour in the wine comes only from pressing; there is no skin contact with the juice, nor any control of fermentation temperatures. Nor was I able to ascertain whether the wine undergoes a malolactic fermentation. Their wine-making is 'as natural as possible' and certainly very rustic. The wine is bottled *'quand il a fait ses Pâques'*, in other words after Easter. As for the taste, it was mouth-wateringly acidic.

Most of the vineyards of the Côtes d'Auvergne are on the volcanic soil of the Massif Central. *Puy* is the local word for the extinct volcanoes whose cones are a dramatic feature of the scenery to the west and south west of Clermont-Ferrand. Most of the vineyards are on hillsides at an altitude of 300–400 metres, generally on south west-facing slopes.

Climatic problems vary. Spring frosts are the biggest hazard and frost protection, except prayers, is financially inconceivable. The winters are long and hard, July and August hot, and the autumns long and sunny. Gamay does well here, as it has a short vegetative cycle, with a late bud-break. There is a small amount of Pinot Noir and a couple of courageous growers have planted Chardonnay, which is not included in the VDQS regulations and so will go to make Vin de Pays de Puy-de-Dôme.

The most flourishing *cru* of the Côtes d'Auvergne is Châteaugay, which takes its name from a hilltop village outside Clermont-Ferrand. Appropriately, the village is dominated by its château. Pierre Lapouge is the most important producer of Châteaugay, as he has 10 hectares there as well as 2.5 hectares in neighbouring Chanturgues. While Châteaugay has a total of 80 hectares in production with 80 *déclarations de récolte*, Chanturgues, which is closer to Clermont-Ferrand, is being eaten up by the building contractors of the tyre city. Pierre Lapouge makes 150 of the tiny 200-hectolitre average annual production of Chanturgues. This is sad, as the wine does merit its status as a *cru*. It was the name most often praised by the nineteenth-century authorities, and it deserves to survive.

There are soil differences between the two *crus*. Châteaugay is a mixture of clay, limestone and basaltic debris, while Chanturgues has a higher proportion of volcanic soil, which gives a more tannic wine. Although Gamay is the main grape variety, there is also a little

Pinot Noir – only 5 per cent in Châteaugay and 10–12 per cent in Chanturgues. There is no precise blend and the two grape varieties are mixed together in the vineyards, which are on very steep slopes. There is a gradient of up to 1 in 4 in Chanturgues which makes mechanization impossible. The vineyards are sheltered from the prevailing winds, and the heat is retained by a kind of amphitheatre of hills. From the edge of the village of Châteaugay you can see steep hillsides of vines broken by houses, and in the distance the plain and the sprawl of Clermont-Ferrand.

Pierre Lapouge is a sturdy farmer, who works with his two sons. He began with 1.5 hectares and gradually developed his vineyard. Back in 1940 everyone grew a few vines alongside their other crops; few do so now, but M. Lapouge believed and still believes that there is a future in wine. He was the first in the area to bottle, some thirty years ago. He also has some cereal, but is more interested in his wines.

His cellars are fairly rustic: the fermentation takes place with whole bunches of grapes in open-topped cement vats and lasts about four or five days. It never goes above 28°C. Chanturgues is a more solid wine and ages better than Châteaugay, so M. Lapouge puts it in wood for twelve months. In contrast, Châteaugay can be drunk when it is young and fruity in the spring. While we compared them in his small tasting-room, the local gendarme came in for a drink and jokingly accused me of industrial espionage!

To the south of Clermont-Ferrand, near the town of Issoire with its evocative Romanesque church, is the village of Boudes. There are slopes of vines as you approach the village, but the *cru* of Boudes consists of only 40 hectares, mainly on black basalt soil. I tracked down Annie Sauvat and her father Claude, who have 6.5 hectares and are one of the two families who make a living from their vines. The other is André Chermensat. I am told he is '*un grand personnage*' in the appellation, but unfortunately I was unable to meet him.

The Sauvats' vineyards consist of a hectare of Chardonnay which was planted in 1983 and was only just coming into production. There is also half a hectare of fifteen-year-old Pinot Noir, and the rest is Gamay, which is vinified according to the *méthode beaujolaise* with a five- or six-day *cuvaison*. They want to increase their Pinot Noir so that they have enough to make a varietal wine, which they would eventually like to age in 225-litre barrels rather than the traditional larger casks. Pure Pinot Noir is permitted in the VDQS regulations, but as yet none is made. At present they make two styles of Gamay, a light one that is pure Gamay, and a more solid wine with up to 30 per cent Pinot Noir.

Their Chardonnay, only in its first year of production, was lightly leafy, with the *bonbons anglais* smell of new wine. The pink, made from Gamay that was pressed and not macerated, had high acidity with a little fruit, while the 1986 red Gamay was light, perfumed and fruity. The blend of Gamay and Pinot Noir was still doing its malolactic fermentation, so was not available for tasting.

Annie and Claude Sauvat are optimistic about the future, for they have established a local reputation and have no problem in selling their wine just from the cellar door. That afternoon they were going to the local prize-giving to collect their gold medals.

Most isolated of the *crus* of the Auvergne is Madargues. It was the hardest to find, for it is not a village but a *lieu-dit* in the village of St-Bonnet-près-Riom on the way to St-Pourçain. The monks of the nearby abbey of Mozac had given Madargues its early reputation, but since then phylloxera, mildew and the First World War have all contributed to the vineyard's decline. Bernard Boulin is the courageous man who is trying to re-establish its reputation. He is a car mechanic by training, but wine has always fascinated him. His parents-in-law made ordinary *vin de table* without any technology. He has just 2 hectares of Gamay in production, has planted some Pinot Noir, is planning some Chardonnay, and is aiming for a total of 10 hectares. His vineyards are on sunny south east slopes on the edge of the Limagne at a height of about 250 metres. In contrast to the rest of the Auvergne vineyards, the soil is not volcanic, but clay and limestone mixed with some sand.

M. Boulin's very first bottling was in 1976 and he admits that it was a bit hit-and-miss. Since then he has learnt from various courses; in 1986 he made two red wines, one from destalked grapes fermented in an open vat for twelve days, and the other from whole bunches fermented *à la beaujolaise* in a closed vat, also for twelve days. This indicates an inquiring mind that is eager to experiment. I preferred the Beaujolais style, as it was more supple and fruitier. Then M. Boulin opened the last bottle of his 1982, a mouthful of mellow fruit, which had, in the manner of Beaujolais, taken on some of the vegetal character of Pinot Noir. His enthusiasm was infectious. Unlike the dreary co-operative at Veyre-Monton, which accounts for a quarter of the production of Côtes d'Auvergne, the independent growers are positive in their attitude. Their appellation may have lost its former reputation and importance, but they are making the best wine they can within their limited means. I felt optimistic for them as I drove towards St-Pourçain.

ST-POURÇAIN-SUR-SIOULE

St-Pourçain is a lively country town, standing where the main road between Vichy and Montluçon crosses the River Sioule. The decaying medieval abbey of Ste-Croix dominates the market square which bustles with colourful activity on Saturday morning, with stalls of fruit and vegetables, cheeses and flowers.

The vineyards of St-Pourçain claim a long history, with Phoenician rather than Roman origins. Certainly the Romans also had vineyards here, and old tools dating back to 50 BC were discovered at nearby Vichy. Viticulture developed during the Middle Ages and the wines were enjoyed by the kings of France, who in the fourteenth century were protectors of the town of St-Pourçain. The wines travelled by river and canal to Paris. The dukes of Bourbon also showed an interest in their local wines.

Wines from St-Pourçain were served at the feast given by St Louis at Saumur in 1241 to celebrate the coming-of-age of his brother Alphonse of France. Philip the Fair enjoyed the wines of St-Pourçain at the beginning of the fourteenth century; and later in the same century, at the papal court of Avignon, St-Pourçain was linked with Beaune ('vin de Biaune et de St-Poursain') and featured among the wines used to celebrate great solemnities. Viticulture continued to flourish till the end of the eighteenth century. Contigny on the Allier was an important port for sending wine to Paris, where it was popular with the many Parisian café-owners from the Auvergne. The installations of the port of Contigny were destroyed in a severe flood in 1893. During the first half of the nineteenth century vines gave way to cereals and fruit trees, and phylloxera completed the shrinkage. Today the vineyards of St-Pourçain consist of about 500 hectares spread out over nineteen villages, mainly to the west of St-Pourçain itself.

Variety is the dominant feature of St-Pourçain, for the regulations of the VDQS, implemented in 1951, include several grape varieties for red, white and pink wines. The historic reputation of St-Pourçain depended upon its white wines and the most characteristic grape of the area is white – the Tresallier, which is the local name for Sacy. Opinions vary as to its quality. Some believe it gives white St-Pourçain its originality, while others consider that it lacks quality and should be quietly abandoned. In fact most people have a little, for they cannot completely give up the traditional grape, but several growers have planted Chardonnay and Sauvignon. There is also some Aligoté, some unsuccessful experimental Gewurztraminer and a grape called St-Pierre Doré which, I was told, makes 'a filthy wine'. The main discussion is for and against Sacy.

Some growers make two wines, a pure Sacy and a *cuvée prestige* of Chardonnay and Sauvignon, while others mix all their white grapes together, saying that Sacy gives acidity, Sauvignon aroma and Chardonnay structure. But Chardonnay can ripen too early and easily becomes overripe; Sacy, by contrast, only ripens properly one year in ten. It has high acidity and gives large yields of a rather neutral-flavoured wine. It does in fact make a good base for champagne-method sparkling wine, and this has become more widespread over the last ten years, but does not yet feature in the VDQS.

Gérard and Jean-Louis Pétillat are the only growers who are brave enough to have no Sacy at all, and as a result they are waging a long-term battle with the authorities of the INAO, who require them to have a minimum of 30 per cent Sacy. They argue that they obtain a better wine from Chardonnay and Sauvignon and that Sacy is not only too difficult to ripen but gives too much juice, while the average yield for Chardonnay is only 40 hectolitres per hectare.

Chardonnay and Sauvignon had always been mixed up in the vineyards, so they were included in the appellation regulations, but it is only in recent years that they have gained importance. The Pétillats were the first to plant them in any quantity and to make a wine without Sacy. They are now reproached for making a commercial wine rather than a characteristic one. The nuttiness of the Sacy certainly has originality appeal, but there is no doubt that Chardonnay and Sauvignon blends are more to the taste of the modern consumer.

Red wine is still a recent phenomenon in St-Pourçain. Roger Chérillat, the president of the wine-growers' association, who has been working in the vineyards for over fifty years, remembers that before the Second World War there was hardly any red wine and what there was did not merit discussion. Gamay and Pinot Noir were planted to meet a post-war fashion for pink wine; when that faded, red wine took its place, so that white grapes now only account for about a quarter of the production of St-Pourçain.

Gamay and Pinot Noir are the two red grape varieties. Sometimes they are vinified separately and sometimes together; the grower's whim decides. Gamay dominates and is described as 'fantastic'. Pinot Noir is difficult to grow and vinify. With its compact bunches it retains humidity and is easily affected by rot, and with a lot of rain the grapes swell and burst. It needs more skin contact than Gamay and some wood ageing. Roger Pétillat is enthusiastic and makes a varietal wine, while Guy Nebout is disappointed with his half-hectare of Pinot Noir. He thought it would improve the Gamay but the promise was not fulfilled, though possibly it should be aged longer.

The co-operative is experimenting with ageing its Pinot Noir in new oak *barriques*, with as yet no positive conclusions. Pinot Noir probably gives better results on its own; a blend with Gamay is not a happy marriage, tasting something like an indifferent Passe-Tout-Grain. Only 60 to 70 hectares of Pinot Noir are planted, so that Gamay is the principal red variety and is used for pink wine as well. No one questions its aptitude, but it seems a pity that red grapes have taken over the vineyards of St-Pourçain, as in my opinion the more enjoyable wines of the area are white. A blend of all three white varieties makes a very attractive wine with character and flavour, whereas the reds are sometimes marred by an excess of acidity and are a little clumsy in taste.

Nineteen villages on the slopes above the Bouble and the Sioule, which flow into the Allier above St-Pourçain, make up the appellation. Saulcet, a few kilometres from St-Pourçain, is the most important village for individual growers. Besson in the north has a large area of vines but is mainly cultivated by co-operative members. There is quite a considerable soil variation in the vineyard. The dominant soil type is a mixture of clay and limestone which is very hard when dry and very heavy when wet. Saulcet and Verneuil are clay and limestone, while there is granite at Meillard and sand at Besson. Fourilles and Chantelle in the south are flinty, with small stones or *galets*. All this is within a stretch of only 30 kilometres. Clay and limestone give lighter wine, while granite is good for Gamay and makes for more solid wines with lower yields.

Cultivation methods vary considerably, too. Rows were tradition-ally narrow, but Joseph Laurent, inspired by Lenz Moser, was one of the first to plant vines in wide rows (3.5 metres apart) and to train them high. Since then he has reduced the height of his vines to less than a metre and the width of his rows to 3 to 2.8 metres, with spacings of about 1.2 metres, giving about 3,000 vines per hectare. As the vine has access to more soil, so you get larger grapes and more juice. Some people, such as Roger Chérillat, grow grass between the rows to prevent too high a yield; grass also eliminates problems with chlorosis. Yields in St-Pourçain average about 55 to 65 hl/ha. Pruning is by the *guyot* system, single on poor soil and double on richer soil.

La Cave des Vignerons de St-Pourçain, with 250 members cultivating 350 hectares of vines, is an important element of the appellation, especially since its quality and techniques have improved noticeably in recent years following considerable financial investment. They have installed stainless-steel fermentation vats and instituted strict controls on the quality of grapes, with appropriate bonuses. They make three qualities of each colour, of which only two are bottled; the lowest category is sold off in cubitainer at their shop, which does a roaring trade.

The better white, Cuvée Printanière, is half Sauvignon and half Chardonnay. I was uncertain how well these two very different varieties can ever marry together in the same wine, as this blend seemed rather unharmonious. I preferred the basic white made purely from Sacy, with its crisp acidity and slightly nutty finish.

Both pinks are made from Gamay. The better one calls itself a *vin gris* and is fresh, with light raspberry undertones. Their standard red is also made from Gamay, with what they describe as a semi-carbonic fermentation, while their better red is pure Pinot Noir, made by a traditional vinification; there are plans to age it in new *barriques*. They also produce a *vin nouveau*, released on 1 December, and a sparkling wine called Anne de Bourbon, made from one-third Sacy and two-thirds Gamay. As yet the champagne-method wines of the area are not included in the appellation, but as most people now make some, there are hopes of rectifying this omission.

Gérard and Jean-Louis Pétillat are among the more adventurous growers of St-Pourçain. I tracked them down at Meillard, one of the northern villages of the appellation. Their white wine is a blend of one-third Sauvignon and two-thirds Chardonnay, bringing them into conflict with the INAO. Their pink is pure Gamay and their red pure Pinot Noir. With 15 hectares they are now one of the larger individual growers. They used to rear beef cattle, but have turned to wine as part of the trend towards specialization. They have a well-run modern cellar. Whites are fermented at as low a temperature as possible and reds at up to 25°C. A centrifuge is preferred to fining. They also make all three colours of sparkling wine.

Joseph Laurent reckons that his is the oldest wine-growing family in the area. There were Laurents at Saulcet before the Revolution, with records going back to 1715 if not earlier. His methods seemed rather haphazard, albeit successful, and his cellar a little disorganized. There was an old wooden vat, 'as it looks nice', and some smaller barrels which are used occassionally. Otherwise he has the standard cement vats, lined with enamel paint, and as yet is not equipped to control his fermentation temperatures very accurately. I suspect things will change when his son comes into the business; he is fresh from oenology studies and has plans for change – a *vin nouveau*, some sparkling wine, and more plantings of Pinot Noir and Chardonnay. His first planting of Pinot Noir is not yet in production, but eventually he would like to experiment with ageing it.

Despite the chaotic cellar, M. Laurent's wines were surprisingly good. His *cuvée prestige* – 15 per cent Sauvignon blended with Chardonnay – was the most successful blend of those two grapes that I tasted. He has half a hectare of just post-phylloxera Sacy and feels that they are condemned to Sacy if they want the appellation. He makes two reds from his Gamay: a wine to age, with solid fruit and structure, and a wine for early drinking. The soil at Saulcet is such a mixture that he can grow the grapes for the wine to age on granite and obtain lighter results with the same vinification method from the grapes grown on clay and limestone. The family also have land under wheat, sunflowers and sugar-beet – the last of which ironically comes back to them as the sugar for chaptalization!

Roger Chérillat, in Saulcet, is the grandfather of the appellation and president of the growers' association. He is a friendly old man who has seen many changes in the vineyards over the last fifty years. Once they used horses, and sprays were carried on their backs. First they made white wine, then pink and now red. His family have been here since the 1850s and Jean Chérillat, another producer in Saulcet, is a cousin.

Roger Chérillat is optimistic about the future of St-Pourçain, considering that they were lucky to be a small vineyard in a good position. Others may worry that there is too much variety at St-

Pourçain, but certainly it seemed a flourishing vineyard, with a strong local following.

M. Chérillat has 12 hectares of vines as well as some cereal. He has replanted all his vineyards over the past ten to fifteen years, introducing Pinot Noir and increasing his area of Chardonnay. He feels that Chardonnay has improved the quality of white St-Pourçain; Pinot Noir, on the other hand, has not been so successful as it needs to be aged, whereas St-Pourçain is above all a wine for drinking early. He uses Pinot Noir for his pink wine rather than for his red. Even a more substantial wine, described as a *vin de garde*, is aged for only two or three years. M. Chérillat is the largest producer of sparkling wine after the co-operative; he makes it from Sacy and Chardonnay, as Sauvignon is too perfumed to be included in the blend. It was a pleasant note on which to leave St-Pourçain.

COTEAUX DU LYONNAIS

The Coteaux du Lyonnais is one of those lost vineyards of France, a small region that is easy to overlook on the country's viticultural map as it nestles between the Beaujolais and the Côte Rôtie. As such it may be seen to be a zone of transition between Burgundy and the Rhône valley, although in fact its affinity is exclusively to the Beaujolais. In effect it is the most southern appellation of Burgundy. The only grape variety for the red wine that dominates the appellation is Gamay Noir à Jus Blanc; a little white wine is made from a blend of Chardonnay and Aligoté.

Vines have been grown in the hills south west of Lyons for centuries. Indeed some say that there were vineyards here even before Roman times, but viticulture certainly flourished after the foundation of Lyons or Lugdunum in 45 BC. In the Middle Ages the Benedictine monks of the now ruined abbey of Savigny continued to extend the vineyards, which reached their peak in the second half of the eighteenth century with 13,500 hectares. Since then phylloxera, the rural exodus and the encroaching urban sprawl of the city of Lyons have reduced the appellation of the Coteaux du Lyonnais to some 200 hectares. The area is limited to the north by the Beaujolais. Indeed it seems a very arbitrary line that separates the appellations. The river Gier forms the southern boundary, and the Monts du Lyonnais, rising towards the Massif Central, mark the western edge of the appellation. In practice the area divides naturally into two parts, with the vineyards of the north grouped around the villages of Sain Bel, Fleuriex, L'Arbresle and Lentilly, while the southern vineyards centre upon the villages of Millery and Givors. The Coteaux du Lyonnais were first recognized as a VDQS in 1952 and were finally granted their appellation in 1984.

I spent a day there. It was one of those wonderful sun-soaked days at the end of summer, that you appreciate all the more for knowing that autumn follows close behind. The vintage had begun a few days earlier. Trailers of grapes were arriving at the co-operative in the village of Sain Bel. One chubby farmer had stopped at the baker's on the way, for there was a *baguette* perched on top of one of his boxes of grapes! The co-operative of Sain Bel accounts for half the production of the appellation, and also makes Beaujolais, as it is very close to the southern limit of Beaujolais and several of its members have vineyards in both appellations. This is a region of polyculture. Very few people make a living from their vines alone. They breed Charollais cattle or grow maize or have fruit trees. The nearby village of Bessinet calls itself 'the capital of the cherry'.

The co-operative was created in 1956 and today works well for its appellation. The cellars were extended a couple of years ago and are now well equipped to control fermentation temperatures and carry out efficient vinifications by what they call semi-carbonic maceration, or the Beaujolais method. The fermentation vats are filled with whole bunches of grapes, but they rarely add any extra carbon dioxide. The grapes are pressed after five to nine days, depending on the style of wine they wish to make, and on the condition of the vintage.

The white wine is made from Chardonnay and Aligoté fermented together. Aligoté grows better in the northern part of the appellation where the soil is lighter, while Chardonnay prefers the heavier clay and limestone soil of the south. The 1987 vintage of white wine was crisp and fresh with grassy overtones. Two qualities of red wine are made, as well as a *vin de primeur* (although they are insistent that they are not trying to imitate Beaujolais Nouveau). Both reds are intended, like Beaujolais, for relatively youthful drinking. They have the attractive freshness of the Gamay grape, while the Cuvée Benoît Maillard, named after an abbot of the monastery of Savigny, is a slightly more substantial wine.

François Descôtes in the village of Millery in the southern half of the appellation is a young man who has recently taken over the family's vineyards. He explained the variations of soil within the appellation. The vineyards in the east, towards the Rhône, consist of glacial sand and *galets* or large stones, while those in the west have the granitic influence of the Massif Central. The wines from the east keep better, although they are lighter in colour, while those of the west have a more distinctive flavour of game and wild fruit, but age quicker. In practice he blends the two to make a single wine.

The southern part of the appellation, closer to the Côte Rôtie, is hotter than the north. The vines here flower some twelve days earlier than those of the Beaujolais. They are usually pruned in the *guyot* system with 6,000 vines per hectare, which contrasts with the Beaujolais where there are usually 10,000 vines per hectare and the pruning is often according to the *gobelet* system. I liked M. Descôtes's wines. His white wine is usually a blend of one-third Aligoté and two-thirds Chardonnay, but in 1988 he was planning to make a pure Chardonnay, as his new vineyards of Chardonnay were coming into production. His 1987 red had some attractive fruit reminiscent of sour cherries and was rounded with good structure, while a 1983, which he opened to demonstrate that Coteaux du Lyonnais need not necessarily be drunk in very early youth, had hints of blackcurrant and was not unlike a Brouilly.

The comparison points straight to the heart of the problem confronting Coteaux du Lyonnais: it is overshadowed by its big brother, Beaujolais. The wines are similar and comparison is inevitable. But Coteaux du Lyonnais is also cheaper and represents in many instances a far better quality/price ratio than an indifferent Beaujolais; it thus deserves wider recognition.

9

Wines of Savoy

The vineyards of Savoy are scattered, with small pockets of vines over a large area of the departments of Savoie and Haute-Savoie, mingling with fields of cereal and pastures of grazing cows. The city of Chambéry is the natural centre of the region. It was the capital of the dukes of Savoy during the Middle Ages, yielding place to Turin in 1562. Savoy was not finally annexed to France until 1860, and so Chambéry retains a very Italian atmosphere. Some of the façades are painted in the warm russet and mustard colours of Italy and there are narrow alleyways and geranium-filled courtyards, while the Place St Léger in the centre of the old city has the fountains and cafés of an Italian town.

The name Savoy comes from the late Latin Sapaudia, meaning a country of fir trees (*sappi* or *sappini* – cf. French *sapins*). Large expanses of fir trees still cover the hillsides, where little else will grow. The Romans probably introduced vines to this region, as they did in so many other parts of France. Then in the Middle Ages monks – Benedictines from Cluny and Hautecombe – played their part.

By 1807 there were 10,109 hectares of vines in the two departments of Savoie and Haute-Savoie; this had increased to 13,000 hectares by 1889. The best wines were said to come from the grape varieties Mondeuse, Cot and Persan, grown around Chambéry. Today Mondeuse is enjoying something of a revival, while Persan has disappeared and Cot is planted more successfully elsewhere in France. Some of the existing *crus*, as well as some unknown names, were praised for exhibiting to a lesser degree the qualities of the light wines of the Médoc.

Guyot attributed the best red wines to Mondeuse. He praised the red wines of Annecy, but generally thought the wines of Haute-Savoie less good than those from around Chambéry. Referring to

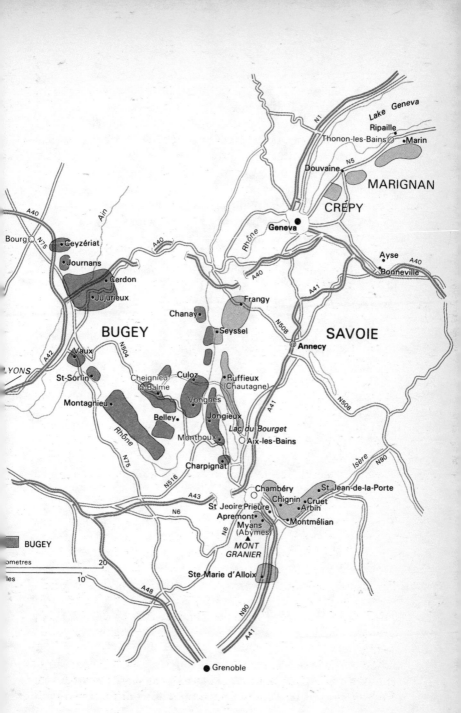

Lake Geneva
Ripaille
Thonon-les-Bains • Marin
Douvaine • N5
MARIGNAN
CRÉPY
Ayse •
Bonneville •
Geneva
A40
N1
Rhône
A40
A41
N508
SAVOIE
Frangy •
Chanay •
Seyssel •
Annecy
Bourg N75
Ceyzériat •
Journans •
Gerdon •
Jujurieux •
A40
Ain
BUGEY
Vaux •
St-Sorlin •
Cheignieu
la Balme
Culoz •
Vongnes •
Ruffieux
(Chautagne)
N504
N508
LYONS
A42
Montagnieu •
Belley •
Jongieux •
Monthoux •
Rhône
N75
Charpignat
Lac du Bourget
Aix-les-Bains
A41
Isère N90
Chambéry
St Jeoire Prieuré
Apremont •
Myans
(Abymes)
Chignin •
Cruet
Arbin •
Montmélian •
St Jean-de-la-Porte •
A43
N6
N6
MONT
GRANIER
Ste Marie d'Alloix •
N90
A41
A48
Grenoble

BUGEY

ometres   20
les   10

Cruet, Montmélian and St-Jean-de-la-Porte, he said that in a good year they did not go to your head or disturb the nervous system. The whites he described rather poetically as wines of fantasy.

Phylloxera first struck in 1887, and by 1905 the vineyard area of Savoy had decreased to 8,940 hectares. It declined still further with the lack of manpower during the First World War, but after the Second World War there was some revival of interest. A shift from red to white wine gradually took place, so that white wine now accounts for 70 per cent of the production of the vineyard. In 1986 there were 1,500 hectares of Vin de Savoie, with Crépy and Seyssel producing a total of around 100,000 hectolitres of wine.

The VDQS, specifying fifteen *crus*, was created in 1957 and an appellation came sixteen years later, but this had little effect on the quality of the wines. But they did become more popular with the growth in summer tourism and winter sports, and as a result the area began to wake up a little. The last ten years have seen a gradual transformation in vineyards and people. The older generation of traditional wine-growers have sent their sons to oenology school, and the sons in turn have improved their techniques and equipment and now bottle their wine. *Appellation contrôlée* was described as 'the great adventure', and viticulture has saved areas like Jongieux and Marin where nothing much apart from vines would grow. Mechanization is still difficult in some areas. Tractors arrived at the end of the 1950s and before then people used oxen and horses. Savoy still remains a region of polyculture, with cereals and dairy farming as well as vines. There is a gentle annual increase of about 50 hectares in the area of vineyards. It is a region of tiny producers with ares rather than hectares, and the three co-operatives of Cruet, Chautagne and Montmélian account for 30 per cent of the production, while half the region's wine is sold by the local *négociants*.

Many growers have been content to let the twentieth century pass them by. Only now are they creating a Comité Interprofessionnel to promote their wines and regulate the market. Attitudes towards such a step are mixed; some believe it has come too late to achieve anything concrete. So far there is little problem in selling Savoy wine for there is a strong regional demand from tourists and holiday-makers, as well as from the local population. A mere 1 per cent of the area's production travels outside France, and for the present there is little need or incentive for that to increase. The multiplicity of *crus* creates confusion; some are no more than names, but were included to satisfy the petty rivalries and jealousies of neighbouring villages.

The principal appellation of Savoy is quite simply Vin de Savoie; this includes at present sixteen possible *crus* of which some are much better known than others. A grape variety usually features on the label and the use of the grape variety Roussette is distinguished by an appellation, Roussette de Savoie; four villages are separate *crus*. In addition there are the older appellations of Crépy and Seyssel. In total there are 1,500 hectares, strung out along a 100-kilometre line stretching from the valley of the Isère south of Chambéry, through the Combe de Savoie and along the shores of the Lac du Bourget as far as the region of the Chablais and Lake Geneva on the Swiss border. This mountainous region naturally generates a number of different microclimates and also grape varieties. Savoy wines can be still, *pétillant* or sparkling; red, white or pink. In addition to the appellations, there are two *vins de pays*, albeit of little importance: Vin de Pays d'Allobrogie, named after the Allobroges, the Gallic tribe who inhabited the region in Julius Caesar's time, and Vin de Pays des Coteaux du Grésivaudan, in the adjoining department of Isère, made mainly from Jacquère and Gamay.

THE COMBE DE SAVOIE

Among the *crus*, the best-known are Apremont and Abymes. I set off in a mild drizzle, heading south from Chambéry. In the distance were the snow-capped mountains of the Chaîne des Bellesdonnes and nearer to my destination the imposing face of Mont Granier. Apremont is a sleepy village. Until the First World War its reputation was for red wine made from Mondeuse, but today the vineyards are planted with Jacquère for white wine. Jacquère rose to prominence with plantings in the 1920s, when it was used for sparkling wine and for vermouth. The vineyards of Apremont now cover 300 hectares, and the area has increased in recent years as the village has given up growing wheat and rearing cattle.

The Jacquère grape is peculiar to Savoy and Bugey. It is an easy vine to cultivate, not susceptible to rot or oidium and only slightly to mildew. It is easy to train too. One grower described it as '*formidable!*' It is also the principal grape variety of the *cru* Abymes and another name for it is Plante des Abymes – a possible indication of its origin. Unlike Apremont, the name is not that of a village. On the night of 24 November 1248 part of the side of Mont Granier collapsed and the landslide destroyed the village of St-André and stopped just short of the village of Myans. It is thought that this disaster may have been caused by water undermining the cliff; certainly, the monks at nearby Montmélian who recorded the event described a cloud of steam, coming presumably from hot water. The resulting debris led to the area being called Abymes, and the vineyards of this *cru* are planted on the rubble from Mont Granier; those of Apremont are on glacial deposits. A small river, the Ruisseau du Glandon, separates the two *crus*. Apremont is on higher slopes and less susceptible to frost damage; Abymes is lower in the valley. The difference between Apremont and Abymes is hard to distinguish. Apremont, as the local saying goes, ripens in the shade, while Abymes ripens in the sun; Abymes therefore tends to be a little softer and more supple, while Apremont is harder and more stony, with overtones of gunflint.

Although Jacquère is the dominant white grape of Abymes and Apremont, there has been some experimentation with Chardonnay. It was originally introduced in the early 1960s with the objective of improving the Jacquère, but has not lived up to expectations and in some places has been pulled up. Sometimes it is vinified separately, as it is also an accepted grape variety for Vin de Savoie. It gives lower yields than Jacquère, but will keep longer. Its local name is Petite Ste-Marie.

Vinification methods have improved enormously in the area in recent years. The cellars of Le Vigneron Savoyard at Apremont are a typical example. This is a group of eight properties accounting for a total of 40 hectares in Apremont. The group was created in 1968 and each member cultivates his vineyards separately and makes common cause only at vintage time. Although they have co-operative status, they are more like a GAEC, a Groupement Agricole d'Exploitation en Commun. Jacquère for Apremont and Abymes occupies most of their vineyards, but they also have 5 hectares of Chardonnay which is vinified as Vin de Savoie and 2 hectares of red grapes, Gamay and Mondeuse. Their cellars have been modernized and are well equipped with stainless-steel vats. Their attitude is more open-minded and experimental than that of many Savoyard wine-growers. Robert Dupraz described himself as '*un passioné de la technique*'. They are equipped to control their fermentation temperature at 18°C and the fermentation lasts a minimum of three weeks. There is no malolactic fermentation as they want to retain an almost aggressive acidity, characteristic of the region's white wines. They bottle all their output themselves and they are one of the few producers who sell on the export market. I liked their wines. The Apremont had a hint of gunflint; in comparison Abymes was more flowery and grassy, with a little more substance.

Across the valley from Abymes and Apremont is the tiny village of Chignin, which does not even boast a café. The vineyards are at an altitude of about 360 metres, on steep hillsides rising sharply from the valley floor. Chignin is one of the *crus* of Vin de Savoie; as with Abymes and Apremont, Jacquère is the most important grape variety, but the wine has a slightly fuller flavour. The vineyards face south and south west, so that the grapes are less acid than those of Apremont where the vineyards face east. The soil is a mixture of clay and limestone.

Chignin has its own speciality, a separate appellation of Chignin-Bergeron. Bergeron is the local name for the Roussanne grape of the northern Rhône. Nobody knows quite how there came to be a pocket of Roussanne in this one village. One story is that a M. Bergeron planted some vines that he had brought from the Rhône valley. Certainly Roussanne has been grown here for over a hundred years, as it is mentioned by nineteenth-century authorities. Now clonally selected plants from nurseries in Savoy are being planted at Hermitage.

The production is tiny, a mere 6 hectares out of a total of 125 hectares of Chignin. The Roussanne is much more difficult to grow than Jacquère as it needs a particularly sunny aspect; indeed not all the delimited area of Chignin can be planted with Bergeron, so there is a separate delimitation for that grape variety. It is also much more susceptible to disease than Jacquère and needs more attention, but it gives more fruit and aroma and, unlike Jacquère, the wine will age. In hot summers it will make very good wine. Out of the fifteen growers who make a living from wine in Chignin, only five or six have Roussanne. Initially there was little financial incentive to grow this more temperamental variety as yields are smaller – 58 hectolitres per hectare versus 68 for Jacquère in 1986 – but now there is more demand and the rewards are greater, with Chignin-Bergeron costing 60 per cent more than Chignin made from Jacquère.

There are differences in the vinification of the two grapes. Experimentation with some skin contact before pressing is being considered for Roussanne. The malolactic fermentation usually occurs and the taste is quite different. The colour is a little deeper, the nose slightly nutty and the palate has more structure, with flavours reminiscent of tropical fruit. As yet no one ages their Roussanne in oak, for the cost would be prohibitive. Raymond Quénard, a leading grower in the village, described Chignin-Bergeron quite simply: 'It's my Rolls!'

Like Apremont and Abymes, Chignin was planted with red Mondeuse before the phylloxera, but was converted to white wines between the two World Wars; only one-fifth of the vineyards of Chignin are now planted with red grapes – Mondeuse, Gamay and a little Pinot Noir. Gamay is the most widely planted red variety in all three *crus*. Vinification methods are the same as in the Beaujolais, with whole bunches of grapes being put into the fermentation vat, but no carbon dioxide added. Maceration is only for a short period, giving a light, fruity wine, with quite high acidity.

The Mondeuse is the most characteristic red grape variety of the area. It is now enjoying something of a come-back, although in France it is found only in Savoy and Bugey, while in north east Italy it is known as Refosco. It needs a longer fermentation. The grapes are crushed but left with the stalks, and after eight to ten days' maceration it has a deep colour with a tough, peppery nose and palate. It can be aged successfully in wood, though in fact no one does this in Chignin.

It is the village of Arbin in the valley of the Isère, a few miles away, that has a reputation for red wine. The village never followed the fashion for white wine and has kept its vineyards of Mondeuse. Louis Magnin is one of the best growers here. His methods are traditional: he ferments in large wooden vats and ages his wine in smaller barrels for a few months before bottling in the spring. The flavour is reminiscent of the pepperiness of Syrah, with some red fruit, tannin and balance.

Pierre Boniface at Domaine des Rocailles, with vineyards in Apremont, is one of the very few growers to experiment with ageing Mondeuse in small oak barrels. The juice is fermented on the skins for seven days at a fairly low temperature of 18–22°C so as not to extract too much colour. M. Boniface's brother is the manager at Château Clarke in the Médoc, so he is able to buy Bordeaux barrels that have only been used for two wines. As yet these experiments are still at the initial stage, although the early results are quite delicious, with peppery, *viandé* fruit and perfume. Michel Grisard, at Fléterive, a village that is better known for its hectares of vine nurseries than for its wine, is the only other grower to use small, newish oak barrels for his Mondeuse. The others have cement vats or traditional old large casks.

The other village *crus* to the south of Chambéry are St-Jeoire-Prieuré, Montmélian, St-Jean-de-la-Porte, Ste-Marie-d'Alloix and Cruet, while the village of Fléterive is an aspiring *cru* whose application for an elevation in status has so far been rejected by the INAO. St-Jean-de-la-Porte and Ste-Marie-d'Alloix exist only on paper as they never ask to use the appellation and prefer to sell their wine simply as Vin de Savoie, while the production of St-Jeoire-Prieuré was a meagre 80 hectolitres in 1986. It could be more, but again the rest was labelled Vin de Savoie. The wines of Montmélian, which are predominantly made from Jacquère, are produced by the village co-operative. Cruet is also dominated by its co-operative, which makes other wines as well as the *cru*; the vineyards of Cruet itself total only about 18 hectares, planted mainly with Jacquère and less commonly with Roussette for white wine, and mainly with Gamay for red. From there I headed north towards the Lac du Bourget.

CHAUTAGNE AND JONGIEUX

To the north of Chambéry, on the eastern shores of the Lac du Bourget, is the *cru* of Chautagne, which is unusual in having a greater reputation for red wine than for white. The most important producer is the Cave Co-opérative de Chautagne at Ruffieux. It was founded in 1953 and today has 220 members with a total of 137 hectares of vines. Only about twenty members have between 1 and 3 hectares – apparently you can earn an adequate living on 3 hectares of vines – while the other 200 members have anything from 10 to 60 ares. The vineyards are in the villages of Chandrieux, Ruffieux, Serrière and Motz, Chautagne being the name of the canton. They are at an altitude of 200 to 250 metres, facing west towards the Lac du Bourget. The soil is very chalky.

Gamay is the most important grape variety but there are Mondeuse and Pinot Noir too, and for white not only Jacquère and Roussette but also Aligoté, which is unusual. Each red grape variety is vinified separately and since 1985 they have made a blend of all three called

Le Chautagnard. To my taste it does not have as much fruit as the single-variety wines. The Mondeuse has an earthy, peppery flavour. The Gamay is a medium-weight, fruity wine and the Pinot Noir has varietal character with some acidity and tannin – a cool-climate Pinot Noir, not unlike an Irancy. The Gamay also makes an attractive pink wine reminiscent of raspberries.

Mondeuse was the main grape variety in the area before the phylloxera, and Gamay was not introduced to the region until afterwards. It has adapted easily, although with its early bud-break it is prone to frost damage. Pinot Noir did not arrive until after the Second World War and is still relatively unimportant in the area. The Mondeuse can be very irregular in both quality and quantity, and the co-operative members earn more for their Gamay or Pinot Noir.

On the west side of the Lac du Bourget is the village of Jongieux near the Benedictine abbey of Hautecombe, where members of the royal house of Savoy are buried. The last was ex-King Umberto II of Italy in 1983. Jongieux became a *cru* of Vin de Savoie in 1988, a status that it deserves as its wines are of more interest and the vineyards larger than several of the earlier *crus*. Some 200 hectares in the villages of Jongieux, Lucey, Billième and St-Jean-de-Chivetin make up the vineyards of Jongieux, which are all on south west-facing hillsides. Also in the area is a tiny parcel of Roussette vines for the Roussette *cru* of Marestel. Not all the vineyards have been included in the *cru* of Jongieux, and those which are not will remain simple Vin de Savoie.

The soil is very chalky and contains glacial debris from the mountain as well as some sand. Jacquère is the principal grape variety for white wine and there is also some Chardonnay, as well as a little Aligoté that has not been accepted for the *cru* and is therefore no longer being planted. Chardonnay, however, is growing in importance as it gives good results, similar to those obtained in the nearby vineyards of Bugey. There is also Roussette for Roussette de Savoie. The red grapes are Mondeuse (which is aged in old wooden barrels for a few months), Pinot Noir and Gamay, which is the most important and makes pink as well as red wine.

ROUSSETTE DE SAVOIE

Roussette de Savoie has qualified as a separate appellation since 1942, and after Jacquère, Roussette is the most characteristic grape of Savoy. It is grown in small parcels all over the region and has four *crus* unrelated to those of Vin de Savoie, namely Marestel, Monthoux, Monterminod and Frangy. The name Roussette comes from the reddish colour of the skin of the ripe grapes, and the local synonym is Altesse, which translates literally as 'highness', implying perhaps that the best wines were kept for the royal court. It is said to have ampelographical links with the Furmint of Hungarian Tokay. The vine may have been introduced into Savoy from the Mediterranean in the fifteenth century, following the marriage in 1432 of Anne of Lusignan, daughter of the king of Cyprus, with Duke Louis of Savoy.

While the *crus* are always pure Roussette, a wine labelled Roussette de Savoie without a *cru* name may in fact contain up to 50 per cent of Chardonnay, which gives higher yields than Roussette, without any mention of it on the label. It depends upon the grower's whim. Otherwise vinification methods are the same as for the other white grapes of Savoy, but the resulting wines are richer and fatter with some residual sugar.

Frangy is the most important of the four *crus*. There are references to viticulture in the area in the eleventh century. In the fifteenth century the wine of Frangy was drunk by the counts of Geneva. Jean-Jacques Rousseau praised the Roussette of Frangy and the nineteenth-century authorities also mentioned it; before the phylloxera at the end of the last century there were 950 hectares of vines. Geneva, only 25 kilometres away, was the obvious market, and the wines were carried there by horse and cart, with two *demi-muids* per cart. Frangy was within the *zone franche*, which was created by Napoleon as a border area with agricultural land for feeding the Swiss population, and was entitled to certain privileges. In 1920 this zone was reduced by 10 kilometres, with the result that Frangy lost its market. People abandoned their vines and turned to dairy farming, for an efficient milk co-operative had been set up at Frangy in 1902. Today restrictive milk quotas have reversed the process and young people are planting vines again, so there are now about 50 hectares of Roussette.

The best place to taste Frangy is in the friendly village bar, La Cave de la Ferme, where François Lupin sells his own wines. There have been Lupins in Frangy since 1670, making them the oldest family of the village. At Frangy we have crossed the departmental boundary into Haute-Savoie, so there is no Jacquère here, nor any Chardonnay, only Roussette and, for sparkling wine, Molette. Red wines are made from Gamay or Mondeuse as Vin de Savoie. M. Lupin has just 2 hectares, 80 per cent planted with Roussette and the rest with Mondeuse. His small, neat cellar is through the courtyard behind the bar.

He ferments his white wine at 20–22°C. It is a long fermentation in cement vats, lasting about thirty days and water-cooled if necessary. A malolactic fermentation is rare and the tartrates deposit naturally during the winter. The wine is bottled in the spring after filtering, but not fining. Roussette tends to have a degree more alcohol than Jacquère at 12–13°, and a similar point of acidity; but it also has traces of residual sugar, which give quite a fat, rounded wine with some substance. Compared to the Jacquère, the Roussette is more difficult to cultivate: it is not so easy to train and it is very susceptible to mildew and oidium.

M. Lupin also gave me my first taste of a traditional speciality, *la chèvre de Savoie*, a sweet, frothing mouthful of mousse. It is made by putting grape juice into a small barrel, usually made of acacia. The juice begins to ferment, but the carbon dioxide cannot escape. It is then flavoured with a small amount of rum or kirsch, about 1 litre to 35 litres of must. Good friends are invited into the cellar to drink *un coup de chèvre* at the end of a meal.

The other three *crus* for Roussette are rarely seen. Marestel, near Jongieux, produces about 100 hectolitres per year, likewise Monthoux on the south western shores of the Lac du Bourget. There is just one producer of Monterminod at the Château de Monterminod to the east of Chambéry, with 7 hectares of vines planted on a steep slope in the village of St-Alban-Leysse.

SEYSSEL

The oldest appellation in Savoy is Seyssel, dating from 1942. There were references to the wines of Seyssel in the eleventh and twelfth centuries and it was the monks of the abbey of Arvières who developed the vineyards in the fourteenth century. The wine was at its apogee in the eighteenth century. The little town of Seyssel is divided between two departments, Haute-Savoie and Ain, by the

Rhône, which also formed the frontier between Savoy and France until 1860. There are vineyards on both sides of the river valley, some 80 hectares in all. They are at an altitude of between 270 and 420 metres, on clay and limestone soil, facing south or south east. The climate is continental with cold, dry winters, hot summers and little humidity, so that the vines remain rot-free and healthy.

The best-known producer of Seyssel, and probably the only Savoy producer with any pretensions to an international reputation, is Varichon & Clerc. A M. Varichon founded a company in 1901 and a M. Clerc also created a company at about the same time; in 1910 they joined forces and began to specialize in sparkling wine, creating a tradition in Seyssel. Roussette always had a slight *pétillant* quality, retaining some carbon dioxide when bottled early. At first they used the original *méthode rurale*, as also found in Gaillac, which was then refined to include the *remuage* and *dégorgement* of Champagne.

The grandson of the first M. Clerc retired in 1986 and the company was bought by a Burgundian, Henri Gabet, who has connections in the Beaujolais. The motive for his purchase was an interest in unknown appellations; he now has the challenging task of resuscitating a company that has been allowed to fall asleep. Evidence of his own energy includes the introduction of *giropalettes* for *remuage*, though manual *remuage* is still carried out and one *remueur* was to be seen puffing contentedly on his pipe!

Varichon & Clerc make four wines. Roussette de Seyssel is a still wine that comes from the Altesse grape alone, and is similar to the *crus* of Roussette de Savoie. According to Georges Blanc at the starred restaurant La Mère Blanc in Vonnas, this is the only wine you can drink with asparagus, with its rich, leafy nose, high acidity and fatness. Their flagship is Seyssel Mousseux, a vintage wine sold under the brand-name of Royal Seyssel, made mainly from Molette but including at least 10 per cent Roussette, which gives the wine finesse. Molette is a Savoy grape permitted only for sparkling wine; it makes an excellent base wine of neutral acidity. Molette gives high yields but is slightly sensitive to rot and oxidizes easily, so that care is needed with pressing and ageing. The method is that of Champagne, with the wine spending at least three years, if not longer, on the lees of the second fermentation.

They are virtually the only people to make a Pétillant de Savoie, which comes mainly from Jacquère, with a pressure of 2.5 kilos per square metre as opposed to 5 kilos for *mousseux*. Finally their basic wine is a champagne-method product without an appellation, a blend of Molette and wines from the Loire valley, plus the second pressing of Roussette.

AYZE

There is only one other place apart from Seyssel with a particular reputation for sparkling or *pétillant* wine, and that is Ayze, one of the *crus* of Haute-Savoie and nearer to Lake Geneva than to Chambéry. Other producers in Savoy make sparkling wine called simply Vin de Savoie Mousseux. No one is really quite sure how the tradition of making sparkling wine developed at Ayze. At the end of the last century, most of the wine of Ayze was sold in wooden barrels in nearby Geneva. Then a café-owner called Joseph Jacquier began making sparkling wine in the village of Marignier just before the First World War. He called his wine Ayze Royal. In all probability the local wine tended to be a little fizzy, with incomplete fermentations, and this was the starting-point for production of a sparkling wine by the traditional *méthode rurale*.

Ayze is a small village outside Bonneville, which on Fridays is a bustling market town. The villages of Marignier and La Côte d'Hyot are also included in the appellation, but the area in production still only totals about 50 hectares.

I went to see Jean and Eric Vallier at La Côte d'Hyot who, with 2 hectares of vines, are amongst the largest producers of Ayze. The characteristic grape of Ayze is the Gringet, which is said to be related to the Savagnin of the Jura and therefore possibly also to the Gewurztraminer, and was brought to the area from Italy in the thirteenth century. It grows well on the south and south east-facing slopes of the Côte d'Hyot with its marl soil. Gringet is blended with 30 per cent of Roussette. Mondeuse Blanche, which is known locally and confusingly as Roussette d'Ayze, is also permitted but is in fact disappearing as it contributes nothing to the wine.

The steep slopes of the vineyards do not allow for any mechanization so they carry sprays for treating the vines on their backs, as in the days before the introduction of tractors.

Nowadays the champagne method has generally superseded the *méthode rurale*, though it is possible to find sparkling Ayze which has not been disgorged. M. Vallier has a neat little cellar with stainless-steel vats. Fermentation takes about a month, as long as possible. There is no malolactic fermentation and the wines are bottled in the spring and spend nine months on the lees. *Dégorgement* is *à la volée*. He makes two wines: a very dry one with just a hint of *dosage*, and – his own innovation – a *demi-sec* with a slightly higher *dosage*, which gives a more rounded wine instead of the crisp, almost austere flavour of traditional Ayze. It is also possible to find still Ayze but, rather as with champagne, when you taste the still wine of Ayze, you can see how much more enjoyable it is with bubbles. The pressure is usually 4 to 4.5 kilos, slightly lower than for a fully sparkling wine.

Ayze was an important vineyard before the phylloxera, but as in many other parts of France, people did not bother to replant their vines and the area has remained 'asleep'. The majority of the growers today are reaching retirement age. Jean Vallier is one of the more energetic as well as one of the younger ones. His parents made cheese and he inherited a small parcel of vines, which he has extended over the last fifteen years, as he says, for love. Today he is optimistic for the future because there is a good local demand for the wine, with summer tourism and winter sports, and the quality and methods are improving.

CRÉPY AND THE VINEYARDS OF LAKE GENEVA

The vineyards on the southern shores of Lake Geneva have more in common with those of Switzerland than with the other wines of Savoy, for the dominant grape variety here is Chasselas. Crépy (an appellation in its own right since 1948), two *crus* of Vin de Savoie, Ripaille and Marignan, and an aspiring one, Marin, are the wines of the lake.

Chasselas has been grown in the region since the thirteenth century. It is also found in Alsace and at Pouilly-sur-Loire, but is generally better known as a table grape. There are, however, several types of Chasselas. At Crépy they grow Chasselas Roux, so called as there is a hint of red in the skins when the grapes are ripe, and the skins are thicker than for a table grape. Yields are good, about 45 hectolitres per hectare. The Chasselas produces a lot of vegetation, which can lead to problems with rot if the autumn is wet. The vineyards of Crépy are on the hillsides of the villages of Loison and Ballaison and of the town of Douvaine, facing west towards the lake and benefiting from a microclimate tempered by it. Hail is the biggest climatic problem. Spring frost can also be a hazard, and prayers are the only possible frost protection. In September storms can cause damage. The soil of the vineyards consists of glacial deposits over heavy clay, and a subsoil of chalk. Crépy is the *lieu-dit* where the three parishes meet.

There have been vineyards in the area since the Middle Ages. In 1264 it was recorded that Richard de Ballaison had bought vineyards from the abbey of Notre-Dame de Filly, whose monks produced wine throughout the abbey's existence. Phylloxera struck the region in 1894, but the wine survived thanks to the demand from Geneva and then succumbed to competition from Swiss wines. There are now 75 hectares in production, an area which remains fairly static. The land is valuable for building and the number of growers is decreasing as people retire.

Vinification methods are those standard to white wines and precise techniques depend upon the modernization or otherwise of the cellar. Chaptalization is usually necessary and fermentation temperatures are controlled. The malolactic fermentation usually occurs and the wines are bottled in the spring for consumption during the summer. Sometimes Crépy is bottled off the fine lees to give it a hint of *pétillance*. Mercier, who are no relation to the champagne house, are the biggest producers with 35 hectares of vines, and did much to establish the appellation. Métral has a reputation as a traditional producer. I enjoyed Crépy from Fichard, with its soft flavour and leafy fruit; it had no strong character and was light in alcohol, '*un vin de toute la journée*'. Chasselas can be criticized for lacking flavour, and the INAO has tacitly agreed to allow some experiments with Chardonnay in an attempt to give the wine more aroma.

The *cru* of Ripaille consists of the vineyards of the Château de Ripaille, a magnificent fifteenth-century château on the shores of Lake Geneva outside Thonon-les-Bains. The château has a long history associated with the counts and then dukes of Savoy. There was a Roman villa with vines on the site from the first to the fourth centuries. Bonne de Bourbon built a hunting-lodge here at the end of the fourteenth century and then it was used by the first duke, Amadeus VIII, who subsequently became the last antipope in the history of the Catholic Church and reigned as Felix V from 1439 to 1449. At the end of the fifteenth century the property was occupied by invading Swiss from Berne, who during their occupation sent wine back to

Berne in barrels. Finally St Francis of Sales asked to be given the buildings for use as a Carthusian monastery, and thus it remained, with its vineyards flourishing, until the Revolution. The château was then bought by General Dupas, who fought battles for Napoleon, and it now belongs to the Neckar family. The kitchen of the monastery remains, with its superb fireplace and examples of the monks' metalwork, for they were skilled locksmiths.

The vineyards are on fairly flat land sloping gently towards the lake. The Swiss town of Lausanne lies opposite. The soil is stony, with glacial deposits brought down by the River Dranse but without the chalk of Crépy. Eighty-nine million cubic metres of water in Lake Geneva cannot fail to give the area a distinctive microclimate.

Vinification methods are standard in a well-equipped cellar, with fermentation at 20°C, no skin contact, a malolactic fermentation, cold treatment for tartrates, filtration and bottling in the spring and early summer. The manager, Claude Guillerez, considers that the wine needs eight to ten months in bottle to show its best. Ripaille has a slightly nutty flavour, with smoky hints and a lot of fruit, and has a touch of carbon dioxide to keep its freshness.

Near Ripaille is the *cru* of Marignan in the village of Sciez. There is just one producer, Bernard Canelli, whose 10-hectare estate is called La Tour de Marignan. Again Chasselas is the sole grape variety.

On the hills above Ripaille is the village of Marin, which will become a *cru* of the appellation of Vin de Savoie in the next year or so. Claude Delalex, the best producer of the village, took me on a tour of the vineyards. There are 57 hectares in the appellation, of which only 24 are actually in production. He has 5 hectares. His vineyards are on steep slopes at an altitude of 400 to 500 metres, facing south west, with a view of the Château de Ripaille and Lake Geneva. You can see the remains of old terraces. Erosion is a problem here and sometimes the soil, consisting of glacial deposits and chalk, has to be replaced.

As well as Chasselas, Claude Delalex admits to 150 Chardonnay plants which he is growing experimentally, with some success. Chasselas has a short vegetative cycle and ripens well here in these high vineyards, which are almost at the altitude limit for viticulture. It gives its best results if the yield is limited to 50–60 hectolitres, for otherwise the flavour is too diluted.

M. Delalex's cellar is small and neat, with wooden barrels each named after parcels of vines like Le Clou, Froget, Tully, and so on. He began bottling his wine when Vin de Savoie became a VDQS. His family also had cows and did market gardening, but he took the decision to concentrate on vines. Red wine can also be made in Marin, from Gamay and Mondeuse, but white wine from Chasselas is the most typical. Vintages vary. Deacidification and chaptalization are both permissible to remedy any defects, and the malolactic fermentation is prevented to keep the youthful freshness of the wine. The 1986, tasted straight from the vat, had a slightly floral nose with a stony acidity. Generally these are wines to drink within a year or so, but 1983 was an especially good vintage and (in the summer of 1987) quite delicious with hints of honey, almonds and *pain d'épice* – a perfect note on which to finish a visit to the vineyards of Savoie.

BUGEY

The town of Seyssel is the link between Savoy and Bugey, for the vineyards of the appellation of Seyssel are on both sides of the Rhône, which separates the department of Ain from that of Haute-Savoie.

The wines of Bugey come from a lost region between Lyons and Chambéry, contained by a large loop of the river in the south east corner of Ain. The lively town of Belley is the centre of the area, and on Saturday mornings there is a colourful market. It was the birthplace of the renowned French gastronome, Brillat-Savarin, who had a vineyard for the *cru* of Manicle and wrote about the wines of his birthplace with affection.

The countryside is green with luscious pastures and grazing cows and there are fields of wheat, maize, rape and even tobacco as well as vineyards, for it is very much an area of polyculture. There are steeper hills, with pine and deciduous woodland, scrub and lakes. Four or five hectares of vines is considered a large holding.

The first vines were planted here by the Romans, but it was monks who gave viticulture a real impetus in the Middle Ages. The earliest monastery in the region was founded at Ambronay in about AD 800; Cistercians came here from Cîteaux in the twelfth century and may have brought grape varieties from Burgundy with them.

Originally part of Savoy, Bugey was ceded along with Bresse to Henri IV of France in 1604. Nevertheless it has remained a sleepy backwater on the way to nowhere. Its wines remained unknown, drunk exclusively within the region and not even travelling as far as Lyons or Chambéry, cities which were watered by Beaujolais or Apremont.

The nineteenth-century authorities gave Bugey scant notice. Cyrus Redding mentioned that the wines of Virieux and Manicle could have the spirit and body of the wines of the Rhône, and Machurraz, Culloz and Cerveyvieux the sweetness and perfume of Beaujolais. Montagnieux was much esteemed and sought after, while Virieux was said to keep thirty or forty years in bottle. Guyot also praised the wine of Manicle. The area enjoyed its heyday in the nineteenth century when it had 30,000 hectares of vines, destined to satisfy the thirst of a large agricultural population.

The recognition of the wines of Bugey as a VDQS in 1957 saved them from oblivion and encouraged the reconstruction of the vineyards; the hybrids for table wine were pulled up and noble grape varieties reinstated.

The grape varieties of Bugey are both borrowed and indigenous. The latter are the same as those of Savoy: Jacquère, Molette, Roussette or Altesse, and Mondeuse; the former are those of Burgundy: Pinot Noir, Chardonnay and Gamay. A little Aligoté is also grown, plus some Poulsard from the Jura. As with Vin de Savoie, wines are named by grape variety. Jacquère is less successful in Bugey than at Apremont and Abymes. It needs a very warm, sunny aspect and ripens late; here it gives a flavour that is too markedly herbaceous. No more is being planted and it is likely eventually to disappear. Molette is grown quite extensively and is replacing Jacquère. Although a late ripener, it gives good yields of neutral, fairly acidic white juice, suitable for sparkling wine.

Roussette has also been diluted by other grape varieties. It is still grown at Seyssel, but is susceptible to frost and rot, gives irregular yields, ripens late and is difficult to cultivate. Roussette du Bugey now tends to mean a type of wine rather than a grape variety, and is more often made from Chardonnay, which has been well established in Bugey for many decades and gives better results than in Savoy.

Mondeuse, too, has a limited future and is much more successful in Savoy. It only does well on the warmest sites of Bugey, as it is another late ripener. Sometimes it can have too much character and tannin.

Gamay has been grown in the region for centuries, although it suffers from rot in the frequently wet climate of Bugey and is vulnerable to a combination of humidity and heat in August and September. There is also a little Pinot Noir which can prove even more temperamental. In cool years the red wines can have too much acidity, and it is undoubtedly the white wines of the region that provide the most interesting drinking.

As with Vin de Savoie, the VDQS of Vin du Bugey has been attributed with various *crus*, namely Virieu-le-Grand, Montagnieu, Manicle, Machuraz and Cerdon; and for Roussette du Bugey there are Anglefort, Albignieux, Chanay, Lagnieu, Montagnieu and Virieu-le-Grand. In fact the only *crus* of any significance are Cerdon and Montagnieu, and there is one brave, solitary grower of Manicle. The others exist solely on paper.

The region being so hilly – almost mountainous – its 300-odd hectares of vineyards exhibit a broad diversity of microclimate, altitude, aspect and soil. Altogether sixty-three villages around Belley are entitled to the appellation, but only about twenty of them are of any significance; of these the most important is Vongnes, with two of the area's largest producers, the Maison Monin and the Caveau Bugiste. Cerdon is quite separate from the rest of the vineyards and closer to Bourg-en-Bresse than to Belley.

Eugène Monin is president of the growers' association and lives in a fifteenth-century house in the village of Vongnes with his family, including a black cat called Sammy and two dogs, Toby and Tosca. His sons Philippe and Hubert help to cultivate the 14 hectares of vines and his range of wines is typical of Bugey. His methods are fairly unsophisticated and that, too, is characteristic. He now has stainless-steel vats to ferment his white wines and cement vats for reds. They abandoned the old wooden vats a few years ago, 'taking photographs of them with tears in our eyes'.

Like most producers of Bugey he considers Chardonnay to be his best wine. His 1985 was good in September 1986, with a leafy nose, some fruit and acidity – but not a wine to age, for none of the wines of Bugey is destined for a long life. His Roussette du Bugey contains 25 per cent of Altesse (Roussette) and the rest is Chardonnay, giving perhaps a more fragrant and fuller wine than pure Chardonnay.

Sparkling wine is also an important part of the family's activity. Eugène Monin began making it in 1960 when he sold all his father-in-law's cows in order to concentrate on wine. He began with just 200 bottles, and now makes between 60,000 and 80,000 every year from 25–30 per cent Chardonnay with equal parts of Jacquère,

Aligoté and Molette – all of which combine to make a crisp, fruity glass of bubbles.

Gamay is vinified in the same way as in the Beaujolais, i.e. the grapes are not crushed, but whole bunches are put into the vat and pressed by their own weight. The fermentation, in contact with the skins, lasts six or seven days. In contrast the Pinot Noir is crushed, but not destalked.

Unlike the secretary of the local growers' association, M. Monin believes that there is some revival of interest in Mondeuse. He describes it as 'the Bordeaux of Bugey'. It is a difficult grape because it ripens so late, especially in a cool year, when you may not be able to pick it before All Saints' Day (1 November). It is also a tannic grape, that might benefit from some wood ageing, but this is not possible for financial reasons. Instead it is bottled within the year, and it is left to the customer to age this solid, stalky, rather inky wine for two or three years.

The most exciting discovery of Bugey was the wine of Manicle, a recognized *cru* of the VDQS, whose tradition is maintained by one family in the tiny village of Cheignien-la-Balme. We met André Miraillet who has just 5 hectares, planted with Chardonnay and Pinot Noir and owned jointly with his father Gabriel and uncle Léon. Their vineyard is outside the village, on a gentle slope at a height of 400 metres, but with a rock face rising steeply behind so that the sun's heat is reflected on to the pebbles in the vineyard. With a south east aspect they obtain very healthy, ripe grapes. The house next to the vineyard once belonged to Brillat-Savarin. It is now owned by a friend of the Miraillet family who took us back to see the old winepress. We sat in the evening sunshine sipping Jacquère, nibbling local Comté cheese and contemplating in the distance the snow-capped peak of Mont Blanc some hundred kilometres away.

André Miraillet is a young man who left school at the earliest opportunity. He says his association with wine began in the cradle, but he has had no formal training. His cellar is underneath his house in the village and he has replaced most of the wooden barrels with small stainless-steel vats for fermentation, though he has kept some hundred-year-old barrels in which he ages both his red and white wine for a few months. Any control of fermentation temperatures is haphazard and the red grapes are crushed by the time-honoured method of human feet. He also has an old-fashioned vertical press. It was on quite a different scale from Monin who was commented on as '*c'est l'industrie déjà*'. The wines are neither fined nor filtered and the results are delicious. The 1985 Pinot Noir, tasted in September 1986, had a strong smell of raspberry jam, with lots of young Pinot Noir fruit, and length on the finish; but the star wine of my visit to Bugey was the 1985 Chardonnay, which had a light, leafy nose with a soft, buttery flavour of the grape. It has continued to develop over the ensuing twelve months.

The village of Montagnieu perches on a steep hillside. A village wedding had just emerged from the church and the bells were ringing in the September sunshine. Fortunately for us, Franck Peillot was not a member of the wedding party and was happy to spend the afternoon explaining the subtleties of Montagnieu.

The development of sparkling wine in Montagnieu is a fairly recent phenomenon. Previously the village was known for its Roussette; this is a difficult grape to vinify and has a tendency to start refermenting, so it seemed a logical step to create a second fermentation deliberately. Franck and his father began making sparkling wine four years ago. They are now well equipped on a small scale for the champagne method, ageing their wine for between eighteen months and two years before disgorging. The pressure is slightly less than for champagne, so they prefer to call their wine *pétillant* rather than *mousseux*, a term which has acquired pejorative overtones.

Unlike most growers in the region they have no Chardonnay, just Roussette, for both sparkling and the small amount of still wine which they continue to make. Unfortunately we could not taste the latter as it was all sold, but the sparkling wine had a slightly honeyed nose, reminiscent of apples and boiled sweets, with light, fresh acidity on the palate. They only make a Brut style.

The vineyards of the *cru* are in the three villages of Seillonnez, Briorde and Montagnieu itself. The chalk hillsides are so steep that tractors are impossible to use and they have pulleys to bring equipment up the slopes. The harvest takes two weekends in October, providing a festive occasion for family and friends.

Cerdon is quite separate from the rest of Bugey. Rosé de Cerdon is made in eight villages south east of Bourg-en-Bresse, of which Cerdon is the largest, surrounded by an amphitheatre of vines. Most of the vineyards are at an altitude of about 400 metres on south east-, south- and south west-facing slopes, on clay and limestone soil. We went to see Georges Martin at Vieillard, a tiny hamlet up a dirt track in the hills near Jujurieux. It was the day of the village *fête des galettes*. The *galettes*, a cross between a loaf of bread and a cake, made with cream, eggs and sugar as well as flour and yeast, are cooked in the village's old bread-oven. The smell was mouth-watering, and the taste of warm, creamy *galette* exceeded expectations. There was bunting and music and the entire village sat down together to lunch, of which the *pièce de résistance* was an enormous roast, also cooked in the bread-oven.

Rosé de Cerdon is a sparkling wine. It is made mainly from Gamay with some Pinot Noir, Pinot Gris and Poulsard. This part of Bugey is nearest to the Jura and Poulsard has been here as long as Gamay. Pinot Gris is rare, although it can give vigour and alcohol to the wine. Poulsard is difficult to grow and its yields are very irregular, but there is a certain prestige attached to it which has encouraged people to plant it. Chardonnay was also allowed from 1986, having already been grown in the area for still wine. It gives a good alcohol level. A Rosé de Cerdon *demi-sec*, with 30 grams of residual sugar per litre, has also been permitted from 1988.

Before the Second World War Cerdon was a region of still red wine, and still wine can be produced here as a *cru* of Bugey even today; but the real interest now lies in the area's sparkling wine, and only that made by the traditional (what they call 'ancestral') method.

There has always been a little sparkling wine at Cerdon. Often the Poulsard did not finish fermenting properly and the resulting wine was kept for special celebrations. The ancestral method developed from this inability to complete the fermentation, but nowadays the process is much more methodical. Georges Martin explained. He is a young enthusiast who has come to wine-making after a brief career in industry. Buying and planting vines over the past eight years, he has developed his father's 70 ares to 3.5 hectares.

Sometimes he vinifies all his grape varieties together, sometimes separately, depending upon the quantity and the conditions of the vintage. His cellar is rustic – he retains his father's old wooden vats. The grapes are pressed, so there is no skin contact. He manages to control the fermentation, stopping it after about two weeks when there are 50 milligrams per litre of residual sugar. This used to be done with sulphur, but now they use refrigeration equipment, blocking the fermentation just long enough to filter and bottle the wine. The bottles are left standing upright and the fermentation starts again; this time the wine is left for three months, after which it is filtered under pressure to remove any remaining deposits, and then rebottled. The best results are achieved with an early first bottling and second fermentation, which make the wine more stable. There is no malolactic fermentation, so the acidity level is quite high; chaptalization is allowed, but there is no further dosage or addition of yeast. The finished wine is low in alcohol, 8.5–9° depending on the level of sweetness – the drier the wine, the more alcoholic it is. In any case, to quote M. Martin, 'It will make you sing, but nothing more!'

Rosé de Cerdon made in the ancestral way is the true wine of the area. Unfortunately there is discord in the vineyards, particularly over the production method. It is also permitted to produce a Rosé de Cerdon by the champagne process; as people do not have sufficiently well-equipped cellars, this is sometimes done for them at nearby Lons-le-Saunier in the Jura. Much more common, even though it is not allowed in the appellation, is a wine into which carbon dioxide has been artificially injected – what I call the bicycle-pump method. Sadly, of the 200 hectares of vines around Cerdon, 85 per cent of the wine is vinified in this industrial way and there is no comparison in the taste. The wine is labelled *vin pétillant gazéifié*, the taste is coarse and the bubbles vicious. The real thing is a delicate pink wine with a deliciously grapy flavour, light and fruity with traces of sweetness.

10

Wines of the Jura

The Jura, in a remote corner of France on the borders of Switzerland, is the home of some of the country's most individual wines. There are not only red, white and pink, still and sparkling, but also the distinctive *vin jaune* of Château-Chalon and elsewhere, which is the nearest France comes to producing anything resembling sherry, and the sweet and luscious *vin de paille*, a remnant of old-fashioned wine-making that has survived in this dramatically hilly region.

Lons-le-Saunier is the centre of the vineyards of the Jura. It is a quiet country town, with a single claim to fame as the birthplace of Rouget de Lisle, the composer of the 'Marseillaise'. The Rue du Commerce is a picturesque street lined with arcades on each side. The town is also an important centre for salt, both as a commodity and as a curative element in the thermal springs.

To the south are the vineyards of the Revermont du Sud, which are part of the overall appellation of Côtes du Jura. To the north there are the appellation of Arbois, where Louis Pasteur spent much of his childhood, and the tiny appellations of L'Étoile and Château-Chalon. The vineyard area has doubled since the 1960s and is now static at around 1,450 hectares. Polyculture has tended to disappear as people have chosen between vines, wheat and cows. Once the vineyards were scattered in numerous tiny parcels, not even the size of an are, let alone a hectare; now the *remembrement* or regrouping of plots, which was carried out in the early 1970s, has greatly facilitated the wine-grower's task.

The vineyards of the Jura have a long and chequered history. The region did not finally become part of France until the reign of Louis XIV; he destroyed all the châteaux here, so it is rare to find any old feudal castles. During the Middle Ages it was part of the county of Burgundy (the 'Franche-Comté') and a pawn in the power struggle

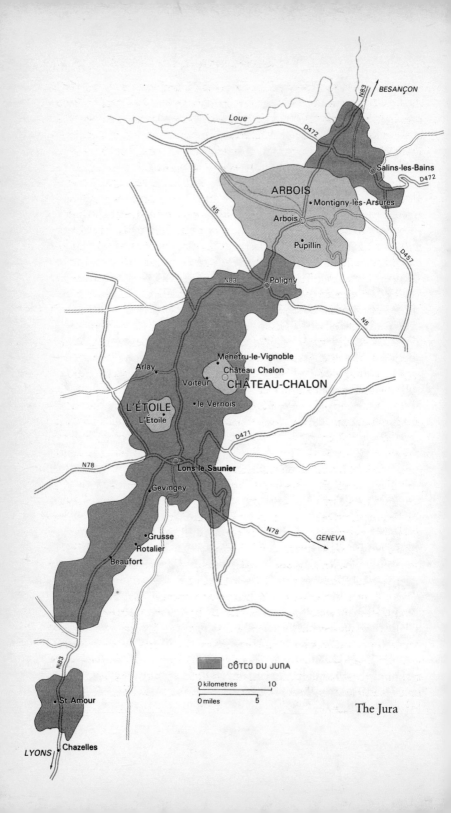

The Jura

between the Holy Roman Emperors and the kings of France. The duchy of Burgundy adjoined the county to the west, and the two provinces periodically found themselves under the same ruler; this association led to the introduction of Burgundian grape varieties, Pinot Noir and Chardonnay, to complement the traditional indigenous ones, notably Poulsard, Trousseau and Savagnin.

The monasteries also played their part in the development of the vineyards. The wines of the Jura were greatly esteemed in the Middle Ages, although the area had the disadvantage of no great navigable river system to facilitate transport. In 1298 Philip the Fair bought 37 *muids* of Vin d'Arbois. Margaret of Flanders, Duchess of Burgundy, bought wine from Arbois for her Paris town house in 1374, and in 1493 the Emperor Maximilian accorded the wine of Arbois the right of free entry into all his heriditary territories. François I ordered a hundred barrels of Jura wine for the French court in 1537. Henri IV enjoyed the wines of Arbois after the end of the siege of the town in 1595, and Sully recorded that at the marriage of Henri IV to Marie de Medici the queen was attended by all the Italian ladies who, being pleased with the wine of Arbois, drank more of it than was necessary!

In the nineteenth century Guyot recorded that there were 20,000 hectares of vines in the department and that vines were the most important crop. Grape varieties included Savagnin as well as Melon and Gamay Blanc (both now local names for Chardonnay), and for red wines Pulsart (the Poulsard of today) and Trousseau, as well as Noirien and Beclan which have now disappeared.

Jullien rated Salins and Arsures as meriting a reputation for red wine, writing that their colour was light rather than dark and that they were very fine, pleasant and alcoholic. Arbois and Poligny were also given a passing mention for producing good red wines, but were much more highly rated for white wine, while Château-Chalon previously used to produce white wine which, after twenty years of ageing, could be compared with the most renowned wines such as Tokay, but the vineyards had been split up and the wine was no longer good. Rendu, later in the century, was more appreciative. The production of *vin jaune* provided the wealth of Château-Chalon. He compared it to Madeira, a real dry French Madeira, and very heady. Cavoleau, while describing the wines of the Jura as being worthy of recommendation but lacking great distinction, rated *vin jaune* as the most esteemed dessert wine of the country, that would keep for at least forty years.

L'ÉTOILE

The smallest appellation of the Jura is L'Étoile, with just 55 hectares. It takes its name from a hilltop village outside Lons-le-Saunier and became an appellation in 1937. Apart from the local co-operative, there are only two producers of any size: the Château de l'Étoile and Jean Cros at Domaine de Montbourgeau. Jean Cros is a jovial man, with a round face and a bushy moustache. He has 16.5 hectares of vines which he runs with his daughter Nicole. L'Étoile is only white or yellow, never red or pink, so M. Cros's vineyards are planted mainly with Chardonnay as well as some Savagnin and a little Poulsard, a small amount of which is allowed in L'Étoile (in fact M. Cros makes his into Côtes du Jura).

The reputation of L'Étoile depends upon its white wine, which is either a blend of Chardonnay and Savagnin, or pure Chardonnay, or occasionally pure Savagnin, though that grape is more likely to be used for *vin jaune*. The white wine is aged in wood for two or three years and takes on a dry, nutty flavour, the distinctive taste of the Jura. Asked what distinguishes L'Étoile from the other appellations of the Jura, Jean Cros thought it had more fruit and finesse, more elegance. The soil is no different from elsewhere, except for starfish fossils which gave the village its name, but the microclimate is kinder. The village is surrounded by hills which protect the vineyards from frost and hail. In the occasional years when the grapes lack sugar and the wine alcohol, they make a sparkling wine at L'Étoile. They also make *vin jaune* in the traditional manner of Château-Chalon, as well as some deliciously sweet, nutty *vin de paille*.

CHÂTEAU-CHALON AND *VIN JAUNE*

The most distinctive wine of the Jura is *vin jaune*. Château-Chalon is an appellation in its own right, making *vin jaune* alone, while *vin jaune* is one of several categories in the regulations for Côtes du Jura, Arbois and L'Étoile. Château-Chalon takes its name from a hilltop village with a ruined abbey and a simple Romanesque church dating from the tenth century, one of the oldest in the Jura. The abbey was founded in 600 and the nuns were all of noble families. To be eligible to enter the abbey, you needed sixteen quarterings on your coat of arms; such connections ensured that the wine of Château-Chalon was sent to all the royal courts of Europe. The abbey, like so many others, was destroyed at the Revolution, but there is a vineyard called Les Dames which remembers the noble nuns. From the village there is a magnificent view of the vineyards below. Vineyards from three other villages are included in the appellation, namely Doublans, Nevy-sur-Seille and Menétru-le-Vignoble. The vineyards are planted on clay and limestone soil, and face south east at an altitude of between 250 and 350 metres, with a suitable microclimate of hot summers, sunny autumns and shelter from the north wind.

One of those who appreciated the wines of Château-Chalon was the Austrian statesman, Metternich. His family is recorded as buying the wines as early as 1750. Morton Shand, in *A Book of French Wines*, tells the story of Napoleon, at the negotiations for his marriage with Marie-Louise, wishing to flatter Metternich by praising the wines of Schloss Johannisberg, of which the Metternich family are still owners. Metternich replied, 'You have in France a white wine that is much finer than my Schloss Johannisberg.' Napoleon professed himself ignorant, and the reply was 'Château-Chalon.'

The differences between Château-Chalon and other *vins jaunes* are minute. There is a higher minimum alcoholic degree for Château-Chalon (12° as opposed to 11.5° for other *vins jaunes*), but in practice at least 13° is preferred for both. Both require a minimum of six years' ageing, so that wine from the 1979 vintage cannot be bottled before 1 January 1986. The wine is kept in small oak barrels of 228 litres, the same size as the Burgundian *pièce*, and is neither racked nor topped up for six years. During this time a *voile*, or 'veil' of yeast, forms which is not unlike the *flor* of Jerez. Experiments are being carried out at the research station in Poligny to determine the exact characteristics of this *voile* and also to study the possibility of seeding it. No one quite knows how *vin jaune* developed in the first place. Probably, as with other discoveries, someone put wine in a barrel in a cellar in Château-Chalon and simply forgot about it. When it was found years later, the results were surprisingly good.

None of the cellars in the Jura is completely below ground. Château-Chalon, in particular, is built on a granite outcrop so that it is impossible to dig deep subterranean cellars. Consequently there are considerable temperature fluctuations – between 8° and 18°C during the year – and these are necessary to encourage the growth of the *voile*. The yeasts become active in the summer and die down in the winter. The *voile* takes at least two, if not three years to develop in the first place, and then it continually renews itself. While the yeasts are alive and multiplying they give nothing to the aroma of the wine. It is when they are dying that the distinctive bouquet of *vin jaune* develops over a period of a couple of months. A new generation of yeasts appears as soon as the temperature is favourable again, but never in a uniform manner.

The *voile* of the Jura is from a similar family to the *flor* of Jerez, but less able to withstand the high alcoholic content of sherry. The *flor* for fino sherry is often as much a centimetre thick or more, compared with the thin *voile* of a millimetre in the Jura. If the *voile* is too thick it becomes too active and can give bad tastes to the wine. Not only temperature, but humidity and the ratio of barrel size to the volume of air in the barrel can also affect the activity of the yeast. The atmosphere in the cellars should not be too damp, and if there is too much air in the barrel, the yeast will become too active. *Vin jaune* can only be made from the Savagnin grape. No one is quite sure of the origins of this variety. Suggestions have been made that it is related to the Gewurztraminer, or that it has associations with Tokay and originated in Hungary. In Savoy it is called the Gringet and makes sparkling Ayze.

It is vinified with great care at a temperature of no higher than 25°C in stainless-steel or cement-lined vats. Chaptalization is permitted up to 1° of alcohol and once the wine has been left to develop into *vin jaune* it is tasted and analysed regularly every six months to ensure that the level of volatile acidity does not rise above 0.4 grams per litre. The risk of the wine turning into vinegar is high, and research is being done in an attempt to reduce the hazards and wastage. Experiments with artificial seeding have so far given good results with the Savagnin, but there are fears that wine made in this way may not age so well. *Vin jaune* produced by the natural method has a very long life. Another problem arising from artificial seeding is that the artificial yeasts may take over and destroy the natural yeast. Chardonnay will develop the flavour of *vin jaune* with artificial yeasts, but it takes four rather than six years to do so and then fades rapidly.

The annual production of *vin jaune* and Château-Chalon is tiny. About 70,000 bottles of Château-Chalon are made in a good year, and in bad years like 1980 and 1984 the twelve growers themselves decide not to sell the wine under the appellation but to declassify it into Côtes du Jura. Every year in Château-Chalon a commission inspects all the vineyards, checking on degree of potential alcohol, yield and how well the vines have been tended. In 1979 someone was refused the appellation for his wine as he had sulphured his vines badly. Although the appellation allows 30 hectolitres per hectare, it is rare that more than 20 hl/ha is made. Savagnin gives tiny yields and suffers badly in cold springs, sometimes failing to produce grapes at all. Work is being done on clonal selection to overcome some of these deficiencies. At Château-Chalon there are only 35 hectares in production, with a further 15 hectares being planted following the *remembrement* or reorganization of the land in the village. The delimitation was first done in 1936 but was 'very whimsical'; it was amended in 1985, and the permitted area is now smaller.

The ageing process reduces the quantity of wine still further. Both *vin jaune* and Château-Chalon are sold in the distinctive *clavelin* bottle of 62 centilitres; this apparently irrational figure is in fact the amount of wine left from 1 litre after six years ageing in barrel.

Jean Macle – described by a colleague as '*lui, c'est vraiment le sommet*' – is one of the most conscientious and talented producers of Château-Chalon, and he explained the intricate details of making *vin jaune*. His small, neat cellar goes back to the seventeenth century and he has 12 hectares of vines, 4 planted with Savagnin and 8 with Chardonnay. With the help of his wife, he has developed this estate from his father's tiny vineyard. Twenty years ago no one had just vines at Château-Chalon. Jean Macle's father had cows, and farmers made cheese or grew wheat. Even with a wine of the reputation of Château-Chalon, it was inconceivable to live from vines alone. Happily, things have changed. Even so, the financial commitment involved in making *vin jaune* is very burdensome. M. Cros at L'Étoile explained how his daughter Nicole had just planted a hectare of Savagnin. It will take four years for those vines to produce grapes for the appellation, and the wine needs six years' ageing. She will not have any wine to sell until the vines are more than ten years old. The cost of financing the ageing of a large stock of wine for six years is almost prohibitive, and the wine is justifiably more expensive than any of the other wines of the region.

Another excellent producer of *vin jaune* is Christian Bourdy, a friendly, expansive man with a welcoming smile. The Bourdy family have been making wine in Arlay since 1781 and that is the date on the cellar wall. He has 5 hectares of vines, but also a *négociant* activity which enables him to buy grapes. He has vines at Château-Chalon as well as in the village of Arlay, and so makes both Château-Chalon and ordinary *vin jaune*. As he explained, oenologically all the wines of the Jura are sick, but we like them like that and we do not want to cure them. *Vin jaune* can only be made through contact with air, which is normally detrimental to wine. His *vin jaune* is kept apart from his other wines, in a separate cellar modelled on that of the abbey of Baume, with a wonderful vaulted ceiling.

Vin jaune is an intrinsic element of Jurassian cuisine, with its dishes like *poulet au vin jaune*. But it is best drunk with Comté, the hard yellow cheese of the region, and with the similar Gruyère which crosses the border from Switzerland. M. Bourdy advised that a bottle should be opened at least six hours before it is drunk, so that the wine can develop its true flavours by gentle oxidation. His wine has a deliciously nutty, salty taste, reminiscent of fino sherry but lighter in alcohol.

ARBOIS

Arbois is a delightful old town. You first catch sight of its russet-coloured roofs and the imposing church tower of St-Just from the top of a long hill. It is possible to visit the house where Louis Pasteur spent much of his childhood. His father was a tanner and this is where he plied his trade; Pasteur later transformed it into a smart town house. Opposite there is a small wine museum, and local pride is summed up in the following dictum:

> *Du vin d'Arbois,*
> *Plus on en boit,*
> *Plus on va droit!*

Arbois prides itself on having been one of the very first appellations of France in 1936 along with Cassis and Châteauneuf-du-Pape. Another claim to fame is that it is the only town in France to have supported the Revolution four times, in 1792, 1830, 1848 and finally in 1870.

Louis Pasteur used the wines of Arbois in his experiments with bacteria and yeast for his treatise on oenology. His vineyard outside the town of Arbois is now maintained by the firm of Henri Maire, which is by far the most important producer in Arbois and the Jura.

Henri Maire has done more for the wines of the Jura than anyone else in this century. It is not an exaggeration to say that he has put them on the map. There are many people who know the name Henri Maire, who would otherwise be unaware of the wines of the Jura. The family goes back to 1632 and they have always been wine-growers, but it is the present head of the family who has placed his company among the top six producers in France by volume. Admittedly a considerable proportion of the turnover is in table wines quite unconnected with the Jura. His best-known wine is probably Vin Fou, a sparkling wine made by the transfer method and without a drop of Arbois in it. When you meet Henri Maire, you can understand the amazing growth of the company. The man exudes energy and everything is done at top speed. We visited the cellars at a run, and a ride in his car was quite unnerving.

The company is responsible for between 50 and 60 per cent of the production of the Jura. They own four sizeable estates and buy the production of 300 hectares of vines in Arbois and the Côtes du Jura. His four estates – Domaine de Montfort, Domaine de la Croix d'Argis, Domaine de Sorbief and Domaine de Grange Grillard, as well as large installations where most of the vinification is carried out – are all close to the town of Arbois. They also vinify at the 65-hectare estate of Domaine de Sorbief where there is a typical Arbois cellar with large barrels, over a hundred years old, for ageing the red wine. M. Maire lives at the Château de Montfort, a twelfth-century château whose cellars contain barrels for ageing *vin jaune*. Here, in March 1986, we were treated to a tasting of 1959 Vin d'Arbois Corail; it was pale rather than deep red, like the colour of coral, and was made from all five Arbois grape varieties – 25 per cent Poulsard, 30 per cent Trousseau, 20 per cent Pinot Noir, 15 per cent Chardonnay and 15 per cent Savagnin. It had the lingering flavour of mature wine and retained some lively fruit. It is unusual for a red wine from the Jura to age so well in bottle, though a longer life is expected of the region's white wine.

The wines of Arbois can be not only red, white and pink, but also yellow or even what they call *corail* or *rubis*, coral or ruby, depending on the depth of colour and the grower's whim. The vineyards cover 766 hectares in six villages, of which Pupillin alone is allowed to attach its name to the label. There is strong local rivalry, typified in the verse:

Arbois le nom;
Pupillin le bon.

To the less informed palate, however, the difference is negligible. The vineyard area is a mosaic of small parcels. Twenty years ago people also had cows, but these have been given up, 'with wine barrels replacing cows', as people have chosen to concentrate on vines; but even so, holdings tend to be quite small and divided.

Red wine is more important than white wine in the appellation of Arbois. The typical grape varieties are Trousseau and Poulsard, while Pinot Noir came from Burgundy centuries ago, brought, some say, by the Prince de Chalon. The exact proportions of each variety depend on the grower's aim and preference. Red wines in the Jura tend to lack colour and in contrast the pink wines are sometimes darker than usual, so that the difference can be hard to make out. Neither the Poulsard nor the Trousseau have much colour in their skins and even a pink wine will be fermented on the skins for at least a week, if not two or even three. The Trousseau tends to be a little more thick-skinned and full-bodied, so a grower like Lucien Aviet at the Caveau Bacchus in Arbois makes his pink wine from Poulsard and his red from Trousseau. He has very little Pinot Noir. Often older vines are used for red wine as they give more body and colour.

Lucien Aviet's 1983 Rosé d'Arbois, a pure Poulsard, destalked and fermented on the skins for three weeks in large oak vats with a daily *remontage*, was then aged in wood for fifteen months. The red, a pure Trousseau, may spend four weeks on the skins and is then aged for about eighteen months before bottling. *Vin de primeur* is anathema in the Jura.

White Arbois tends to be predominantly Chardonnay, with some Savagnin, and occasionally Poulsard vinified as white wine. Savagnin is usually destined for *vin jaune*, though it is also possible to find an Arbois from pure Savagnin. White wines, especially those made from Savagnin, tend to have the slightly maderized nose of *vin jaune*, while pure Chardonnay usually has a more marked varietal character.

Sophistication of method varies from grower to grower, and one finds a mixture of the modern and the traditional. Inevitably, Henri Maire's cellars are streamlined, while those of the small family growers are more typical. For some, temperature control is perhaps a little hit-and-miss and often unnecessary, as it is rarely that hot at vintage time. Few people can afford elaborate cooling equipment, and most prefer to let nature take its course. In any case, temperature control is much less important than in other parts of France. Chaptalization is permitted; some practise it and others do not, depending on the year. A minimum natural alcoholic content of 10° is necessary. Some people use cultured yeast. Virtually all wine is aged in wood, usually large old oak casks, small 228-litre *pièces* being only for *vin jaune*.

The other significant producer of Arbois is Rollet Frères, a GAEC or group of father, two sons and a daughter. We met one of the sons, Pierre. When they began in 1968 they had 20 hectares, and today they have 50: 15 in the Côtes du Jura and 35 in Arbois, which makes them the second largest company in the Jura after Henri Maire. They have abandoned their traditional but impractical cellars and now have a streamlined warehouse with modern equipment and a 26,000-hectolitre capacity in wood. Unlike the majority of Jura producers, they concentrate on wines of a single grape variety and have made that something of a house speciality, with pink Poulsard, red Trousseau and red Pinot Noir. Whites include Chardonnay, aged in small new oak barrels, while Savagnin is only aged in old wood. Poulsard is the most important grape variety of Arbois and red is the dominant colour, though Poulsard can be included in white wine. Poulsard likes heavier, marly soil, while Trousseau likes warm gravel and is found particularly in the village of Montigny outside Arbois. I liked the Trousseau, with its gentle flavour, reminiscent of raspberries.

CÔTES DU JURA

Côtes du Jura is the all-embracing appellation of the region, covering all the vineyards that are not Château-Chalon, L'Étoile or Arbois. It extends to the north and south of Lons-le-Saunier over seventy-two villages, with a mixture of soil and a variety of microclimates. Generally more white than red grapes are grown. The small town of Poligny is an important centre today, while the village of Arlay was of historical significance. To the south of Lons-le-Saunier is the Revermont du Sud, a rather overlooked area, where some dynamic growers have joined together to promote their wines. We spent a friendly morning with them going from one cellar to the next.

First stop was to see Claude Bernard, a rather shy young man who cultivates 7 hectares of vines with his brother. Their vineyards are planted mainly with Chardonnay, though they also have Poulsard, as well as a little Pinot Noir, which gives wine with a good colour, but can suffer quite severely from frost. Although it has been grown in the Jura for a long time, especially around Arlay, some people do not consider it typical and want it suppressed. There is no Trousseau, as it does not do so well in the south and is more suited to the soil and microclimate of Arbois. They had their first vintage of Savagnin in 1984 and have just started to make *vin jaune*. They have old vaulted cellars in the village of Givengey. Most of the wine ferments in wood in a rather haphazard way, just as it pleases, without much attention being paid to temperatures. Volumes are small and the weather is cool, so there is little danger of overheated fermentations.

The most surprising aspect of the vinification of Jura wines is that during the ageing process many of the growers do not top up the barrels, and this gives the typical oxidized taste of Jura. My first impression of the white wine was that it was maderizing; but no, it had a curious nutty flavour. The Chardonnay had even developed a *voile* too, and if left could turn into *vin jaune*. It tasted of the vinification process rather than of the grape. As they pointed out, Pasteur came to some erroneous conclusions in his oenological researches as a result of basing them on Jura wines. He believed it was oxygen that made the wine and that some aeration was essential, whereas in most other regions that is not at all the case.

From Claude Bernard we went on to Michel Rameaux at Grusse and Pierre de Boiseau at the Château de Gréa, whose vinification methods were very similar to M. Bernard's.

Jacques Richard, the president of the growers' association, concentrates on sparkling wine. His 10 hectares are planted mainly with Chardonnay as well as a little Savagnin for *vin jaune*. The best Chardonnay is kept for still wine and the rest turned into bubbles. Sparkling wine is included in the appellations of Arbois and Côtes du Jura and production has increased considerably over the last ten years. Établissements Armand Jacquier, at Couliège outside Lons-le-Saunier, have a thriving *champenisation* business; they provide the equipment and technique to produce most of the sparkling wine of the Jura, and seem to enjoy considerable success. Certainly the wines we tasted were fruity and well made, with a good *mousse* and an attractive yeasty, nutty tang. Most of the wine is Brut, without any dosage. There is a little *demi-sec* and some pink from Poulsard.

Another important property in the Côtes du Jura is the Château d'Arlay, which is owned by Count Renaud de Laguiche, whose brother is the Laguiche of Montrachet fame. We were shown round by his son Alain who is better informed about the history of the estate than its vinification methods. Arlay was once a fortified village, on account of its position on the border between Burgundy and Franche-Comté. There are now two villages. The lower village has a church dedicated to St Vincent, the patron saint of wine-growers, and at the top of the hill there is an eighteenth-century château built on the site of an old monastery. The park was also laid out in the eighteenth-century, and incorporates the ruins of a medieval castle. There are wonderful views towards Château-Chalon. Part of the old monastery now houses the ageing cellars of the estate, while the offices are in the former monastic kitchens and the fermentation vats stand where once there were stables.

Château d'Arlay, with 30 hectares of vines, is one of the oldest estates in the Jura and is planted with all five grape varieties of the area, Chardonnay, Savagnin, Poulsard, Trousseau and Pinot Noir. Their white wine usually consists of 90 per cent Chardonnay with 10 per cent Savagnin, blended just before bottling after two years' ageing. This wine had the more usual leafy flavour of Chardonnay, in contrast to a wine with 25 per cent Savagnin which had a more sherry-like tang.

Their pink wine is a blend of 50 per cent Pinot Noir with Trousseau and Poulsard; they call it *corail*, as pink (*rosé*) has acquired pejorative connotations. It is aged in wood for two years and like most Jura pink wines is fairly substantial. Their red wine is unusual in being pure Pinot Noir, but then Arlay is the main area for that variety. In contrast, Christian Bourdy in the village below makes his red wine from a maximum of 50 per cent Pinot Noir. The soil at Arlay is quite heavy, clay and limestone, producing wines that demand more ageing than in other areas.

Another curiosity of which the region is proud is its *vin de paille*, which is included in three appellations, but not in Château-Chalon. Most people make a little for family and friends, and it is a treat and a privilege to be offered some at the end of a tasting. The grapes were once dried on straw, hence its name, from October to January, so that the juice is rich and concentrated. One hundred kilos of grapes will normally give about 70–75 litres of juice, but for *vin de paille* this is reduced to 20 or 25 litres. The fermentation is very slow, taking as long as four years in a small barrel. The final taste is rich and nutty, and the wine brown in colour. It can come from red or white grapes and is considered an excellent accompaniment to *foie gras*; I am not so sure.

A postscript to the wines of the Jura is the Vin de Pays de Franche-Comté, which covers the two departments of Haute-Saône and Jura. There is an example of three growers at Champlitte in the north near Dole, who make red wine from Pinot Noir and Gamay and white from Auxerrois and Chardonnay. Production is tiny and the wines a cross between Jura and Burgundy in style.

There is no doubt that the wines of the Jura are amongst the most distinctive of France, sharing very little with wines from other regions in either method or taste.

Wines of the North

CÔTES DE TOUL

The vineyards of Lorraine must be the most isolated vineyards of France, a forgotten backwater on the country's wine map. Like so many other parts of France, Lorraine has a tradition of viticulture which goes back to the Romans. The extensive vineyards of the nineteenth century have now been reduced to a few pockets which are easy to overlook in a survey of France. One can only admire the tenacity of wine-growers who maintain their region's wines in the face of climatic difficulties, for these, with Champagne, are the most northern vineyards of France. They come in two VDQS, Côtes de Toul and Vins de Moselle.

The town of Toul is the centre of the VDQS of Côtes de Toul, with a Gothic cathedral whose bishops did much to establish viticulture in the region in the Middle Ages. Although there are eight villages within the VDQS, only three are of any importance – Buligny to the south of Toul and Bruley and Lucey to the north. Lucey has a slope of vines called Les Vignes de l'Évêque; grapes from the village were taken to the episcopal cellars in Toul for vinification, so that none of the houses in Lucey was built with a cellar – but this was not so in Bruley, which was part of the kingdom of France, and not on episcopal land. The area is unusual in having had no great abbeys to play their part in the development of the region's wine; this role was filled by the bishops of Toul. Later, in about 1700, the Duke of Lorraine established the Code Viticole de Lorraine, which forbade the planting of Gamay (because it was too productive) and encouraged the cultivation of Pinot Noir.

By 1850 there were 45,000 hectares of vines in the four departments of Lorraine: Vosges, Meuse, Moselle and Meurthe-et-Moselle. Toul is the departmental capital of Meuse. Guyot was the most flattering of the nineteenth-century authorities. He described the grandeur and the beauty of the vineyards, saying that the vine at Toul was the subject of all possible care and attention, the queen of agriculture. Previously Pinots had been masters of the vineyards of Toul, but then the vulgar varieties had tended to replace them completely. He noted Brulay for its white wine from Aubin, a grape which has now disappeared.

Phylloxera did not touch the area until 1895 and did not cause much damage until 1910, much later than in most other parts of France; so for a while the region enjoyed a certain advantage, supplying wine to areas where it was lacking. A lot of wine went to Champagne before the champagne revolts of 1907 which led to a delimitation of the region's vineyards. Reims is only 170 kilometres away.

It was the First World War rather than phylloxera that destroyed the vineyards of the Côtes de Toul. The Germans came within 20 kilometres of Toul and the front line of Verdun went through vineyards which were never replanted after the end of hostilities, as there was no money available. In addition, the development of the railways and more efficient means of transport meant that the region's traditional markets disappeared. By 1920 half the vineyards had gone and they continued to decline until about 1960, when the region was granted a provisional VDQS. This was confirmed in 1962, offering some incentive to the achievement of a gentle increase in the vineyards over the last twenty years. Even so, the area of Côtes de Toul remains at only about 60 hectares, producing an average of 4,000 hectolitres of wine per year. In 1962 the average production was only 1,000 hectolitres.

There is an enormous theoretical potential for growth, to the extent that about 100 hectares per village has been delimited. In reality, however, the area is now fairly static, and there are only a few growers of any size – that is, with the four or five hectares necessary for making a living. Of the sixty-odd growers in the VDQS, twelve are responsible for 40 hectares and many of the smaller growers are giving up their vines on retirement.

The principal grape variety is Gamay for the decree of the Duke of Lorraine has long since been forgotten, and there is also some Pinot Noir and a little Auxerrois Blanc for white wine. Aubin is allowed in the regulations for white wine, but in practice has disappeared. A little Pinot Blanc has also been introduced into the area and is similar to Auxerrois in maturity and acidity.

The overriding problem of a northern vineyard is one of climate and the ability of the grapes to ripen properly. For this reason red wine production is of very uncertain success. The Côtes de Toul have developed their own speciality, Gris de Toul, a delicate pink wine. The colour comes from the grape skins, but there is no skin contact with the juice, just crushing and a fairly hard pressing. Gris de Toul is nearly always made from Gamay and the small amount of Pinot Noir is generally kept for red wine.

The vineyards are on slopes, facing south and east. The soil is clay and limestone. At Bruley there is more clay and less limestone so that the wine tends to be lower in acidity and higher in alcohol, while at Lucey the wine is more delicate.

Weather is the main problem. Spring frost can cause considerable damage and it costs too much to protect the vines with oil-fired heaters or *chaufferettes*. Cold weather at the flowering can also diminish the yield, so that while 1982 produced 100 hectolitres per hectare, in contrast 1985 only made 57 hl/ha.

The most unexpected wine of the area is the sparkling wine. Given that the Côtes de Toul have historical connections with Champagne and is not so far from Épernay, perhaps it should not have been a surprise, but it certainly was a delicious discovery. One of the largest producers is the GAEC des Coteaux de Toul, run by the three Lelièvre brothers at Lucey. Roland, the youngest, studied oenology at Avize in Champagne. He did not want to waste his expertise, especially as he likes champagne, and he began making his own sparkling wine for fun. He started with 1,300 bottles in 1975 and now produces about 15,000 each year. The method follows that of champagne and the wine stays on the lees of the second fermentation for two and a half years. The base wine is vinified in the same way as *vin gris*, with no malolactic fermentation or fining, as the must is centrifuged to clean it before fermentation. It is made from the excess production of Gamay above the permitted 60 hl/ha, so in theory it is only a *vin de table*, but none the worse for that. It is sold under the brand-name Leucquois, a reference to the Leuci who were the early Gallic inhabitants of the area.

The only other producers of any size are the Laroppe Frères, otherwise known as the Société Vinicole de Toul, and they are also *négociants*. Michel Laroppe's grandfather was associated with a local co-operative which made sparkling wine here when the champagne outlet was closed. They now make *vin gris* as well and are also developing their red wines from Pinot Noir. I was lucky, for I visited them in the spring of 1986 when there were wines of the ripe 1985 vintage to taste. I fear that the 1984s would have been a less happy experience. The fermentation lasts two to three weeks to extract the maximum amount of colour. The basic red wine has no wood ageing as it is intended for relatively early drinking. For better wines they are conducting their first tentative experiments with ageing in new wood, using new Burgundian *pièces*. After five months in wood the 1985 had quite a delicate raspberry flavour of young Pinot Noir, with some new wood influence. The 1983, drunk at dinner, was rather harder, with a stalky, astringent flavour. I suspect the success of red Côtes de Toul depends entirely on a warm summer. In unripe years the grapes are best vinified as *vin gris*, while the 1985 must not be decried for it certainly had some potential.

As well as wine, Toul produces plums for mirabelle liqueur. There is a well-signposted 'Route du Vin et de la Mirabelle'. Some people have their own stills, but there is a public still in each village and mirabelles are more important to the region's economy than grapes. The adjoining villages of Lucey and Bruley both show off their vinous associations. At Lucey, in the Maison de Lorraine, there is a small museum showing how wine used to be made in the area, as well as the typical furnishings and design of a Lorraine house of the seventeenth century. At Bruley there is a *caveau de dégustation* run by a group of growers from each village and offering wines for tasting and sale, again with a small museum of vinous artefacts in restored vaulted cellars.

The future of this isolated vineyard is somewhat uncertain. A few passionate enthusiasts will always ensure its survival, but it is unlikely ever to make an impact outside the region. Michel Laroppe summed up the problem when he said that with 600,000 to a million bottles to sell every year, they are too big for the region and too small for France. There is not enough wine to promote on a national scale, but the good producers will continue to make interesting wines with their own individual characteristics. Certainly a Gris de Toul or the sparkling equivalent is a wonderfully refreshing drink on a warm summer's day. The members of the wine brotherhood, the Confrérie des Compagnons de la Capucine – a *capucine* is a tiny barrel-shaped container filled with wine, which the wine-grower took with him when he was working in the vineyards – swear:

> *Fidelité au vin toulois,*
> *Qu'il soit Aubin, Pinot, Gamay,*
> *Buvons-le frais, plutôt que froid,*
> *Et ne l'abandonnons jamais.*

VIN DE MOSELLE

Even more off the beaten track is Vin de Moselle, a tiny, struggling VDQS near Metz, towards the Luxembourg border. Much of its history is similar to that of Côtes de Toul. The wines were important in the Middle Ages, and Metz Cathedral was built with revenues raised from the vineyards.

In the nineteenth century this was still an important viticultural area. Pinot Noir from the Côte de Metz was used for champagne. Rendu said that the most esteemed wine of the Moselle came from Scy-Chazelle near Metz, where they grew Pinot, Petit Noir and Auxois Gris. Guyot described a few good proprietors who courageously maintained their fine grape varieties. The best wines were from Pinots, Riesling and Meunier, not from the vulgar varieties. It was an area of light, delicate wine that was hygienic and nourishing. In 1871 the region became German and the traditional champagne outlet was blocked, so that Vin de Moselle was used instead for Sekt. Any incentive to produce wines of quality completely disappeared. The nineteenth century also saw the beginning of the Industrial Revolution, with effects more marked in this part of France than in the strongly agricultural areas elsewhere. People sold their vineyards to invest in industry and labour problems developed on the land as people were lured to work in factories. When it came to replanting the vineyards after the phylloxera, the wine-growers of Lorraine made the wrong choice, choosing prolific hybrids instead of quality grape varieties; they ignored the overwhelming competition from the Midi, which was facilitated by the development of the railways.

This is the most northerly of all French vineyards. It is actually closer to the vineyards of Luxembourg than to any other vineyards of France. The climate is not always kind. Frost can be a problem, but the valley of the Moselle provides a suitable microclimate, with a good aspect on south- and south east-facing slopes. Temperatures are the same as in Reims and rainfall is low (except the day I was there). The vintage comes late, after a warm autumn. The vines are planted on slopes and not too low down in the valley, in order to avoid the spring frosts. Nevertheless, to make wine here you have to be dedicated, tenacious or possibly a little eccentric.

Today there are just three small areas of vines for Vin de Moselle. The first is at Vic-sur-Seille north east of Metz, where there is one serious wine-maker, a M. André. Everyone else grows cereals too in the valley of the Seille. More important is the area around Metz, with villages such as Vezon, Ancy-sur-Moselle and Vaux along the Moselle. Thirdly there are vineyards close to the Luxembourg border around Sierck-les-Bains where the grape varieties and methods are more akin to those of Luxembourg than France, and indeed where several vineyards are owned by Luxembourgeois. Müller-Thurgau and Rivaner are grown here, and with Luxembourg interest this area perhaps has more of a future than the other islands of vines in the industrial wastelands around Metz. The area was first delimited in 1951 and again in 1984, to cover a total of about 1,000 hectares in eighteen villages. In fact only about 200 are planted, though there seems to be a slight tendency towards expansion as declining opportunities in industry divert interest to the area's viticultural potential.

Jean Jaspard at Vezon has maintained Burgundian traditions in the Moselle. He learnt to make wine at Chassagne-Montrachet during the Second World War and planted vines on his parents' land on his return. His cellars are rustic, with wooden barrels and one or two steel vats, and he has a basic conception of wine-making: a little chaptalization, and no fining or filtering – he firmly insisted that his wine is natural. He thought it did a malolactic fermentation, but was not too sure. He used a horse, a white mare called Paulette, rather than a tractor, until only about ten years ago, and his treatment of the vines is absolutely traditional. He is against such 'new-fangled' ideas as chemical sprays and so on. His white wine, made from Auxerrois, was rustic, too – light and flowery, with some acidity.

Most dedicated of all was Jean-Marie Diligent, an eccentric history teacher and an idealist. His aim is to resurrect the old viticultural traditions of Lorraine, and he has some money to achieve it. He has bought the château at Vaux outside Metz in the Moselle valley. There were always vines at the château, and when the area was part of Germany there was a Sekt cellar, Weingut Schloss Vaux. So far M.

Diligent has planted 2 hectares of Auxerrois and Pinot Noir, but he also plans Chardonnay, Pinot Blanc, Pinot Gris and some Müller-Thurgau. He is fervently convinced of the possibility of resurrecting the reputation of Vin de Moselle. We talked over a bottle of 1984 Auxerrois which was quite perfumed and flowery, with some crisp acidity. The grapes were picked in November. M. Diligent also dreams of noble rot. He had also had some sparkling wine made for him, by Bernard Massard, the Luxembourg sparkling wine producers.

There is another oasis of vines, Vin de Pays des Côtes de Meuse, about 60 kilometres west of Metz around Vigneuille-lès-Hattan-châtel. The grape varieties are Pinot Noir and Auxerrois and there is little difference from Vin de Moselle.

None of these wines is likely to attain anything more than local interest, but it would be sad if they were to disappear completely under building-sites and fruit trees.

PARIS

It was twenty years after my first visit to Paris that I found the vineyard of Montmartre. Few Parisians are aware of its existence, either. It is one of the few remaining vestiges of the considerable medieval vineyards of the Ile de France. The Clos de Montmartre has been reduced to just 1,800 square metres – a walled garden at the corner of the Rue des Saules and the Rue St-Vincent behind the basilica of the Sacré-Coeur. During the Middle Ages there was an abbey at Montmartre and the first abbess, Adelaide of Savoy, is credited with extending the vineyard over the slopes of Montmartre at the beginning of the twelfth century. At the end of the sixteenth century Henri IV is said to have enjoyed the wine during the siege of Paris. Subsequently the vineyard was greatly reduced, but did offer some resistance to urban encroachments as Montmartre was incorporated into the city of Paris in the nineteenth century.

Between the two World Wars the vineyard was more or less abandoned until the mayor of the 18th *arrondissement* took the initiative and replanted it with 3,247 vines of Chasselas de Thomery, which produce a light *clairet* style of wine. The meagre production of 500 bottles is auctioned every year for local charities. No tasting was available, but hearsay has the wine to be thin and acid.

The vintage at the Clos de Montmartre is an excuse for a local celebration. On the first Saturday in October is the *fête de la vendange*. Most of the grapes have already been picked and they are vinified in the cellars of the local town hall. However, a few symbolic bunches are kept for picking on the day. There are speeches, to which little attention is paid, songs by people who try to sound like Édith Piaf, and processions. The chief participants are members of the wine brotherhoods of many of the other vineyards of France, with a colourful Bacchic figure leading the way. By the end of the afternoon the vines, which already look far from healthy in their struggle against carbon monoxide, are overwhelmed by an invasion of people on their tiny slope, and a good time is had by all.

France is full of unexpected vineyards, though perhaps none more surprising than this one in the heart of the capital. It provides a fitting epilogue to a journey through the lesser-known vineyards of the world's greatest wine country.

APPENDIX I

What is Grown Where

────────

ALIGOTÉ

Alpes-de-Haute-Provence
Bugey
Coteaux du Lyonnais
St-Pourçain
Savoie

CABERNET FRANC

Béarn
Bergerac
Buzet
Charente
Côtes du Brulhois
Côtes de Duras
Côtes de Gascogne
Côtes de la Malepère
Côtes du Marmandais
Côtes de St-Mont
Entraygues
Estaing
Fronton
Gaillac
Haut-Poitou
Hérault
Irouléguy
Lavilledieu
Madiran
Tursan

CABERNET SAUVIGNON

Alpes-de-Haute-Provence
Aude
Béarn
Bergerac
Buzet
Cabardès
Charente
Coteaux d'Aix-en-Provence
Côtes du Brulhois
Côtes de Duras
Côtes de Gascogne
Côtes de la Malepère
Côtes du Marmandais
Côtes de Provence
Côtes de St-Mont
Entraygues
Fronton
Gaillac
Gard
Haut-Poitou
Hérault
Irouléguy
Madiran
Pyrénées-Orientales
Tursan
Var
Vaucluse

CARIGNAN

see Grenache Noir
except Bandol and Bellet

CHARDONNAY

Alpes-de-Haute-Provence
Aude
Bellet
Bouches-du-Rhône
Bugey
Charente
Corsica
Coteaux du Lyonnais
Côtes de Gascogne
Gard
Haut-Poitou
Hérault
Jura
Limoux
Moselle
Puy-de-Dôme
Pyrénées-Orientales
St-Pourçain
Savoie
Urfé
Vaucluse

CHENIN BLANC

Charente
Corsica
Entraygues
Estaing
Hérault
Limoux
Pyrénées-Orientales

CINSAUT

see Grenache

GAMAY

Alpes-de-Haute-Provence
Bugey
Cerdon
Charente
Côte Roannaise
Coteaux du Lyonnais
Côtes d'Auvergne
Côtes du Forez
Côtes du Marmandais
Côtes de Toul
Entraygues
Estaing
Fronton
Gaillac
Glanes
Haut-Poitou
Lavilledieu
Marcillac
St-Pourçain
Savoie
Vaucluse

GRENACHE NOIR

Bandol
Banyuls
Bellet
Cabardès
Cassis
Collioure
Corbières
Corsica
Costières de Nîmes
Coteaux d'Aix-en-Provence
Coteaux du Languedoc
Coteaux de Pierrevert
Coteaux Varois
Côtes du Lubéron
Côtes de la Malepère
Côtes de Provence
Côtes du Roussillon
Fitou

Hérault
Maury
Minervois
Palette
Pyrénées-Orientales
Rivesaltes
Roussillon-Villages

Gaillac
Gard
Glanes
Hérault
Pyrénées-Orientales
Vaucluse

MALBEC–COT–AUXERROIS

Aude
Buzet
Cabardès
Cahors
Côtes du Brulhois
Côtes de Duras
Côtes de la Malcpère
Côtes du Marmandais
Fronton
Hérault
Pécharmant

MARSANNE

Aude
Cassis
Costières de Nîmes
Coteaux de Pierrevert
Hérault

MERLOT

Alpes-de-Haute-Provence
Aude
Bergerac
Buzet
Cabardès
Cahors
Charente
Côtes de Brulhois
Côtes de Duras
Côtes de Gascogne
Côtes de la Malepère
Côtes du Marmandais

MOURVÈDRE

Bandol
Banyuls
Cabardès
Cassis
Collioure
Corbières
Costières de Nîmes
Coteaux d'Aix-en-Provence
Coteaux du Languedoc
Coteaux de Pierrevert
Coteaux Varois
Côtes du Lubéron
Côtes de Provence
Côtes du Roussillon
Fitou
Hérault
Minervois
Palette
Roussillon-Villages

PINOT NOIR

Alpes-de-Haute-Provence
Aude
Bugey
Cerdon
Côte Roannaise
Côtes d'Auvergne
Côtes de Toul
Hérault
Jura
Moselle
St-Pourçain
Savoie

SAUVIGNON

Aude
Bandol
Bergerac
Bouches-du-Rhône
Buzet
Cassis
Charente
Coteaux d'Aix-en-Provence
Côtes de Duras
Côtes de Gascogne
Côtes du Marmandais
Côtes de Provence
Gaillac
Haut-Poitou
Hérault
Monbazillac
Pacherenc de Vic-Bihl
Pyrénées-Orientales
St-Pourçain
Tursan
Vaucluse

SÉMILLON

Bergerac
Buzet
Charente
Coteaux d'Aix-en-Provence
Côtes de Duras
Côtes du Marmandais
Côtes de Provence
Gaillac
Monbazillac
Pacherenc de Vic-Bihl

SYRAH

Aude
Banyuls

Cabardès
Collioure
Corbières
Corsica
Costières de Nímes
Coteaux d'Aix-en-Provence
Coteaux du Languedoc
Coteaux de Pierrevert
Coteaux Varois
Côtes du Lubéron
Côtes de la Malepère
Côtes du Marmandais
Côtes de Provence
Côtes du Roussillon
Fitou
Fronton
Gaillac
Hérault
Lavilledieu
Minervois
Pyrénées-Orientales
Roussillon-Villages

UGNI BLANC

Aude
Bandol
Cassis
Charente
Corsica
Costières de Nímes
Coteaux d'Aix-en-Provence
Coteaux de Pierrevert
Côtes de Duras
Côtes de Gascogne
Côtes du Lubéron
Côtes du Marmandais
Côtes de Provence
Hérault
Palette
Pyrénées-Orientales

Outline List of Vins de Pays

AGENAIS from Lot-et-Garonne; covers the appellations of Côtes de Duras and Côtes du Marmandais, from similar grape varieties.

AIN vineyards near Seyssel; very similar to the wines of Bugey.

ALLOBROGIE covers vineyards in Ain, Savoie and Haute-Savoie, and makes mainly white wine from Jacquère, in a light Savoy style.

ALPES-DE-HAUTE-PROVENCE covers that department, notably the experimental wines of the Coteaux de Pierrevert and France's highest vineyards around Digne and Gap.

ALPES-MARITIMES covers that department and comes from the traditional Provençal grape varieties, including Rolle for white wines.

ARDAILHOU from the coastal area of Hérault; mainly red, from traditional Midi grape varieties.

ARDÈCHE covers the whole department to the east of the Rhône valley and is based on Gamay, Syrah and Chardonnay.

ARGENS from Provence, covering the valley of the Argens river in the department of Var, making mainly red and some pink wine from the usual Provençal grape varieties.

AUDE covers the whole department, coming from both traditional Midi and innovatory grape varieties.

BALMES DAUPHINOISES from the department of Isère; consists of reds from Gamay and whites from Jacquère. *Balme* is a dialect word for 'valley'.

BÉNOVIE one of the many *vins de pays* of Hérault, from vineyards around the village of St-Christol. Bénovie is the name of a small stream that crosses the area.

BÉRANGE comes from Hérault, around Lunel, and is made from traditional grape varieties.

BESSAN from Hérault, around the town of that name; made from the usual Midi grape varieties.

BIGORRE covers red wine from young vines within the appellation of Madiran.

BOUCHES-DU-RHÔNE covers the whole department, including the three large areas of the Coteaux d'Aix-en-Provence, the Côtes de Provence and the Camargue.

BOURBONNAIS comes from the department of Allier and from the same grape varieties as St-Pourçain, but in practice is rarely found.

CASSAN from Hérault; takes its name from the old abbey of Cassan, but in practice is rarely seen.

CATALAN from Pyrénées-Orientales, south and west of Perpignan; made from both traditional and experimental grape varieties.

CAUX from Hérault, around the village of that name in the Coteaux du Languedoc.

CESSENON from Hérault; makes mainly red wines from traditional Midi grape varieties, within the appellation of Coteaux du Languedoc.

CHARENTAIS born of the surplus of wine for Cognac; covers the whole of Charente and Charente-Maritime.

CHER covers that department in the Loire valley, with white wines from Sauvignon and red wines from Gamay.

COLLINES DE LA MOURE in Hérault, in the hills behind Sète and Montpellier. The Abbaye de Valmagne is one of the best producers.

COLLINES RHODANIENNES comes from the northern part of the Rhône valley, and stretches across the departments of Isère, Loire, Ardèche, Rhône and Drôme; uses all the grape varieties traditional to those areas.

COMTÉ DE GRIGNAN from the department of Drôme; name inspired by the Château de Grignan. The wines resemble a light Côtes du Rhône.

COMTÉ TOLOSAN covers several department of the south west, namely Haute-Garonne, Gers, Pyrénées-Atlantiques, Tarn and Tarn-et-Garonne, centred on the city of Toulouse; uses any of the many grape varieties of the south west.

CONDOMOIS red and white wines from around the town of Condom in Gers.

CÔTE VERMEILLE one of the newer *vins de pays*, covering vineyards on the coast of Roussillon around Banyuls and Collioure.

COTEAUX DE L'ARDÈCHE from the southern half of the department of Ardèche; very similar to the departmental *vin de pays*, with traditional Rhône grape varieties, plus Chardonnay, Cabernet Sauvignon and Merlot as *cépages améliorateurs*.

COTEAUX DES BARONNIES from the department of Drôme in the southern Rhône; mainly red from traditional grape varieties, with some white from Chardonnay.

COTEAUX DE BESSILLES one of the newer *vins de pays*, from vineyards near Montagnac in Hérault.

COTEAUX DE LA CABRERISSE from Aude, within part of the appellation of Corbières, with similar grape varieties.

COTEAUX CÉVENOLS comes from the foothills of the Cévennes in Gard, north east of Alès.

COTEAUX DE CÈZE comes from the north east part of Gard, from vineyards along the banks of the Rhône which produce a lighter version of Côtes du Rhône.

COTEAUX CHARITOIS comes from Nièvre, with white wines from Sauvignon and Chardonnay and reds mainly from Gamay.

COTEAUX DU CHER ET DE L'ARNON comes from vineyards adjoining the appellations of Reuilly and Quincy in the Loire valley.

COTEAUX DE LA CITÉ DE CARCASSONNE from Aude; comes from vineyards near the medieval city, close to Cabardès.

COTEAUX D'ENSÉRUNE from Hérault, east of Béziers, with mainly red and pink wine from the usual Midi grape varieties, enlivened by some Syrah and Cabernet Sauvignon.

COTEAUX DES FENOUILLÈDES from Pyrénées-Orientales; makes wines similar to a light Côtes du Roussillon.

COTEAUX FLAVIENS covers vineyards south of Nîmes in the Costières de Nîmes, from grape varieties of that appellation.

COTEAUX DE FONTCAUDE from Hérault, west of Béziers, around the abbey of Fontcaude, within the appellation of St-Chinian.

COTEAUX DE GLANES an island of vines in the northern part of the department of Lot, made from Merlot and Gamay.

COTEAUX DU GRÉSIVAUDAN from the departments of Isère and Savoie, around Grenoble; mainly white from Jacquère.

COTEAUX DE LAURENS from Hérault, north of Béziers, with the usual grape varieties of the Midi as well as some *cépages améliorateurs*.

COTEAUX DU LÉZIGNANAIS from around the town of Lézignan in Aude; made from the traditional grape varieties of the Midi.

COTEAUX DU LIBRON comes from Hérault, north of Béziers, where the vineyards are crossed by the River Libron. The grape varieties are those traditional to the Midi, with some *cépages améliorateurs*.

COTEAUX DU LITTORAL AUDOIS comes, as the name implies, from the coastal region of Aude.

COTEAUX DE MIRAMONT a traditional wine of Aude, east of Carcassonne, making a lighter style of Minervois.

COTEAUX ET TERRASSES DE MONTAUBAN comes from the hills around Montauban in Tarn-et-Garonne. The main producer is the co-operative at Lavilledieu.

COTEAUX DE MURVIEL comes from vineyards around the town of Murviel-lès-Béziers, within the appellation of St-Chinian.

COTEAUX DE NARBONNE around Narbonne in Aude; includes some vineyards within the appellation of La Clape.

COTEAUX DE PEYRIAC   covers a large part of the appellation of Minervois and is made from similar grape varieties.

COTEAUX DU PONT DU GARD   comes, as the name implies, from vineyards around the famous Roman aqueduct; uses grape varieties traditional to Gard.

COTEAUX DE QUERCY   one of the better *vins de pays* of the south west, from the southern part of Lot and northern part of Tarn-et-Garonne; uses the traditional grape varieties of the south west.

COTEAUX DU SALAGOU   comes from near Lake Salagou in Hérault and has a tiny production from traditional Midi grape varieties.

COTEAUX DU SALAVÈS   from the department of Gard, east of Nîmes; made from the traditional grape varieties of Languedoc.

COTEAUX DU TERMENÈS   one of the many *vins de pays* of Aude, from the centre of the department; in practice, rarely seen.

CÔTES DE BRIAN   from Hérault; named after the river in the south west of the department. Grape varieties are traditional.

CÔTES CATALANES   from the north east part of the department of Pyrénées-Orientales; makes a lighter-style Côtes du Roussillon.

CÔTES DE CERESSOU   from Hérault; covers vineyards of the Coteaux du Languedoc.

CÔTES DE GASCOGNE   covers the Armagnac area.

CÔTES DE LASTOURS   from Aude, using traditional Midi grape varieties.

CÔTES DE MONTESTRUC   a disappearing *vin de pays* from vineyards around the town of Montestruc in the Armagnac region of Gascony.

CÔTES DE PÉRIGNAN   from Aude, close to the appellation of La Clape.

CÔTES DE LA PROUILLE   from Aude; planted with the same grape varieties as for Côtes de la Malepère.

CÔTES DU TARN   covers the appellation of Gaillac, producing similar wines, notably whites from Mauzac.

CÔTES DE THAU   covers vineyards around the Etang de Thau in Hérault, with both traditional varieties and some successful experimentation, notably for white wines.

CÔTES DE THONGUE   one of the many *vins de pays* of Hérault, from the centre of the department; as well as traditional grape varieties, there is some successful experimentation.

CÔTES DU VIDOURLE   from the valley of the Vidourle in Gard, west of Nîmes. The grape varieties are those traditional to Languedoc.

CUCUGNAN   from Hérault; mainly red from the traditional grape varieties of the Midi, produced by the co-operative of Cucugnan.

DEUX-SÈVRES   from the Loire valley department of the same name; made from grape varieties traditional to the area.

DORDOGNE   comes from the same grape varieties as Bergerac.

DRÔME   covers the department of that name on the east bank of the Rhône and is mainly red from Syrah, with some Grenache and Cinsaut, and is similar to Coteaux du Tricastin.

FRANCHE-COMTÉ   covers the departments of Haute-Savoie and Jura. The white comes from Chardonnay and Auxerrois, and the red and pink from Pinot Noir and Gamay.

GARD   covers the whole department, making a lighter style of Costières de Nîmes from the grape varieties of the Midi.

GIRONDE   concentrated in the northern part of the department, with wines made from Colombard and Ugni Blanc; more akin to the neighbouring Vin de Pays Charentais than to Bordeaux.

GORGES DE L'HÉRAULT   as the name implies, comes from the dramatic region of gorges in the northern part of the department. Grape varieties are traditional.

GORGES ET CÔTES DE MILLAU   made by a co-operative at Aguessac on the banks of the Tarn above Millau; comes mainly from Gamay and Syrah.

HAUTE-GARONNE   a departmental wine, covering Fronton and other small parcels of vines.

HAUTERIVE-EN-PAYS-D'AUDE   one of the many *vins de pays* of Aude; comes from south of Narbonne, with mainly red wines made from the usual Midi grape varieties.

HAUTE VALLÉE DE L'AUDE   from the Limoux area of Aude, is mainly red made from traditional Midi grape varieties and from introductions from the south west.

HAUTE VALLÉE DE L'ORB   one of the many *vins de pays* of Hérault, from vineyards in the valley of the Orb; in practice, rarely seen.

HAUTS DE BADENS   from the village of Badens in Aude, in the appellation of Minervois; mainly red, produced in a small quantity from traditional grape varieties.

HÉRAULT   covers the whole department, and is produced both from traditional Midi and from innovatory grape varieties.

ILE DE BEAUTÉ   covers the whole of Corsica and includes innovatory as well as traditional grape varieties.

INDRE   covers the department of that name in the Loire valley, with wines from the traditional Loire grape varieties.

INDRE-ET-LOIRE   covers that department, with red, white and pink wines from the traditional Loire grape varieties.

JARDIN DE LA FRANCE   covers the whole of the Loire valley, including the departments of Cher, Indre, Indre-et-Loire, Loir-et-Cher, Loire-Atlantique, Loiret, Maine-et-Loire, Deux-Sèvres, Vendée, Vienne and Haute-Vienne; uses all the grape varieties of the region, though Sauvignon and Gamay are the most successful.

LANDES   a departmental *vin de pays* covering pockets of vines in the pine forests of the south west, in particular around Tursan; uses traditional south west grape varieties.

LOIRE-ATLANTIQUE one of the departmental *vin de pays* of the Loire valley, making an inferior Muscadet from the same grape variety.

LOIRET one of the departmental *vins de pays* of the Loire valley, with vineyards mainly around the towns of Orléans and Gien.

LOIR-ET-CHER covers the whole department of that name, especially around the châteaux of Blois and Chambord, with red, white and pink wines from traditional Loire grape varieties.

MAINE-ET-LOIRE one of the departmental *vins de pays* of the Loire valley, with wines from the same grape varieties as the appellation Anjou.

MARCHES DE BRETAGNE from the Atlantic end of the Loire valley, south of Ancenis and Nantes; mainly white wine with a small amount of red.

MAURES covers the southern part of the department of Var, between St-Tropez and St-Raphaël; mainly red from Provençal grape varieties.

MEUSE from the department of that name in northern France; red and pink or *gris* from Pinot Noir and Gamay, and white from Auxerrois, Aligoté and Chardonnay.

MONT BAUDILE from Hérault; takes its name from the mountain that dominates the skyline near Montpeyroux. The wine is mainly red from traditional Midi grape varieties.

MONT BOUQUET from Gard, south east of Alès; mainly red wine from traditional grape varieties, plus some experimental plantings of Merlot and Cabernet Sauvignon.

MONT CAUME comes from Var, from vineyards around Bandol; made from Provençal and some experimental grape varieties.

MONTS DE LA GRAGE from the western part of Hérault, around St-Chinian; made from traditional grape varieties, improved by some Syrah.

NIÈVRE one of the departmental *vins de pays* of the Loire valley, with vineyards mainly around La Charité-sur-Loire and Tannay.

OC covers the whole of the Midi, including Aude, Gard, Hérault, Pyrénées-Orientales, as well as Ardèche, Bouches-du-Rhône, Var and Vaucluse. The grape varieties are all those allowed within that area.

PETITE CRAU from the northern part of Bouches-du-Rhône, around St-Rémy-en-Provence; uses the usual Rhône grape varieties.

PÉZENAS comes from vineyards around the town of the same name in Hérault, and uses grape varieties traditional to the Midi.

PRINCIPAUTÉ D'ORANGE from the department of Vaucluse in the southern Rhône; comes from typical Rhône grape varieties to make a feebler Côtes du Rhône.

PUY-DE-DÔME covers vineyards around the city of Clermont-Ferrand that are not included within Côtes d'Auvergne. Production is tiny.

PYRÉNÉES-ATLANTIQUES covers the whole department of that name, notably vineyards around Jurançon and Madiran, being made from the same grape varieties as those appellations.

PYRÉNÉES-ORIENTALES   comes from all over the department of that name, from the same grape varieties as Côtes du Roussillon, with some experimentation.

RETZ   covers the area south of the mouth of the Loire; mainly pink wine from Grolleau, with a little red from Cabernet Franc.

SABLES DU GOLFE DU LION   covers the coastal dunes of the Gulf of Lions, stretching across the departments of Bouches-du-Rhône, Gard and Hérault. Les Salins du Midi is the principal producer.

ST-SARDOS   comes from vineyards in Tarn-et-Garonne and Haute-Garonne, around the town of St-Sardos near Montauban. The wine is mainly red from the traditional grape varieties of the south west.

SARTHE   one of the departmental *vins de pays* of the Loire valley; very limited production, from Chenin Blanc.

SERRE DU COIRAN   comes from Gard, south east of Nîmes; now called Vin de Pays des Côtes de Libac, after a river in the area, and made from traditional Midi grape varieties, it resembles a light Costières de Nîmes.

TARN-ET-GARONNE   covers the department of that name in south west France, making mainly red wine from the grape varieties of the south west.

TERROIRS LANDAIS   a more strictly defined version of Vin de Pays des Landes, covering vineyards in the valley of the Adour, on the Coteaux de Chalosse, the Sables Fauves and the Sables de l'Océan. The grape varieties are those of the south west.

THÉZARD-PERRICARD   the newest *vin de pays*, from near Agen in Lot-et-Garonne; only red, from Cabernet, Merlot and Tannat.

TORGAN   has replaced Coteaux Cathares and is one of the *vins de pays* of Aude, resembling a lighter version of Corbières.

URFÉ   takes its name from the Château d'Urfé and covers the two VDQS of Côte Roannaise and Côtes du Forez.

UZÈGE   from Gard; centred on the attractive town of Uzès north of Nîmes, with wines from traditional Midi grape varieties.

VAL DE CESSE   comes from the department of Aude, making a lighter style of Minervois; includes some experimental Cabernet and Merlot.

VAL DE DAGNE   covers vineyards in Aude, south east of Carcassonne; makes a lighter style of Corbières, and includes some Cabernet and Merlot.

VAL DE MONTFERRAND   covers the northern part of Hérault, producing mainly red wine from traditional grape varieties.

VAL D'ORBIEU   from the eastern part of the department of Aude; produces mainly red wine from traditional Midi grape varieties.

VALLÉE DU PARADIS   a wine with a wonderfully evocative name from the valley otherwise known as that of the Berre, in the Corbières part of Aude.

VALS D'AGLY   from Pyrénées-Orientales; makes a lighter style of Côtes du Roussillon from vineyards in the river valleys.

VAR   covers the department of that name, with vineyards mainly in the north, and produces red wine and some pink from traditional Provençal grape varieties.

VAUCLUSE   covers the department of that name at the southern end of the Rhône, and produces wines similar to Côtes du Rhône and Côtes du Lubéron.

VAUNAGE   comes from north west of Nîmes; produced by growers who also make Coteaux du Languedoc, using the typical Midi grape varieties and some new introductions.

VENDÉE   covers the department of that name and is very similar to the VDQS of Fiefs Vendéens.

VICOMTÉ D'AUMÉLAS   from Hérault; comes from thirteen villages which in the twelfth century belonged to the Vicomte d'Aumélas. A mixture of Midi and south west grape varieties is grown.

VIENNE   one of the departmental *vins de pays* of the Loire valley, with a tiny production of wine that is similar to Haut-Poitou.

VISTRENQUE   a tiny area in the north east corner of Gard, on the plain of the Vistre, producing wine from traditional Midi grape varieties.

YONNE   covers the department of that name and can be used for wine from young Chardonnay vines that will eventually produce Chablis.

Glossary

Most of the viticultural and wine-making terms are explained in the introductory chapter. However, a few words that occur elsewhere in the text may remain unaccounted for.

BOURRUT   the new wine that has not quite finished fermenting, so that it still retains at least 10 grams of sugar per litre. It tastes slightly sweet and is dangerously drinkable.

CAUSSES   a term used in Cahors to describe the arid plateau above the valley of the Lot.

CÉPAGE   a grape variety; so *vin de cépage* is a varietal wine, and the *encépagement* is the mixture of grape varieties allowed in a wine. A *cépage améliorateur* is one which is imported from another area to improve the quality of a blend.

CLAIRET   a light red wine.

GARRIGUES   the term used in the Midi to describe the wild scrub in the foothills of the Massif Central. In many areas it is now being cleared for vineyards.

LIQUOREUX   descriptive of a very sweet wine such as Monbazillac.

MOELLEUX   descriptive of a medium-sweet wine, as in Jurançon, rather than a very sweet one.

RANCIO   descriptive of the oxidized taste of fortified wine.

SOLERA   a system for ageing fortified wine, in particular sherry. The barrels of wine are arranged in a series of scales or tiers, each containing the same style of wine, with each scale younger than the last. As the wine is drawn off from the oldest barrels, they are refreshed with a slightly younger wine. The *solera* system depends upon the fact that the younger wine takes on the characteristics of the older.

VÉRAISON   during the ripening process the grapes reach a point when they turn colour, so that black grapes are no longer green and white grapes become golden. This is called the *véraison*.

VIANDÉ   translates literally as 'meaty' and is descriptive of the typical taste and smell of the Mourvèdre grape, with its animal overtones.

VIN DE PAILLE   literally 'straw wine', made notably in the Jura, from grapes that have been dried (traditionally on straw mats).

Abbreviations

ANTAV   Association Nationale Technique pour l'Amélioration de la Viticulture
CIVAM   Centre d'Information et de Vulgarisation pour L'Agriculture et le Milieu Rural
GAEC   Groupement Agricole d'Exploitation en Commun
GICB   Groupement Interproducteurs du Cru Banyuls
INAO   Institut d'Appellation d'Origine
INRA   Institut National de la Recherche Agronomique
ONIVIT   Office National Interprofessionnel des Vins
SAFER   Société d'Aménagement Foncier d'Etablissement Rural
SICAREX   Societé d'Intérêt Collectif Agricole des Recherches Expérimentales
UCCOAR   Union des Caves Coopératives de l'Ouest Audois et du Razès
UCOVIP   Union Coopérative Vinicole du Pic St-Loup
UVAL   Union des Vignerons de l'Ile de Beauté
VDQS   Vin Délimité de Qualité Supérieure

Bibliography

Asher, Gerald, *On Wine*, Jill Norman and Hobhouse, London, 1983

Baillaud, Robert, and Clavel, Jean, *Histoire et Avenir des vins en Languedoc*, Privat, Toulouse, 1985

Baudel, José, *Le Vin de Cahors*, Luzech, 1977

Boissieu, Jean et al., *Les Vins du Rhône et de la Méditerranée*, Éditions Montalba, Paris, 1978

Brown, Michael and Sybil, *Food and Wine of South West France*, Batsford, London, 1980

Busby, James, *A Tour through some Vineyards*, 1833

Capdeville, Pierre, and Nespoulous, Jean-Louis, *Le Vin de Cahors des origines à nos jours*, Éditions Milan, Toulouse, 1983

Casamayor, Pierre, *Vins du Sud-Ouest et des Pyrénées*, Éditions Daniel Briand/Robert Laffont, Toulouse, 1983

Cavoleau, Jean-Alexandre, *Œnologie française*, Paris, 1927

Dion, Roger, *Histoire de la Vigne et du Vin en France des origines au XIXe siècle*, Flammarion, Paris, 1959

Dorozynski, Alexandre, *Les Vins des Alpilles*, Éditions Barthélemy, Avignon

Duyker, Hubrecht, *Grands Vins du Rhône et du Midi*, Nathan, Paris, 1985

Enjalbert, Henri, *Un vignoble de qualité en Languedoc*, 1985

Girel, Roger, *Le Vignoble savoyard et ses vins*, Glénat, Grenoble, 1985

Guyot, Jules, *Études des vignobles de France*, Paris, 1868

Imbert, Christian, *Historique de la Vigne en Corse*, 1984

Jullien, André, *Topographie des vins de France*, Paris, 1816

Lichine, Alexis, *The Wines of France*, Cassell, London, 1952
  Guide to the Wines and Vineyards of France, 3rd edn, Papermac, London, 1985

Mouillefert, *Les Vignobles et les Vins de France*, 1891

Office interprofessionel des vins, *Les Vins de pays, une tradition nouvelle*

Pomerol, Charles (ed.), *Terroirs et Vins de France*, Total-Édition-Presse, Paris, 1984

386

BIBLIOGRAPHY

Puel, Hugues, *Gaillac AOC, Vignoble singulier à déguster au pluriel!*
Redding, Cyrus, *A History and Description of Modern Wines*, Whittaker, Treacher and Arnot, London, 1833
Rendu, Victor, *Ampélographie française*, Paris, 1857
Réol, Jean, *Le Vignoble de Gaillac*, Paris, 1910
Robinson, Jancis, *Vines, Grapes and Wines*, Mitchell Beazley, London, 1986
Rouget, *Les Vignobles du Jura*, 1897
Seward, Desmond, *Monks and Wine*, Mitchell Beazley, London, 1979
Shand, P. Morton (revised and edited by Cyril Ray), *A Book of French Wines*, Penguin, Harmondsworth, 1968
Spurrier, Steven, *French Country Wines*, Collins, London, 1984
Vizetelly, Henry, *The Wines of France*, 1908
Weston, Michael, *Where the Mistral Blows*, Wine and Spirit Publications, London, 1981

Index

Abbaye de St-Hilaire, 231
Abymes, 329–31, 343
Adissan, 190
Agde, 117, 230
Agen, 38, 43, 62
Aignan, 82
Aigues Mortes, 231, 234
Aix-en-Provence, 240, 255, 272
Ajaccio, 291, 292, 293–4, 298
Alaigne, 181, 182
Albas, 47
Albi, 69, 71–2, 198
Albignieux, 344
Aléria, 298–9
Ambierlé, 311
Ancy-sur-Moselle, 368
Anglefort, 344
Anhaux, 113–14
Antignac, 204
Appietto, 293–4
Apremont, 329–31, 343
Apt, 240
Aragon, 185
Arbin, 332
Arbois, 244, 349, 352, 356–9, 360
Arlay, 355, 361
Armagnac, 9, 80, 81, 82–3
Aspiran, 190
Association des Crus de la Côte d'Azur, 271
Association Nationale Technique pour
 l'Amélioration de la Viticulture,
 (ANTAV), 126
Auchan, 124
Ayze, 338–9
Azillanet, 167

Bages, 159
Baixas, 144
Bandol, 1, 171, 189, 240, 246–55
Banyuls, 133, 134, 140, 143, 149–54
Banyuls-sur-Mer, 134, 149
Béarn, 9, 93, 103, 115–16
Beaujolais, 311, 323, 325
Beaupuy, 36–7
Bellegarde, 238
Bellet, 240, 258–61, 271, 292
Bellocq, 115–16

Bergerac, 8, 9, 15–19, 21, 24–7
Bergerac Rosé, 21, 27
Bergerac Rouge, 27
Bergerac Sec, 24, 26, 27
Berlou, 199–201
Besson, 320
Billième, 334
Blanquette de Limoux, 176–81
Blaslay, 13
Boën-sur-Lignon, 309
Boudes, 313, 316–17
Bourgueil, 14
Boutenac, 161, 165
Brantôme, 19
Brignoles, 280, 282
Briorde, 346
Broze, 72
Bruejouls, 91
Bruley, 364, 365, 366
Bugey, 342–8
Buzet, 8, 9, 35, 38–42

Cabardès, 167, 184–6
Cabrières, 187, 190, 208
Cahors, 1, 8, 9, 42–62
Cahusac-sur-Vère, 72
Calvi, 291, 304–6
Camplong d'Aude, 159
Caramany, 134, 135
Carcassonne, 176, 181
Cascastel, 155
Casinca, 299
Casino, 124
Cassagnes, 135
Cassis, 240, 241–6, 271, 356
Castanet, 72
Castelmaure, 159, 160
Castelnau, 108
Castelnau-de-Guers, 207
Castelnau-Rivière-Basse, 106
Castelreng, 176
Castel Roubine, 263
Caunes Minervois, 167
Caveau Bacchus, 358
Caveau Bugiste, 344
Cave Co-opérative de Bellegarde, 238
Cave Co-opérative de Chautagne, 333

Cave Co-opérative de Duras, 31–2
Cave Co-opérative d'Embrès et de Castelmaure, 161
Cave Co-opérative de Gan, 97, 99
Cave Co-opérative de Labastide-de-Levis, 75–6
Cave Co-opérative de Limoux, 178
Cave Co-opérative de Monbazillac, 20
Cave Co-opérative de Pinet, 207
Cave Co-opérative des Producteurs de Mont Tauch, 156
Cave Co-opérative de St-Gilles, 235–6
Cave Co-opérative de St-Mathieu-de-Tréviers, 213
Cave Co-opérative de St-Mont, 112–13
Cave Co-opérative de St-Saturnin, 209
Cave Co-opérative de Salies-de-Béarn-Bellocq, 115
Cave Co-opérative de Técou, 76
Cave Co-opérative de Vignerons Foréziens, 307
Cave Co-opérative du Haut-Poitou, 12
Cave de Berlou, 199
Cave des Vignerons de St-Pourçain, 321
Cave Poquet, 296
Cave Rabelais, 222
Caves de Treilles, 155
Caves d'Olt, 51–2
Caves St-Antoine, 56
Cazes Frères, 139–40
Cellier de Marrenon, 284
Cellier des Templiers, 152
Centre d'Information et de Vulgarisation pour l'Agriculture et le Milieu Rural (CIVAM), 292, 303
Cerbère, 149–50
Cerdon, 344, 346–8
Cerveyvieux, 343
Cestayrols, 72
Ceyrac, 190
Chablis, 49
Chambre de l'Agriculture de l'Aude, 182
Champlitte, 362
Chanay, 344
Chandrieux, 333
Chantelle, 320
Chantovent, 170
Chanturgues, 313, 315–16
Château Arricau-Boudes, 109
Château Ausone, 16
Château Belingard, 25–7
Château Bellevue-la-Forêt, 67
Château Boucassé, 107
Château Boudigand, 25
Château Caix, 52
Château Calissanne, 277
Château Cayrou d'Albas, 52
Château-Chalon, 349, 351, 352–6
Château Chasse-Spleen, 169
Château Chayne, 25
Château Coujan, 201
Château Court-les-Mûts, 28
Château d'Agié, 62
Château d'Aguilar, 156

Château d'Arboras, 210
Château d'Arlay, 360–1
Château d'Aydie, 108, 109
Château de Barbeyrolles, 271
Château de Bellet, 259–61
Château de Bouchet, 41
Château de Cabriac, 186
Château de Caix, 61
Château de Campuget, 236–7
Château de Castelmaure, 161
Château de Chambert, 56–7, 61
Château de Corneilla, 136
Château de Craussac, 67
Château de Crémat, 259, 260–1
Château de Duras, 34
Château de Flaugergues, 214
Château de Fonscolombe, 278–9
Château de Gourgazaud, 170
Château de Grammont, 214
Château de Gréa, 360
Château de Grezel, 54
Château de Gueyze, 41
Château de Haut-Fabrègues, 205
Château de Jau, 138–9
Château de Jonquières, 210
Château de la Crémade, 255
Château de la Peyrade, 220
Château de l'Étoile, 352
Château de Malviès, 183, 184
Château de Mercuès, 52
Château de Mille, 284
Château de Monbazillac, 21
Château de Monterminod, 336
Château de Montferrand, 213
Château de Montfort, 357
Château de Moujan, 227
Château de Notre-Dame-de-Quatourze, 192–3
Château de Nouvelles 156–7
Château de Pamplonne, 267
Château de Paraza, 173
Château de Parnac, 52
Château de Pau, 95
Château de Paulignan, 168, 173
Château de Rasque, 270
Château de Rayssac, 186
Château de Ripaille, 340–1
Château de Routier, 183
Château de Rozier, 237
Château de Selle, 263, 264, 267–8
Château des Bouysses, 52, 61
Château du Cayrou, 54
Château du Grès-St-Paul, 217
Château Fabas, 172
Château Grillet, 256
Château Haute-Serre, 49, 52–3, 61
Château Isolette, 284
Château Jolys, 97, 98, 101
Château Jonquières, 124
Château La Baronne, 163
Château La Bastide, 37, 63
Château La Brie, 21
Château La Canorgue, 284–5
Château Lafite, 34

Château La Gordonne, 231
Château Lagrange, 173
Château Lagrezette, 52, 61
Château la Jaubertie, 24–5
Château La Lagune, 273
Château La Liguière, 204
Château La Plante, 27
Château La Rouquette-sur-Mer, 195–6
Château Larroze, 74–5
Château Lastours, 78
Château les Astous, 100
Château Margaux, 57, 107, 226
Château Marguerite, 67
Château Marsalet, 21
Château Minuty, 263, 264, 266, 270–1
Château Montus, 107
Château Moujan, 196–7
Château Mouton-Rothschild, 20
Château Nalys, 196
Château Pennautier, 185–6
Château Pion, 21
Château Puypezat, 28
Château Renaudie, 21
Château Romassan, 253, 267
Château St-André de Figuère, 271
Château St-Auréol, 164
Château St-Didier, 53–4
Château St-Martin, 263
Château St-Mayne, 25
Château Ste-Rosaline, 263, 264, 265, 270
Château Septy, 21
Château Simone, 240, 255–8
Château Tiregand, 19–20, 198
Château Treilles, 61
Château Treuil de Nailhac, 22–3
Château Val Joanis, 286–7
Château Vannières, 249, 254–5
Château Vignelaure, 273–5
Châteaugay, 313, 315–16
Châteauneuf-du-Pape, 196, 215, 239, 244, 278, 286, 356
Chautagne, 328, 333–4
Cheignien-la-Balme, 345
Chignin-Bergeron, 331–2
Chinon, 14
Claira, 143
Clairet de Pierrevert, 283
Clairette de Bellegarde, 233, 235, 238, 249
Clairette du Languedoc, 187, 190–2, 208
Clairvaux, 91
Clos Cibonne, 263
Clos de Gamot, 54–5
Clos de la Bernarde, 269–70
Clos de la Coutale, 58–9, 61
Clos de Montmartre, 369–70
Clos de Morta Maio, 303–4
Clos du Pech de Jammes, 52
Clos du Relars, 263
Clos Fontindoule, 21–2
Clos Joliette, 98, 103
Clos Landry, 305
Clos Mireille, 263–4, 265, 267, 268–9
Clos Nicrosi, 300
Clos Reginu, 305

Clos Triguedina, 56, 61
Clos Uroulat, 101
Cocumont, 36–7
Cognac, 9, 80–1
Collioure, 133, 134, 140, 149–54
Colombier, 21
Combe de Savoie, 329–33
Comigne, 159
Comité Interprofessionnel des Côtes de Provence, 272
Comité Interprofessionel des Vins du Région de Bergerac, 28
Commanderie de la Peyrassol, 271
Condom, 81, 83
Confrérie des Compagnons de la Capucine, 366
Corbières, 124, 129, 144, 147, 158–65, 186
Corbières Centrales, 159
Corbières du Roussillon, 134
Corbières-Maritimes, 159
Corbières Supérieures du Roussillon, 134
Cordes, 71, 75
Corent, 313, 314–15
Corneilla, 136
Costières de Nîmes, 233–9
Costières du Gard, 234, 235, 237, 239
Côte de Metz, 367
Côte d'Hyot, 338
Côte Roannaise, 307, 310–13
Côte Rôtie, 323, 325
Côte St-Pierre, 42
Coteaux d'Aix-en-Provence, 240, 256, 271, 272–80
Coteaux d'Ajaccio, 291
Coteaux de Cap Corse, 300–301
Coteaux de la Méjanelle, 187, 214–15
Coteaux de l'Aude, 172
Coteaux de Peyriac, 172
Coteaux de Pierrevert, 241, 282–4
Coteaux de Quercy, 64
Coteaux de Vérargues, 187, 216–17
Coteaux des Baux, 240, 273, 275–6, 280
Coteaux des Ferrages, 263
Coteaux du Cap Corse, 291
Coteaux du Languedoc, 124, 126–30, 187–90, 191–2, 207, 210, 217, 234, 235, 282
Coteaux du Lyonnais, 323–5
Coteaux du Roy René, 272
Coteaux et Terrasses de Montauban, 64
Coteaux Varois, 231, 240, 264, 280–2
Côtes d'Auvergne, 307, 313–18
Côtes de Bergerac, 19, 21, 24
Côtes de Bergerac Moelleux, 24, 27, 28
Côtes de Buzet, 39–40
Côtes de Castillon, 27
Côtes de Ceressou, 192
Côtes de Duras, 8, 30–4
Côtes de la Malepère, 176, 181–4, 185
Côtes de Montravel, 29
Côtes de Provence, 231, 240, 256, 261, 262–72, 282
Côtes de St-Mont, 9, 106, 111–13
Côtes de Thongue, 192

Côtes de Toul, 363–7
Côtes du Brulhois, 8, 62–3
Côtes de Cabardès et de l'Orbiel, 185
Côtes du Forez, 307–10
Côtes du Frontonnais, 65–9
Côtes du Jura, 349, 352, 359–62
Côtes du Lubéron, 240, 282, 283, 284–7
Côtes du Marmandais, 8, 33, 34–7, 49
Côtes du Rhône, 237, 285, 296
Côtes du Rhône-Villages, 271
Côtes du Roussillon, 133, 134–42, 147
Côtes du Roussillon-Villages, 133, 134–5, 139
Côtes du Ventoux, 284
Couliège, 360
Crémant de Limoux, 178
Crépy, 328, 329, 339–41
Crouseilles, 106, 108
Cruet, 328, 333
Culloz, 343

Damazan, 38
Dauliac, 52
Delta Domaines, 229–31
Domaine Barroubio, 175
Domaine Cauhapé, 99, 100
Domaine Clos Ste-Magdeleine, 245
Domaine Colombu, 304–305
Domaine Condamine-Bertrand, 190
Domaine de Boudéry, 269
Domaine de Bregançon, 263
Domaine de Cagueloup, 255
Domaine de Castèle, 93
Domaine de Cazes, 182
Domaine de Crampilh, 110
Domaine de Dauliac, 52
Domaine de Deffends, 282
Domaine de Ferrant, 33
Domaine de Fontsainte, 165
Domaine de Frégate, 255
Domaine de Froin, 180
Domaine de Gaudou, 60
Domaine de Gaujal, 207
Domaine de Gourgueil, 29
Domaine de Grange Grillard, 357
Domaine de Jarras, 231, 232–3
Domaine de la Bastide Blanche, 255
Domaine de l'Abbaye de St-Hilaire, 282
Domaine de l'Amarine, 238
Domaine de l'Arjolle, 132, 227
Domaine de l'Aumérade, 263
Domaine de la Bernarde, 265, 266, 269–70
Domaine de la Capelle, 222
Domaine de la Clapière, 263
Domaine de la Croix, 263
Domaine de la Croix d'Argis, 357
Domaine de l'Espiguette, 126
Domaine de la Fadèze, 230
Domaine de la Gardie, 230
Domaine de la Grande Loube, 263
Domaine de la Grange Rouge, 230
Domaine de l'Herbe Sainte, 173
Domaine de la Jalousie, 82
Domaine de la Laidière, 251–2

Domaine de la Pineraie, 57
Domaine de la Senche, 173
Domaine de la Source Ste-Marguerite, 263
Domaine de Labarthe, 77–8
Domaine de Landes, 52
Domaine de Léret-Monpezat, 52, 61
Domaine de Martinolles, 179–80
Domaine de Massable, 52
Domaine de Mauvanne, 263
Domaine de Montbourgeau, 352
Domaine de Montfort, 357
Domaine de Paviglia, 294
Domaine de Pech Céleyran, 19, 198
Domaine de Peraldi, 293
Domaine de Perchade-Pourruchet, 92–3
Domaine de Pibarnon, 252
Domaine de Plantérieu, 82
Domaine de Quattre, 61
Domaine de Régusse, 283
Domaine de Rieux, 82
Domaine de Rimauresq, 263
Domaine de St-Césaire, 280
Domaine de Ste-Eulalie, 170
Domaine de St-Jean-de-Villecroze, 280–1
Domaine de St-Louis-la-Perdrix, 238, 239
Domaine de St-Maur, 263
Domaine de Sorbief, 357
Domaine de Tanella, 296
Domaine de Tarriquet, 82
Domaine de Terrebrune, 254
Domaine de Teston, 107
Domaine de Torraccia, 297
Domaine de Trévallon, 273, 275–6
Domaine de Versailles, 41–2
Domaine de Villemajou, 162
Domaine de Villeroy, 231–2
Domaine des Chaberts, 282
Domaine des Pourthié, 230
Domaine des Rocailles, 332
Domaine des Savarines, 59
Domaine des Trois Cantous, 76–7
Domaine du Belouvé, 253
Domaine du Bosc, 229
Domaine du Bosquet, 231, 233
Domaine du Château Bas, 279
Domaine du Galoupet, 263
Domaine du Grand-Mayne, 34
Domaine du Jas d'Esclans, 263
Domaine du Loou, 281–2
Domaine du Mas Blanc, 151
Domaine du Mas de Carrat, 215
Domaine du Noyer, 263
Domaine du Paternel, 245
Domaine Durand, 32
Domaine Eugénie, 58, 61
Domaine Fiumiccioli, 295
Domaine Genson, 207
Domaine Guiraud-Boyer, 203
Domaine Jean Cros, 74–5
Domaine La Blasque, 283
Domaine La Grave-Béchade, 33–4
Domaine La Rivière-Haute, 194
Domaine La Voulte-Gasparets, 161
Domaine Labarrade, 52

Domaine Laurens-Teulier, 90–1
Domaine Meste Duran, 83
Domaine St-André, 191
Domaine St-Aunès, 214
Domaine Ste-Lucie, 214
Domaine St-Martin-de-la-Garrigue, 228
Domaine St-Victor, 230
Domaine Sarda-Malet, 147
Domaines Ott, 253, 263–4, 267–9
Domaine Tempier, 247–8, 249–51, 254
Donzac, 62
Doux, 13
Duras, 9, see also Côtes de Duras
Durban, 159

Entraygues et du Fel, 9, 87–8
Entre-Deux-Mers, 30–1, 35
Estaing, 9, 89
Établissements Armand Jacquier, 360
Eugénie-les-Bains, 92, 101
Évenos, 248

Faugères, 127, 130, 187, 198, 203–206
Fayssac, 72
Fédération Nationale des Producteurs de
   Vins de Table et des Vins de Pays, 128
Feuilla, 155
Figari, 291, 296
Fitou, 129, 144, 147, 154–7, 160
Fitou de Hautes-Corbières, 155–6
Fitou-Maritime, 155–6
Fléterive, 333
Fleurieux, 324
Fontcouvert, 163
Fontès, 190
Fouqueyrolles, 29
Fourilles, 320
Frangy, 335–6
Frontignan, 18, 219
Fronton, 8, 65, 66–8

GAEC des Coteaux de Toul, 365
GAEC des Vignerons du Haut-Quercy, 84
Gageac, 28
Gaillac, 8, 9, 65, 69–79
Gaillac Perlé, 74, 76
Gaillac Premières Côtes, 72, 75
Gaillac Rouge, 79
Gan, 100
Givors, 324
Glanes, 84–5
Grand Roussillon, 144
Graves, 35
Groupement Agricole d'Exploitation en
   Commun (GAEC), 3
Groupement Interproducteurs du Cru
   Banyuls (GICB), 150, 152–3
Grusse, 350

Hautes-Corbières, 159
Haut-Minervois, 167
Haut-Montravel, 29
Haut-Pays, 9, 16, 30, 35, 38, 43, 69
Haut-Poitou, 9, 13–15

Hérault, 46, 50, 117, 120–2, 124

Ile de Ré, 80
Ile d'Oléron, 65, 80
Impernal, 52
Institut National de la Propriété Industriale,
   41
Institut National de la Recherche
   Agronomique, 184
Institut National des Appellations d'Origine
   (INAO), 25, 37, 49, 125, 135, 139, 159,
   168–9, 173–4, 216, 263, 285, 314, 319,
   321, 340
Irouléguy, 9, 113–14

Jongieux, 333–4
Jonquières, 210
Jurançon, 95–104, 110
Jurançon moelleux, 9, 98, 99, 101, 102, 111
Jurançon Noir, 64, 83, 85
Jurançon Rouge, 47–8, 74
Jurançon Sec, 99, 101–102

L'Arbresle, 324
La Cadière, 248, 252, 253, 254
La Clape, 130, 187, 194–8
L'Étoile, 349, 352
L'Étoile co-operative, 153
La Lavinière, 167, 168–9, 173
La Palme, 155
La Rochelle, 12, 80
La Roque, 255
La Ville-Dieu-du-Temple, 63
Labarrade, 52
Lagnieu, 344
Lagrasse, 159
Landerouat, 31
Landes, 52
Langlade, 187, 188–9
Languedoc, 18, 46, 120, 160
Laroppe Frères, 365
Latour-de-France, 134, 135, 140
Laurens, 204
Lavilledieu, 8, 63–5
Layac, 62
Le Beausset, 248, 251
Le Bosc, 190
Le Castellet, 248
Le Fel, 87
Le Puy-Ste-Réparade, 278
Le Viala, 89
Lentigny, 311, 312
Lentilly, 324
Léret-Monpezat, 52
Les Arcs, 272
Les Cosporons Levants, 154
Les Piloums, 154
Lesquerde, 124, 135, 145
Leucate, 155
Limoux, 72, 176
Lisle-sur-Tarn, 72
Listel, 231–3
Lucey, 334, 365, 366
Lunel, 216–18

Machuraz, 343, 344
Madargues, 313, 317
Madiran, 8, 104–109, 112
Magrie, 176
Maison Monin, 344
Maîtres Vignerons du Presqu'île de St-
  Tropez, 267
Malras, 176
Malviès, 181
Manicle, 342–3, 344, 345
Marcillac, 9, 90–1
Marcilly, 309
Marcoux, 309
Marestel, 336
Marignan, 341
Marin, 341–2
Marmande, 34–5
Mas Amiel, 148–9
Mas Chichet, 141
Mas de Daumas Gassac, 98, 223–6
Mas de la Dame, 276–7
Mas de la Rouvière, 253
Mas des Pigeonniers, 222
Mas Pignou, 79
Massable, 52
Maubourget, 108
Maury, 133, 143, 148–9
Médoc, 25, 51, 273
Meillard, 320, 321
Menjucq, 102
Meyragues, 278
Meyreuil, 255
Mèze, 207
Millery, 324
Minerve, 166
Minervois, 124, 129, 166–74
Mireval, 222
Monbazillac, 9, 17–19, 20–4, 26–7
Monestier, 28
Montagnac, 207
Montagne d'Alaric, 158, 159, 163
Montagnieu, 344, 346
Montels, 72
Monterminod, 336
Monthoux, 336
Montmélian, 328, 333
Montolieu, 185
Montpeyroux, 187, 208, 210–11
Montravel, 19, 29
Motz, 333
Moulidars, 80
Moulin des Costes, 253
Moussette d'Astrée, 310
Murviel, 199
Muscat de Beaumes-de-Venise, 145, 218,
  221
Muscat de Frontignan, 219–21, 222
Muscat de Mireval, 222
Muscat de Lunel, 217–18
Muscat de Rivesaltes, 136, 142, 143, 144–5,
  156, 220
Muscat de St-Jean-de-Minervois, 174–5

Nérac, 38, 95

Neuville-de-Poitou, 12–15
Nicolas, 135
Nizas, 190

Oletta, 303
Ollioules, 248, 254
Olonzac, 167
ONIVIT, 84
Ordre de la Dive Bouteille de Gaillac, 74

Pacherenc de Vic Bihl, 9, 98, 104, 106,
  109–11, 112
Palette, 240, 255–8
Paris, 369–70
Parnac, 53
Patrimonio, 291, 292, 301–4
Paulan, 190
Pauligne, 176
Paziols, 155
Pécharmant, 18, 19–20, 24, 27, 198
Pépieux, 167
Pérat, 190
Périgueux, 19
Perpignan, 125, 132, 134, 144
Pétillant de Savoie, 337
Pézanas, 190–1
Pic St-Loup, 187, 213–14
Picpoul de Pinet, 187, 206–8
Pierrerue, 199
Pierrevert, 282–3
Pieusse, 176
Pineau de Charente, 81, 146
Pinet, 207
Plaimont, 82, 106
Plaisance, 82
Planèz, 135
Poligny, 351, 359
Pomerols, 207
Pomport, 21
Portel, 159
Portet, 155
Porto-Vecchio, 291, 296–8
Port-Vendres, 149
Pouzolles, 227
Pralong, 309
Prieuré de Cénac, 53, 61
Prieuré de St-Jean-de-Bébian, 187
Puy-l'Évêque, 47, 57

Quatourze, 187, 192–4
Quercy, 43, 44
Queyssac-les-Vignes, 86–7

Rancio, 144, 152–3
Rasiguères, 135
ratafia, 86
Razac-de-Saussignac, 28
Reutnauer, 51
Revermont du Sud, 349, 359
Ribaute, 159
Rieux-Minervois, 167, 172
Rigal, 51, 53
Ripaille, 340–1

Rivesaltes, 133–4, 136, 139, 142, 143–9, 156
Roanne, 310
Rollet Frères, 359
Roquebrun, 199
Rosé d'Arbois, 358
Rosé de Béarn, 115
Rosé de Cerdon, 346–8
Rosé de Corent, 314
Rosette, 19, 28
Rouffignac, 21
Rouge de Béarn, 100, 116
Rouillac, 28
Roussette de Savoie, 329, 334, 335–6
Roussette de Seyssel, 337
Roussette du Bugey, 343, 344
Roussillon, 132–4
Roussillon des Aspres, 134
Routier, 181, 183
Ruffieux, 333

SAFER, 127
Sain Bel, 324
St-André-de-Sagonis, 190
St-Aunès, 214
St-Chinian, 124, 187, 198–203
St-Christol, 187, 216
St-Cyr-en-Bourg, 14
St-Cyr-sur Mer, 248
St-Drézery, 187
St-Émilion, 16, 18, 27
St-Étienne-de-Baigorry, 113–14
St-Florent, 301–302
Ste-Foy, 17
Ste-Foy-des-Vignes, 18
St-Georges d'Orques, 187, 211–13
St-Guiraud, 210
St-Haon-le-Châtel, 311
St-Haon-le-Vieux, 311, 312
St-Hilaire, 176
St-Jean d'Angély, 80
St-Jean-de-Chivetin, 334
St-Jean-de-la-Porte, 333
St-Jean-de-Minervois, 124, 167, 174–5
St-Jeoire-Prieuré, 333
St-Laurent-des-Vignes, 21
St-Lessans, 18
Ste-Marie-d'Alloix, 333
St-Mathieu-de-Tréviers, 213
St-Mont, 82, 106, 111–12
St-Paul-des-Fenouillèdes, 140
St-Polycarpe, 176
St-Pourçain-sur-Sioule, 307, 318–23
St-Romain-de-Bellet, 258, 261
St Saturnin, 187, 208–10
Saintes, 80
Salies-de-Béarn, 115–16
Salins du Midi, 125, 131–2, 231–3, 282
Sanary, 248
Sance, 18
Sarlat, 18, 19
Sartène, 291, 292, 294–5, 298
Saturargues, 217
Saulcet, 320, 322

Saussignac, 19, 28
Sauternes, 9, 18, 101
Sauvignon du Haut-Poitou, 13
Sciez, 341
Seigneurs de Cahors, Les, 61
Seillonnez, 346
Senouillac, 72
Serrière, 333
Seyssel, 328, 329, 336–8
Seyssel Mousseux, 337
Sigean, 155, 159
Sigoulês, 28
Société d'Intérêt Collectif Agricole des Recherches Expérimentales (SICAREX), 126
Société Vinicole de Toul, 365
Syndicat de la Défence des Vins des Côtes de Buzet, 38
Syndicat du Vic-Bihl, 105

Terrasse, 18
Tiregand, 19
Toul, 363–4
Tour de Marignan, La, 341
Tourreilles, 176
Tourtour, 280
Trausses, 173
Treilles, 155
Trélins, 307, 309
Tuchan, 147, 155–7
Tursan, 9, 92–4

Union Co-opérative Vinicole du Pic St-Loup (UCOVIP), 124, 125
Union de Plaimont, 82, 106
Union des Caves Co-opératives de l'Ouest Audois et du Razès (UCCOAR), 182
Union des Maures et de L'Esterel, 267
Union des Vignerons Associés du Levant (UVAL), 299
Union des Vignerons de l'Ile de Beauté, 298
Union des Vins du Var, 267
Uva Corse, 297

Varichon & Clerc, 337
Vaux, 368–9
Verneuil, 320
Veyre-Monton, 317
Vezon, 368
Vias, 229
Vic-Bigorre, 108
Vic-sur-Seille, 368
Vieillard, 346
Vieille-Tursan, 92, 93
Vigneron Savoyard, 330
Vignerons Catalans, 125, 136, 139, 140, 142
Vignerons du Val d'Orbieu, 124, 125, 157, 164
Vignerons Foréziens, 307–309
Vignerons Réunis des Côtes de Buzet, 39
Vigneuille-les-Hattan-châtel, 369
Vigouroux, Georges, 49, 51, 52–3
Villars-sur-Var, 264
Villaudric, 65–8

Villefranche du Queyran, 38
Villeneuve-les-Corbières, 155
Villerest, 311
Villeveyrac, 126–7
vin clairet, 262
Vin d'Arbois, 351
Vin de Corse, 291, 298
Vin de Lavilledieu, 64
vin de médecin, 9, 62, 71
Vin de Monein, 103
Vin de Moselle, 363, 367–9
vin de paille, 86, 349, 352, 361
vin de pays, 2, 130–2, 223
Vin de Pays Catalan, 136, 140
Vin de Pays Charentais, 79–81
Vin de Pays d'Allobrogie, 329
Vin de Pays de Bigorre, 108, 132
Vin de Pays de Franche-Comté, 362
Vin de Pays de Hauterive en Pays d'Aude, 163
Vin de Pays de l'Agenais, 33, 35
Vin de Pays de l'Aude, 131, 171, 173, 177, 185
Vin de Pays de la Bénovie, 216
Vin de Pays de la Côte Vermeille, 140
Vin de Pays de la Haute Vallée de l'Aude, 177
Vin de Pays de l'Hérault, 131, 169, 192, 213, 215, 223
Vin de Pays de l'Ile de Beauté, 291, 292, 298–300
Vin de Pays de la Vaunage, 189
Vin de Pays de Mont Caume, 253
Vin de Pays d'Oc, 131, 171, 232
Vin de Pays de Puy-de-Dôme, 315
Vin de Pays d'Urfé, 312
Vin de Pays de Vaucluse, 284, 285, 286–7
Vin de Pays des Alpes-de-Haute-Provence, 283
Vin de Pays des Bouches-du-Rhône, 273, 280
Vin de Pays des Coteaux Cathares, 156
Vin de Pays des Coteaux de Bessilles, 131, 228–9
Vin de Pays des Coteaux de Glanes, 84–5
Vin de Pays des Coteaux de la Cité de Carcassonne, 185
Vin de Pays des Coteaux de Murviel, 201
Vin de Pays des Coteaux de Narbonne, 197
Vin de Pays des Coteaux de Peyriac, 170
Vin de Pays des Coteaux de Quercy, 51
Vin de Pays des Coteaux des Fenouillèdes, 140

Vin de Pays des Coteaux du Grésivaudan, 329
Vin de Pays des Coteaux Flaviens, 234, 235
Vin de Pays des Côtes Catalanes, 140, 142
Vin de Pays des Côtes de Gascogne, 81–3, 98, 112
Vin de Pays des Côtes de Meuse, 369
Vin de Pays des Côtes de Montestruc, 81–2
Vin de Pays des Côtes de Pérignan, 198
Vin de Pays des Côtes de Prouille, 183
Vin de Pays des Côtes de Tarn, 76
Vin de Pays des Côtes de Thau, 207
Vin de Pays des Côtes de Thongue, 132, 226–7
Vin de Pays des Côtes du Condomois, 81, 83
Vin de Pays des Landes, 92
Vin de Pays des Pyrénées-Atlantiques, 106, 114, 116
Vin de Pays des Pyrénées-Orientales, 140–1
Vin de Pays des Sables du Golfe du Lion, 131–2, 231–3
Vin de Pays des Vals d'Agly, 140
Vin de Pays du Comté Tolosan, 64, 66
Vin de Pays du Gard, 234, 235
Vin de Pays du Jardin de la France, 131
Vin de Pays du Lot, 85
Vin de Pays du Mont Baudile, 209, 211
Vin de Pays du Tarn, 74
Vin de Pays du Torgan, 156
Vin de Pays du Val de Montferrand, 213
Vin de Pays du Var, 280, 281
Vin de Rivière Basse, 104
Vin de Savoie, 328, 330, 333, 334, 336, 343
Vin de Savoie Mousseux, 338
Vin de Vic-Bihl, 104
vin d'une nuit, 6, 14, 209–10, 268
vin doux naturel, 7, 133, 143, 145–7, 148
Vin du Haut-Poitou, 12–15
vin du sable, 92
vin jaune, 349, 351, 352–6
Vin Muscat de Claira, 143
Vingrau, 135
vins cuits, 262
vins de chaudière, 120
vins paillets, 96
Vire, 60
Virieu-le-Grand, 343, 344
Vongnes, 344
Vonzailles, 13

Wineshare, 34